Classical
Myth &
Culture
in the
Cinema

Classical Myth & Culture in the Cinema

Edited by
Martin M. Winkler

OXFORD
UNIVERSITY PRESS

2001

OXFORD
UNIVERSITY PRESS

Oxford   New York
Athens   Auckland   Bangkok   Bogotá   Buenos Aires   Cape Town
Chennai   Dar es Salaam   Delhi   Florence   Hong Kong   Istanbul   Karachi
Kolkata   Kuala Lumpur   Madrid   Melbourne   Mexico City   Mumbai   Nairobi
Paris   São Paulo   Shanghai   Singapore   Taipei   Tokyo   Toronto   Warsaw

and associated companies in
Berlin   Ibadan

Copyright © 2001 by Oxford University Press

Published by Oxford University Press, Inc.
198 Madison Avenue, New York, New York 10016

This volume is a revised edition of *Classics and Cinema* published 1991 by
Associated University Presses, Inc.

Oxford is a registered trademark of Oxford University Press

Library of Congress Cataloging-in-Publication Data
Classical myth and culture in the cinema / edited by Martin M. Winkler.
p.   cm.
Includes index.
ISBN 0-19-513003-0; ISBN 0-19-513004-9
1. Myth in motion pictures.   2. Mythology in motion pictures.
I. Winkler, Martin M.
PN1995.9.M96 C59 2001
791.43'615—dc21   00-056665

9 8 7 6 5 4 3 2 1

Printed in the United States of America
on acid-free paper

Contents

Contributors

JAMES R. BARON is Associate Professor of Classical Studies at the College of William and Mary. He frequently writes, lectures, and teaches courses on the classical tradition in European and American culture, often with special attention to Scandinavian authors.

MICHAEL CACOYANNIS is one of the leading Greek film directors. His most recent film is *The Cherry Orchard* (1999), an adaptation of Anton Chekhov.

MARY-KAY GAMEL is Associate Professor of Classics, Comparative Literature, and Theater Arts at the University of California, Santa Cruz. She has published articles on Roman literature in performance and on feminist productions of ancient drama and is coeditor and cotranslator of *Women on the Edge: Four Plays by Euripides*. She teaches courses on theater history and film and stages annual productions of ancient drama, often in her own translation and adaptation.

ERLING B. HOLTSMARK is Professor of Classics Emeritus at the University of Iowa. His chief interests are in Homer, Ovid, and the continuity of the classical tradition, especially in its popular forms. He is the author of *Tarzan and Tradition: Classical Myth in Popular Literature* and *Edgar Rice Burroughs*.

MARIANNE MCDONALD, Member of the Royal Irish Academy, is Professor of Classics and Theater at the University of California, San Diego, and the founder of the *Thesaurus Linguae Graecae* and *Thesaurus Linguarum Hiberniae* projects. Her books include *Terms for Happiness in Euripides*; *Euripides in Cinema: The Heart Made Visible*; *Ancient Sun, Modern Light: Greek Drama on the Modern Stage*; and *Star Myths: Tales of the Constellations*.

FRED MENCH is Professor of Classics at the Richard Stockton College of New Jersey and the author of articles on ancient literature and the classical tradition. He is also the editor of *Fictional Rome*, an electronic resource for historical novels set in ancient Rome.

J. K. NEWMAN is Professor of Classics at the University of Illinois and holds Oxford degrees in both Literae Humaniores and Russian. His books include *Augustus and the New Poetry*, *The Classical Epic Tradition*, *Roman Catullus and the Modification of the Alexandrian Sensibility*, and *Augustan Propertius: The Recapitulation of a Genre*. With his wife, F. S. Newman, he has published *Pindar's Art: Its Tradition and Aims* and edited *Latin Poems of Lelio Guidiccioni*. He has won four silver medals in the *Certamen Vaticanum* for his original Latin poems.

HANNA M. ROISMAN is Professor of Classics at Colby College. She is the author of *Loyalty in Early Greek Epic and Tragedy*, *Nothing Is As It Seems: The Tragedy of the Implicit in Euripides'* Hippolytus, and, with Frederick Ahl, *The* Odyssey *Re-Formed*.

PETER W. ROSE is Professor of Classics at Miami University of Ohio. He has published articles on classical literature and on Cuban cinema and has written analyses of films for various leftist political newsletters. His book *Sons of the Gods, Children of Earth: Ideology and Literary Form in Ancient Greece* applies Marxist critical perspectives to various works of the Greek literary canon.

JANICE F. SIEGEL, a comparatist by training, is Assistant Professor of Classics at Illinois State University and has taught in the Intellectual Heritage Program at Temple University. She is the editor of the year 2000 "Survey of Audio-Visual Resources for Teachers of Classics" in the journal *Classical World* and maintains an electronic network of resources devoted to classical literature, history, and archaeology.

JON SOLOMON is Professor of Classics at the University of Arizona. He is the author of *The Ancient World in the Cinema* and the editor of two collections of essays, *Accessing Antiquity: The Computerization of Classical Studies* and *Apollo: Origins and Influences*. He has also published a translation, with commentary, of Ptolemy's *Harmonics*.

The late J. P. SULLIVAN was educated at Oxford and Cambridge Universities, where he also taught, and was a film reviewer for *The Oxford Magazine*. His last appointment was as Professor of Classics at the University of California, Santa Barbara. He is the author, among other books, edited collections, and articles, of *Ezra Pound and Sextus Propertius: A Study in*

Creative Translation, The Satyricon of Petronius: A Literary Study, Literature and Politics in the Age of Nero, and *Martial, the Unexpected Classic: A Literary and Historical Study.* His last book, published posthumously, was the anthology *Martial in English,* coedited with A. J. Boyle.

MARTIN M. WINKLER is Professor of Classics at George Mason University. His classical education began in Münster, Germany, at the Gymnasium Paulinum (founded A.D. 797). His books are *The Persona in Three Satires of Juvenal, Der lateinische Eulenspiegel des Ioannes Nemius,* and the anthology *Juvenal in English.* He has also published articles on Roman literature, on the classical tradition, and on classical and medieval culture and mythology in film. He frequently lectures on and teaches courses in classical literature and cinema and has presented two extensive film programs at the National Gallery of Art in Washington, D.C.: "Greek Tragedy from Stage to Screen" and "Hollywood's Rome."

*Classical
Myth &
Culture
in the
Cinema*

Introduction

The mythology and culture of ancient Greece and Rome have been a staple of cinema since its earliest beginnings. Between the extremes of unabashed embraces of the lurid and the ridiculous on the one hand and committed attempts at the accurate and, on occasion, the sublime on the other, films that are set in antiquity or reflect its mythical or literary themes express the fascination the ancient world has always exerted on the popular imagination.

This volume examines some of the connections between antiquity and our own society as revealed in the cinema. Ancient myths and archetypes recurring in films attest to the vitality of our cultural tradition. Retellings of classical stories on film may show that filmmakers have used the ancient material consciously in order to comment on their own times or that they unconsciously reflect cultural trends. Ancient myths can also provide instances of more or less imaginative entertainment. In such processes the classical sources may become imbued with a creative art and intelligence not readily apparent to a casual viewer. Openly commercial films set in antiquity, whose historical or mythological accuracy may leave much to be desired, can still reward a close engagement with their underlying qualities. Genre cinema, such as the western, gangster, war, or science-fiction film, which at first sight has nothing in common with the ancient world, may still adapt plots or patterns familiar from antiquity, particularly those relating to heroic myth. This volume examines all these areas. It addresses not only scholars and students but also interested readers of any background.

1. Teaching and Research

The pervasive presence of cinema throughout the twentieth century and, concurrently, its wide range in quality from exploitation "quickies" to acknowledged works of art have made the traditional separation of "high" and "low" or "popular" culture questionable, if not impossible. But this is not as dire a consequence of modern culture as many traditionalists readily assume, for throughout the history of Western civilization great artists and their works have been popular during and after their lifetimes. The plays of the Greek dramatists of the fifth century B.C. are a case in point. We have come to regard them as being among the highest points of high culture, but they were written and performed for the average and upper-class Athenian alike. The same is true of the Elizabethan and Restoration stages and their audiences. It is therefore only appropriate for us today to widen our perspectives on culture, history, literature, and the visual arts. The *Annales* school of historiography has already demonstrated the gains that derive from such broader views. Consequently, this book deals with both "high" and "low," but it also addresses a diachronic parallel, that of "then" and "now."

Awareness of the importance of popular culture, both ancient and modern, for all of culture, society, and the arts helps us bridge the gap between antiquity and today. And not only that. If we approach our common cultural history in this way, we may throw new light on both the past and the present. We may illumine the present by revealing the influence of the past even where it may not have been suspected to exist, just as we may illumine the past by examining it from our modern vantage point. It goes without saying that, to do this sensibly and successfully, both sides must be approached fairly and equably. It will not do, as happens only too often, to force the past into the straitjacket of fixed modern theories so that results may be shown to exist which the theoretical framework had postulated a priori, or to deplore the present as falling irredeemably short of the great standards of the past. In either of these cases, the conclusions reached are not only predictably one-sided and distorted but also hopelessly dull. Much academic writing regrettably does not avoid these traps.

One of the goals of this book is to demonstrate, in the area of film, what shapes an approach such as the one outlined here may take in connection with ancient Greece and Rome. In the process the book also shows that classical studies is a versatile academic discipline, capable of combining long-established methods of scholarship with openness to modern approaches to the ancient cultures and their traditions. There now exists widespread interest in such endeavors. In colleges and universities, courses on classical mythology, civilization, and literature in translation incorporate film screenings on a regular basis. The programs of academic associations list topics involving film more and more frequently. At a time when humanities in general and the ancient classics in particular are no longer the bedrock of Western education they once were, the use of film within a traditional and largely nonvisual curriculum can provide an excellent means to keep Greece and Rome alive.

Teachers of the classics became aware of the educational potential of film early on. Two examples are worth considering in some detail. In 1915, B. L. Ullman, well-known classicist and editor of the *Classical Weekly*, made the point very emphatically about films set in Greece or Rome:

> Moving pictures are an excellent means of showing that the Classics are not dead. The classical teacher not only makes Latin and Greek alive, but makes the Greeks and Romans seem like living beings (if he does not do so, he should). He contributes matters of lively interest to the life of today and he draws on the same life to make his subject alive. The circle is perfect. Here is where the cinematograph plays its part. . . . An institution which seems to some only an evil may be turned into useful channels. I have heard several teachers complaining that their students do no work because they are at the 'Movies' much of the time after School hours. This is undoubtedly true and will remain true. There is no question that the cinematograph is to become an even more important factor in our civilization than it is. . . . As classical teachers, let us seize an opportunity . . . the cause of the Classics will be greatly benefited, for the people as a whole will become familiar with classical life and history. It is to the advantage of the Classics that these [photo-]plays be seen by the greatest possible number of persons, and that more and more plays of this sort be produced.[1]

Five years later, George Hadzsits of the University of Pennsylvania restated Ullman's confidence in the cinema from a more alarmist perspective. In the same journal he wrote about the state of classical education in terms that sound like the cri de coeur of today's educator:

> The present status of our High School and College curricula but mildly reflects the menace of an ignorance almost incredible and indescribable . . . . the comparatively brief time with difficulty snatched from other innumerable obligations for the joy of research is ill-spent, if there be no appreciation of such work in a world turning away from the totality of those things, of which each piece of research represents but a small fraction. The pathos of research work that does not gain a hearing will soon become bathos.

For classical education to continue, Hadzsits calls for "enlightenment on the subject of the value of the Classics, after which the will may assert itself

1. B. L. Ullman, *The Classical Weekly*, 8 no. 26 (May 8, 1915), 201–202 (editor's letter). Ullman quotes a contemporary newspaper: "The classicists have a new ally. They have labored in vain to get the public to listen to them . . . , but now people are flocking by the thousand to the theater to see what they would not read or hear about in the classroom. Teachers may now be seen on a Saturday afternoon leading schoolboys who have refused to be driven" (202).

to return to the Classics." One of the most effective ways to achieve this goal, he believes, are screenings of feature films with classical subjects:

> If these great films were exhibited in every High School, there would be a revival of interest which no other means would accomplish. After all, our work suffers from its fragmentary nature, and mere glimpses of reality through individual pages of Latin do not, in the nature of things, satisfy any normal or natural human craving. Great film spectacles, even though it may be said that their educational value is ephemeral, ought at least to arouse the slumbering synthetic process which alone can energize knowledge. Whatever historical inaccuracies may mar one or another of these great moving pictures, their value, on the whole, is incalculable in stimulating enthusiasm. In place of the mosaic representations of human life and its problems, extracted from one page, one paragraph, and even one sentence, a brilliant revelation is brought to mind and to eye of the totality of ancient life in all its vitality.[2]

Eighty years later we know that such an optimistic belief in the power of narrative cinema as an educational tool has been fulfilled only to a far more modest extent. Films have not significantly aided classical—or, for that matter, English—scholars and teachers to stem the tide of illiteracy. But as Umberto Eco has emphasized, we are "a civilization now accustomed to thinking in images. . . . It is the visual work (cinema, videotape, mural, comic strip, photograph) that is now a part of our memory." The fragmentary nature of classical scholarship and teaching to which Hadzsits had pointed finds its parallel in the fragmentary state in which most of antiquity itself has come down to us. In Eco's words: "In the case of the remains of classical antiquity we reconstruct them but, once we have rebuilt them, we don't dwell in them, we only contemplate them as an ideal model and a masterpiece of faithful restoration."[3] Films that recreate antiquity, rebuild its ruins even if their restoration is rather fanciful, and give the ruins life by making them inhabited by both historical and fictional people, can go a long way toward showing what life back then could have been like and what some of it actually *was* like, provided that we are able to abstract from the worst stereotypes or anachronisms present on the screen. In the words of Anthony Mann, director of two of the most

2. George Depue Hadzsits, "Media of Salvation," *The Classical Weekly*, 14 no. 9 (December 13, 1920), 70–71.

3. Umberto Eco, *Travels in Hyperreality: Essays*, tr. William Weaver (San Diego: Harcourt Brace, 1986; rpt. 1990), 217, 213, 67. On the modern dichotomy between word and image and its cultural implications cf. Mitchell Stephens, *The Rise of the Image, the Fall of the Word* (New York: Oxford University Press, 1998). On the impact of earlier technology on the word cf. the standard work by Walter J. Ong, *Orality and Literacy: The Technologizing of the Word* (1982; rpt. London: Routledge, 1991).

accomplished—and accurate—historical films: "if . . . *everything* [in such films] is historical, then you don't have [dramatic] liberty . . . inaccuracies from an historical point of view . . . are not important. The most important thing is that you get the feeling of history."[4]

Modern historians bear out Mann's perspective. As John Tosh has put it recently:

> Historians are not . . . only concerned to explain the past; they also seek to reconstruct or re-create it—to show how life was experienced as well as how it may be understood—and this requires an imaginative engagement with the mentality and atmosphere of the past. . . . historians are time and again confronted by gaps in the evidence which they can make good only by developing a sensitivity as to what might have happened, derived from an imagined picture that has taken shape in the course of becoming immersed in the surviving documentation.[5]

Scholars and creative artists equally strive to achieve the feeling of history, but there is no better medium than the cinema to reach this goal, whether the subject of a particular film is historical—dealing with an era of the past—or literary—based on a past work of fiction or myth.[6]

Even so, the presence of antiquity on film, television, or computer screens has become, by and large, no more than a pleasing diversion to most viewers. But there is another, and equally important, aspect. Many films that at first sight seem to have nothing to do with Greece or Rome reveal narrative structures or archetypal themes familiar since antiquity. Finding such thematic connections where viewers at first do not even suspect them is an especially fascinating and rewarding way to bring the continuing presence of antiquity and its influence on modern culture to people's consciousness. If appreciation of our own culture—and this includes popular culture—can be enhanced by an examination, from a classical perspective, of our primary visual art form, the cinema, then the

4. Anthony Mann, "Empire Demolition," in *Hollywood Directors 1941–1976*, ed. Richard Koszarski (New York: Oxford University Press, 1977), 332–338; quotation at 336. Mann's article was originally published in *Films and Filming* (March 1964) in connection with the release of his film *The Fall of the Roman Empire*. Mann had earlier directed the medieval epic *El Cid* (1961). His perspective on historical cinema is in keeping with Aristotle's on the superiority of tragedy, to him the representative of all creative arts, over historiography (*Poetics* 1451a37–1452a11).

5. John Tosh, *The Pursuit of History: Aims, Methods and New Directions in the Study of Modern History*, 3rd ed. (Harlow: Longman, 2000), 115–116 (in a chapter entitled "The Limits of Historical Knowledge"). See also David Lowenthal, *The Past is a Foreign Country* (Cambridge: Cambridge University Press, 1985; rpt. 1993), especially 210–238.

6. On the subject of historical cinema see in particular Robert Rosenstone, *Visions of the Past: The Challenge of Film to Our Idea of History* (Cambridge: Harvard University Press, 1995).

rationale for opening the curriculum to include film is obvious; the educational as well as aesthetic rewards to teachers and students can only increase. Incorporating feature films, especially the works of acknowledged filmmakers, into classical course offerings need not represent a sellout to the lowest common denominator or a trivialization of culture; rather, it is an effective means to make antiquity more readily accessible and to throw light on our own age as well. The cinema is certainly not the panacea for the educational ills Ullman and Hadzsits had envisioned, but it *is* an ally to the teacher just as much as it is, in general, an index of social and cultural currents.[7]

In the humanities no less than in the sciences, teaching cannot be separated from research. The contributors and editor of the book in hand therefore hope that the work presented here will suggest further avenues for both. As readers will notice immediately, we deal with films as cultural artifacts deserving consideration as works of high or popular art or, sometimes, of both. Our primary intent is to interpret, and we approach the films we discuss with certain thematic concerns. At the same time we intend to represent different approaches and to indicate the range which explorations such as ours may take. Our book is thus in the nature of what Romans called a *satura lanx*, a "well-filled dish," containing a variety of items on films that overtly deal with antiquity and on those that contain archetypal mythical or literary themes. But this does not make the volume a mere mélange. Readers will be able to trace thematic connections between and among our chapters. For instance, all of us emphasize the cinema's importance as a narrative medium. That is to say, we "read" films as "texts." (More on this later.) In doing so, of course, we each have different perspectives and priorities. But the very diversity of both content and approach will, we believe, make our work interesting not only to aca-

---

7. Here are a few examples for the nature of cinema as a kind of cultural seismograph: Expressionist films revealed the instability and anxiety of Germany in the wake of World War I, just as Neorealism reflected the harsh situation of Italy at the end of World War II. The Soviet cinema of montage illustrated both mass society and the machine age in postrevolutionary Russia. In the United States, government-conspiracy and rogue-cop films characterized the Nixon era. More recently, the films of Mike Leigh and Ken Loach exposed the social Darwinism of Margaret Thatcher's England. The genre of the western film in particular has shown great flexibility in commenting on contemporary issues: Numerous films in the 1950s, 1960s, and early 1970s, from Fred Zinnemann's *High Noon* (1952) and Allan Dwan's *Silver Lode* (1954) to Sam Peckinpah's *The Wild Bunch* (1969) and Michael Winner's *Chato's Land* (1972), are obvious allegories of the McCarthy era or the Vietnam war. Italian westerns with their frequent exhortations to revolution provide a popular parallel to the high-culture Marxism of 1960s intellectuals like Luchino Visconti and especially Pier Paolo Pasolini.

demic specialists in classical studies and related areas within the humanities, such as comparative literature, film studies, English, or cultural studies, but also to general readers and to amateurs—in the original sense of the word—of literature and film.

2. Theoretical Background

In juxtaposing works or periods from classical antiquity to those of cinema across a time span of roughly 1,800–2,800 years, we proceed from some basic critical assumptions. These are primarily those of the reader-oriented theories of literature that developed in the wake of hermeneutics in general and the work of German philosopher Hans-Georg Gadamer in particular. Although referring to literary texts rather than to cinema, such theories apply beyond language to narratives in any media whenever presentations of a plot proceed in analogous ways. With the exception of experimental or deliberately nonnarrative films, the storytelling in mainstream cinema follows longstanding literary traditions.[8] Our volume presents, among other things, a test case for the applicability of modern literary theory to cinema.[9]

Raman Selden has provided the following concise summary of the hermeneutical approach to literature:

> Gadamer argues that all interpretations of past literature arise from a dialogue between past and present. Our attempts to understand a work will depend on the questions which our own cultural environment allows us to raise. At the same time, we seek to discover the questions which the work itself was trying to answer in its own dialogue with history. Our present perspective always involves a relationship to the past, but at the same time the past can only be grasped through the limited perspective of the present. Put in this way, the task of establishing a *knowledge* of the past seems hopeless. But a hermeneutical notion of 'understanding' does not separate knower and object in the familiar fashion of empirical science;

8. See, for example, Seymour Chatman, *Story and Discourse: Narrative Structure in Fiction and Film* (Ithaca, N.Y.: Cornell University Press, 1978; rpt. 1989), or David Bordwell, *Narration in the Fiction Film* (Madison: University of Wisconsin Press, 1985). The literature on cinematic storytelling is extensive.

9. A model exposition of a literary approach to film appears in Robin Wood, *Hitchcock's Films Revisited* (New York: Columbia University Press, 1989), 1–51, from the critical perspective of F. R. Leavis. The argument of Helmut Kreuzer, "Trivialliteratur als Forschungsproblem: Zur Kritik des deutschen Trivialromans seit der Aufklärung," *Deutsche Vierteljahresschrift für Literaturwissenschaft und Geistesgeschichte*, 41 (1967), 173–191, a study of popular German novels, is relevant as well.

rather it views understanding as a 'fusion' of past and present: we cannot make our journey into the past without taking the present with us.[10]

To this we may add Terry Eagleton's observation that

> the meaning of a literary work is never exhausted by the intentions of its author; as the work passes from one cultural or historical context to another, new meanings may be culled from it which were perhaps never anticipated by its author or contemporary audience. . . . All understanding is *productive*: it is always 'understanding otherwise', realizing new potential in the text, making a difference to it.

As a result, hermeneutics "sees history as a living dialogue between past, present and future." The reader

> makes implicit connections, fills in gaps, draws inferences and tests out hunches; and to do this means drawing on a tacit knowledge of the world in general and of literary conventions in particular. The text itself is really no more than a series of 'cues' to the reader, invitations to construct a piece of language into meaning.[11]

This theoretical perspective is helpful when connections among works of popular culture—or between those of popular and high culture—either from one time or from different periods of time are to be examined and interpreted. Frequently, popular authors and other creative artists do not acknowledge direct or specific influences but instead let their works speak on their behalf; many do not even possess any conscious knowledge or awareness of what has shaped their creative impulses. Consequently, any critical venture, ranging from traditional scholarly research into a work's or author's sources to modern "intertextuality," as it is now generally called, becomes more difficult to undertake but also more fascinating. Several of the essays in this volume illustrate such an approach. Its academic readers, at least those with a theoretical inclination, will keep this or related perspectives in mind; no doubt they will also occasionally dissent or prefer to have encountered additional or different theoretical frames. In such cases the contributors and editor hope that they will take their readings in this book as an incentive to make further and broader inroads into its terrain. Nonacademic readers may rest assured that no

10. Raman Selden, Peter Widdowson, and Peter Brooker, *A Reader's Guide to Contemporary Literary Theory*, 4th ed. (Lexington: University of Kentucky Press, 1997), 54–55. See also Umberto Eco, "*Intentio Lectoris*: The State of the Art," in *The Limits of Interpretation* (Bloomington: Indiana University Press, 1990; rpt. 1994), 44–63.

11. Terry Eagleton, *Literary Theory: An Introduction*, 2nd ed. (Minneapolis: University of Minnesota Press, 1996), 61–63 and 66.

expertise in academic theory is a prerequisite for reading—and, we hope, enjoying—our work. For this reason we have done our utmost to keep the volume free of specialized terminology and academic jargon.[12] Throughout, we quote ancient texts in translation (our own, unless otherwise credited); on the rare occasion that a Greek or Latin word, phrase, or passage appears in the original language (although transliterated, if Greek), it is accompanied by an English translation.

3. Greco-Roman Cinema?

To complement the foregoing, primarily academic, side of this introduction, now a different question: Was there, in a manner of speaking, a cinema in classical antiquity? (Not literally, of course, but. . . .) I broach this subject, which deserves more detailed treatment, only briefly, limiting myself to a discussion of one Greek and one Roman text. Partly this is for reasons of space. But partly it is also to whet readers' appetite for the volume. The next few pages are then, as it were, the verbal equivalent of a film's preview or trailer, a "teaser" to get readers hooked on the whole subject of antiquity and film.

The situation described in the following ancient dialogue should provide an answer in the affirmative to our question:

> "Imagine people in a cavernous dark hall; at the far end of the hall, a long way off, there's an entrance open to the outside world. They've been there for a long time, riveted to their seats in a way which keeps them in one place and allows them to look only straight ahead, but not to turn their heads. There's a light a long way further up the hall behind them, and the people see shadows cast by the light on to the wall directly opposite them. And what if sound echoed off the wall opposite them? Don't you think they'd be bound to assume that the sound came from those shadows?"
> "I'm absolutely certain of it," he said.
> "All in all, then," I said, "the shadows would constitute the only reality people in this situation would recognize."
> "That's absolutely inevitable," he agreed.

The preceding is part of Plato's famous Allegory of the Cave, somewhat shortened and adapted to reinforce the cinematic analogy.[13] For example,

---

12. G. R. Elton, *The Practice of History* (1967; rpt. London: Fontana, 1987), 135–146 (a section entitled "Style"), is a concise older, but by no means outdated, defense of clarity in academic writing. Elton's standards for writing history apply, with some adjustments, to all areas of scholarship in the humanities.

13. *Republic* 514a–515b; quoted from Plato, *The Republic*, tr. Robin Waterfield (Oxford: Oxford University Press, 1993; rpt. 1998), 240–241.

I have substituted "dark hall" for the translator's "cavernous cell," and "for a long time" replaces "since childhood." Plato's point is to provide an analogy to human life as a whole in connection with education and the attainment of philosophical knowledge; my focus is on the *setting* of the allegory to which he resorts to make his point immediately comprehensible. My changes in the text do not interfere with the situation Plato conjures up before his readers' mental eyes, not even when I replace the original's mention of "firelight" with a neutral "light" or when I substitute Plato's description of people literally immobilized by chains with a figurative immobilization ("riveted to their seats") of the kind which film audiences sometimes experience and which enthusiastic journalists promise them in their rave reviews of new films.

Others saw the analogy between Plato's allegory and the cinema long ago. F. M. Cornford pointed to cinema as a modern parallel in his 1941 translation of the *Republic*:

> A modern Plato would compare his Cave to an underground cinema, where the audience watch the play of shadows thrown by the film passing before a light at their backs. The film itself is only an image of 'real' things and events in the world outside the cinema. For the film Plato has to substitute the clumsier apparatus of a procession of artificial objects carried on their heads by persons who are merely part of the machinery, providing for the movements of the objects and the sounds whose echoes the prisoners hear.[14]

That the shadowy existence of actors on the screen is a close parallel to the existence of the people who carry these objects in Plato's Cave and whose shadows appear on its wall becomes clear in the following description by Luigi Pirandello, one of the first modern authors to address this aspect of cinema. In his novel *Si Gira*, written before the advent of sound and the spread of color in the cinema, Pirandello put the case in terms strongly reminiscent of Platonic philosophy and its distinctions among images, reality, and the realm of ideas:

> The film actor feels as if in exile—exiled not only from the stage but also from himself. With a vague sense of discomfort he feels inexplicable emptiness: his body loses his corporeality, it evaporates, it is deprived of reality, life, voice, and the noises caused by his moving about, in order to be

14. Francis MacDonald Cornford, *The Republic of Plato* (Oxford: Oxford University Press, 1941), 228 note 2. A French scholar had been there before Cornford: Jean Przyluski, "Le théatre d'ombres et la caverne de Platon," in *Deuxième congrès international d'esthétique et de science de l'art*, vol. 1 (Paris: Alcan, 1937), 297–299, dealt with Plato's Cave in connection with cinema and its predecessor, the shadow play.

changed into a mute image, flickering an instant on the screen, then vanishing into silence. . . . The projector will play with his shadow before the
public, and he himself must be content to play before the camera.[15]

If Plato's Cave parallels the physical environment of the cinema, is there
also an ancient text that shows us what an ancient film, if I may put it in
such an anachronistic term, might have looked like? Indeed there is. The
Roman poet Lucretius describes the different sense perceptions in Book 4
of his philosophical-didactic epic *On the Nature of Things*. A central passage
on dream visions begins with a statement that reminds us of Plato's Cave:

> it is not wonderful that images move
> And sway their arms and other limbs in rhythm—
> For the image does seem to do this in our sleep.
> The fact is that when the first one perishes
> And a new one is born and takes its place,
> The former seems to have changed its attitude.
> All this of course takes place extremely swiftly,
> So great is the velocity and so great the store
> Of them, so great the quantity of atoms
> In any single moment of sensation
> Always available to keep up the supply. . . .
> And what when we see in dreams the images
> Moving in time and swaying supple limbs,
> Swinging one supple arm after the other
> In fluid gestures and repeating the movement
> Foot meeting foot, as eyes direct? Ah, steeped in art,
> Well trained the wandering images must be
> That in the night have learned such games to play! . . .
>   It sometimes happens also that the image
> Which follows is of a different kind: a woman
> seems in our grasp to have become a man.
> And different shapes and different ages follow.
> But sleep and oblivion cause us not to wonder.[16]

15. I quote Pirandello from Walter Benjamin, "The Work of Art in the Age of Mechanical Reproduction," in *Illuminations*, ed. Hannah Arendt, tr. Harry Zohn (1968;
slightly different new ed. New York: Schocken Books, 1969; rpt. 1986), 217–251; quotation at 229. The English translation of *Si Gira* (1916) is *Shoot! The Notebooks of Serafino
Gubbio, Cinematograph Operator*, tr. C. K. Scott-Moncrieff (1926; rpt. New York: Garland, 1978). In the context of Platonic thought it might be amusing to note that the quotation from Pirandello here given is several times removed from its original. I quote from
an English translation of Benjamin's German translation of a French version of Pirandello's
Italian.

16. Lucretius, *On the Nature of Things* 4.768–776, 788–793, and 818–822. The quotation is from Lucretius, *On the Nature of the Universe*, tr. Ronald Melville (Oxford:
Oxford University Press, 1997; rpt. 1999), 122–124.

In passages such as these, in certain texts of Greek and Roman narrative literature, and in much of ancient visual art we are justified to recognize the precursors of film—what some French scholars have termed "le pré-cinéma." In an essay first published in 1946, André Bazin, the influential critic and theoretician of film, has made this point explicitly:

> The cinema is an idealistic phenomenon. The concept men had of it existed, so to speak, fully armed in their minds, as if in some Platonic heaven, and what strikes us most of all is the obstinate resistance of matter to ideas rather than of any help offered by techniques to the imagination of the researchers.

Bazin adduces a felicitous analogy from Greek mythology: "the myth of [Daedalus and] Icarus had to wait for the internal combustion engine before descending from the Platonic heavens. But it had dwelt in the soul of every man since he first thought about birds."[17]

4. Cinema and the Other Arts

If Lucretius could maintain in the first century B.C. that the occurrence of moving images in our subconscious mind is far from remarkable, modern technology has extended this phenomenon into our waking life. Cinematography and even more the ubiquity of television and now the computer no longer cause us to wonder that moving images surround us in our waking state as well. In the final paragraph quoted, Lucretius even anticipates the editing technique fundamental to cinema when he observes that a sequence of images can present completely different figures in quick succession. So a major twentieth-century poet, himself an accomplished painter and filmmaker as well, repeatedly called the cinema the Tenth Muse. Jean Cocteau, writer-director of films on both modern and classical subjects, hailed the youngest Muse in encomiums such as these: "FILM, the new Muse" (1920); "the Muse of Cinema, whom the nine sisters have accepted into their close and strict circle" (1953); and: "The Muse of Cinema is the youngest of all Muses" (1959).[18]

---

17. André Bazin, "The Myth of Total Cinema," in *What Is Cinema?*, tr. Hugh Gray, vol. 1 (Berkeley: University of California Press, 1967; rpt. 1974), 17–22; quotations at 17 and 22 (slightly altered and corrected).

18. Jean Cocteau, *The Art of Cinema*, ed. André Bernard and Claude Gauteur, tr. Robin Buss (London: Boyars, 1992; rpt. 1999), 23, 123, and 56 (with slight corrections); see also 176–177 and 192–193. Cocteau's best-known films on classical subjects are *Orpheus* (*Orphée*, 1949) and *The Testament of Orpheus* (1959). His 1946 observation on cinema as both commercial and artistic medium is worth remembering: "Mediocre films are not

Another Frenchman, film pioneer Abel Gance, best known today for his epic *Napoleon* (1927), provides us with details, describing cinema in poetically charged language:

> It is *music* in the harmony of its visual turns, in the very quality of its silences; *painting* and *sculpture* in its composition; *architecture* in its construction and ordered arrangements; *poetry* in its gusts of dreams stolen from the soul of beings and things; and *dance* in its interior rhythm which is communicated to the soul and makes it leave your body and mingle with the actors of the drama [on screen].[19]

The earliest implementation of such a view of the cinema, which demands an epic subject treated on an appropriately huge scale, was D. W. Griffith's *Intolerance* (1916), a celebration of what the new medium could achieve by combining the traditional arts of epic and dramatic narrative, painting and photography, sculpture and architecture, music and dance. The spectator's soul may well have been caught up in this film's hitherto unparalleled mixture of lyricism, realism, psychology, and sentimentality. Griffith's direct inspiration for *Intolerance* was Giovanni Pastrone's *Cabiria* (1914), an epic melodrama on ancient Carthage and Rome, with intertitles by Gabriele d'Annunzio. In general, however, Griffith was

---

an indictment of cinema, any more than painting, literature and theatre are compromised by mediocre canvasses, books or plays. It would be madness not to think of this incomparable medium for poetry as an art, even as a very great one" (*The Art of Cinema*, 32).

19. I have translated Gance as quoted in G.-Michel Coissac, *Les coulisses du cinéma* (Paris: Les Éditions Pittoresques, 1929), 4. Gance's description reflects futurist Ricciotto Canudo's pyramidal model of cinema and the arts as published in the Paris *Gazette des Beaux Arts* in 1923: Painting and sculpture, poetry and dance provide the basic layer, next come architecture and music, crowned at the top by cinema, the seventh art. Connecting lines between the individual arts form triangles and illustrate the mutual influence among the first six. On the subject in general see Rudolf Arnheim, *Art and Visual Perception: A Psychology of the Creative Eye*, rev. ed. (Berkeley: University of California Press, 1974), especially chapter 8 ("Movement"). The interrelationship of the arts was well known in antiquity; it received an influential restatement in Gotthold Ephraim Lessing's *Laocoon* of 1766. See also Arnheim, "A New Laocoön: Artistic Composites and the Talking Film," in *Film as Art* (Berkeley: University of California Press, 1957; rpt. 1971), 199–230. In general see Ralph Stephenson and Guy Phelps, *The Cinema as Art*, 2nd ed., rev. (London: Penguin, 1989). Detailed further references to and introductory essays on the connections between film and the individual arts are in *Film and the Arts in Symbiosis: A Resource Guide*, ed. Gary R. Edgerton (New York: Greenwood, 1988). On the religious, or quasi-religious, nature of cinema and of experiencing film, another link to the traditional arts, see, for example, Geoffrey O'Brien, *The Phantom Empire: Movies in the Mind of the Twentieth Century* (New York: Norton, 1993; rpt. 1995), 51–53, 85–86, 98, and 109–111. O'Brien, 97, quotes director Eric Rohmer: "There is alarm over the disappearance of sacred art: what does it matter, if the cinema is taking over from the cathedrals!"

strongly influenced by the narrative techniques of Charles Dickens, as none other than Sergei Eisenstein has shown in detail.[20] Eisenstein in turn has acknowledged the unbroken tradition of Western art as formative for the art of cinema:

> our cinema is not altogether without parents and without pedigree, with-
> out a past, without the traditions and rich cultural heritage of the past
> epochs. It is only very thoughtless and presumptuous people who can erect
> laws and an esthetic for cinema, proceeding from premises of some incred-
> ible virgin-birth of this art! . . . Let Dickens and the whole ancestral
> array, going back as far as the Greeks and Shakespeare, be superfluous re-
> minders that both Griffith and our cinema prove our origins to be not solely
> as of Edison and his fellow inventors, but as based on an enormous cul-
> tured past; each part of this past in its own moment of world history has
> moved forward the great art of cinematography.[21]

5. Cinema and Modern Culture

Before Eisenstein wrote this, Walter Benjamin had commented on the quali-
tative change which modern technology has brought on the very nature
and status of art, especially through mechanical reproduction of art works
in photographs and films and, beyond this, of photography and cinematography as themselves new forms of art. Their capability of being end-
lessly reproduced alters, fundamentally and irrevocably, the tradition of art
and the concept of what constitutes an original. As Benjamin puts it:

> the technique of reproduction detaches the reproduced object from the
> domain of tradition. By making many reproductions it substitutes a plu-
> rality of copies for a unique existence. And in permitting a reproduction
> to meet the beholder or listener in his own particular situation, it reacti-

20. Sergei Eisenstein, "Dickens, Griffith, and the Film Today," in *Film Form: Essays in Film Theory,* ed. and tr. Jay Leyda (1949; rpt. San Diego: Harcourt Brace Jovanovich, 1977), 195–255. See also Eisenstein, "Word and Image," in *The Film Sense,* ed. and tr. Leyda (1942; rpt. New York: Harcourt Brace Jovanovich, 1975), 1–65. Cf. William C. Wees, "Dickens, Griffith and Eisenstein," *The Humanities Association Review/La Révue de l'Association des Humanités,* 24 (1973), 266–276, and Ana L. Zambrano, "Charles Dickens and Sergei Eisenstein: The Emergence of Cinema," *Style,* 9 (1975), 469–487. Perhaps the most Dickensian of Griffith's films is *Broken Blossoms* (1919), set in a dark and squalid London straight out of *Oliver Twist, Bleak House, Little Dorrit,* or *Our Mutual Friend.*

21. Eisenstein, "Dickens, Griffith, and the Film Today," in *Film Form,* 232–233. The literal translation of the title of Eisenstein's 1944 essay is "Dickens, Griffith, and Us"; cf. *Film Form,* 267. Literature on the artistic prehistory of cinema is extensive; the locus classicus is the 1933 essay by Arnheim, "The Thoughts That Made the Pictures Move," in *Film as Art,* 161–180.

vates the object reproduced. These two processes lead to a tremendous shattering of tradition. . . . Their most powerful agent is the film. . . . In the case of films, mechanical reproduction is not, as with literature and painting, an external condition for mass distribution. Mechanical reproduction is inherent in the very technique of film production. This technique not only permits in the most direct way but virtually causes mass distribution.[22]

From such mass production derives, in large part, the modern critical division into high and popular culture. Traditionally, the one is to be studied, appreciated, or imitated, the other despised or avoided. But as Benjamin already made clear, with the rise of photography in the nineteenth century such a division became largely untenable. An observation by Charles Dickens concisely anticipates Benjamin: Those living in a machine age, Dickens wrote in a letter regarding the Coketown of *Hard Times*, want *"something in motion"* for their entertainment.[23] Dickens had acrobats and performing animals in mind, but we may also think of the popular theater of his time. Eventually, the presentation of images of motion on the screen was to eclipse the real motions on the stage. Since then, the worldwide popularity of moving photographic images—first in the cinema and then on television and computer screens—has made the distinction of high and low culture even more questionable. Umberto Eco, following Benjamin, concludes:

> Our relationship with mass-produced goods has changed and also with the products of "high" art. Differences have been reduced, or erased; but along with the differences, temporal relationships have been distorted, the lines of reproduction, the befores and the afters. The philologist is still aware of them, but not the ordinary consumer. . . . The distances have been reduced, the critics are puzzled. Traditional criticism complains that the new techniques of enquiry analyze Manzoni and Donald Duck with the same precision and can no longer tell them apart (and it's a cheap lie, contrary to all the printed evidence) without realizing (through lack of attention) that it is, on the contrary, the development of the arts itself, today, that tries to obliterate this distinction. . . . And this situation tells us that when such shifts of horizon occur, they don't have to mean things are going better or worse: Things have simply changed, and even value judgments must be formed according to different parameters.[24]

22. Benjamin, "The Work of Art in the Age of Mechanical Reproduction," in *Illuminations*, 221 and 244 note 7. Although it strongly reflects the historical situation prevalent at the time of its original publication in 1936, Benjamin's essay has preserved its importance well beyond its political aspects.

23. Quoted from Peter Ackroyd, *Dickens* (San Francisco: Harper, 1990), 698.

24. Eco, *Travels in Hyperreality*, 147.

6. Film Philology

Eco's description of modern culture, of its academic interpreters, and of its discontents contains an implicit but strong exhortation to classical scholars and to anyone interested in antiquity to reexamine our temporal relationships to Greece and Rome across the reduced distances that technology and technologically based art have made available. By the very nature of its images, film provides the viewer with only a minimum of information about characters, their thoughts, emotions, and motivations, and about the atmosphere prevailing in a given scene. So viewers must themselves draw the appropriate conclusions; that is to say, they must interpret the film with the help of the visual and verbal clues that director, writer, editor, or actors provide in a given scene's action and dialogue. Much of such an interpretive approach is also required for all modern readers of classical texts, who often rely on an expert's introduction or commentary even when they can read a Greek or Latin work in the original. Anyone who has studied the classical languages knows that the closest attention to every detail, to each word, even to a word's ending or one single letter, is necessary for a correct understanding and appreciation of the text. All classical literature and all cinema of substance call on us to pay close attention if we wish to appreciate a work's true quality, its accomplishments and creative dimensions. Rigorous training in philology of the kind classical scholars undergo is the best conditioning for film analysis—for what we might call, in analogy to the well-established philologies, the philology of film.[25] "The camera," director Elia Kazan has observed, "is more than a recorder. It's a microscope that penetrates. It goes into people, and you see their most private and concealed thoughts."[26] To this we could add: and their emotions. Literature, especially the novel, and narrative film are analogous: the one may be a verbal, the other a visual representation of consciousness. The camera becomes "an instrument for photographing the invisible."[27] The viewer must look at the visible that

25. I take the term *Filmphilologie* from Axel Sütterlin, *Petronius Arbiter und Federico Fellini: Ein strukturanalytischer Vergleich* (Frankfurt a. M.: Lang, 1996), 173.

26. I quote Kazan from Part Two of *A Personal Journey with Martin Scorsese through American Movies*, written and directed by Scorsese and Michael Henry Wilson (British Film Institute/Miramax Films, 1997).

27. O'Brien, *The Phantom Empire*, 87. O'Brien, 87–88, mentions the work of Robert Bresson, Carl Theodor Dreyer, Kenji Mizoguchi, and Roberto Rossellini as examples. Other directors' names could be added. See also the study by future screenwriter and director Paul Schrader, *Transcendental Style in Film: Ozu, Bresson, Dreyer* (1972; rpt. New York: Da Capo, 1988). A comparable perspective informs Bruce F. Kawin, *Mindscreen: Bergman, Godard, and First-Person Film* (Princeton: Princeton University Press, 1978). Earlier, and on a significantly larger scale, Siegfried Kracauer, *From Caligari to Hitler: A Psycho-*

the camera presents on the screen to be able to reach and interpret the invisible. After all, as Christian Metz has pointed out: "A film is difficult to explain because it is easy to understand."[28]

But the analogy between literary texts, especially classical ones, and films extends even further. Digital technology now makes it possible for philologists of the cinema to treat a film as traditional philologists have always treated *their* materials. We can now view a film again and again at any time we wish, jump from any scene to any other within seconds, select a scene for particular scrutiny at slow motion, or even look at individual frames. In other words, we are now in the position to "read" a filmic work in ways similar to those in which we read a literary one. The new technology even enables us to find a particular moment in a film faster than we could find a certain passage or line in a work of literature by turning back the pages of a book, and so the term "chapters" for a film's individual sequences or scenes in videodisc editions seems entirely appropriate.

Since the ready availability of digital technology, an increasing number of films have begun to receive critical attention no less philological than that accorded literary texts. Just as practically all works of ancient literature exist in scholarly editions, videodiscs of films are now appearing in comparable form. Editors of classical texts consult the manuscript traditions of the works they are editing and weigh the importance of textual variants in the manuscripts and those proposed by earlier scholars; they emend and restore the text to come as closely as possible to the original work as its author intended it. Frequently, an extensive commentary accompanies such a critical edition; a case in point is Eduard Fraenkel's monumental edition and commentary of Aeschylus' *Agamemnon* (1950). Now films, too, exist in critical editions alongside earlier incomplete, reedited, or variant prints. For example, the different versions of Fritz Lang's *Die Nibelungen* of 1924 or Sergei Eisenstein's *Battleship Potemkin* of 1925, which had circulated for decades, have now been superseded. A

---

logical History of the German Film (Princeton: Princeton University Press, 1947; rpt. 1974), had made the case for German cinema between World War I and 1933. As Kracauer writes: "Inner life manifests itself in various elements and conglomerations of external life, especially in those almost imperceptible surface data which form an essential part of screen treatment. In recording the visible world—whether current reality or an imaginary universe—films therefore provide clues to hidden processes" (7). Those he analyzes "expos[e] the German soul" (1). A more recent individual example is the description by Michael Chapman, director of cinematography for Martin Scorsese's *Taxi Driver* (1976), of this film being "a documentary of the mind"; quoted from *Making* Taxi Driver, written and directed by Laurent Bouzereau (1999), a documentary included in the digital videodisc of the film ("collector's edition").

28. Quoted from Stephenson and Phelps, *The Cinema as Art*, 28.

"director's cut" of a film originally released in a different form or severely cut by a studio now restores deleted scenes and "outtakes," often including different camera "takes." In some cases, even whole scenes or individual moments intended for television broadcasts as alternatives to those shown theatrically, especially if sex and violence are an issue, are now included. Roughly, all these are the equivalents of the "variant readings," the *variae lectiones*, of ancient texts. Faded colors and washed-out black-and-white images are restored to their original appearance through recourse to the camera negative or an exceptionally well-preserved print in combination with digital image enhancement. Widescreen films are restored to their original aspect ratio as well, sometimes supplemented by the familiar—and compositionally ruinous—"pan and scan" format. Unlike ancient texts, however, the process of restoration can today involve the original author, usually the director. Terry Gilliam's cooperation on the three-videodisc set of his film *Brazil* (1985) is a representative example. A videodisc may even present the different versions of an entire film for scholarly study, as is the case with Howard Hawks's *The Big Sleep*. For the first time, we can now compare the film's original prerelease version of 1944, shown only overseas to American soldiers, with the different general-release version of 1946. Since Hawks was involved in making both, the question of authorship and of what constitutes the best "text" of his work becomes especially complex and fascinating in this case.

The videodisc of *The Big Sleep* contains a film scholar's commentary on its two versions and their origins. Here, too, we may see parallels to the editing of ancient texts. Videodiscs of particularly significant films frequently include detailed comments by film historians or, for more recent films, by directors, screenwriters, or others involved in their making. Documentaries on such films, behind-the-scenes footage, production stills, and other materials round off the editions—just as classical editors include all available historical and textual information in theirs. Beyond such work on the text, classical and later literature on the one hand and films on the other have come to share a tradition of extensive interpretation in books and articles. Modern technology has made possible a convergence of these two traditions to the extent that they have become analogous. Originally, film scholars and others writing about film found themselves in a situation similar or identical to that which philosopher Stanley Cavell describes in connection with his work on *The World Viewed*:

> I wrote primarily out of the memory of films . . . [later] I had begun the practice of taking notes during and after screenings. . . . I was always aware that my descriptions of passages were liable to contain errors, of content and of sequence. . . . in speaking of a moment or sequence from a film we,

as we might put it, cannot *quote* the thing we are speaking of. The fact is not merely that others might then not be sure what it is we are referring to, but that we ourselves might not know what we are thinking about. This puts an immediate and tremendous burden on one's capacity for critical description of cinematic events.[29]

Fortunately for all concerned, this situation is no longer the norm.

7. The Present Volume

The book in hand provides sample interpretations of a varied body of cinematic texts, illustrating different critical and philological approaches. It is a revised edition of *Classics and Cinema*, which appeared in 1991.[30] Although published by a small academic press, the book quickly took its place in the forefront of scholarly work on the importance of classical Greece and Rome in today's culture, on the pervasive influence of antiquity on the medium of film, and on the new perspectives which film can afford the interpretation of literature. Previously, the academic establishment had generally ignored or disdained the new lease on life which the cinema has given to antiquity outside the ivory towers. Not least through the example set by *Classics and Cinema*, less confined comparative approaches to the study and teaching of antiquity are now proliferating in secondary and higher education.

High-school, college, and university teachers widely consulted the book for developing new courses and carrying out their own research. In 1991, interdisciplinary approaches to antiquity by means of cinema were still in a stage of infancy, despite occasional earlier signs that film and literature could together provide a strong impulse to a fresh view of both classical antiquity and this modern medium. Since then, the situation has changed, and "classics and cinema," as it has frequently come to be called, is now a well-established and still expanding area of classical studies in the United Sates, Europe, and elsewhere. When it went out of print, the book left a considerable gap. It is here published again in an updated edition, reflecting recent academic and cultural developments.

The original volume's essays have been thoroughly revised and a few new ones added. As editor, I regret that three of the original contributors were unable to participate again. Untimely death prevented J. P. Sullivan.

29. Stanley Cavell, *The World Viewed: Reflections on the Ontology of Film*, enlarged ed. (Cambridge: Harvard University Press, 1979), ix–x. The book's first edition appeared in 1971.

30. *Classics and Cinema* (*Bucknell Review*, 35 no. 1; Lewisburg, Pa.: Bucknell University Press/London and Toronto: Associated University Presses, 1991).

The other two are Frederick Ahl ("Classical Gods and the Demonic in Film") and Kristina M. Passman ("The Classical Amazon in Contemporary Cinema"). Given the proliferation of films on both topics, the former profiting from an ever-advancing special-effects technology that makes any and all forms of the supernatural visible, the latter reflecting the increasing number of women taking the place of male heroes in action and adventure films, these essays are still important foundations for future examinations of their subjects. The new volume is thus not an entire replacement of the earlier one, and readers interested in the topics of these two essays are urged to look for a copy of *Classics and Cinema* in secondhand bookstores.[31] New in this volume are contributions by Hanna Roisman, Fred Mench, and Janice Siegel and my own on *Star Wars*. I have included the essay by Mench on Virgil's *Aeneid* because it was the first detailed interpretation of an ancient text from the perspective of cinema on the part of an American classical scholar, and as such it deserves a new appreciation. To his and Sullivan's work I have made some additions, corrections, or revisions.

The absence of film stills from our chapters deserves a word of explanation. This was a deliberate choice on the part of some authors regarding their "texts." Moreover, from a practical point of view, the cost of even black-and-white illustrations to accompany the essays was prohibitive, to say nothing of color plates. While this is an unfortunate aspect of academic publishing, the ready availability of films on videotape and videodisc has somewhat compensated for this loss. We are aware that watching a film on tape, or even on a digital disc, which gives better-quality images and preserves the original format intact, is not the ideal way of approaching an artistic work that, for its full impact and beauty to be appreciated, must be watched in a good print on the large screen for which it was intended. We therefore hope that some of our readers will make the effort to watch the one or the other film in a revival or art-house theater or in a museum. A volume about the cinema, however, should not be entirely without images. Hence the visual essay by writer-director Michael Cacoyannis on his film *Iphigenia*, one of the most accomplished translations of Greek tragedy to the screen.

It remains for me to express my thanks to the contributors, new or returning, for making this revised volume possible. If it induces readers to watch a particular film again or for the first time, if it persuades them to read or to think anew about a film or a classical text, or if it aids academic colleagues in teaching or research, the book will have accomplished its purpose. In a wide variety of ways, classical myth and culture are alive and well in the cinema. Certainly this bodes well for our modern culture.

31. The essays by Ahl and Passman are in *Classics and Cinema*, 40–59 and 81–105.

I

The *Katabasis* Theme in Modern Cinema

Erling B. Holtsmark

To the extent that it adheres to a genre of film criticism, this chapter comes closest to the tenets of Russian Formalism.[1] It is true that the material I examine assumes a vaguely Proppian shape in that my analysis is based on a study of repeated motifs and themes, but my concern is not merely to catalogue such repetitions in order to construct an idealized *katabasis* film. The films I discuss are all formulaic in the sense that they fit, and draw on, patterns of narrative expectation that are of great antiquity. Yet their very formalism need not detract from their originality, which in fact lies in their creators' capacity to manipulate audience expectation. As John Cawelti has noted:

> A successful formulaic work is unique when, in addition to the pleasure inherent in the conventional structure, it brings a new element into the formula, or embodies the personal vision of the creator. If such new elements also became wildly popular, they may in turn become widely imitated stereotypes and the basis of a new version of the formula or even a new formula altogether.[2]

1. On this see, in general, Vladimir Propp, *Morphology of the Folktale*, 2nd ed., ed. Louis A. Wagner (Austin: University of Texas Press, 1968). On the relevance of Formalism to film criticism see, for example, Peter Wollen, *Signs and Meaning in the Cinema*, 4th ed. (London: British Film Institute, 1998), 29, 60, and 163–173. Although my essay is an analysis of a crossgeneric "template" derived from classical myth, it is not, strictly speaking, genre criticism although it has connections to this approach. Readers may wish to consult, for example, the essays in *Film Genre Reader II*, ed. Barry Keith Grant (Austin: University of Texas Press, 1995).

2. John G. Cawelti, *Adventure, Mystery, and Romance: Formula Stories as Art and Popular Culture* (Chicago: University of Chicago Press, 1976), 12. Although this work is not oriented toward film, it contains much insightful information relevant to the kind of study here undertaken, and the first chapter ("The Study of Literary Formulas") in particular is strongly recommended.

And in connection with the Vietnam genre, which I will take up in detail later, the following truism has been advanced:

> The Vietnam film has not yet settled into the ripe generic dotage of the private eye or western genre, but it has reached the point where previous Vietnam films as much as Vietnam memory determine its rough outlines. As with any genre, a recurrent set of visual motifs, narrative patterns, and thematic concerns has emerged.[3]

The broadly classificatory approach at the start of my discussion is meant to serve as a convenient template of the conventional formulas of which the reader (and viewer) should be aware in thinking about and looking at the kinds of cinematic narratives treated here.

Although it may well be possible to investigate this or that corpus of katabasis films through an auteur approach, this has not been my choice here. The reason is obvious. The underpinning pattern I am concerned to elucidate is so widely dispersed—vastly more so than is suggested by the necessarily selective group of films I consider—and has been so common a literary property since the time of earliest antiquity that it is simply inappropriate to think of it in the more restrictive terms that the auteur theory would demand.

Because, for reasons of plot, character, and allusion, among others, myth is a central feature of ancient Greek literature, it has appeared tacitly axiomatic from the time of antiquity that myth informs most narrative literature. To reinforce this truism one may point further to the ubiquitous and wholesale adaptation of Greek myth by Roman and early medieval writers. The literature of the High Middle Ages and the Renaissance, not to mention that of European Classicism and Romanticism, continues to bear eloquent testimony to the durability of myth as a vehicle for shaping versions and visions of reality in texts and images.

What is perhaps not so generally observed or consciously recognized is the astonishing extent to which the mythic patterns of classical antiquity have worked themselves into the very marrow of the cinematic skeletons that support plot, action, and characterization. Film may historically be regarded as a development of theater, which has ancient and classical foundations in its own right. And since, prior to the emergence of film, legitimate theater was essentially a literary mode, it is not too surprising that much the same thematic and narrative patterning of literature, including that deriving from myth, should have made itself felt in the cinema.[4] In

3. Thomas Doherty, "Full Metal Genre: Stanley Kubrick's Vietnam Combat Movie," *Film Quarterly*, 42 no. 2 (1988–1989), 24–30; quotation at 24.

4. Such obvious links between film and literature as the screenwriting careers of William Faulkner, F. Scott Fitzgerald, and many lesser luminaries (e.g., Erich Segal, Joseph

this connection I am not concerned with such obvious mythic heirs as film versions of Homer's *Odyssey*, the heroic exploits of Heracles and other mythic heroes, or adaptations of Greek tragedy but with films that have no overt relationship to the mythic background which informs them.

Although they are not restricted to any one type, katabasis films tend to fall into certain genres: westerns, detective thrillers, war stories, and science fiction. These are also the literary genres that most frequently have recourse to mythic patterns in their story lines. This is not to say, however, that other genres fail entirely to offer examples of mythically conceived plots. A good instance is Blake Edwards's comedy-satire *10* (1979), whose middle-aged protagonist undertakes his own odyssey in search of a meaningful relationship. More specifically for the purposes of my essay, I am interested in that narrative, ancient even by the time of the archaic Greeks of Homer's world, that portrays the hero's descent into, and ascent from, the underworld—the journey to hell.

1. The Pattern

The Greek word *katabasis* literally means "a going down, a descent," capturing the imagined physical orientation of the other world relative to this one. The following generalizations can be made about the katabasis.[5] The entryway to the other world is often conceived as lying in caves or grottos or other openings in the earth's crust into the nether regions, such as chasms or clefts. Further, since that other world lies beyond a boundary separating it from our realm, such natural topographical delimiters as rivers, bodies of water, or even mountain ranges may be the physical tokens of demarcation. It is well known, for instance, that the underworld of classical mythology is penetrated by a number of rivers, most notably Styx and Acheron, which have to be crossed in a skiff punted along by the old ferryman Charon. The lower world is generally dank and dark, and the journey usually takes place at dusk or during the night. The realm itself is inhabited by the wealthy king and queen of the dead and by the

---

Wambaugh) underscore the overt relationship. For a theoretical exploration of this connection see Gerald Peary and Roger Shatzkin, *The Classic American Novel and the Movies* (New York: Ungar, 1977), 1–9, or Joy Gould Boyum, *Double Exposure: Fiction into Film* (1985; rpt. New York: New American Library, 1989), 3–20. For classical literature see Kenneth MacKinnon, *Greek Tragedy into Film* (Rutherford, N.J.: Fairleigh Dickinson University Press, 1986), 4–21.

5. More extensive analyses of the typology of the hero's descent appear in my *Tarzan and Tradition: Classical Myth in Popular Literature* (Westport, Conn.: Greenwood, 1981), 97–99 and 137, and *Edgar Rice Burroughs* (Boston: Twayne, 1986), 18–20.

innumerable spirits of the dead, by monsters (e.g., Cerberus) and evil-doers (e.g., Tantalus). The usual purpose of the journey is to obtain spiritual or material wealth—wisdom, gold, flocks, or some other form of treasure—or to rescue a friend or friends, often a woman or wife. The katabatic hero is often accompanied and helped by a companion (who may be female) or by a loyal retinue of retainers, some or all of whom may be lost in the course of the journey so that the protagonist returns alone. Virtually all katabasis stories might carry as their epigraph the famous lines which the Sibyl addresses to Aeneas as he prepares to undertake *his* great descent:

> facilis descensus Averno . . .
> sed revocare gradum superasque evadere ad auras,
> hoc opus, hic labor est.

> the way down to Hell is easy . . .
> but retracing your steps and getting back up to the upper air:
> there is the task, there is the job! (*Aeneid* 6.126, 128–129)

After his return, the hero sometimes assumes roles of increased responsibility and leadership (for instance, as a teacher or ruler) on the basis of his experience underground during his harrowing in hell.[6] From the time of Odysseus' descent in the *Odyssey*, katabasis seems inevitably to entail at some level a search for identity. The journey is in some central, irreducible way a journey of self-discovery, a quest for a lost self.

A critical point to appreciate for our purposes is the protean nature of the displacements to which the underlying paradigm is subject and this paradigm's sometimes tenuous association with the cinematic product in question. For example, without too much imagination we can appreciate how the underlying "reality" of the cavernous entrance to the underworld may manifest itself associatively in any given narrative, whether literary or cinematic, as claustrophobic defiles or narrowing mountain passes, or how the underlying motif of the demarcating body of water may appear inversely as a scorching desert, given the geographical exigencies of a particular narrative.[7] And just as these paradigmatic elements undergo

6. Further discussions may be found in Raymond J. Clark, *Catabasis: Vergil and the Wisdom-Tradition* (Amsterdam: Grüner, 1976), and A. D. Leeman, "Aeneas' Abstieg in das Totenreich: Eine Läuterungsreise durch Vergangenheit und Zukunft," in *Form und Sinn: Studien zur römischen Literatur (1954–1984)* (Frankfurt a. M.: Lang, 1985), 187–202.

7. See Jarold Ramsey, "From 'Mythic' to 'Fictive' in a Nez Percé Orpheus Myth," *Western American Literature*, 13 (1978), 119–131. On such suggestive associations or antitheses in myth in general see Joseph Fontenrose, *Python: A Study of Delphic Myth and Its Origins* (Berkeley: University of California Press, 1959; rpt. 1980), 6–9.

such transformations, so do the objectives. Thus the journey is no longer a literal descent into the actual underworld, as in Book 11 of the *Odyssey* or Book 6 of Virgil's *Aeneid*, but becomes a displaced trek into such emblematic hells as enemy terrain (e.g., the Vietnam of Michael Cimino's *The Deer Hunter* [1979]), prison (as in Stuart Rosenberg's *Brubaker* [1980]), the sleazy world of the Times Square area (as in John Schlesinger's *Midnight Cowboy* [1969]), the urban universe of drugs and crime (as in Richard Donner's *Lethal Weapon* [1987] and its sequels), or the futuristic outworlds of science fiction (as in George Lucas's *The Empire Strikes Back* [1980]).

Any hero who, like Odysseus, literally descends into hell in a sense dies and is then reborn when he ascends once more to the upper world. This theme of the katabatic hero as "dying" before being "reborn" gives rise to numerous variations, all displacements to a greater or lesser degree of the underlying idea. In the detective or police thriller, for example, the protagonist goes "under cover," that is, he is no longer the real he but some concoction dreamed up by his superior or control.[8] In John Irvin's *Raw Deal* (1986) a discredited FBI agent seeks to reinstate himself with the Bureau by undertaking an undercover mission that requires him first to burn to death in an explosion.

I now turn to a more detailed consideration of some specific films in order to note how this ancient and pervasive concept of the katabatic hero is worked out. I begin with the most archetypally heroic genre.

2. The Western

The western undoubtedly has the most readily available material for transformation and remapping: unbroken deserts and delimiting mountain ranges stretching ceaselessly westward and filled with hostile Indians, Mexican bandits, or greedy outlaws bent on rape, pillage, and murder.[9] *100 Rifles* (1969), directed by Tom Gries, contains some good elements of the type as well as an interesting inversion at the end.

A black lawman, Lyedecker, comes from Arizona to Mexico to bring back a bank robber, a half-breed named Yaqui Joe. Mexico here functions as the displaced underworld. The point is underscored by its mountains

8. Some of the terminology for such heroes is highly suggestive, such as "mole," an animal that burrows down and lives under the earth, the standard location of the underworld, or "sleeper," sleep readily being understandable as a displaced form of death. In Greek mythology, Thanatos (Death) and Hypnos (Sleep) are brothers.

9. On the mythic aspects in westerns see Martin M. Winkler, "Classical Mythology and the Western Film," *Comparative Literature Studies*, 22 (1985), 516–540.

and sere deserts and by the graphic hanging and the displays of suspended corpses at the beginning of the film. The sheriff, a kind of combination of Hermes and hero, has entered this realm in order to return Yaqui Joe to Phoenix, an antithetical variant on the search for a friend. One is tempted to see the choice of town as intentional, evoking, as the name does, the idea of rebirth. This quest in turn undergoes mutation within the katabasis proper, and the film's focus comes to rest on the rifles Joe had purchased for the Yaqui Indians with the stolen money. Thus, typologically speaking, both treasure and "friend" are the motives for this particular journey into hell.

Joe and Lyedecker get on the wrong side of the savage Mexican general Verdugo (Spanish for "executioner") and are almost killed by him on several occasions, most dramatically in front of a firing squad before the brutalized Yaqui Indians come to their rescue. These near-deaths, like unconsciousness, sickness, or sleep, are thematic displacements of death itself; as such they are emblematic of the larger realm of death in which the protagonists move.

A katabatic inset also occurs, recapitulating the larger katabasis theme of the narrative and foreshadowing its successful resolution. After some Yaqui children are taken hostage by Verdugo's men, Joe and Lyedecker organize the Indians for a raiding party into the outpost to which the general is moving. They kill the men and stage an ambush on the column escorting the children. The action is set in nocturnal darkness, and after the enemy are slain, the outpost is turned into a fiery inferno from which the Indians escape with their children. This use of the parallel, even embedded, mininarrative that reflects or somehow comments on the core tale is a familiar literary device; from classical literature, for example, we may think most prominently and immediately of the *Odyssey* and of Ovid's *Metamorphoses*, not to mention the ancient romances and novels. In the *Odyssey*, for example, the journey of Telemachus is set off against the journey of Odysseus, and the banqueting scenes at Ithaca, Pylus, and Scheria are set off against the banquet, as it were, in the Cyclops' cave. In Virgil's *Aeneid* the hero's journey to the underworld is a culmination of his other journeys in the preceding books to seek information about his future.

Toward the film's end Lyedecker is transformed into the unwilling leader of the Indians in their final conflict with Verdugo and his militia. The katabatic hero has in effect become a leader in the nether realm and leads his companions into a successful defense against Verdugo. In the end the hero relinquishes this role as unbecoming to himself and turns it over to the half-breed, Yaqui Joe. Contrary to typological expectation, the hero does not bring back the "friend" he was sent for but decides to return alone to Phoenix and bequeathes to Joe the leadership of the Yaqui Indians.

100 Rifles is an interesting variation on the katabasis theme. Among its more unusual aspects are its defiance of thematic expectations and the repeated suggestion that Joe and Lyedecker are split aspects of one persona, each of which, as a result of this particular harrowing of hell, achieves a deeper awareness of himself. Both are nonwhite, the one black and the other half-Indian; both are leaders (Joe steps right into Lyedecker's role at the end); and, most dramatically, for a portion of the film they are handcuffed to each other, at one point engaging in a ferocious fight while attached to each other, as if, metaphorically speaking, components of the persona were at odds with its entirety. Lyedecker several times comments gnomically on knowing who he is and doing the kind of job he is best suited for, while Joe, at the end, is made to realize what *he* is best suited for—leading his people.

Set in the same general time and place as *100 Rifles*, southern Texas and northern Mexico at the beginning of the twentieth century, Sam Peckinpah's *The Wild Bunch* (1969) likewise lends itself to analysis as an extended katabasis. In fact, the "underworld" becomes an unusually fluid concept in this film. Initially it is represented by the south Texas town that Pike Bishop's marauders enter in order to steal railroad funds. After mutual slaughter among the townsfolk and Pike's band, they meet up with old man Sykes, a gang member who functions typologically as a kind of Charon-Hermes figure. He knows the terrain and has had a lot of experience in it, and he is good with horses and wagon. He is also the only member of the gang who does not die at the end. When the Bunch cross a demarcating river into Mexico, a kind of topographical reversal takes place. The United States subsequently becomes the place to which they must journey in order to secure their particular version of treasure, a trainload of rifles for the Mexican revolutionary general Mapache. In a dramatic return from this displaced hell they cross desert and a bridge spanning the riverine boundary between the two realms, making it back safely to Mexico with the weapons, for which Mapache pays them ten thousand dollars. One of their group, the Mexican Angel, is taken prisoner by Mapache after the delivery of the rifles. In a fashion predictable from the type, Pike and Dutch, who fills a subordinate leadership role in the Bunch, decide to ignore the lethal dangers of confronting Mapache and his two hundred soldiers in their stronghold, and the four surviving members of the Bunch enter it to rescue their companion. Thus the locus of hell shifts once more, although the mapping conforms to the type. They ride down from the mountains, cross the desert, and enter through the portals, offering to buy Angel back from the drunken and darkly dressed Mapache.

When the latter slits Angel's throat, a fierce gun battle erupts in which most of the townspeople, Mapache's soldiers, and all four of the Bunch are killed.

Enclosing these katabases is a larger one, in which an unwilling agent of the railroad and former member of the Bunch, Deke Thornton, has been pursuing Pike's gang and, after the train robbery, is trying to intercept the rifles and capture the thieves. From Thornton's point of view, Mexico is the underworld he is forced to enter with a useless crew of miscreants, a group reminiscent of Odysseus' often less than helpful companions who, like Thornton's, are killed because of their greed long before they make it back to *their* "upper" world. Typologically speaking, it is the hero who survives the journey through hell, and therefore Thornton emerges at the end as the protagonist. He alone survives the "descent" and will assume a leadership role in helping Sykes rebuild Angel's village after the film's narrative has concluded.

Why this unusual shift in the locus of hell, and the different points of view about hell? As abbreviated katabasis narratives in their own right, they provide parallel accounts, a multiplication of the pattern. Conceptually, however, the viewer is left with the sense that hell is where you make it, and for the likes of Pike's gang hell is wherever they are, as Mexico certainly proves to be for them. Lest there be any doubt about this point, the camera, after its nightmarish panning and crosscutting among the combatants' dances of death, lingers suggestively over the strewn corpses and waiting buzzards. It is also worth noting that the film is organized in classical ring composition, with the winning of treasure at its center and the two extended sequences of slaughter framing the whole.[10] Minor thematic moments enhance this sense of almost paradigmatic structure: after being bumped by an old woman at the start Pike helps her; after being shot by a young one at the end he shoots her. The innocent and mindless cruelty of children at the start is echoed by the consequential and deliberate cruelty of a child at the end; the *Iliad*-like despoiling of the corpses of the slain at the start, albeit by clear antiheroes, involves only clothing and personal effects, but at the end the stakes have been raised to gold-filled teeth. The bloody slaughter of innocents is portrayed in graphic slow motion at both ends.

The katabatic subtheme of the rescued woman occurs in Richard Brooks's *The Professionals* (1966). A wealthy older man, Grant, hires four individuals to cross the desert into Mexico to recover Mrs. Grant, kidnapped by the Mexican revolutionary Raza. The four adventurers each have an

10. On ring composition in film see my "Films and Ring Composition," *KLEOS: Estemporaneo di Studi e Testi sulla Fortuna dell'Antico*, 2 (1997), 271–274.

area of expertise: Rico is an arms expert with leadership ability; Dolworth is an explosives man with considerable inventiveness; Ehrengard is a natural horse handler; and Sharp is a tracker par excellence.

In terms of the ancient prototypes, these four men distributively represent the typological constants familiar from the katabasis narrative. The hero is of course a fighter, clever as well as strong, and frequently has special abilities or associations with animals. The black man, Sharp, as often in modern cinematic incarnations, is a Hermes figure, the *psychopompos* ("escorter of the dead") who not only guides the hero into hell but also helps him return to the upper world.[11] In the ancient tales sometimes the hero is alone, as when Heracles rescues Alcestis, and at other times he has companions who may be especially helpful (e.g., Peirithous trying to get Persephone back from the lower world for Theseus) or not (e.g., Odysseus' journey to the Cyclops' cave). From a typological point of view it matters little whether we are dealing with many capabilities condensed into a single hero or with several heroes who have split among themselves the varied abilities of a single personality. In any event, at the end of *The Professionals* our thematic expectations, as well as Grant's hopes, are foiled in that the ostensibly rescued woman turns out to have been Raza's willing "victim," who wanted out of Grant's clutches; she is finally returned to Mexico. The suggestion emerges that Grant is in effect the real Hades from whom she had to be rescued.

Although certain film genres such as westerns and detective narratives seem to lend themselves more intuitively to patterning on the katabasis theme than others, even such films do not, of course, all fall into the general type. Yet even where the overarching design is lacking, it may manifest itself in smaller segments that inform or enhance the plot as a whole.

A good example is *The Long Riders* (1976), directed by Walter Hill, the story of the James-Younger gang in post–Civil War Missouri. The film is structured as a series of parallel episodes of bank robbery followed by celebration and involvement with women. The first and last bank robberies in the film create a ring-compositional frame. The last robbery is relevant to my discussion. For once the gang decides to leave the familiar territory

11. As such, blacks typically have roles as escorts or trackers to point the way. They pilot the boat, as in *Apocalypse Now* (a film discussed later), or bring the hero back to his world, as the black drummer does in Richard Fleischer's *The Jazz Singer* (1980) by driving into the desert. Consistent with this is the inverted use of albinos as monster types. The freaky albino in *Lethal Weapon* is a transcendent Death monster, with whom the hero wrestles at the end. The equally crazy albino in Burt Reynolds's *Stick* (1985), a Death demon suitably dressed completely in black, is a twist on the same inversion. The etiolated death figures are evil incarnate, while the black ones embody the instructive psychopompic function of the Hermes figure.

of Missouri and do their robbing in distant Minnesota. They leave home for a place far from home that they reach by train, shown traveling at night. They are going to this distant place in search of treasure, as one of the gang has learned that the bank in Northfield, Minnesota, is full of money. Appropriately the bank is located next to the town mortuary, a point emphasized not only in dialogue but also visually; a shot of Cole Younger waiting outside the bank places him prominently and lingeringly against the mortuary in the background. As it turns out, the town knows that the gang are on their way, and they are unable to get any money. In addition, they are ambushed as they try to escape. All but Jesse James are wounded or killed, and Jesse, along with his brother Frank, abandons the rest of the men. He is himself later betrayed and shot.

The importance of this minor instance of the theme lies in the fact that it is played off against the expectations we have of the standard tale. It is a kind of anti-katabasis, fully understandable as such only against the backdrop of familiarity with the general tale. For here the hero neither gains treasure nor, certainly, any wisdom. (Jesse returns to Missouri and wants to start a better gang to rob banks.) Rather than bringing back friends from the dead, he leaves them dying or destined for long prison terms. Thematically, then, it seems appropriate that Jesse is shot at the end, since he never really escaped from the harrowing journey to hell in Northfield, where the rest of the gang came to their end.

George Stevens's classic western *Shane* (1953) has a memorable katabasis narrative at its end. In a resolution of the fierce range war that has divided the film's world, Shane rides into town late at night, crossing the river that separates the settled, civilized homestead, on whose behalf he is fighting, from the corrupt town. Little Joey, his friend, follows him and is shown crossing a graveyard on the way. We assume that Shane did also, although this does not appear on screen. For the final showdown with the land-hungry Ryker and his hired gun Wilson, Shane enters a tavern through swinging doors. These saloon doors have appeared numerous times before and have become a kind of iconic shorthand for entrance into a zone of danger, that is, a katabatic realm. One may note that a common euphemism in classical myth for the underworld was *pylae* ("gates, entryway").[12] The classical hero is not infrequently associated with cattle or is involved in a confrontation with an owner of cattle, as in the case of Odysseus and the cattle of the Sun, Heracles and the cattle of Geryon, or Amphitryon and the stolen cattle of the Taphians.[13] Ryker is a ruthless

12. Fontenrose, *Python*, 329–330.

13. For this cattle owner as a Death demon see Fontenrose, *Python*, 335–336 and 346; see also G. S. Kirk, *The Nature of Greek Myths* (London: Penguin, 1974; rpt. 1990), 189–190.

cattle baron and, typologically speaking, Shane, in overcoming him and his henchmen, embodies the role of the hero as master of cattle. As if to underscore the contrast between the hero and the murderous agent of this lethal cattle owner, Shane is dressed in white, Wilson in black.[14] Shane shoots both Ryker and Wilson, and as he begins to walk out of the saloon, Joey, who has been watching, alerts him to a man with a rifle aiming at him from the upper story. It is not unusual for the hero to receive help at some point in his journey from a woman, child, animal, or other kind of escort, and the aid Joey gives Shane may be seen as a form of this element of the narrative. Although Shane is ostensibly helping Joey's father and the homesteaders in the valley, his confrontation with Wilson reinforces in himself the self-knowledge to which he has come and which he now carries out of the gunfight. Appropriately, the emaciated Wilson looks like a figure of death with an especially menacing grin. As Shane tells Joey before he rides off: "A man has to be what he is, Joey. You can't break the mold. I tried it, and it didn't work for me." A man of violence is a man of violence, just as a man of peace is a man of peace. Shane knows, finally, what he is.

Katabasis aside, this sentiment is itself strongly classical. Its underlying meaning is captured in the Delphic injunction "Know thyself," repeated in countless guises throughout Greek literature. Dress plays an important part in orchestrating this shifting of roles by Shane. When we first meet him, he wears his "armor," his gunfighter outfit complete with six-shooter and gunbelt; as he tries to fit into the homesteaders' civilized society, he buys farmer's clothing and a new belt, which he wears until he starts on his trip into town to deal with Ryker and Wilson. At that point he once more dons his "armor." This emblematic use of clothing is common in film; a well-known deployment of it in a katabatic setting is the opening of John Schlesinger's *Midnight Cowboy* (1969), where a country hick from Texas gets himself outfitted for his descent into the dark netherworld of male prostitution in the urban hell of New York City.

Another western, Robert Aldrich's *Ulzana's Raid* (1972), which deals with the pursuit of renegade Apaches into the Arizona territory, is structured as a typical katabasis but accommodates certain shifts toward the end. A young lieutenant, Garnett, full of peaceful Christian pieties quite inappropriate to the infernal desert where the Indians live, leads an army party in pursuit of Chief Ulzana and his band of horse raiders. Garnett's commanding officer sets the tone at the film's start by recalling General

---

14. On this imagery see Andrew Tudor, "Genre," in *Film Genre Reader II*, 3–10, especially 5.

Sheridan's observation that if he owned hell and Arizona, he would live in hell and rent out Arizona.

Into this harsh and uncompromising land goes the naive lieutenant, escorted by a white scout named MacIntosh and by Ke-Ni-Tay, an Apache in the service of the army. The searing desert and the mountainous defiles through which they pass conjure up the western version of the katabic landscape filled with the Apaches' pillage, burning, and rape.[15] For the lieutenant this campaign proves to be as much the emblematic journey for practical knowledge of the world as it is the ostensible pursuit of horses and thieves. Throughout, he questions MacIntosh and Ke-Ni-Tay about the land, the Apaches, their customs, and the reasons for their cruelty. MacIntosh is the Hermes figure who at the start conducts the lieutenant and his men into the wilderness, but the native scout Ke-Ni-Tay gradually comes to assume that role. Indeed, since MacIntosh is dying at the end, Ke-Ni-Tay escorts the corpse of Ulzana, whom he has killed, to burial. The white and the Indian scout teach the lieutenant about the land as much as they teach him about his need to learn that Christian charity, while laudable in the fort, is a dangerous delusion in the desert. By letting Ke-Ni-Tay have his way, Garnett symbolically lays aside his Christian arrogance and, the film implies, begins to learn how to accept the land on its own terms as he sets out for the "real" world of the fort.

3. The Thriller

Now for a different venue. *Narrow Margin* (1990), written and directed by Peter Hyams, sketches a brief for the duty of citizens to bear witness against those who corrupt society, but this message tends to get blown away in the general rush of the film's action. The plot is quite simple. A deputy district attorney must bring back a witness to a murder in order to convict a major crime figure.

The katabic landscape, the displaced underworld, is in this case the rough and dangerously beautiful terrain of the Canadian Rockies. Caulfield, the deputy D.A., travels by helicopter to the remote cabin where his companion, a detective, has traced the woman who had inadvertently witnessed a crime czar's presence at a murder and whose testimony can put this man behind bars for good. The immense grandeur of snow-covered peaks, among which the helicopter threads its precarious way, provides a splendid example of contemporary displacement of the tra-

---

15. Topography clearly assumes such a role in American Indian katabasis narratives. See Ramsey, "From 'Mythic' to 'Fictive'."

ditional boundaries demarcating the "other" world. And the detective accompanying Caulfield is an Elpenor figure, the sacrificial victim who pays with his life for the hero's journey to the beyond. Homer's Elpenor, the youngest of Odysseus' men, lost his life at Circe's palace (*Odyssey* 10.552–560).

Most important for the journey shown in this film is the train, the film's clearest emblem of the hero's journey. We first see it in a distant shot snaking like a great silver dragon through the wild and mountainous terrain of western Canada. Since antiquity the underworld has been almost always located toward the west. Most of the action takes place on this train, at night and in the dark. The train traverses a spectacular katabatic world of steep mountainsides, narrow defiles, still lakes, rivers, and dark tunnels.

The hero brings the woman back to the real world, gains the knowledge she has, which is necessary to convict the crime boss, and secures his own version of treasure, this time measured not in dollars or gold but in the satisfaction of doing his job well. And like Odysseus and practically all archetypal heroes, he overcomes foes and obstacles by physical daring and by cunning and resourcefulness. The mythical underpinnings will no doubt escape the viewer's conscious awareness in all the excitement, but they are there.

Recent years have seen, ad nauseam, scandals and upheavals involving no less than the very president of the United States. Many citizens have come to believe that the country's highest office has, well, gone to hell as a result. So we may be justified to wonder if in the Clinton years films dealing with even a fictional U.S. president did not exhibit at least some katabatic features as well. No surprise: some—political thrillers—do.

A katabatic interlude occurs in the last half hour of Dwight Little's *Murder at 1600* (1997). Although the film is not strictly plotted as a katabasis, its ending involves the successful attempt of the hero and his two buddies to save the presidency for the president. They achieve this by descending into the tunnels that will conduct them underground into the White House, naturally in the nick of time. The cinematography lovingly exploits all the standard furniture of the katabatic descent, here through a sewer grill, into dank and dark subterranean passageways. The trio is pursued by a demonic opponent, who almost kills the hero but is shot dead by the hero's female companion. The waist-deep waters coursing through these tenebrous warrens evoke the riverine topography of the classical underworld.

Like *Murder at 1600*, Clint Eastwood's *Absolute Power* (also 1997) is not essentially a katabasis film. Its plot revolves around a detective's search for a young woman's killer. Yet an early sequence is clearly mapped on the particulars of the katabasis tale, replete with some intriguing high-tech updates.

A thief, Luther, breaks into the mansion of wealthy Walter Sullivan during the night. This house contains vast treasure in the form of price-less paintings and, in the secret vault next to the master bedroom, coins, cash, and a variety of jewelry. Sullivan, a multibillionaire and political kingmaker, is a kind of Hades figure who is married, as was his mythi-cal predecessor, to a younger woman. Sullivan even has specific asso-ciations with the earth; as we learn later, his father was a miner, and the son had become his heir. Lording it over all the earth's underground treasures, the Greek Hades was a god of extreme riches, as his Greek eponym, Ploutos ("Wealth"), and his Latin one, Dis ("Rich") make clear. There is no Cerberus guarding Sullivan's house, but there is, as the in-vestigating detective later puts it, "a zillion-dollar security system." Luther gets around this electronic watchdog with a sophisticated elec-tronic device. And rather than going down, he climbs the stairs to the bedroom, enters the vault, and robs the old man. While he is so occu-pied, Sullivan's wife and her lover—yes, the president—come home. Luther hides in the vault and becomes an unwilling witness to drunken foreplay that turns into rough sex and ends in the woman's murder. (It's that kind of president.)

Luther escapes with his treasure and with the knowledge of presiden-tial complicity in crime and coverup. In the rest of the film, which con-sists of the murder investigation, the katabatic overtones introduced by the opening sequence reverberate throughout, both in the parallel plot of Luther rescuing another woman from death (his daughter) and in his emergence into safety from Sullivan's attempt on his life. Reinforcing the analogy to Hades, Sullivan is a death-dealer who hires an assassin to take out the man whom he erroneously believes to have murdered his wife. And he himself, we are forced to conclude, kills the president at the end. *Absolute Power* is a solid example of how the *katabasis*, while not cen-tral, can effectively strengthen a film's plot.

4. Science Fiction

The 1986 film *Cherry 2000*, directed by the relatively unknown Steve De Jarnatt, offers a flashy variation on the basic katabasis pattern. Sam Treadwell owns a Cherry 2000 robot, which is his beautiful live-in mis-tress. She is actually an android, externally indistinguishable from a real human being (an evocation of Michael Crichton's *Westworld* [1973] and Ridley Scott's *Blade Runner* [1982]). After she shorts out during a love session on the floor and water clogs her circuits beyond repair, Sam realizes he loves her. When she cannot be fixed at the repair shop, Sam is given her miniaturized "personality disc" and told that a replacement husk is in all probability stored at a "Graveyard" in Zone 7, a dangerous land beyond civilization. His journey to the Graveyard to find a new Cherry husk for his disc is thus a replaced form of the hero's search for a lost woman. His guide is one of the most famous trappers of Zone 7, a woman, as it turns out, called E. Johnson. A large part of the film is given over to the katabatic journey proper, which they make in this sexy sybil's souped-up Thunderbird.

This journey is replete with and remarkably faithful to the ancestral themes we have come to expect for this part of the descent tale. The two travel mainly at night, avoiding the various marauding outlaw bands that dot the barren landscape through which they move. The Nevada desert scenery spectacularly embodies the theme of a barrier separating this world from the one below. In a striking scene, Johnson and Sam cross a vast chasm at whose bottom lies a great river. Plunging down through a cavernous hole into the "underworld," they are met by an old man fittingly attired as a spelunker, Six-Fingered Jake, a friend of Johnson and arch-trapper reputedly killed by the outlaws but still alive. This character, with his emblematic underworld attire and knowledge of the underground caverns, is a guide figure of the sort often encountered by the katabatic hero, an incarnation of Charon. Jake transports Sam and Johnson across the river on his spare barge, powered by two outboards in place of Charon's traditional punting pole.

Johnson reconditions an old plane and flies Sam to the Graveyard ahead of the pursuing outlaws. When they have arrived at the repository, the guide leads the hero in a final descent through a skylight into a ghostly, pale chamber where countless husks hang etiolated and lifeless in the eerie gloom. We cannot help but think of Anticleia's description of the spirits to her son Odysseus:

> The flesh and bones are no longer possessed of strength,
> but the powerful might of blazing fire overpowers them
> as soon as the personality has abandoned the white bones.
> And the spirit goes flying, flitting off like a dream.
> (*Odyssey* 11.219–222)

It is perhaps relevant to this ancient passage to note that, when the original Cherry shorted out electrically, she was enveloped in crackling flashes and fiery sparks and that her miniaturized laser disc containing the complex program for all her emotions and feelings ultimately traces its ancestry back to Homer's *thumos* ("personality, life-force"). Sam had removed the disc from the original, the whole point of his journey being to find another husk in which to insert it.

As soon as he does, the new Cherry pops alive. But Sam soon recognizes that all her emotions are mere programs. In a climax fraught with shoot-outs with the outlaws and narrow escapes from disaster, Sam jettisons the newly activated Cherry and makes it back to earth with Johnson, with whom a romantic relationship had been developing as they proceeded deeper into the "underworld."

Needless to say, this particular twist on the typical ending, in which the hero abandons the woman he searched for and takes up with the sibyl, has no counterpart in Greek and Roman myth. In this film, however, it emerges naturally out of the paradigm and will strike the viewer as an ingenious and organically motivated innovation on a design now some five thousand years old.

Finally, the hero, who was at first a moping and rather helpless individual, undergoes a transformation as a result of his journey and, typologically speaking, returns with enhanced wisdom. For Sam learns, largely through the agency of Johnson, his sybil, to fend for himself and to improvise daringly as circumstances require. He comes to recognize what love is all about—at least in the American cinema of the 1980s.

Although this is not a well-known film, it should be. It adheres believably to the katabasis type but allows for some clever adaptations. Played with gentle humor, primarily thanks to Melanie Griffith's laid-back portrayal of the psychopompic sibyl, it succeeds admirably as an example of the genre. A katabatic sleeper, as it were!

The concept driving *Johnny Mnemonic* (1995), directed by Robert Longo and written by cyber-guru William Gibson, author of *Neuromancer*, extrapolates from contemporary technology and earlier films, such as *Westworld* and Mike Hodges's *The Terminal Man* (1974). As his name tells us, Johnny Mnemonic has some kind of plug-in interface in his skull and can upload several gigabytes of data. He turns himself into a data courier; once he has arrived at his destination, he plugs in and downloads. The only catch is that Johnny had to lose some of his original core memory to make room for this new ability—in his case, his childhood. On a long delivery trip from Beijing to Newark, his head is so crammed that he has periodic seizures and desperately needs to download, but the access code has gone astray.

What follows is a standard katabasis narrative, even if its hero is a technofreak of the 2020s. All the katabatic territory is there: the night journeys through smoke-shrouded alleys in the urban wasteland of Newark, a descent into tunnel-like sewers, a female aide, a black Hermes who guides and protects the hero, the obstructing minions of the underworld, literally and figuratively, and the harmer who in the end turns helper. Johnny's ostensible search for a computer to download his data is really a hunt for his missing childhood, a far-out trip that quite literally blows his mind before it is rearranged the way it used to be and his past comes into focus again.

The film is a 1960s acid trip morphed for the cyber generation of the 1990s. But despite its intriguing premise, which weds ancient narrative typology to modern computer technology, the story crashes, largely because of the film's mindless iteration of dazzling technique. The special effects, however, are already outdated.

Johnny Mnemonic is a katabasis, so to speak, to a narrative nadir. But it prompts me to consider some of the dangers inherent in too close a reliance on typology and formula, even when they are as seemingly inexhaustible as those of the *katabasis*. My example is another thriller, *Conflict of Interest* (1993), directed by Gary Davis. It deals with a rogue cop, who is wound too tight and is stepping outside procedures in order to get a job done, and with a son and father getting to know each other. The typology is clearly there; in this case it takes the story of a father's search for and exculpation of his son who is unjustly accused of murder.

Everything we can expect from the pattern is present: the helping woman, the otherworldly landscape of a rock music club (named "The Wreck") of dark and dancing souls that gyrate, a nasty Hades figure with the biblical name Gideon, who has his thugs in constant attendance, a huge bouncer as guardian of the gates, and a Persephone-like dark woman named Eve, who belongs to Gideon but is rescued by the son. The hero's talisman, his police badge, enables him to enter this nightmarish underworld. He also receives the crucial help of a black cop friend. A twist on our expectations occurs when the son, initially the object of the father's frantic quest, becomes himself the quester and saves his father from making a huge mistake. In the end, as we expected, father and son are reconciled, and the detective validates himself in the eyes of son and society. His rehabilitation is a kind of rebirth.

The danger of excessive reliance on pattern, however, is that spontaneity and inventiveness run the risk of being forgotten; as with *Johnny Mnemonic*, form triumphs over substance. *Conflict of Interest* is ultimately uninteresting because it is too categorical in the way it unfolds its story. There is no deepening of the plot nor any apparent concern about the characters, who are merely generic types. The father's uncontrollable rage, for example, shows up too often and with far too limited variation in the acting and becomes quite tedious. We almost agree with the crooked cops that he is a pain in the ass.

5. Contemporary Drama

40

CLASSICAL

MYTH &

CULTURE

IN THE

CINEMA

John Boorman's *Beyond Rangoon* (1995) rings a variation on the heroic quest in that this narrative is not for treasure, friend, or spouse but rather the recovery of oneself. One of the most intense of the films dealt with in this essay, it is a hauntingly beautiful study of death and rebirth, of loss and recovery, of the interplay between the microcosms of personal desire and a macrocosm of political tyranny. It is not, I am sure, a film soon to be showing in today's Myanmar, the former Burma.

Laura, a doctor whose child and husband have been murdered, has gone on a trip deep into Burma in an effort to forget her grief. This proves to be as harrowing a journey into the katabatic heart of human darkness as any considered here. Tellingly, the photography in *Beyond Rangoon* is so lush as if to ask pointedly how a landscape of such exquisite beauty can nurture such sinister malevolence. A similar landscape, haunting and beautiful, serves the same thematic function in Terrence Malick's *The Thin Red Line* (1998), a film set in World War II.

This displaced underworld is represented by the despotic military of Burma and by a soldier's attempt to rape Laura in a village hospital. Here, emblematically, she as a doctor would heal and save lives, but she murders her assailant in cold blood in order to save herself. At last she has awakened from her lethargy and begins her extraordinary ascent to the safety of the upper world, symbolized by her desperate crossing over into Thailand.

The familiar geography of the katabasis is almost oppressive: thick, clinging jungles, swift and rapacious rivers demarcating zones of reality, swaying bridges across high gorges, maleficent soldiers, and helping denizens of this otherworld, which lies beyond the relative civilization of Rangoon but reveals a deeper reality of how lives are lived.

Laura, sleepless, goes out into the Rangoon night to watch the Democracy Movement and the courage of its leader in facing down an armed militia. But during her night foray she loses her passport. This loss suggests a loss of identity and accurately reflects her emotional state. She must wait until the American Embassy can issue her a replacement. While waiting, she walks around Rangoon and meets an older gentleman, Aung Ko, a former professor at the University of Rangoon who fell afoul of the military and now takes foreigners on tours. He is a Hermes figure, escorting Laura not only into the interior of Burma but also into the unknown territory of her inner self. In an example of ring composition at the end of the film, Aung Ko with dignity and fortitude faces down a soldier denying the refugees access to the bridge to Thailand and impresses Laura so much that this moment becomes the start of the descent that will lead to her return to herself and to her acceptance of a grief that is as inconsolable as its cause is inexplicable.

While they are out in the countryside, the military cracks down on "hooligans," and a return to Rangoon is imperative. But the soldiers are after Laura and Aung Ko. The plot now shifts to that of an escape film and becomes a journey within a journey. When she sees Aung Ko being beaten by soldiers and one of his former students getting shot for trying to protect him, Laura comes to his help. Now she turns into her own Hermes, guiding herself and the wounded Aung Ko back to safety. Crashing their car into a river while being pursued by soldiers, she must rescue Aung Ko; in the process she loses her replacement passport. Drenched by the river and covered in shoreline mud, she is no longer Laura, American citizen grieving for her loss, but a survivor and rescuer who initiates a process of spiritual rebirth from the riparian slime.[16]

On a raft heading for Rangoon Laura nurses Aung Ko back to health. Back in Rangoon, she is arrested in front of the American Embassy and barely escapes in the chaos of a huge demonstration. With Aung Ko and others she finally makes it across the river to a camp in Thailand, where she begins to help in the hospital compound.

At the start of the film, Laura is preoccupied with herself to the point of obsession with her grief. She constantly wears dark sunglasses, as if she wished to shut out the world and not see it the way it is in both its ugliness and beauty. Her soul itself is blind. In the last dream she has about her murdered son and husband, just before crossing over to Thailand, her boy comes to her in the night and tells her that she has to let go of him. Laura then tells Aung Ko that she can no longer hold on to her child. Nobody can remain with the dead. (We are reminded of Odysseus' meeting with his mother in Book 11 of the *Odyssey*.) But this does not mean that Laura will ever forget her child. Indeed, children are a leitmotif throughout the film, at every turn reminding her of her own lost son and of hope for the future.

In an early scene Laura buys a small bird and sets it free, but the birder whistles it back and cages it again. At this stage Laura is not ready herself to be free, but she will be after she has gone through all that is in store for her. Observing and moving among an oppressed and suffering people who are able to endure inspires her. Their fight for freedom from external dictatorship parallels her own struggle, at first clumsy but later intense, to liberate herself of interior tyranny.

16. For the emergence of a similarly "encrusted" rebirth hero see my "Spiritual Rebirth of the Hero: *Odyssey* 5," *The Classical Journal*, 61 (1966), 206–210, especially 209 (on *Odyssey* 5.455–457 and 6.224–226): Odysseus is "bespattered with the unsightly dross that still clings to him from his watery womb."

Boorman's moving film works out the katabasis theme intricately and persuasively. *Beyond Rangoon* could certainly lend itself to postcolonial or feminist analysis. The former would revolve around the oppressive political character of the regime in Burma and its collusive maintenance by Western oil companies, a point never broached in the film itself, of course. The latter could focus on the clear oppression of the female protagonist or underscore the fact that all the doctors in the film are women. But the film strikes me as much more rewardingly explored in terms of its katabatic design.

Pure Country (1992), directed by Christopher Cain, is superficially rather different from *Beyond Rangoon* but at a deeper level pointedly similar. It, too, deals with the quest not for friend or treasure but for self.

A burned-out country-and-western artist, played by a real-life performer, walks away from it all to find out who he is and what he values. True, we have seen this before—herein actually lies the interest in this film. How is the variation played out this time? The hero has something akin to a nervous breakdown on stage, trapped in a dazzle of stage lights, fireworks, and crazed fans screaming in the dark arena like the souls of the damned. After the show, he tells his drummer and boyhood friend that he needs to go for a walk. The journey begins.

When the protagonist sings in the opening number about the heartland, the meaning of his song is not the American Midwest but the territory of the emotions, the land his journey will let him explore. First he returns to his childhood home. With a shave and a haircut he divests himself of his old life. His grandmother, a kind of sibyl ("there are no answers, only the search"), can hardly recognize him in his changed appearance. This is the first of a series of Odyssean recognition scenes in which he alternatively hides and reveals himself, until in a final recognition scene he proves to the woman he loves who he really is. Sound familiar—from about three millennia ago? There is even a seductive and willful woman reminiscent of Homer's Circe, although she here embodies both the helping and the hindering female, characters common in tales of journeys and quests since the time of Odysseus. This film is an urbane reworking of the classical katabasis paradigm in a story about the pressures of contemporary musical tours.

6. The Vietnam War Film

I come finally to a consideration of the katabasis in films based on the collective American descent into the hell of Vietnam. For example, the graphic portrayal of a displaced underworld in *Platoon* (1986), written and directed by Oliver Stone, is striking. The topography of hell is the Vietnamese landscape of a clinging, claustrophobic jungle, crawling, like any katabatic terrain, with impeding monsters, here shown as preying insects and leeches, venomous snakes, and murderous Viet Cong. The film emphasizes the idea of rebirth after the ascent, which is an underlying assumption of the whole katabasis narrative, both verbally and visually by the frames that enclose the narrative. At the start of the film, new infantry are seen disembarking through dust and smoke from a transport plane, and we hear the new recruit Taylor muttering that it feels like hell here. At the very end, as he ascends in a helicopter from the jungle charnel house created by the great firefight he has just survived, he observes sotto voce that he feels like a child who has been born of two fathers: Barnes, the psychopathic sergeant, and Elias, the crusading sergeant. These two have condensed into his personal *psychopompos* guiding him through hell; in order for him to become his own self, both are killed. The child must be freed of paternal influences before he can grow up to be an adult in his own right.

Elias is consistently portrayed as a thoughtful and caring soldier and comes to represent a model of good soldiering for Taylor, but Barnes shoots Elias in cold blood and leaves him for dead. When Taylor realizes what Barnes has done, he gets into a fight with the sergeant and is almost killed by him in the "underworld," an underground bunker that some of the soldiers have built for relaxing and indulging in drugs. Shortly thereafter, as if to cancel the potentially evil influence of Barnes that he might bring back from Vietnam, Taylor kills him. Because this film has strong overtones of a *Bildungsroman*, it seems appropriate that the hero should be seen as liberated from the continuing intrusion of the spiritual ancestry of Elias and Barnes on his life after he returns to America.

Although this is perhaps fortuitous, Taylor's first name is Chris. While he is no more a saint than anyone else, the name of this katabatic protagonist nevertheless evokes the name of Christ, the katabatic protagonist of Christianity's central myth of death, descent, and resurrection. And the major engagement that leads to Taylor's "rebirth" begins on New Year's Day, a symbolic day of renewals and beginnings, when, in Taylor's words, they are all marching through the jungle like "ghosts in a landscape," a phrase that recalls the ghosts who inhabit the Homeric underworld.

At the start of the film Taylor is an inexperienced grunt. Indeed, he makes an issue of this point in a letter he is writing to his grandmother. Like the other soldiers, most of whom he sees as American society's underclass forced to fight in Vietnam, he thinks of himself as a loser at the bottom of the barrel; since he is so far down in the mud, he can only go up.

(This metaphorical direction has immediate relevance to the katabatic themes of going down and up again.) He emerges from his journey through hell as someone who has learned to refashion himself and his values out of the meaninglessness of war, and he will live with this awareness in the world to which he returns.

There are, moreover, a number of incidents throughout the film that function as katabatic insets that comment by way of parallelism or antithesis on the overarching katabasis informing the film as a whole. An early parallel is the minor inset when Taylor thinks he has been shot and is dying from what is only a slight head wound; however, another soldier is killed, and Barnes takes the opportunity to make of him a memento mori for the rest of the soldiers who did not die this time. Shortly after this first baptism of fire, a black soldier, who should be understood as a psychopompic figure, introduces Taylor into the "underworld"; his introduction of Taylor to the others is significant, for he calls him not "Taylor" but "Chris." This abbreviated evocation of the Christian archetype of death and resurrection parallels the larger theme of the katabasis and foreshadows the hero's ultimate return from the harrowing experience of Vietnam. For in both this small "underworld" and in Vietnam as a whole, he enters an innocent, passes certain ritualized initiation ceremonies, and emerges a different character: from the "underworld," as accepted by the other grunts, and from Vietnam, accepted by himself.

Parallel to this is the incident in which Elias descends into the cavernous, riverine tunnels of a Viet Cong underground bunker, where he confronts and kills the enemy deep in their lair; his safe ascent again signals the emergence of the katabatic hero from the underground enemy entrenched in this part of the countryside. In antithetical fashion, in one inset the soldiers cross a river and climb up a hill to invade a village, brutalize some peasants, almost rape some of the children, torch the entire compound, and drive off the still living as though they were cattle. This invasion of a microcosm of Vietnam can also be seen as an inverted katabatic episode in that the directions are reversed, enemies rather than friends are led back, and the hero, along with Elias, opposes rather than promotes the operations undertaken. As in most films about Vietnam, much of the action takes place either in nocturnal darkness or in the tenebrous passageways beneath the covering jungle canopy, and fires burn everywhere in a land scored by rivers large and small.

The shape of Stanley Kubrick's *Full Metal Jacket* (1987) owes a diffused but unmistakable allegiance to the katabasis type. Indeed, although it is less schematic than *Platoon* in its overt deployment of the specific details characterizing the pattern, the film involves two katabases: the sojourn of the young men at Parris Island and Joker's campaign in Vietnam. Each complements and comments on the other.

The boot camp is a world unto itself, separated from the mainland by a body of water. It proves to be a harrowing hell for the raw recruits who, during the opening sequence, are emblematically shorn of their connections to "this world" by the barbers trimming their hair down to the skull. The sadistic drill sergeant Hartman, who runs their "other world," has set himself up as a minor deity empowered to remold them into killing-machine Marines, and they must do constant obeisance to him and his torturous training regimen. One of them, Pyle, finally snaps and, at night in a communal toilet room, with Joker, the film's protagonist and narrator, looking on helplessly, takes a kind of communal vengeance on Hartman by killing him and then himself.[17] Cut to Saigon.

This world, ten thousand miles from the United States, is steeped in deceit, corruption, and death. On several occasions the men characterize it implicitly as the otherworld when they speak of eventually "rotating back to the world" if they are not first killed. Joker works for the army newspaper and is sent upcountry to join the platoon of his boot camp buddy Cowboy. The topography of his journey is consistently infernal: dark billowing smoke, flames, bombed-out buildings, death, killing, a demarcating Perfume River, corpses, a mass grave, and a virtually invisible enemy. Entering an urban shell of concrete rubble, the men are pinned down by sniper fire, and some of them are killed. A rescue party is sent to "take out the gooks" and recover the corpses of the dead, a resonatingly Homeric motif, as is seen in the mutilation of Sarpedon's corpse (*Iliad* 16.545–546) or the fight over the body of Patroclus (*Iliad* 17.700–736).[18] In the final confrontation with the enemy, Joker enters a cavernous edifice of twisted girders and pitted foundations eerily lit by dancing fires, only to discover that what appeared to be a large concentration of hostile

17. A persistent metaphor for the otherworlds of boot camp and Vietnam is the word "shit"; to endure the horrors of being in either hell is, with an appropriate awareness of direction, "to be in deep shit." Doherty, "Full Metal Genre," comments sensibly on this use of language and speaks of "a veritable fecal obsession" (27). Aristophanes uses the same metaphor in *Peace*, where the "world without peace . . . is visualized in images of excrement," among others; quoted from Jeffrey Henderson, *The Maculate Muse: Obscene Language in Attic Comedy*, 2nd ed. (New York: Oxford University Press, 1991), 63. See also Kenneth J. Reckford, "'Let Them Eat Cakes'—Three Food Notes to Aristophanes' *Peace*," in *Arktouros: Hellenic Studies Presented to Bernard M. W. Knox on the Occasion of His 65th Birthday*, ed. Glenn W. Bowersock, Walter Burkert, and Michael C. J. Putnam (Berlin: De Gruyter, 1979), 192–193; and C. H. Whitman, *Aristophanes and the Comic Hero* (Cambridge: Harvard University Press, 1964), 110.

18. On this theme in general see Charles Segal, *The Theme of the Mutilation of the Corpse in the "Iliad"* (Leiden: Brill, 1971).

troops who have been decimating the Americans' ranks turns out in reality
to be a single woman, really not much more than a girl. Joker, acting for
the men, kills her after she has been mortally wounded.

The narrative is unified by Hartman's death at the end of the boot camp
sequence, during which emphasis had repeatedly been placed on equat-
ing rifles with girlfriends and even valuing weapons over penises, and by
this final scene of the killing of the woman sniper.[19] The men have already had a number of debasing encounters with Vietnamese prostitutes,
and whether it is literally with a military weapon or symbolically with a
bodily tool, they end up raping and destroying the country. And herein
lies the chilling irony of the film, for in reversing the normal katabatic
pattern in which heroes rescue a woman abducted into hell, Kubrick has
the men prove themselves by killing a woman who is an inhabitant of hell,
her real home. The ironic parallel with Pyle's shooting of Hartman is
unmistakable. Like Pyle, Joker now becomes a liberator in that he, too,
destroys a communal nemesis, but in so doing he invalidates the whole
point of the traditional journey down, which is to *save* the woman. The
frightening inversion of values in *Full Metal Jacket* becomes clear when
Joker turns out to be the one who *kills* the woman. If we understand Joker
as a Pyle and the sniper as a Hartman, we realize that there is little if any
difference between the Vietnamese and the American persecutor and apparently little difference between the deadly actions of Pyle and Joker. In
Joker's case the murder is justified by the murderous behavior of the
Oriental woman, now close to death, but in Pyle's case the justification of
murdering the white man who had turned them all into state-sanctioned
killers is morally ambiguous at best. When, within the larger narrative
perspective of the katabasis, the killing of a woman is right, something is
very much wrong. What does America stand for? Where is hell?

Apocalypse Now (1979), written and directed by Francis Ford Coppola,
is an inverted katabasis tale. Its protagonist, Willard, is sent upriver in
Vietnam not to rescue a friend but rather to kill an American officer who
has come to be seen as an enemy of his country's interests. He is to cross
over into Cambodia and "terminate with extreme prejudice" a renegade

19. Throughout the story there is much talk about "cocks," "queers," "jerking off,"
and "pussy." Although this use of language is only peripherally related to the katabasis
theme, the film develops the terminology of nonnormative sexual behavior as metaphor
for nonnormative behavior in general to a remarkable degree. Similarly, war as nonnormative behavior is the topic of Joker's discussion with a superior who objects to his
wearing a symbol of peace, a normative form of human interaction. The language as such
is typical of soldiers and hence consistent with their realistic portrayal. In general, sex
and talk about sex in the film seem to function as subtext for male initiation into man-
hood, an important result of the hero's return from his katabasis.

field commander, Kurtz, a highly decorated hero and former leader of the Special Forces. The man has carved out a small empire for himself deep in the jungle, and his native troops worship him like a god. The film is steeped in such typical emblems of the katabasis as enclosing jungles, nocturnal patrols, and bridges and borders typically demarcating this world from that.

Most striking, however, is the centrality of the patrol boat that takes Willard on a perilous passage up a broad river snaking through the dense and enclosing Vietnamese jungle. The vessel takes Willard both geographically and symbolically farther and farther away from the civilized security of Saigon into an increasingly dangerous landscape. Passing the last American outpost, itself a bombed-out encampment of lost and leaderless G.I.s, he continues across the border into Cambodia. The black chief who skillfully guides the patrol boat past one danger after another is a mix between Charon and Hermes, being both the helmsman of the infernal skiff and the conductor into the underworld. The fact that he is killed before Willard and his men reach their destination underscores the inverted nature of this narrative.

The film is based on Joseph Conrad's *Heart of Darkness* and is also influenced by T. S. Eliot's *The Waste Land*, and a brief but highly significant camera pan of a copy of James Frazer's *The Golden Bough* in Kurtz's corpse-filled precinct is crucial for an appreciation of the film's conclusion. This, then, is a mythic tale of sacrificial death and ritual resurrection, appropriately linked to the katabasis of a dying-and-rising god, Willard. A famous scene at the end intercuts the ritual hacking to death of a sacrificial bull by the montagnards with Willard cutting up Kurtz and thus serves to point out the latter's death as sacrifice on the barbaric altar of American political and military expediency. The pattern deployed here relies heavily on the theories of Frazer: *Rex est mortuus, vivat rex* ("The king is dead, long live the king"). No sooner has Willard completed his mission and killed Kurtz than the natives bow down to him and offer precisely the kind of religious obeisance they once offered Kurtz, as described at the beginning of the film by the general briefing Willard.

In a manner of speaking, Willard has been resurrected. At the start of the film he was lost to home and family and half crazy as well; now he is a god. Yet in the very last scene, as he starts off downriver on the patrol boat in the utter black of night, his grotesquely camouflaged face fills the screen—dark eyes staring, the last words of Kurtz echoing in his mind: "The horror! The horror!" This is a katabatic protagonist who will never return to "this world" a psychically whole individual, ready to assume roles of responsibility and leadership.

Platoon and *Full Metal Jacket* stick to the fundamental katabasis theme of the hero's death and rebirth. But *Apocalypse Now* takes a grimmer view and examines the effect of the descent on an individual man who, as noted, is not likely, in any wholesome sense of the word, to return, as did Odysseus, for example. The other two films show us protagonists who seem to have been able to internalize and appropriate their harrowing otherworld experiences without being overwhelmed by them, but *Apocalypse Now* elaborates a much bleaker vision of the hero's future, leaving him stuck forever in his own private inferno.[20]

The recent revival of the war film genre—Steven Spielberg's *Schindler's List* (1993) and *Saving Private Ryan* (1998), Malick's *The Thin Red Line*—gives us additional examples of katabases, here set in World War II. *Saving Private Ryan* begins with what may well be the most harrowing portrayal yet made on film of a living hell. With only some warning from the film's exposition of what is to come, viewers are more or less forcibly thrust into the nightmare world of Omaha Beach. They, and the hero, survive and ascend from it only to be thrown into another descent, that of a dangerous mission behind enemy lines. (This one the hero does not survive.) If, in General Sherman's words, "war is hell," then cinematic katabases such as those in the films here mentioned come closer than any other creative medium to bringing this point home to people who have not themselves undergone such experiences.

7. Conclusion

I have looked at some cases of a rather common vision informing narratives, the mapping of the katabasis typology onto essentially non-underworld stories set in modern times and even in the future. It remains for me to consider briefly why the concept is so widespread in a medium so hugely popular and culturally international.

20. Much the same may be said about Brian de Palma's *Casualties of War* (1989). On this film and on Vietnam war films in general see, for example, Stephen Hunter, "Changing Film Images of Vietnam," in *Violent Screen: A Critic's 13 Years on the Front Lines of Movie Mayhem* (Baltimore: Bancroft, 1995), 213–218. On literature and film dealing with the return from the war see James Campbell, "Coming Home: Difference and Reconciliation in Narratives of Return to 'the World,'" in *The United States and Viet Nam from War to Peace*, ed. Richard M. Slabey (Jefferson, N.C.: McFarland, 1996), 198–207. On Vietnam narratives see also Andrew Britton, "Sideshows: Hollywood in Vietnam," *Movie*, 27–28 (1981), 2–23; *Inventing Vietnam: The War in Film and Television*, ed. Michael Anderegg (Philadelphia: Temple University Press, 1991); and Milton J. Bates, *The Wars We Took to Vietnam: Cultural Conflict and Storytelling* (Berkeley: University of California Press, 1996). For analogies between the Vietnam war and Greek myth see Jonathan Shay, *Achilles in Vietnam: Combat Trauma and the Undoing of Character* (1993; rpt. New York: Simon and Schuster, 1995).

As I indicated at the outset, the genealogy of film suggests that the thematic as much as the narrative devices of drama and literature are built into the medium. And since these elements in literature go back largely to ancient sources, it is not surprising that some of the strictly mechanical patterns are embedded in numerous films. Since there appears to be a tacit and, in my view, erroneous assumption that ancient literature—the classics—is inaccessible to all but those with extensive knowledge of ancient Greek and Latin, how can it be that such a prevalent aspect of a supposedly inaccessible body of works is so pervasive in the most popular of popular media? Obviously the pattern speaks to something deeply human, for whether the mass audiences or the filmmakers consciously recognize it as such or not, the cinematic katabasis continues to entertain viewers not only brought up in the Western tradition but in practically any other culture as well. This may simply be a less than compendious way of saying that what is at heart mythic is at heart universal. The whole concept of C. G. Jung's *Tiefenpsychologie* and its archetypes is a complex elaboration on such a view, and if one accepts, as many do not, his articulation of the innateness of these psychic operators, then the appeal of the katabasis type is freed from any kind of anchoring in specific cultural traditions.

Whatever one's larger attitude to this question, I offer, on a less theoretical scale, the observation that the thematic displacement of katabasis themes shifts onto the narrative the power of a death tale, or part of a death tale, and hence lends to it a certain urgency and import beyond the surface structure of the story presented. For example, when Heracles takes the cattle of Geryon, although there is no reference to a physical descent into a lower world, the adventure clearly takes him beyond the normative world and forces him to confront, in Geryon, a death demon (in triplicate at that!), whom he must overpower before being able to abscond with his new-found wealth.[21] Of the films examined here, this associative connection is most evident in the ones about Vietnam and lifts them out of the particular to a more universal application. Not everyone may have been a Willard in Vietnam, but everyone has journeyed into the dark and perilous Cambodia of the self or the heart of his or her own darkness—some not as deeply, some more so; some with less success, others with more. The protagonists of the western as well as of the science-fiction tale and the detective thriller likewise make their descent into the varied katabatic landscapes to which their quests bring them. The pattern endures because it has been our own since Gilgamesh first went in search of

---

21. See G. S. Kirk, *Myth: Its Meaning and Functions in Ancient and Other Cultures* (Berkeley: University of California Press, 1970; rpt. 1974), 185–186.

immortality in the fourth or third millennium B.C. Extrapolating from the last five thousand years, we may assume that the pattern will in all likelihood continue to be central to how we tell our stories, in word or in image, and to our vision of ourselves. The enduring nature of this underpinning myth with its origins in the earliest Western narratives seems to be beyond dispute.

II

Verbal Odysseus: Narrative Strategy in the *Odyssey* and in *The Usual Suspects*

Hanna M. Roisman

In 1905 the American anthropologist Matilda Stevenson reported the following case, which had occurred among the Zuñi Indians of New Mexico: A teen-age boy was accused of witchcraft when a twelve-year-old girl was stricken with a nervous seizure right after he had taken her by the hands. At his trial before a court of priests, the boy initially pleaded his innocence and denied having any occult powers, but his truthful defense was of no avail. Sorcery was a crime punishable by death, and, despite his youth, the boy was in great danger. So he changed his strategy. He admitted to having inherited magic powers, which even enabled him to assume the shapes of animals. When asked to demonstrate these powers, he gave a sad speech in which he regretted their loss after the incident with the girl. Relieved that he was no longer a sorcerer, the priests set him free.[1]

This story is instructive. The clever boy realized that telling the truth would not save him from death, but that fabricating a story which upheld the Zuñi system of beliefs would. By both admitting and denying that he had supernatural powers, he brought his story into accord with what the people believed and were able to understand. They certainly were unable to believe or understand that his touching of the girl's hands had not produced her seizure since they could not figure out any other cause for it.

---

1. Matilda Coxe Stevenson, *The Zuñi Indians: Extract from the Twenty-Third Annual Report of the Bureau of American Ethnology* (1905; rpt. New York: Johnson, 1970), 398–406. Claude Lévi-Strauss, *Structural Anthropology* [vol. 1], tr. Claire Jacobson and Brooke Grundfest Schoepf (New York: Basic Books, 1963; rpt. 1978), 172–175, provides an analysis. I am grateful to Lauris A. McKee for drawing my attention to this story.

But they were willing to accept that he had suddenly lost command of his occult powers after touching the girl.

This modern episode reminds us of a classical rhetorical strategy, one often encountered in modern fiction as well. At times it is more advantageous for characters, especially first-person narrators, to use the cultural framework of their audiences for their purpose than to oppose it. In his *Rhetoric*, Aristotle phrased it aptly: "what is convincing is what one can be convinced by" (*pithanon tini pithanon*).[2] The story of the Zuñi boy brings home the general truth that a story or claim is convincing only within its specific context, and that there is no point in telling the objective truth if the hearer cannot accept or understand it.

I will demonstrate the validity of Aristotle's observation by discussing and juxtaposing one classical and one modern example, the Phaeacian episode in the *Odyssey* and the film *The Usual Suspects* (1995), a mystery-thriller written by Christopher McQuarrie and directed by Bryan Singer. Both employ a strategy whereby a narrator adapts his claims to the cultural reality and expectations of his audience.

The Phaeacian episode covers roughly six books of the *Odyssey* (Books 6–12).[3] After receiving the Phaeacians' hospitality on their island of Scheria, Odysseus reveals his name and tells the story of his adventures on his journey home from the Trojan War. Most famously, he tells the Phaeacians about his visit to the island of the Cyclopes, where he defeated and blinded the monstrous Polyphemus. None of his tales corresponds to the dimensions of everyday human life.

The plot of *The Usual Suspects* is set in an entirely realistic portrayal of the modern world. A freighter, believed to have ninety-one million dollars' worth of cocaine on board, explodes at a pier in San Pedro, California. Twenty-seven people die in the explosion, but there are two survivors: Arkosh Kovash, a Hungarian gangster now hospitalized with severe burns, and Roger "Verbal" Kint, a crippled, small-time con man. (His nickname, as we will see, is a major clue to his character: "People say I talk too much," he explains.) U. S. Customs agent David Kujan conducts a grueling interrogation of Verbal. In a series of flashbacks, Verbal tells Kujan how everything began six weeks earlier at a police lineup in New York. Five known criminals, among them Kint, were brought in on a charge of hijacking a truckload of gun parts. Since the police could not

2. Aristotle, *Rhetoric* 1356b28. The subject of *to pithanon* appears several times in his *Poetics* as well (1451b15–19, 1460a26–27, 1461b9–12).

3. My discussion is based on the analysis in Frederick Ahl and Hanna M. Roisman, *The* Odyssey *Re-Formed* (Ithaca, N.Y.: Cornell University Press, 1996), especially 67–105.

substantiate the charge, the five were released. But while they had been locked up together, they had hatched the scheme that eventually led to their involvement in the explosion of the freighter. About halfway through his story, Verbal tells Kujan how the five discovered that they had all been hand-picked by the fearful and elusive Keyser Soze, an international master criminal, whom Kovash names as being behind the bloodbath. Although none of the five has ever laid eyes on him, Soze has a complete file on each. The only character in the film who can identify Keyser Soze is Arkosh Kovash. While the FBI is trying to get a description of Keyser Soze from Kovash, Verbal Kint sits in Sergeant Rabin's office, where the interrogation takes place, and weaves his intricate tale of the heist he and the other four had been engaged in.

Although the plots of the ancient epic and the modern film are utterly different, the heroes of both adopt similar rhetorical strategies. Reinventing themselves as they speak, Odysseus and Verbal Kint adapt their accounts of their pasts to their hearers' preconceptions in order to obtain the upper hand and to ensure their safety.

1. Truth and Persuasion

Odysseus' and Verbal's strategy is predicated on the conception that the truth may be fluid and that language is a vehicle not of objective fact but of persuasion.

In the Phaeacian episode, King Alcinous voices the concept of fiction that underlies Odysseus' account of his adventures:

> Odysseus, we as we look upon you do not imagine
> that you are a deceptive or thievish man, the sort that the black earth
> breeds in great numbers, people who wander widely, making up
> lying stories, from which no one could learn anything. You have
> a grace upon your words, and there is sound sense within them,
> and expertly, as a singer would do, you have told the story
> of the dismal sorrows befallen yourself and all of the Argives.[4]

The fantastic adventures Odysseus has recounted to the Phaeacians are not lies, the king declares, but poetic fictions ("as a singer would do"). Conflating Odysseus' character and his stories, Alcinous praises both for their beauty and grace and Odysseus for that nobility of mind which reflects the poet's ability to use words to express, even shape, reality. The

---

4. *Odyssey* 11.363–369. The quotation is from the translation by Richmond Lattimore, *The Odyssey of Homer* (New York: Harper and Row, 1967; rpt. 1999), 177.

comparison between Odysseus' fictional telling and that of the poets is made quite explicitly. It is reinforced by the presence of Demodocus, the Phaeacian singer, whose poetry is appreciated without any question as to its literal truth, although there is an obvious difference between Demodocus' and Odysseus' renditions. The court bard does not insert himself into his fictional accounts as Odysseus does. But this fact is immaterial to the king's point.

In contrast to Odysseus' fabulous tales, the yarn that Verbal spins is technically within the realm of possibility, although colored by the genre of the police procedural and crime thriller to which the film belongs and with whose formulae it plays. Here, too, a sphere of discourse is established that is beyond the mundane distinction between truth and lies. In his commentary on the film for the digital videodisc edition, director Singer put it this way:

> It was . . . from an editorial directorial point of view an exciting opportunity to get into the text and to convince and to bring to the audience one thing, and then five minutes later you reach back into the same text and bring out a new set of elements and show them to light . . . [to] convince the audience of something completely different.

Similarly, scriptwriter McQuarrie reveals in his audio commentary that he set himself the challenge of writing "a script . . . in which in the opening scene I show you something that happened, and spend the next two hours trying to convince you that you didn't actually see what you saw and in the end convince you yet again that you actually did see it."

In both the Phaeacian episode of the *Odyssey* and in *The Usual Suspects*, fiction and fact are intertwined in such a way that it is impossible to unravel the knot. Odysseus swears to the truth of his tale to the Phaeacians (*Odyssey* 16.226–232), but, as Alcinous had recognized, it is a poetic rather than a literal truth. In *The Usual Suspects*, neither the internal audience— Agent Kujan—nor the external audience—we, the spectators—will ever know what exactly is true and what is false in Verbal's description of events. Both Homer and the filmmakers immerse us in a world which continuously reinvents itself as the plot evolves.

2. Convincing the Phaeacians

Odysseus' aim is to obtain the Phaeacians' assistance in getting home. Although they have voluntarily promised to help him, there remains the disconcerting possibility that the king and queen, who see Odysseus as a more than suitable husband for their daughter Nausicaa, may decide to prevent his departure. It is important for Odysseus to present himself to them in such a way that they will not be tempted to keep him.

To this end, he goes to some lengths to make sure that his hosts know who he is. This behavior is unusual for him. In most of his encounters with others in the *Odyssey*, he tends to be rather oblique about his identity. While explicit enough in his wish to return home, he is cautious about disclosing who he is or where this home is. For the sake of his safety, he often provides no more than clues for his interlocutors to infer his identity.

His initial expectation seems to be that the Phaeacians will help him on his way if they learn that he is the great hero of the Trojan War. He seems to think that they will be impressed by his valor and respectful of his feats and, as a result, expedite his way back. Thus, as Demodocus sings at the banquet table about a quarrel between Odysseus and Achilles before the Trojan War (*Odyssey* 8.75–82), our hero draws attention to himself by crying and covering his head.[5] The blind bard's song is the first indication that the Phaeacians are not as ignorant about his world as Odysseus had feared. It also indicates to Odysseus that he has become a mythic hero. In the convention of Greek epic poetry, to be the subject of a song is to be acknowledged as heroic and immortal.[6]

But his efforts to attain recognition for himself as he sits at Alcinous' banquet table fall flat. The only one who even realizes that something is amiss is Alcinous himself, who decides that the way to cheer up his grieving guest is to change the entertainment and suggest some sports. After proving his prowess in discus throwing, Odysseus asks Demodocus to sing another song about the Trojan War, stipulating the specific incident to make sure that the tale is about him and no one else. It is to be a song, he says, about Odysseus leading the wooden horse to the Trojan citadel (8.487–498), an incident which demonstrates the ingenuity and valor that Odysseus wants his hosts to know he possesses. As Demodocus sings, Odysseus again cries and covers his head, pausing only to eat and drink at the intervals. He repeats this action until Alcinous finally asks him who he is, where he is from, and how he came to the Phaeacians' shores.

5. I provide a detailed discussion of this scene in "Like Father Like Son: Telemachus's *kerdea*," *Rheinisches Museum für Philologie*, 136 (1993), 1–22. The note on *Odyssey* 8.75 in Alfred Heubeck, Stephanie West, and J. B. Hainsworth, *A Commentary on Homer's Odyssey*, vol. 1 (Oxford: Clarendon Press, 1988; rpt. 1990), 351, on the quarrel between Odysseus and Achilles, of which this line is the only mention, is important for my argument.

6. On this subject in general see, for example, Gregory Nagy, *The Best of the Achaeans: Concepts of the Hero in Archaic Greek Poetry*, rev. ed. (Baltimore: Johns Hopkins University Press, 1999).

The assumption guiding Odysseus' tales in response to Alcinous' questions is that his hosts will expedite his way home if they know who he is and what he is capable of doing to his opponents. However, he also realizes that they are not greatly moved by historical events. In the course of the banquet, he has observed that they were more impressed by Demodocus' song about the gods—the love affair between Ares and Aphrodite. Instead of a historical narrative telling of his victories against mere men, Odysseus launches into an ahistorical narrative which draws on the associations that govern the Phaeacians' world.

From the sketchy information he had previously obtained from Nausicaa, from Alcinous' addresses to the Phaeacians, and from his own observations, Odysseus derives some sense of his hosts and their beliefs about themselves and the world. Among other things, he learns that they regard the world as inhabited by monsters and themselves as a quasi-mythical people in close and frequent contact with the gods. Such people, he knows, will be inclined to accept quasi-mythical stories and will be more impressed by a man who vanquishes monsters than one who vanquishes men. So he presents himself as a dauntless adversary not of human enemies but of the monsters who, in the Phaeacian worldview, embody evil and danger.

Among the various adventures he relates, the most complex and troubling is that of his encounter with the Cyclops Polyphemus. This is the first episode of which Odysseus tells at any length. It is important because the Cyclopes form part of the Phaeacians' national history. As we are informed at the beginning of Book 6, they fled to Scheria after having been plundered and bullied by these giant one-eyed monsters.

Odysseus tells in detail how he outwitted the man-eating Polyphemus and graphically describes the bloody act of blinding him (*Odyssey* 9.105–566). His account of this adventure has two purposes. One is to provide the Phaeacians with an explanation for his wanderings over many years after the fall of Troy. The reason he gives is Polyphemus' call upon his father Poseidon for revenge. For several years, the wrath of Poseidon has prevented Odysseus from reaching his kingdom of Ithaca. Odysseus' other purpose is to make the Phaeacians believe that he is capable of vanquishing creatures they themselves had to flee in order to convince them that it is in their best interest to get rid of him as soon as possible; indeed, to expedite his journey by taking him home on one of the "magical" ships with a highly skilled crew of which they had boasted. His message comes across, and Odysseus receives his safe passage home.

To get his message across to the Phaeacians, however, Odysseus must make his story convincing. He uses several ploys to achieve this goal. One is to make his story accord with what the Phaeacians believe. They regard themselves, he knows, as people of culture and technical skill, far superior to the boorish and savage Cyclopes. Odysseus begins his account by implying the Phaeacians' superiority, describing the Cyclopes as "arrogant" and "lawless" (106). He goes on to draw an implicit contrast between the Cyclopes' uncivilized way of life and the civilized ways of the Phaeacians. The Cyclopes, he says, do not have assembly places (*agorai*) for discussion and consultation or a system of government with prerogatives for rulers. They make their homes in hollow caves on high mountain peaks. Each rules his own children and wives with no concern for the community (107–115). These are things the Phaeacians can be counted on readily to believe of the people whose barbarity they fled. They are even more likely to believe Odysseus' account if it confirms their favorable view of their own culture, as it does, for Odysseus already knows that the Phaeacians have a king and queen whose rule they recognize, a spectacular royal palace, an elaborately built agora, and a rich community life.

Another ploy Odysseus uses to make his story convincing is to weave in details that seem familiar to the Phaeacians. He begins with a description of the Cyclopes' idyllic rural life. They are a people, he says, who live on wheat, barley, and the fruit of the vine, but they do not need to plow or sow because the gods provide them with crops. This recalls the Phaeacians' fields, which similarly do not require the toil of agriculture. Along the same lines, Odysseus' description of Polyphemus' court (9.184–185) recalls the Phaeacians' own agora near the temple of Poseidon (6.266–267). This god is the divine ancestor of both the Cyclopes and the Phaeacians. Odysseus capitalizes on what he has learned about the Phaeacians' history and way of life; for instance, he uses architectural parallels to make his story more plausible and thus more convincing. Ironically, such parallels and contrasts are among the indications to us, the readers of the epic, that Odysseus is weaving a fiction. They are too neat and structured to accord with the messiness of reality.

With the tale of his exploits among the Cyclopes, Odysseus engages in a kind of psychological warfare with his hearers. At the same time that he flatters them he methodically whittles down their self-confidence. The outward similarities between the Phaeacians and the Cyclopes which Odysseus creates in his story serve only to undercut the Phaeacians' boasts about the superiority of their civilization. So does Odysseus' description of the island inhabited by goats, on which he and his crew had landed before he and some of his companions went on to the island of the Cyclopes. The importance of Goat Island, as we might call it, is never explicitly stated in the text. A close look at its description, however, indicates that Odysseus is capitalizing on the technological accomplishments the Phaeacians boast of and that he is doing so in order to throw into question the story of their origin. His description of Goat Island is worth quoting in full, because it shows that he is building on the Phaeacians' own beliefs to keep them at bay:

> There is a wooded island that spreads, away from the harbor,
> neither close in to the land of the Cyclopes nor far out
> from it; forested; wild goats beyond number breed there,
> for there is no coming and going of human kind to disturb them,
> nor are they visited by hunters, who in the forest
> suffer hardships as they haunt the peaks of the mountains,
> neither again is it held by herded flocks, nor farmers,
> but all its days, never plowed up and never planted,
> it goes without people and supports the bleating wild goats.
> *For the Cyclopes have no ships with cheeks of vermilion,*
> *nor have they builders of ships among them, who could have made them*
> *strong-benched vessels, and these if made could have run them sailings*
> *to all the various cities of men, in the way that people*
> *cross the sea by means of ships and visit each other,*
> *and they could have made this island a strong settlement for them.*
> For it is not a bad place at all, it could bear all crops
> in season, and there are meadow lands near the shores of the gray sea,
> well watered and soft; there could be grapes grown there endlessly,
> and there is smooth land for plowing, men could reap a full harvest
> always in season, since there is very rich subsoil. Also
> there is an easy harbor, no need for a hawser
> nor anchor stones to be thrown ashore nor cables to make fast;
> one could just run ashore and wait for the time when the sailors'
> desire stirred them to go and the right winds were blowing.
> Also at the head of the harbor there runs bright water,
> spring beneath rock, and there are black poplars growing around it.[7]

Odysseus says that he and his men came upon this marvelous place by divine guidance since it was pitch-black night, their ships were enveloped in thick fog, and the moon was covered by clouds. No one had spotted the island before they beached their ships on it (143–148). Nor did anyone note the current necessary for landing.

If we pay attention to the lines dealing with navigation in the passage quoted, we see that Odysseus is obliquely but effectively ridiculing the tradition of the Phaeacians' migration to Scheria. We learned at the beginning of Book 6 that the Phaeacians had to leave their former home in Hypereia ("Beyondland") for Scheria because of the violence of the more powerful Cyclopes. Yet there was, Odysseus says, a fabulously rich island nearby. Although inaccessible to the Cyclopes, who cannot build

---

7. *Odyssey* 9.116–141, quoted from Lattimore, *The Odyssey of Homer*, 140–141; italics added.

ships, the island was within reach of the Phaeacians' miraculous vessels. The Phaeacian emigration to the ends of the earth, far from other humans (6.8), when a safe, uninhabited, and fertile land was practically no more than a stone's throw away from their home, now appears, if not entirely incomprehensible, at least superfluous, perhaps even ridiculous. One may, of course, object that the Phaeacians' myth-history, familiar to the external audience, is not explicitly said to be known to Odysseus. But he had been told that the Phaeacians were descended from Poseidon and that they were close kin to the Cyclopes and the Giants (7.56–66 and 205–206). He may also reasonably infer that the land of the Cyclopes is some distance from Scheria or at least that the Phaeacians view it as such.

We cannot know whether Odysseus entirely invented the paradisal Goat Island or whether he adapted the details of his stay there in order to take the Phaeacians down a notch. In any case, his account contains several contradictions, whose cumulative effect is to point to the fictional nature of the entire Cyclopes episode in his tale. To begin with, there is a conflict in some important details in his two accounts of the anchorage that Goat Island affords his ships. First, Odysseus says that the harbor was so tranquil that there was no need to tie the ships by the stern with cables (9.136–139). They simply ran the ships on shore, beached them, lowered the sails, and went to sleep. Some forty lines later, however, as they depart, Odysseus commands his men to loosen the stern cables and set sail (177–180).

The next contradiction involves Odysseus' presentation of the Cyclopes. Odysseus had claimed that the Cyclopes were ignorant of basic agricultural skills, which they had no need to know (108–111). Yet, describing Goat Island, he says that the land, although it is fertile and would bear all things in season, is unworked because the Cyclopes do not have ships to get there. Since the Cyclopes do not know how to sow and till, their inability to reach the island is of no consequence and need not be mentioned. The point of the statement appears to be that the seafaring Phaeacians could have easily avoided the Cyclopes by moving to nearby Goat Island with its rich and fertile soil instead of migrating to out-of-the-way Scheria.

Both these contradictions may be seen as no more than narrative slips stemming from the oral transmission of early Greek epic, or they may be excused as stemming from Odysseus' faulty memory of his experience— the latter a "realistic" kind of reason. But they can also be understood as deliberate indications provided by a sophisticated literary text that, instead, Odysseus is making up the episode as he goes along, inventing details to suit his purpose.

A similar hint at the fictional nature of the episode is evident in Odysseus' account of his approach to Polyphemus' cave (181–186). It is marked by

constant prolepsis—that is, anticipation of later events in a narrative—
and by a confusing overlay of perspectives, mixing the hero's and the poet's
voices. Odysseus says that he and his company sighted the Cyclops' cave
when they had arrived at a place close by—that is, while they were still at
sea. Then he goes on to describe the cave and its surroundings: the laurel
trees with which the cave is roofed over, the sheep and goats that slept in
the cave, the courtyard at its mouth, and the surrounding fence built with
stones set deep in the earth and held together by tall pines and high-crested
oaks. The description is extraordinary in its details. And it is utterly im-
probable. Although Odysseus says that the cave is on the land's edge, it
is questionable whether he or any of his men would have been able to
distinguish types of trees and types of animals before they even dis-
embarked. It is entirely impossible that they would have been able to see
the cave's roof covering, since the sea is lower than the mountain into
which the cave was set.

Moreover, Odysseus could not possibly have known whom he was
about to meet on the island or in the cave, yet he tells the Phaeacians
that a monstrous man—whom he has not yet seen—slept in the tall cave
and shepherded his flocks alone over a great range, not mingling with
others but living apart, his heart set on lawlessness. He even adds that
this monster was not like a man who feeds on bread but like a wooded
peak of lofty mountains, standing out in solitary splendor, apart from
the rest (187–192).

Like the previous inconsistencies, these, too, can be explained away as
oral suturing or poetic license. But they can be much better explained by
Odysseus' aims in using them. They raise questions about perspective and
perception. If his ship was close enough to the cave for Odysseus to observe such details on his arrival and to overhear Polyphemus' conversations, prayers, and soliloquies on his departure, how did Polyphemus fail
to see the ship when Odysseus first arrived, and how did Odysseus get away
with his lie to Polyphemus that his ship had been dashed to pieces on the
rocks (283–286)? There is no mention of a promontory or a cliff overhang
that might obscure the view from Polyphemus' cave. (In Euripides' *Cyclops*,
85–88, Odysseus' ship is in full view from the cave, and Silenus sees the
company ascending before they arrive there.) The implication seems to
be that what and how one sees is related to one's size. From a Cyclopean
perspective, Odysseus and his ship are so tiny, and Polyphemus is so huge,
that the arrival of the Greeks could easily pass unobserved.

This point, of course, is true for the Phaeacians as well. If they are of
ordinary human dimensions, and the text gives no indication that they
are not, they, too, could have evaded and outwitted the Cyclopes. But if
they are not, there is even more reason that they had no need to flee to

the far ends of the earth. Odysseus strongly implies to his listeners that he knowingly approached and eventually subdued a monster from whom the Phaeacians had fled in fear.

The story of the Cyclopes tells the Phaeacians that Odysseus is a man of destructive potential, whom it might be better not to have on their island. To convince the Phaeacians of this and to induce them to provide him with speedy transportation home, it would have done Odysseus no good to tell of his feats at Troy or his victories over other human enemies. What he had to do was to make his point from within his hearers' cultural truths, involving familiar architecture, magical geography, unreal agriculture, and monsters. Although the Phaeacians do not comment on this or any of the stories Odysseus tells them, it is clear that they got his message. They made good on their promise to facilitate his departure from their land.

A major problem in scholarship on the *Odyssey* is the distinction that scholars draw between truth and lies. They treat Odysseus' realistic stories, in which he variously claims to be a Cretan, as "Cretan" lies—doubtless because in antiquity Cretans were stereotypically considered to be liars—but accept without any question his supernatural stories. That is to say, they accept Odysseus' fantastic tales simultaneously as truths within the context of their mythological framework, the *Odyssey*, and as fictions, that is, mythical adventure stories not to be held up to mundane or realistic standards of truth or realism.

Such a distinction, however, is no more than spurious. In both cases, Odysseus is technically lying. Other than the Phaeacians, no one believed in the literal existence of one-eyed monsters like the Cyclopes. In the second century A.D., the Greek satirist and fabulist Lucian observed:

> The founder of this school of literary horseplay is Homer's Odysseus, with his stories at Alcinous's court, of winds enslaved and men with one eye and cannibals and wild men, of many-headed beasts and of how his crew were drugged and transformed; he spun many such fanciful stories to the Phaeacians, who knew no better.[8]

At the same time that Odysseus is bamboozling and manipulating the Phaeacians with his tales, he is also telling a kind of truth that his hearers can understand and accept.[9]

8. Lucian, *A True Story* 1.3; quoted from "A True Story," tr. B. P. Reardon, in *Collected Ancient Greek Novels*, ed. Reardon (Berkeley: University of California Press, 1989), 621–649; quotation at 621.

9. My interpretation addresses Lucian's criticism and resolves apparent inconsistencies in the Phaeacian episode, but I am aware that it is occasionally at odds with other parts of the *Odyssey* narrative, which probably reflect other mythic versions. For example,

3. Verbal Kint: Man of Tiny Mind?

Even more than his great deeds, Odysseus' special claim to fame is his verbal mastery, his ability to invent himself anew before each audience he addresses. Verbal Kint possesses the same mental agility. As did Odysseus, who fashioned his tales of fantastic feats in order to get away from Scheria as quickly as possible, so Verbal creates an intricate story to extricate himself once and for all from the police. His tale, too, is tailored to the specific assumptions and mental capacities of his audience.

The film itself explicitly refers to the two principles that guide Verbal's narrative strategy. Ironically, the first of these, that the aim of Verbal's account is to persuade rather than to render an objective truth, is introduced by his interrogator, Kujan. Intent on getting Verbal to confirm his own conviction that Dean Keaton, one of the other four in the police lineup, is the mastermind behind the freighter fire, Kujan is exasperated with Verbal's insistence that Keaton was no more than a reluctant participant in the affair and imperiously commands him: "Convince me!" Significantly, Kujan does not order Verbal to tell him the truth. His command reveals Kujan's fundamental naiveté in believing that what is convincing must also be true and that only the truth can carry conviction, an assumption the film proceeds methodically to undermine. More generally, this is the film's very justification for Verbal to create a plausible story to convince his interlocutor.

The second principle is that fashioning a story to the hearer's expectations achieves a plausibility that is utterly convincing. Verbal himself voices this principle when he explains to Kujan why he did not tell his fellow criminals his belief that they could manage to escape from Keyser Soze. Keaton, the ex-cop among them, Verbal says, would never have believed him. His next words are not only an explanation intended for Kujan but also an indirect intellectual challenge to the film's audience:

---

outside the Phaeacian episode the blinding of Polyphemus is at times mentioned as narrative fact. Odysseus treats it as such in his talk to himself when he readies his heart to confront the suitors after returning to Ithaca (20.17–24). So does Zeus, when he explains to Athena why Poseidon is angry with Odysseus (1.68–71). Another unresolved inconsistency involves Poseidon's anger at the Phaeacians for providing humans with safe conduct over his seas (13.146–183). The passage about Poseidon's anger, however, nowhere states specifically that he is or will be angry at the Phaeacians for ensuring Odysseus' safe passage to Ithaca. Yet Odysseus was the last whom they were able to help cross the seas. It seems that in an epic of such magnitude as the *Odyssey* it is hardly possible to iron out all inconsistencies.

To a cop, the explanation is never that complicated. It's always simple. There's no mystery on the street, no arch-criminal behind it all. If you got a dead guy and you think his brother did it, you're going to find out you're right.

Here we find a daring assertion of Kujan's lack of intelligence and imagination and a modern version of the Aristotelian rhetorical strategy mentioned earlier.

As with the Phaeacian episode, *The Usual Suspects* provides clear signs that fact and fiction are inextricably intertwined in the telling of the plot. In the opening scene, the audience sees Keaton being shot. In contrast to much else in the film, which is a series of flashbacks in which Verbal gives his version of events to Kujan, this, the frame of the whole story, appears as objective truth. The opening anchors Verbal's account, in which Keaton's murder is a salient point, in "facts." At the same time, Verbal's narrative is introduced by a cinematic device that first only hints at but eventually confirms the fictional nature of his story. While Verbal is waiting in Sergeant Rabin's office for the questioning to begin, the camera follows his gaze as he looks around the room and eyes the bulletin board on the wall behind the desk where Kujan will sit down. This board is in utter disarray. The film script describes it as "a breathtaking catastrophe of papers, wanted posters, rap-sheets, memos and post-its," apparently collected over decades. In the next hour and a half Verbal will look again and again at this bulletin board behind Kujan's back. At the end of the film, Kujan will realize that the board has furnished Verbal with some of the names of people and places for his tale. The purpose of this revealing shot, as scriptwriter McQuarrie says in his commentary, was to structure the whole film around the board in order "to play with the idea of the audience's perception watching a film"—in other words, to indicate that we are not in a world of reality but of artifice, in which truth is a construction. Verbal does no less than to play Odysseus to Kujan's Alcinous, building his story from the items in the immediate environment and giving Kujan what he expects.

From the very beginning, Kujan is quite clear about what he expects Verbal to tell him. Alhough Rabin, who has already interrogated Verbal, lets him know that further questioning will be pointless since Verbal has been granted complete immunity, Kujan correctly insists that Verbal knows more than he has revealed so far:

> there's a lot more to his story. I want to know why twenty-seven men died on that pier for what looks to be ninety-one million dollars worth of dope that wasn't there. Above all, I want to be sure that Dean Keaton is dead.

The crucial point here is that Kujan is not really asking Verbal for new information since he firmly believes that he already knows the answers. As he tells Verbal, he is certain that Dean Keaton, the cop gone bad, masterminded the operation and is using Verbal to make the police believe that he is dead but that Verbal is too stupid to realize that he is Keaton's pawn. Kujan does not mince words about his opinion of Verbal's intelligence, his "tiny mind," as he calls it, and declares peremptorily: "According to your statement you are a short-con operator. Run of the mill. Seems everything you do, you learned from somebody else." He repeats this opinion a little later: "I'll get right to the point. I'm smarter than you. I'll find out what I want to know and I'll get it from you whether you like it or not."

Taking his cue from these assumptions, Verbal presents himself to Kujan as a harmless and not very intelligent cripple, forced to admit the truth to a persistent and astute questioner. Before the investigation gets under way, he draws attention to his disability, flatteringly telling Kujan that "I would have liked to have been a Fed myself" and, shortly afterward, clumsily dropping his cigarette lighter so that Kujan has to light his cigarette for him.

Verbal lets Kujan believe that he, Kujan, is scaring him into talking. After insisting that he is "not a rat," Verbal goes on to play the fool by, for instance, feebly trying to change the subject to the coffee he is drinking and to the coffee beans he once picked in Guatemala. Such a ploy is obvious, meant for Kujan to notice and stop. What Kujan sees is a subdued small-time con man, reluctantly beginning to disclose what he knows.

Verbal plays on Kujan's assumption that he is fond of Keaton and will try to protect him. He goes to great lengths to draw a picture of a reformed Keaton, reluctantly drawn into the criminal proceedings only when he has become convinced that he has no chance of going straight. This is at odds with Kujan's view of Keaton as a corrupt cop and "cold-blooded bastard . . . indicted . . . on three counts of murder before he was kicked off the force"—that is, exactly the kind of person to carry out, even mastermind, the bloodbath on the freighter. But it accords with his assumption that Verbal, gullible cripple that he is, would stand up for his friend and confirms him in his view that Verbal is withholding information. His gratuitous digs about Verbal's intelligence repeatedly tell the viewer that Kujan considers himself far superior to the hapless cripple. But Kujan does not realize that he is revealing to Verbal exactly what he wants to hear:

> you say you saw Keaton die. I think you're covering his ass and he's still out there somewhere. I think he was behind that whole circus in the harbor. My bet is he's using you because you're stupid and you think he's your friend.

Again Verbal plays up to Kujan's sense of superiority by trying, or rather, pretending to try, to change the subject, this time by talking about having once been in a barbershop quartet in Skokie, Illinois. Again, this is a transparent ploy, the sort of thing only a fool would attempt, and naturally does not work—or so it seems. Verbal looks at Kujan with utter contempt, and the audience may suspect that Verbal is not as stupid or incompetent as Kujan thinks. But as Verbal continues to relate the complicated story of his and his accomplices' exploits, Kujan can again congratulate himself, smugly and wrongly, that he has brought Verbal to making disclosures which he had kept from his previous questioners. Verbal's aim is not to convince Kujan of his own version of events, which Kujan will not believe, anyway, but rather to reinforce Kujan's preconceptions. To strengthen Kujan's conviction that he is extracting new information from him, Verbal now names, for the first time, the lawyer Kobayashi. The revelation of this name serves Verbal as an irresistible bait to hook Kujan. To reinforce Kujan's conviction that he is not telling the entire truth, Verbal makes his story increasingly violent, increasingly intricate and suspenseful, and increasingly unlikely. Throughout this, Verbal continues to play the part of Keaton's none-too-bright friend and defender. Among a plethora of information, he relates with all the fluency that his nickname suggests that Keaton could not even bring himself to pulling the trigger on someone who attacked him. The very disparity between the "facts" that Kujan has on Keaton and Verbal's too-good-to-be-true depiction confirms Kujan's presupposition that Verbal is too dimwitted to see through the wily ex-cop.

The pattern continues, with variations, when Verbal admits that he knows of the notorious supercriminal Keyser Soze. Earlier, Kovash had named Keyser Soze as the ruthless mastermind behind the freighter's explosion and as the man who personally killed Verbal's four associates aboard. Verbal's admission comes only in response to new information to which Kujan seems to force him to react. Having just learned from an FBI agent that the purpose of the freighter massacre was to eliminate the one person on the ship who could identify Soze, Kujan abruptly demands of Verbal: "Who is Keyser Soze?" He poses his question triumphantly, certain of having found out something Verbal had kept back. Verbal, of course, plays along by pretending that Kujan has cornered him into disclosing yet more of what he knows.

Kujan's question poses a grave danger to Verbal, for the end of the film reveals that Verbal and Soze are one and the same. The immunity granted him notwithstanding, as long as he is in police custody Verbal cannot allow himself to be identified as Soze, given Soze's extensive and bloody criminal history. Soze, as we learn from Kovash and others, including, primarily, Verbal himself, has created a terrifying reputation for himself in order to maintain power over his empire of crime and to deter anyone from meddling with him. So Verbal now faces a complex challenge: to avert an identification while perpetuating the fearful image of Soze in order eventually to lead Kujan to believe that Keaton is Soze—in other words, that Keaton, whom Kujan wants to be the one who pulled the strings on the dope caper, is also the one who is the ultimate puller of strings, the world's greatest criminal mind. Obviously, if Verbal succeeds in setting up Keaton as the smartest and most dangerous gangster of all to Kujan, Kujan will be too satisfied with himself for getting the truth, as he thinks, out of Verbal and for being the first law enforcement officer ever to get a lead on the elusive Soze. At the same time, of course, Verbal will get himself off the hook for good.

Odysseus had faced a similarly complex task: to convince the Phaeacians both that he was a worthy leader of men and an individual who could be very dangerous. While bragging about his triumph over the monsters the Phaeacians feared, he was careful to diminish his culpability for the deaths of most of his men. Verbal's strategy closely parallels that of Odysseus.

First, he makes sure to maintain Kujan's view of Verbal as hopelessly inept, someone who could not possibly be identified with a master criminal. Trembling at the mere mention of Soze's name, he launches into a fake confession of how he and the others involved in the attack on the freighter were victims of Soze's machinations, forced to participate in the dangerous operation by his hold over them. To avoid identification with the archcriminal, Verbal is careful not to place Soze anywhere near where he, Verbal, had been caught himself. He makes Kobayashi Soze's representative and go-between and focuses most of his narrative on the five men's dealings with the lawyer.

At the same time, Verbal takes pains to depict Soze as a man who will stop at absolutely nothing. Going beyond anything that is required to make his story cohere, and far beyond anything the police might know or suspect, he relates in gory detail how Soze had killed his own wife and children so that they could not be used to pressure him or undermine his will and that he then went after not only his family's attackers but everyone associated with them, whether innocent or guilty: "He kills their kids, he kills their wives, he kills their parents and their parents' friends. He burns down the houses they live in and the stores they work in, he kills people that owe them money."

This depiction has several functions. The most obvious is to furnish him with a convincing explanation of why he participated in the operation and why he had not mentioned Keyser Soze before. When Kujan asks about this latter point, Verbal can simply say that he feared the vengeance of the ruthless and unforgiving criminal. Kujan in turn takes this admission as proof that the weak and crippled Verbal is succumbing yet further to the pressure of his interrogation.

At the same time, in anticipation of the moment when Kujan realizes who Verbal really is, this depiction lets Kujan know that Keyser Soze does not forget, does not forgive, and does not possess a shred of mercy or compunction. This is parallel to Odysseus' account of his resourcefulness, determination, and bloody victory over Polyphemus. Like Odysseus, Verbal intends to warn his hearer: Beware of a man whose survival depends on his ability to evoke terror.

Verbal's portrayal of Soze reveals a man so inhumanly terrible and so elusive that one doubts his existence. As McQuarrie has said, echoing Verbal himself: "Keyser's greatest defense is essentially convincing the world that he doesn't exist." Verbal takes care to plant this doubt himself, telling Kujan that after doing his bloody work of revenge, Soze disappeared and became a myth:

> And like that [*he emits a puff of air from his lips*] he was gone. Underground. No one has ever seen him again. He becomes a myth, a spook story that criminals tell their kids at night. "If you rat on your pop, Keyser Soze will get you." And nobody really ever believes.

The defense works. Kujan, believing that the pathetic Verbal has been taken in by this myth, asks him: "Do you believe in him, Verbal?" Verbal answers in the affirmative, but Kujan, feeling superior, remains skeptical.

Every time Kujan exerts pressure on him, Verbal further develops his story to confirm Kujan in his conceit that he has gotten the better of him. The last instance occurs toward the end of the film, when it becomes clear that Kujan will never abandon his idée fixe about Verbal. After Verbal describes how he heard, but did not see, Keaton being shot, Kujan lets him know that he is certain that Soze is none other than Keaton, that Keaton tricked Verbal into believing him dead and saying so to the police, and that Keaton rewarded him for being his pawn by obtaining immunity for him. He lets him know yet again that he considers him to be far too stupid, crippled, and weak "to see far enough into him [Keaton] to know the truth." This is Verbal's moment of triumph. Playing on Kujan's misconceptions of both Keaton and himself, Verbal now breaks down sobbing and confesses to having been Keaton's fool: "It was all Keaton. We followed him from the beginning." Kujan takes this confession at face value, asks Verbal why he had told all those lies until now, and happily accepts his explanation that Verbal, being the stupid cripple he is, wanted at least to keep the code of honor among crooks and not betray his friends. A smug Kujan is greatly pleased with himself over Verbal's bitter assertion, when he leaves the police station a free man, that he, Kujan, has robbed him of his dignity by forcing him to "rat" on the others. Kujan is fully satisfied that he has gotten the better of the weak-minded and pathetic cripple and is convinced that Keaton was the mastermind behind the dope heist, as he had wanted to believe all along.

4. Convincing Two Audiences

As we have seen, the *Odyssey* provided some clues to its external audience that Odysseus was creating tales for the Phaeacians. This is not the case with *The Usual Suspects*. Singer and McQuarrie both emphasize in their commentaries on the film that it was important for them not to depict Kujan as an "idiot," since this would detract from the hero's accomplishment. Although they gave Kujan a vested interest in proving Keaton's guilt, at least to himself, they were careful to present him as a decent cop doing his job. To this end, it was necessary that Kujan not be the only one taken in by Verbal's story. The film's viewers also had to be convinced, if in a different manner.

The first clear lie in which a viewer could catch Verbal occurs in the film's first scene. There, in one of the rare moments of the freighter story that is not filtered through Verbal's perspective, we witness Keaton being shot and killed. So we know that Verbal is lying when he says at the end that Keaton had been behind everything and that he was still alive. But we can attribute this lie to Kujan's obstinate battering of Verbal and need not understand it as part of a pattern of deception. On the contrary, we may take Verbal's repeated insistence that Keaton is dead as evidence of his forthrightness. The film's creators went out of their way to make Verbal appear credible to the viewer. They kept the audience on his side by presenting him as the helpless victim of Kujan's smugness, arrogance, and bullying—and as a cripple to boot. The gripping visual rendition of Verbal's story, which we not only hear, as does Kujan, but also see in every detail, reinforces to us its apparent reality and truthfulness. Indeed, Singer and McQuarrie specifically cast actor Kevin Spacey as Verbal because, in McQuarrie's words, he was "the last actor that you suspect." Their strategy, of course, paid off.

The extent of the double deception, Verbal's of Kujan and the filmmakers' of the viewers, is revealed to both audiences only at the very last moment. Verbal has left the police station a free man and is beyond the reach of the law. Kujan and we, the viewers, now look at the bulletin board at which Verbal, facing Kujan, had been peering throughout his interrogation. Together with Kujan we read, among other things, "QUARTET" and

"SKOKIE, IL. 60077" on the manufacturer's plate and then "Redfoot," an alias of a wanted criminal whose description is pinned up on the board. Redfoot was Verbal's name for the man who had brought the five criminals to Soze's representative, the lawyer Kobayashi. Kobayashi, we learn at the climax of this scene, is the manufacturer's name printed on the bottom of the coffee mug that Kujan had repeatedly held before Verbal's face, tilting it as he drank. It now dawns on Kujan, as it does on us, what the nature of Verbal's tale had been all along and that he had been taking his inspiration for his story from his immediate surroundings in the office. To drive home the point that his deception worked, Kujan's earlier challenge to Verbal—"Convince me!"—is heard repeatedly in a voice-over during these moments.

As Verbal is about to enter the car come to collect him (driven by his associate, the man we know as Kobayashi), we witness his metamorphosis from pathetic cripple bereft of the last shred of self-respect to a deft operator in full possession of his wits and dignity and of all his physical powers. The crowning touch is that he is now able to work the cigarette lighter that had earlier dropped from his hand. The dim and pathetic cripple Verbal Kint now reveals himself as the clever and victorious crime lord Keyser Soze. Soze, we were told earlier in the film, is of Turkish origin. His last name is close to the Turkish word for "talk" or "speech," an indirect confirmation of Verbal's true identity. The fax, which proves it, arrives in Rabin's office a moment too late.

5. What Is Truth?

Both Verbal and Odysseus are mythmakers, reinventing themselves in accord with their hearers' expectations. Odysseus tailors his rendition of events to the world of the Phaeacians, for whom literal truth would have little meaning or appeal. Verbal similarly adapts his account to the understanding of his interrogator, who, certain from the outset that the man he is interrogating is no more than a stupid, small-time criminal, would have been most unlikely to believe that Verbal is the legendary Keyser Soze, even if Verbal had been inclined to tell him so—as, of course, he was not.

The plots of both works incorporate the idea that the heroes are creating myths. King Alcinous praises Odysseus for his poetic powers. Verbal creates the horrifying story of Keyser Soze to manipulate Kujan and then goes on to announce that Soze is a mythical bogeyman used to scare children. Both epic and film thoroughly mix the realms of myth and reality. In the *Odyssey*, however, while the inner audiences are taken in by

Odysseus' tales, the outer audience is, or should be, able to distinguish both his fabrications of impossible and superhuman feats and his more mundane deceptions from literal truth, although the distinction is not crucial for an appreciation of the work and its sophisticated narrative progressions.

In *The Usual Suspects*, the distinction seems to be meaningful enough for the film's creators to take pains to point out how impossible it is to make. Even at the film's close, when it is clear both to Kujan and to the spectators that Verbal has fabricated much of his story from cues in the office and from those that Kujan had fielded him, fact and fiction remain inextricably intertwined. Verbal has borrowed names from bulletin board and coffee cup, but does this mean that the people he spoke of do not exist? Or did they do what Verbal said they did under different names? Is the man we have come to know as Kobayashi in Verbal's story and who drives the car in which Verbal escapes really a lawyer, really a high-ranking associate and henchman of Keyser Soze, and really called Kobayashi? (The part is played by an Irish actor.) Singer has said that the man previously known as Kobayashi is at the end driving Verbal's car "to show that in every lie there is some truth." Similarly, the film's opening scene verifies for the audience Verbal's insistence that Keaton is dead, but Kujan's suppositions about Keaton are based on verifiable facts: Keaton's criminal record and his documented history of apparent deaths and reappearances. So who is the real Keaton? Is he the reformed criminal of Verbal's account or the incorrigible and wily brute drawn by Kujan?

As the plot unfolds, the film's audience may begin to suspect that Verbal is inventing his story as he goes along, for whenever Kujan challenges him with new information, Verbal modifies his account accordingly. But we cannot know whether what Verbal tells Kujan at each point is a disclosure of information withheld till then or a new invention.

In the course of his tale, Verbal repeatedly taunts Kujan with truths that Kujan is too stuck in his preconceptions to accept. That Keaton is dead is perhaps the most obvious instance. Another is Verbal's affirmation of his own intelligence, initiative, and leadership; in his telling, for example, two of the gangsters call him the man "with the plan." Such boasts serve him in his efforts to make Kujan see him as an idiot, for who but a moron would brag about planning criminal acts while he is in police custody? (The same goes for a murder we see Verbal commit during a robbery shown in flashback.) But at the end of the film, although we know that Verbal was the one who planned the freighter fire and massacre, we have no way of knowing whether or not he planned certain heists or what his precise role was in the events leading up to the fire. Which of the happenings he described did actually occur? Which did he fabricate, and to what extent?

Verbal taunts Kujan with the impossibility of ever catching Keyser Soze—that is, himself: "You think you can catch Keyser Soze? If he comes up for anything, it will be to get rid of me. After that, my guess is you'll never hear from him again." At the end of the film, we learn that this is indeed the case. Soze, through Kobayashi, comes to fetch Verbal, and it is more than likely that Kujan will never see him again. But who is Keyser Soze? At the moment of Verbal's transformation we are supposed to witness the "truth" emerging from the "lies" he has been telling. But this transformation also raises the question of which is the real Verbal, the pathetic, inept cripple or the sharp, cold-blooded murderer? How much of each is genuine, how much an assumed persona? Reality metamorphoses into fiction and fiction into reality, and who is to say which is which?

Regarding both the *Odyssey* and *The Usual Suspects*, we would do best to think like the ancient Greeks and to consider "that which persuades" rather than "that which is." The Greek word *aletheia* means "truth," but its etymological meaning refers not so much to factual truth as to "something that does not elude."[10] To this conception, the idea of historical or factual truth is as good as irrelevant. From a Greek perspective, the task of the narrator in a work of literature is not only to show that things have not eluded him but to present events in such a way that they do not elude his audience, either—that is to say, in a way that the audience will understand and be inclined to believe the speaker. This principle governs the narration of both the Phaeacian episode in the *Odyssey* and *The Usual Suspects*. The concept of truth at the heart of both means that the narrator must adapt what he says to what the audience can understand and is prepared to believe. Both Odysseus and Verbal Kint do so. The modern hero's nickname, then, is particularly apt, for the acceptance of what he sets out to achieve depends on his clever use of language. Odysseus, too, had been famous throughout antiquity for his rhetorical prowess, indeed invincibility, since the *Iliad*.[11]

In the *Odyssey*, the impossibility of knowing the truth, and the very question of whether there is such a thing, appears to be taken for granted. In *The Usual Suspects*, it is one of the central themes and the main idea that the viewer takes away from the film. The story of the Zuñi boy, with which I began, shows us a verbal Odysseus in the making. In connection with the *Odyssey* and *The Usual Suspects* it also reminds us that the old question "What is truth?" is indeed fundamental to human culture and civilization, both archaic and modern.

10. On the idea of truth in archaic Greek literature see Ahl and Roisman, *The Odyssey Re-Formed*, 92–96 and 301 notes 4–6 (references).
11. See especially *Iliad* 3.221–223.

III

Michael Cacoyannis and Irene Papas on Greek Tragedy

Marianne McDonald & Martin M. Winkler

EDITOR'S NOTE: The following interviews were conducted by Marianne McDonald via telephone in November and December 1988 from a list of questions prepared by both of us. Mr. Cacoyannis and Ms. Papas then reviewed the transcripts. They appear here somewhat abridged from their earlier version in *Classics and Cinema*. Material unrelated to the subject of tragedy and to their films of Euripides has been omitted.

As writer, director, editor, and producer, Michael Cacoyannis has been instrumental since the 1950s in making Greek cinema internationally renowned. He was the first to star Melina Mercouri (*Stella* [1955]), and his 1964 film of Nikos Kazantzakis's novel *Zorba the Greek*, which won three Academy Awards, has become a classic, making the title character's name a household word. Besides this film, Cacoyannis is best known for his three adaptations of tragedies by Euripides: *Electra* (1961), *The Trojan Women* (1971), and *Iphigenia* (1977). These films were made in the order in which Euripides wrote his plays, although the mythological chronology is reversed. Classical scholar Hugh Lloyd-Jones has said about the first of them: "Cacoyannis has a touch of genius. He's kept the spirit of Euripides' play and put it into film terms. In fact, he may have improved it."

With his films, and in his stage productions of tragedy, Cacoyannis has provided new accounts of some of the central Greek plays and demonstrated their timeless appeal. *The Trojan Women*, made abroad when Cacoyannis was in exile from Greece, which at the time was under a military dictatorship—what he has called "the Fourth Reich of Greece"—carries clear overtones of modern history. His early film *The Girl in Black*

(1955) had already told a modern story in terms of ancient tragic themes. Cacoyannis has also staged operas and plays by Shakespeare, Tennessee Williams, and Luigi Pirandello, among others, both in Europe and in the United States.

The year she played the eponymous heroine in Giorgos Tsavellas's film *Antigone* (1961), Irene Papas achieved stardom with the title part in Cacoyannis's *Electra*. Among numerous other films, both Greek and international, she played Helen in *The Trojan Women* and Clytemnestra in *Iphigenia*. Irene Papas also acts on the stage, appearing, for instance, in Cacoyannis's production of Euripides' *Bacchae* in New York City. In television films of the *Odyssey*, she was Penelope in Franco Rossi's international European production of 1969 and Anticleia in Andrei Konchalovsky's American version of 1997. She has had memorable roles in Costa-Gavras's political thriller *Z* (1968) and in Ruy Guerra's *Eréndira* (1983), written by Gabriel García Márquez. She acted for Cacoyannis again in *Sweet Country* (1986) and *Up, Down and Sideways* (1993).

1. Michael Cacoyannis

Could you say something about your use of the ancient classics and of history as a means of artistic expression in the medium of film? You are actually dealing with two different things, mythology and history.

Yes, except that Greek mythology is to a great extent based on history, so its characters are not necessarily mythological inventions. Take, for instance, Agamemnon and the whole family of the Atridae. One could certainly say these were historical figures elevated to mythical stature. They were used by poets, especially tragic poets, as dramatic characters and invariably elevated out of their true historical contexts. And that is what I find fascinating. The way they were presented, say, in the fifth century B.C., did not evoke any dim past, but powerfully reflected the cultural and philosophical climate of a civilization that transcended time. The mythical characters, in the way they are made to express themselves in the tragedies, do not come across as primitive people of the twelfth century B.C., the time in which their stories took place. They are not imprisoned in their age or in any age. And that's why they are still alive today and can speak basic truths. That's why they touch us.

Why do you think this would touch us more than a modern work which directly addresses current reality? What can the classics add to this?

The Greek plays are among the greatest texts ever written. The characters are only the means for great minds like Aeschylus, Sophocles, and

Euripides to express their attitude toward universal human problems. I am not interested in the "true" Agamemnon, Clytemnestra, or Oedipus. I know them through Sophocles and the others. I don't know what the "real" Oedipus was like. The Oedipus who means something to me is Sophocles' Oedipus.

Why did you choose Euripides rather than Aeschylus or Sophocles for the basis of your films?

It's because of the way Euripides explores the human condition. He attacked social evils of his time and shaped the historical legends to serve his ends. He was deeply concerned with the corrosion of human values in Athens during the Peloponnesian War. Parallels between the myths and his time easily spring to mind. I find the psychological makeup of his characters more multifaceted than in the other playwrights, who were more bound by traditional forms, although, within these, Sophocles struck a perfect dramatic balance. The ritualistic aspect of Aeschylus' masterworks is very difficult to put on the screen, to transpose cinematically. I think there is a great film to be made of *Oedipus*, but not necessarily of *The Persians*, which is a great play for the theater.

Do you think Euripides is more concerned with psychology than with history?

Yes, he is concerned with our faults, with the fractured aspects of human nature. Man being mortal, being arrogant and selfish, imposing his will on others—these are all things that concern us to this day. That's why, in effect, Euripides is closer to modern audiences.

Why, out of the whole body of Euripides' works, did you choose Electra, The Trojan Women, *and* Iphigenia in Aulis?

The idea of a trilogy wasn't there from the beginning. In fact, the whole concept started with *Iphigenia*, which reflected my feelings about war. Although it's the last of the three films, it was the first of the tragedies I had scripted. It had to wait quite a long time. But having made *Electra* I became convinced that the films could work as a unity. Unfortunately, we have lost their companions, the other plays in their individual trilogies, but here, although the films are drawn from different trilogies, there is an inexorable sequence of events within them. Euripides was a pacifist. He exposes the futility and folly of all wars, where there can be no clear-cut victor or defeated; he shows that everybody suffers. The idea that evil begets evil and revenge begets revenge is a predominant theme in all three plays. Also, I think that they may be his best works, alongside *The Bacchae*, which, to me, is a mind-boggling masterpiece.

The three plays, as well as The Bacchae, *also deal prominently with women. Are you particularly interested in the theme of suffering women? Do you have some feminist concerns with all this?*

Women in Greek tragedy have an important role to play. Feminist concerns predominate in Euripides, and this is why I never understood why some scholars have called him a misogynist. That is really outrageous.

What are your views about the situation of women in modern Greece? Do you see any connections to ancient Greece, and is there some kind of commentary on women's place in modern Greek society in your films of the tragedies?

I think there are connections between ancient and modern Greece. Women in Euripides are always raising their voices against oppression. And— well, who could be more liberated, from a modern point of view, than Helen or Clytemnestra, who rules with an iron will and a harsh tongue? Even though Clytemnestra paid the price for it, nobody would call her "poor Clytemnestra." There is, in fact, an interesting parallel between Medea and Clytemnestra: they both did a great deal to help Jason and Agamemnon. And they both paid their men back in blood for their betrayals.

Both men took up with another woman, Creusa and Cassandra. Agamemnon had even been prepared to kill Iphigenia.

When confronting Agamemnon in Aulis, Clytemnestra reveals that she never loved him. But over the years she accepted her role and became a good wife and mother. As far as the people were concerned, she was a model wife, mother, and queen. She even warns Agamemnon about the monster he will release in her if he should kill Iphigenia. She had compromised because she had come to believe that he was worth it, in a sense. And then she finds out. . . . From her point of view he is a murderer, corrupted by power.

Did you find that working with Irene Papas made it easier to convey these aspects of Clytemnestra's character?

I had identified Clytemnestra with her before I made the film. She wasn't really cast, she was part of the decision to make the film. I'd had no other image of Clytemnestra in my head. It's that extraordinary physique of hers, and the power that goes with it. When Irene cracks, it's like a stone that cracks. There is no sentimental self-pity. Her cries are not hysterical; they are defiant cries against the order of things. When I was working in America, staging tragedies, I always found it very difficult to explain this to American actresses—that there is a kind of impersonal anger bottled up inside. It's not a narrow anger; it's like a challenge to the injustice of life. I think people who experienced centuries of oppression—I don't want to narrow it down to Greeks—know much more about this. Certainly Jewish people do. It's almost like a national trait handed down from generation to generation. It's not a question of having suffered personally; it's as if the voice of suffering echoes through time. You can hear it in Greek and Armenian laments, for instance.

Where did you find the actress who played Iphigenia?

That was luck. From the moment I decided that Iphigenia should be a very young girl, that narrowed down the field and made it an extremely difficult part to cast. I started searching for a young actress who wouldn't look older than sixteen, then I accidentally met a girl of twelve who had actually no acting experience but who happened to have that quality I mentioned before in regard to Irene, the looks, which are very important, the physical framework, shall we say. To go with this, she had a natural intelligence and poise beyond her years. Emotionally, she was immature. But I cast her anyway. I thought, if I can use that immaturity and push her to the level of subtle maturity that Iphigenia herself achieves through suffering, within a matter of hours practically—if I could work such a trick with the actress [*laughs*]—it would be a wonderful correspondence with the role. In a sense I had to violate, temperamentally and psychologically, a young girl to make her able to absorb and cope with the emotional demands of the part. In that I was very lucky; I could do it without hurting her.

Her interaction with Irene Papas as Clytemnestra was most interesting: the experienced actress and the inexperienced. It worked perfectly.

Yes, it did.

What do you think about stage plays being translated into films?

Obviously, I have nothing against that. Plays, after all, are based on dialogue and character, and very often they lend themselves even more to the screen than do novels. Novels often express philosophical states and attitudes which are very difficult to translate to the screen. As long as filmmakers are not absolutely tied down by a text, they are not making "film theater," which was never my intention.

You transformed the plays into something new, rather than merely illustrating a play on the screen.

I also took liberties. I edited or rearranged the text. I took liberties particularly with the chorus.

You added characters, too.

Yes, sure. In *Iphigenia* I added Calchas, I added Odysseus; I had to. In *Electra* I had peasants talking. I didn't add any characters unrelated to the plot, but visually I explored what on stage only happens in the wings.

In Iphigenia, *the viewer is very much aware of the army and of the power it possesses. You certainly have enough people there; it's an oppressive mass.*

Yes.

Why did you add Odysseus and Calchas and give them such large roles?

The way they come across to the audience is as Euripides evoked them via the characters who discuss them, especially Menelaus and Agamemnon. With film, I don't feel limited to the few actors of ancient theater. I can bring in the people who are being mentioned and make them real. If Euripides had written the script himself, I don't think he could have left those characters off-screen.

How do you see the character of Achilles in Iphigenia? *You have kept his self-involvement. But don't you see a change in him, in that mutual affection grows between him and Iphigenia, as when they look at each other in the courtyard at the end?*

That I preserved absolutely intact, the way it is in the play. When I staged the play in New York, this feeling came through the moment they looked at each other. There is no question that, once he has seen her, Achilles is willing to defend her to the death. And I think love is a strong motivation in her, too. Not wanting him to risk his life for her sake conditions her acceptance of death. All that makes sense. Achilles is the only character in *Iphigenia* whose whole text I used. His arrogance and the reasons for it are in the original. Until he sets eyes on Iphigenia, his outrage is provoked not by pity but by the insult to his honor, to a hero's inflated ego.

His philotimo?

Yes, it's *philotimo*, but in the most negative sense. It's a narrow, arrogant pride. And I think that was one thing that came across about him on the screen. He tells Clytemnestra: "If only Agamemnon had asked me personally, I would not have hesitated for the sake of Greece." That's his response to a mother's desperate pleas. Not a thought at the moment for the trapped girl. What also comes across is that Clytemnestra can't get back at him and has to accept his help, even if it is for the wrong motives. All that matters to her is her daughter's life.

Concerning Iphigenia's decision: Weren't there several paths which you could have taken in interpreting Euripides? Do you think you took a positive one when she falls in love with Achilles?

What she does is crystal clear to me. What you could call negative in my approach is not to accept that Euripides can be interpreted in such a way that she becomes infused with sudden patriotism. Strength, yes—and defiance toward the army clamoring for her blood. She says: "I won't give them the pleasure of seeing me being dragged off and wailing. If I have to go, I shall go proudly, and of my own free will."

Do you see her as having a sense of loyalty to her father as well?

Yes, I do, but compassion even more than loyalty, stirred by his anguish and remorse. Once you are trapped and you know you are going to die, something happens inside you, something that gives you the armor to cope with that passage to nothingness, or to the other world.

In other words, if she has to die, she might as well die heroically?

Well, perhaps not heroically, but with dignity. She is aware that her refusal to die would plunge everybody into bloodshed. Not only would she herself be killed, but also her mother, her father, Achilles. In the film you feel this even more because of the power and danger which the surrounding army represents. I made a point of establishing the threat of a discontented mob in the opening sequence, just as I wanted to make clear Iphigenia's first instinct: fear and the desire to escape. So I had her run off into the woods and be hounded down and dragged back. All this is not in the play.

The way you direct the hunt for her parallels the deer hunt at the beginning of the film. A little girl being ruthlessly hunted down—this involves the audience emotionally, particularly if they remember the deer's frightened eyes when they see Iphigenia's. And then her transformation, her change of mind, becomes all the more effective. But this is contrary to Achilles saying that she made a virtue of necessity: "You see there is no way out, so you are determined to be heroic."

At face value, certain parts of her last speech might be considered patriotic: "They will teach the barbarians a lesson." But to anyone who knows Euripides' views about the Greek motives for the Trojan War—I touched upon this earlier in connection with the Peloponnesian War—this kind of rhetoric lacks conviction.

Is she not simply repeating her father's words?

Yes, I think she is, but even his are spoken in desperation. He says, "I would let you off if I could . . ." And this is probably the only thing Clytemnestra by that point cannot absorb: that he is a broken man. If he could call off the expedition, he would, but by that time Odysseus has told the army. There is no escape for Agamemnon.

You bring out this ambiguity in him, and we even pity him.

Still, he does pay an altogether inhuman price for his ambition. He was confronted with the choice of being the supreme general or of refusing to sacrifice his daughter. It's a tormenting choice, but he makes it. Not, I think, because he is swayed by an oracle which, to him, reeks of political intrigue. He clings to the hope that nature will prove the oracle wrong after all: "By the time I send for her and she gets here, the winds are bound to blow and we'll be off." He's playing for time.

Why did you eliminate the gods? Did you try to convey the force of the gods—necessity, retribution, fate—or any of these concepts?

My aim was to interpret Euripides. Fate, which involves human responsibility, is a recurring theme in his plays, but he does not relegate it to the whims of the gods and is very critical about the way his characters behave in order to appease their conscience. He invariably uses the gods to diminish their stature and what they reflect about human nature. We know his philosophical position on religion very well. One doesn't have to resort to his satirical evocation of the gods, in whom he clearly did not believe, in order to get that across. To show them on the screen would be alienating to modern audiences, who should identify with the characters and be as moved as Euripides intended his audiences to be. And they are—deeply moved, I know. It is not a question of any particular religious faith. That can keep changing. Euripides' faith transcended the concept of the gods and soared above and beyond them, not only with reverence but also with the humble awareness that human knowledge, whatever its achievements, can never fathom the supreme power, the divine justice, which shapes our mortal destiny. In *The Bacchae*, the message is clear: "Knowledge is not wisdom." No doubt Euripides would have something to say about the hubris of our scientific exploits today and about the violation of nature. Of course he understood the need for religion. People cannot cope with the unknown; for instance, their fear of death. What he warned against was using the gods as scapegoats for one's own evil deeds.

Do you have a political message in your films? Are they, for instance, anti-junta?

They are against any form of political oppression. I made *Electra* before the junta.

What about Iphigenia?

That it is antimilitaristic, antiwar, goes without saying, but dramatically, not didactically. It exposes the arrogance of rulers who, in their thirst for power, have no regard for the lives of others—they bring about death arbitrarily and senselessly. The depiction of such situations and of the suffering that results is what makes Euripides so uniquely powerful.

Do you see a parallel in Iphigenia *to the Cyprus situation, as* The Trojan Women *might have related to the Melian disaster as recounted by Thucydides?*

Every major crisis or conflict, every tragic situation that happens in the world can be related to Greek tragedy. It covers the whole range of the human condition—as does Shakespeare, of course. You can relate everything, at any time, to Shakespeare's plays. They and the Greek plays are like mirrors in which you can see all of life.

Do you think art can influence politics?

I wish I could say it does. If it were so, after *The Trojan Women* there should have been no more wars. But the greatness of art is that it goes on raising its voice regardless, to quote Edith Hamilton.

Do you see a connection between your Euripides films and some more openly political films, such as Z?

No, because the tragedies are not dealing with transitory political problems. What comes across when we watch them is that history repeats itself. Political upheavals are simply part of the universal pattern of human folly.

What about the use of modern languages? Does modern Greek express tragedy as well as classical Greek? And what about English, the language you used for The Trojan Women?

Great texts survive in any language. My earlier parallel to Shakespeare applies here, too. Some of the best Shakespeare productions, especially on film, were not made in English or by the English. In Greece the plays are performed not in the original but in modern Greek, and translating them is almost as challenging a task as it is to translate them into English. Edith Hamilton's translation of *The Trojan Women*, I think, is masterly. I doubt that the play has been translated into any language as well, including modern Greek. Sartre, who had been commissioned to do the

French translation which I staged in Paris, did a freer adaptation, brilliant in parts but not as consistent in power.

When you film in Greece, do you feel that the countryside can add something to the film? Mycenae, obviously, seems to do just that.

Certainly with *Iphigenia* and *Electra*, which is a pastoral tragedy, but it depends on the subject matter. With *The Trojan Women* it was less so, because I saw its setting as a parallel to a concentration camp in a foreign country, in this case Troy. I made the film in Spain, where I found a better location than I could in Greece, a huge expanse of walls surrounding a city in ruins. Making films of that quality is problematic, and not only in Greece, because they do not fit into any accepted commercial patterns. Afterwards everybody says: "How wonderful," but believe me, such films are made with spit and blood. They are not produced with enough money. It's like begging for favors to get any backing for them.

What is your working relationship with Giorgos Arvanitis, who was the cinematographer on Iphigenia? *Were you influenced by his visual sense or style?*

I don't think he imposes his style. No man other than the director can, or at least should, do that.

So you basically tell your cinematographer what to do?

Well, you do, but you also rely on his talent to deliver what you want. I ask for a certain light, for example, to convey the harshness of the landscape.

In Iphigenia, *that worked very well; both the landscape and the heat came across with great power.*

The degree of stylization in my films is dictated by the emotional impact I am aiming at. I don't just want to dazzle people's eyes. I want to get to their hearts, to move them—shock them and move them. That way I arrive at a kind of cathartic experience.

What do you think about the cinematic treatments of tragedy by other directors?

I don't believe in updating the tragedies, forcing the characters into modern dress, which amounts to diminishing their dramatic power, or in setting them in some mythical limbo. There is a serious misunderstanding in that approach. For instance, Pasolini and Greek tragedy: Pasolini did not make Greek tragedy. He made very striking films about the myths on which tragedy is based. My aim was to make films about the tragic dimension given to the myths by great writers, not to discard it for the bare bones of a plot. What makes the plots work from my point of view is the timeless power given to them by the playwrights. Pasolini's *Oedipus* is set in a very primitive society. And absolutely no inner torment of Oedipus is suggested. But, of course, he was aiming at something totally different. It has nothing to do with Greek tragedy. It has to do with mythology. There is a great confusion about the two.

Why did you create such a striking death scene for the widow in Zorba the Greek? *In ancient tragedy acts of violence occurred offstage.*

Yes, but you had to be aware of the violence because you saw its end results. You were supposed to be tremendously shocked. To see Oedipus staggering out, bleeding, is a culmination of the horror which occurs offstage but is transmitted by the messenger in mercilessly realistic detail, building up to a final cathartic scream.

What is your opinion about eliminating masks, which you don't use in your films? Without them you would see blood running down Oedipus' face.

To me, the human face seen in huge close-up on the screen is even a kind of mask. The ancient Greeks used a lot of effects by way of their stage machinery, which was very advanced. They loved spectacle. Of course, I don't know to what extent they used blood streaming down masks and clothing. But I would not imagine that they evoked pity by downplaying the horror.

Tyrone Guthrie used masks in his Oedipus Rex.

Guthrie only filmed his theatrical production. When he staged *Oedipus* with Laurence Olivier in London, mercifully he didn't substitute a mask for his face.

Tony Harrison's Oresteia, *the BBC production by Peter Hall, was also filmed with masks.*

Again, they only filmed the play. That's a different thing. A mask on the screen would be an absurdity. Even in the theater I don't like using masks. Masks were used in ancient times because they were shaped in such a way that they could project the actors' voices and also because the parts of women were played by men. So they had to use masks. When today's directors use masks, they even put them on the women. So it doesn't really make any sense. The mask was a convention, acceptable to audiences at that time. When staging the plays today, you have to take into consideration the sensibilities of today's audience. I don't use masks because that way I would only tell the audience: "You are looking at a museum piece."

Why should I put such a barrier between audience and author? I would in effect be saying: "I'm doing a conducted tour for you, an academic reproduction of how the tragedies were done." We don't even know exactly how they were done, because we have no record of that. What is certain is that the authors aimed at the most immediate impact.

When you look back on your work with Greek tragedy as a whole, what overall impression do your films give you?

You know, people forget, or rather, they are allowed to forget by the distributors' neglect. It's already been so many years since I made these films, and sometimes I feel as if the tide had swept over them. Every now and then they are shown on late-night television or in art theaters, but I don't believe that their appeal is restricted to an elitist kind of audience. In France, for instance, *Electra* was a big success, playing for nine months in the center of Paris, yet you can't get the distributor to revive it. That's the disheartening thing about film: It is the most popular art, if you want; at the same time, it is the most expendable. You have to keep reprinting copies at great expense, and the print itself is very easily damaged and useless after a time. One can't help feeling a little frustrated, after all [*laughs*]. I desperately want to preserve my films. On the other hand, I am thinking of what I can still do, not of what I have done. That's what keeps me alive, in a sense, not to sit down and say, "Well, you haven't done too badly," and stop creating. There is comfort to be drawn from the fact that all three playwrights—Aeschylus, Sophocles, and Euripides—were active until a ripe old age. And they created masterpieces. But they, one adds with a sigh, were geniuses. And they didn't have to waste their energy chasing after vulgar moguls for funds.

2. Irene Papas

How do you feel about the role of the classics in modern cinema? Do you think they still speak to us today?

By producing and acting in them, you show what you feel about them. This means that you trust the philosophy that exists in the words and the plot situations, and these can be transferred into modern means of communication because "cinema" is a modern word for communicating. But when you express the emotions and thoughts of ancient people, they need modern means of expression. The classics have the same things to say, in a different way, in any period. I believe that, because a classic is a classic, it is also the most modern, the most appropriate for any time. Otherwise the classics wouldn't be alive. If these texts didn't tell people the same truths all the time, they wouldn't be meaningful. There have been many writers whose works survived because of their quality and their truthfulness, and, as art, they are the most timeless and most important things in the world.

Do you think their quality lies in the poetry?

Well, these works can't be put into categories. They have everything, they are not one-dimensional. They have poetry, they have ideas, they have truthfulness, they have form, they have emotions. They are very much a whole. That's why they have been imitated so much. My father used to say that one phrase of ancient wisdom was worth volumes of modern words because the modern world likes to dilute things. Ancient thought is a concentration in the most simple and direct way. As the Greeks say, the best and shortest road to a point is the direct one.

Do you think special acting techniques are necessary in dealing with these texts?

No, I don't believe that. I believe that there is the same way of feeling, then and now. On the classical stage you might have used a louder voice, because some people were seated far away, but you always use the same soul. On the other hand, sometimes you need certain powers that otherwise you don't need. The power of the voice to convey the power of emotions is extremely important. An actor needs to be at his best, physically and mentally, to perform well. We have to. If you don't have your body, the instrument of your profession, always at your disposal, you are limited.

You have great physical power and presence in your roles.

Japanese do in their theater. I know that in Japan you must have training, so it's like polishing the roots of your soul.

Do you use methods different from your stage technique when you are acting in films?

Not at all. It's the same process; the only difference is that you decide about the appropriate means at the particular moment of filming.

Do you have a different technique for ancient and modern parts, such as Electra or the politician's widow in Z?

Again, no. The method of expressing yourself is the same. It may take different shapes or forms.

You have said that you prefer films to the stage.

That's because I can see what I do, and I like to have a record of it—you can give your best and correct what you don't like. And you can give the public what you think is the best you can do at the time. Once you have done that, it's like a finished work of art; it exists by itself. You don't have to repeat it. And you don't later ruin it by an inferior performance, either. On the stage you do the same thing again and again, and once you have squeezed out of yourself whatever you can do, it becomes forced work. You do your best for your audience, but soon you become a machine repeating the same thing every night.

On both stage and screen, you often impress your audience with the independence and zest which you bring to your work. Is there a driving force inside you, a particular creative principle?

I have no secret. I think it is your attitude to death that makes you behave and act in certain ways. Death is the greatest catalyst in human life—how you approach it, what it means to you. All people have to face it and make a decision about it which affects their lives: whether to go on living or to commit suicide, whether to wait for death or not to wait for it. While you're waiting, what are you doing with your life? Are you doing right, or are you doing wrong?

Do you think ancient literature, especially tragedy, can help answer this question?

I don't know. When I was doing *Iphigenia in Aulis* in New York and the Vietnam War was raging, I felt that Euripides hadn't done a thing to stop wars. Poor Clytemnestra was shouting "Murder, murder!" while people in Vietnam were being killed. So what good did Euripides do? None. And he was the best of all.

Aristotle speaks about the pleasure of tragedy in his Poetics. *Doesn't a tragedy present its audience with both a learning process and a pleasurable experience?*

It is not that pleasurable. I don't like to act, to tell you the truth.

You don't like to act?

No, it's nerve-racking. But then life doesn't usually permit me to be as truthful as I can be doing tragedy.

When you are playing a part in a tragedy, do you think you strike a universal chord in human beings?

I don't know if I do. I have no means to know that. I only know when I feel right. Then something happens.

Do you see a political message in the ancient plays?

I believe in everyday life, in everyday decisions. Of course, you act politically, and this is the same thing in the films and in the ancient dramas. But party politics is a completely different matter. It's one thing to be a Republican, Democrat, Communist, or whatever; it is another thing to be a political human being. As Aristotle said, man is a political creature, and every decision you make is political. I think ancient Greek drama goes beyond mere behavior; it addresses human existence itself. There are political films or plays which deal only with questions of behavior, so they last a decade or twenty years, but when the political system changes, they are forgotten.

Costa-Gavras makes political films, such as Z, in which you acted.

Costa-Gavras uses situations that are factually true, so it is very natural that he will make overtly political films. His talent is to take situations chronicled in a newspaper and to turn them into tragedies, not simply politics. He's very talented that way and makes beautiful films because he extends bare facts beyond their time, making them eternal and addressing lasting truths. Michael [Cacoyannis] takes things that are both political and mythic-eternal in form, but Gavras takes a political event and from that he extends it into a tragedy. Really, however, both deal with something which goes beyond mere reality.

Michael Cacoyannis has said that the mythology he uses is, in a sense, also historical.

That is his talent. He takes myth and makes it true, and Gavras takes truth and makes it myth.

When you acted the part of the wife of the politician who is assassinated in Z, did you feel or experience something different from playing Clytemnestra in Cacoyannis's Iphigenia?

In *Iphigenia*, I had a challenging part. Z was much easier, because it was a small and very definite part. I think that Clytemnestra is a victim of the situation.

Does playing a realistic, modern role affect your acting?

If I don't play a realistic Clytemnestra, I am done for. I don't play her like somebody who doesn't exist. I play her as if she were existing right now, as a real person.

So you make the women in both kinds of parts our living contemporaries?

That's right.

Do you have the freedom to create your parts?

That depends on how closely you work with the director—how you coincide with the point of view the director has, because he's the one who decides in the end. So you are not the absolute creator, but you are part of a creation that is also somebody else's. But I had the great fortune to work with Michael close to his point of view. So I participate in bringing out what a particular role means, what we are going to make out of it, which choices we are going to take.

So the two of you shape your roles together?

Oh, sure. I bring in ideas and practical suggestions, and we talk at length about how he sees the part and the whole situation. Of course, I cannot say I am the director, but I contribute to the creation of my role, also theoretically. Sometimes you are called on to interpret only practically, and the theoretical framework is decided by the director. But with Michael I have both.

Cacoyannis has told us that he made certain of his films with you in mind.

Yes, Michael likes my way of acting. The realism. And he prefers me because I'm not an obstacle to his way of seeing things. Sometimes an actress, even if she is very, very good, may have a technique that is incompatible with the director's; it can be an obstacle inhibiting the director's passion. In such a case the creative passion of Michael cannot function.

Cacoyannis implied that you have certain physical qualities besides your acting ability, and when you portray somebody pushed to extremes you can feel it inside yourself.

Well, I cannot see myself from the outside, but I know that I don't hold back. In a way, the responsibility of an actress is to be generous. It's like a confession, an emotional generosity. Why should you be an actor if you are hiding something? That would be impossible.

Is there a difference between Cacoyannis's and Costa-Gavras's directing styles?

Of course, people are different, but I love them both, and in one way or another I was creative with both of them because I liked the subjects they were filming and, in general, the way they make films. Michael has peaks of passion; he is masterly with moments of strong passion. On the other hand, Gavras has what could be described as a cool passion, which creates emotional peaks in the audience. He treats his subject matter with detachment. He presents more of a counterpoint; Michael just throws himself into the fire. But both are very passionate people. With Michael I played the most beautiful roles I have ever had.

Would you tell us something about your roles in his films of Euripides?

The first part I played was Electra, and it was very exciting. It was breathtaking for me, and I was there from the beginning to the end. I saw every shot as it was done, and I would participate. At the end, when we finished shooting, I had a fever for three days! It was too intense for me. In *The Trojan Women*, I had a smaller responsibility for reasons that had to do with the production. I wasn't there all the time. I had a very big part again in *Iphigenia*, and I was closer and participated a lot more.

Did you prefer playing one particular role to any other?

I can't answer that, because it is not possible to answer. To prefer Electra to Clytemnestra, to prefer Clytemnestra to Electra—you just can't do that.

You once mentioned that you wanted to play Andromache in The Trojan Women, *but that Cacoyannis saw much more of Helen in you. Would you have preferred playing Andromache?*

I wanted Andromache because she has that terrific scene with the boy [her son Astyanax]. For an actress, that is a gift. But the other part, Helen, was a very big challenge for me. So, finally, Michael was right because that part needs more acting; more meaning had to be put into it. Andromache would have been easier. It's difficult when you play a role that is more ambiguous. It is not advantageous, the role of Helen. Andromache by nature takes your heart away. As Helen, you really have to sweat.

As Helen, you have a kind of burning, intense beauty. The audience can understand why men would die for you.

Well, but that's not acting. I don't believe that physical attributes are either your fault or your merit. What you choose to do with them, and how you approach your part, that is your art.

Is there a feminist strain in Cacoyannis's films, in the way he deals with the women who are at the center of the tragedies?

It is Euripides who's for women. He saw the underdogs in them, just as in the slaves. That's because they were a kind of suffering animal.

In Electra, *he portrayed Clytemnestra more sympathetically than Cacoyannis did in his film version.*

Sometimes, when I see *Electra*, I think that Euripides might be angry with us because we gave Electra all the rights. It's a modern interpretation. When I played the Sophoclean Electra [on the stage], I felt it was not that her mother is not right, but that her mother in being so afraid of revenge behaved very badly to her children—conflicting rights and duties, as so often in tragedy. When you become a dictator you can become subject to what you wanted to rectify. When you kill somebody for doing something evil you yourself become a killer, somebody evil, so what you wanted to avoid you actually become. Revenge is a vicious circle.

Do you think that Euripides' Electra is more concerned about her own position and her inheritance than about revenge for her father?

Well, why should she have to marry a peasant? Clytemnestra just throws her out. In Euripides sometimes nobody's completely right and nobody's completely wrong. Especially in *The Bacchae*. Nothing is simple. And this is one of the challenges for me.

What in particular would you teach other actresses?

I would try to facilitate their souls to be free. But to teach a soul is very difficult—to teach truth or truthfulness. I believe that art is the truest thing in the world. And that's what an actor should strive for.

IV

Eye of the Camera, Eye of the Victim: *Iphigenia* by Euripides and Cacoyannis

Marianne McDonald

Michael Cacoyannis has produced and directed three films based on plays by Euripides: *Electra* (1961), *The Trojan Women* (1971), and *Iphigenia* (1977).[1] The last of these, after Euripides' play *Iphigenia in Aulis*, is severe and forbidding, challenging its audience to struggle for an appreciation of ancient tragedy and the patterns of experience it represents rather than reducing its source to an easily understood story. Cacoyannis makes things strange to us, for instance in our comprehension of Clytemnestra. How, and to what extent, do we understand, imaginatively even become, Clytemnestra? Do we bring our own experience of war and human suffering to Cacoyannis's version of Euripides' artistic vision? Is this process itself reductive, so that all we are left with is one more depiction of how women and children suffer when men rattle their swords?

A film adaptation renders this suffering more concrete than is possible in a production of Euripides' play on the stage. Siegfried Kracauer's claim that film redeems physical reality is applicable here.[2] Cacoyannis's camera allows us first to identify with Iphigenia, the frightened child. Near the opening of the film, the Greeks are hunting a deer, and the camera follows it through the underbrush, focusing on its eye bulging in panic.

---

1. On these films, and others based on Euripides, see my *Euripides in Cinema: The Heart Made Visible* (1983; rpt. Boston: Greek Institute, 1991). In general see Kenneth MacKinnon, *Greek Tragedy into Film* (Rutherford, N.J.: Fairleigh Dickinson University Press, 1986). See further MacKinnon's and my "Cacoyannis vs. Euripides: From Tragedy to Melodrama," *Intertextualität in der griechisch-römischen Komödie*, ed. Niall W. Slater and Bernhard Zimmermann (Stuttgart: M and P: Verlag für Wissenschaft und Forschung, 1993), 222–234.

2. Siegfried Kracauer, *Theory of Film: The Redemption of Physical Reality* (1960; rpt. Princeton: Princeton University Press, 1997).

Later we see the same landscape and similar camera movements when Iphigenia is hunted down. Cacoyannis forces us to identify with the oppressed, especially women and children, perhaps even more than Euripides had done. (Cacoyannis's Electra, for instance, had been more sympathetic than Euripides'.) With film, our identification with a character or characters is different from the emotional involvement the theater offers its audience. Tragedy on the stage moves us to an emotional and even intellectual pleasure which arises from our watching the play. But in a play it is mainly the language and its delivery that elicit and shape our response, while film gives more emphasis to the visual and, in this way, to a more immediate, visceral experience on the part of the spectator.

If we identify first with Iphigenia as an innocent victim and then with Clytemnestra as an elemental avenging force, what happens to our own individuality and theirs? In the spurious ending of Euripides' play Iphigenia is replaced on the sacrificial altar by a deer.[3] We readily think of Isaac replaced on the altar by a ram and of all the theories that attempt to explain the evolution of ritual sacrifice. The great resonance of film adaptations of Greek tragedy, however, derives from the sense they give us of the fundamental and unchanging, but also inescapable, patterns of experience. The more elemental the style and texture of the adaptation, giving the semblance of faithful adherence to the original, the more shocked we are to see ourselves as victims and our leaders as oppressors.

Cacoyannis presents us with a complex work. The story is set in the mythic-historical period just before the Trojan War, but in addition Cacoyannis makes us think of Euripides' time, that of Athens during the Peloponnesian War (431–404 B.C.), and even of his own, the Greek Civil War after World War II (1946–1949) and the rule of the colonels (1967–1974). The myth's two most powerful dramatic treatments besides Euripides', those by Aeschylus and Seneca, also condemn Agamemnon's arbitrary and arrogant abuse of power, but Cacoyannis makes of Euripides' already poignant depiction of Iphigenia's suffering the fulcrum to arouse moral outrage in his audience. We come to wonder about the relation between the universal and the historically specific: What is the power of the modern adaptation of a classical text that can move us more forcefully than contemporary fact, such as news reports of wars and civil wars,

---

3. Euripides may have died before writing the ending. Most scholars agree that the ending we have is late. There is also much dispute about how much of the play was written by Euripides and how much by others making an actable version of what Euripides may have left unfinished. And who today would believe that a deer was substituted for Iphigenia at the last minute?

or contemporary fiction? To a large extent, the answer lies in the way Cacoyannis creates his audience's identification with the sufferers.

Cacoyannis, who was born on the island of Cyprus, dealt with the Turkish invasion of Cyprus in 1974 in his only documentary film, *Attila '74*, made that year and named after the arbitrary line that divided the island into Turkish and Greek parts. Cacoyannis knew what the power and madness of an invading army could be like and repeatedly shows the faces of the victims: men, women, children weeping, mourning their dead and missing, forced to leave their land. With its emphasis on the suffering of the war victims, the film carries thematic overtones of *The Trojan Women*. Like Euripides, Cacoyannis understood the passion and fickleness of the mob, not least of a military mob. Three years later, when his Iphigenia says that she is volunteering her life to keep Greece free of barbarians, her words acquire a resonance well beyond their mythical context. Both *Attila '74* and *Iphigenia* are works about betrayal, accommodation, and collaboration: Iphigenia is sacrificed with the collusion of Calchas, Odysseus, Menelaus, Agamemnon, and the whole army; Cyprus was betrayed, Cacoyannis suggests, by the Greek junta in collaboration with the United Nations, Turkey, and the CIA.

Both Euripides' and Cacoyannis's versions of the Iphigenia myth show us how ostensibly civilized men can turn barbaric. The characters who exhibit true heroism are women, slaves, and children, usually as victims of men in power. Euripides was a critic of his society, and his dramas were not popular in Athens. (He apparently won only four victories during his lifetime, in contrast to Aeschylus' thirteen and Sophocles' twenty-four.) Unpopular critics, such as Euripides' friend Socrates, are rarely appreciated in their own countries. We can accept their truths only when we are not under the influence of political counterpressures. Euripides and Cacoyannis are closely allied in spirit with their powerful criticism of war and the corruption of martial, religious, and political leaders. Both create moving drama. They lead us beyond a feeling of frustration and resentment against corrupt regimes to empathy with the suffering of individual victims. That is where the real tragedy occurs. There is a vast difference between our moral outrage at the idea of injustice and the rising horror we feel when we see the imminent death of a particular child. In Euripides, conventional male "heroes" constantly betray *aretê* ("excellence"); instead, true *aretê* is often found in women, slaves, and children. The same is the case with Cacoyannis.

It is a truism, but one worth repeating, that war has been a constant concern for mankind. When not in thrall to its ideology, we question its goals and the price it exerts. War and its consequences intrigue Cacoyannis, particularly the question of power: Who holds it and over whom, and what are its abuses? What is a noble war (the Persian Wars of the fifth century B.C.), and what is an ignoble one (civil war)? Is a noble war ever possible? Almost twenty-five hundred years ago, these were Euripides' questions, too. Both Euripides and Cacoyannis make political statements, derived from their own experiences of war and exile. Even more than Homer, who besides showing the horrors of war also extolled the glories of battle and the honor of its heroes, Euripides emphasizes the heroism of the victims, futile as it often is. The wages of war are earned by blood, and in this case the honor gained by Iphigenia as victim is honor lost by Agamemnon.

The issues in Euripides' play are clear. He shows us the price we pay for war: the lives of our children, whenever a country sends its young to fight its wars. Agamemnon's agreeing to slay his own daughter is, fundamentally, the decision all political leaders make when they declare war. Only they think war's tragedies will strike others, and the deaths they suffer will not be their own or their children's. As the herald says in Euripides' *The Suppliants*: "When a people vote for war, no one thinks of his own death, but thinks this misfortune is someone else's, for if death could be seen at the time of voting, never would spear-mad Greece destroy itself" (482–486). In several of his plays, Euripides exposed the Athenians' moral corruption. He questioned the gods by depicting them as more callous and irresponsible than humans. Political leaders often used them for their own ends. Sometimes Euripides also showed the disaster of an arrogant or ambitious man behaving like a god. Euripides had seen the Athenians, after their victory over the Persians, form an oppressive empire under the pretext of protecting Greece from a renewed Persian threat. In 416 B.C., when the island of Melos refused to support Athens, the Athenians reacted by killing all adult men and selling the women and children into slavery. It seems likely that Euripides wrote *The Trojan Women* in response, since the play was performed in 415 B.C. Sparta eventually inflicted total defeat on Athens in 404 B.C., two years after Euripides' death and after the posthumous performance of *Iphigenia in Aulis*. In this play, Clytemnestra recognizes the decision of the Greeks to kill her daughter for the crime that it is and clearly states that this "unholy murder" was an evil choice (1364). Calchas, Odysseus, Menelaus, and the army consider Iphigenia's sacrifice a "good," but its evil nature is clear to Clytemnestra always and to Agamemnon at times. Agamemnon had been torn by conflicting responsibilities and interests but eventually had opted for power; the longer he waited, the more restricted he became in his ability to choose or to change his mind. By the time the army knew, it was altogether too late. When Agamemnon made the excuse to Iphigenia and Clytemnestra that their whole family could be murdered (1264–1268), he was probably right. But earlier he had had a choice.[4]

Euripides' plays reveal his growing awareness of the realities of war and the prevarication of the leaders who had to pander to a mob. The word "mob" (ochlos) occurs more often in the late plays Orestes and Iphigenia than in any other of Euripides' plays. He gradually realized the power of the mob and its demagogues. In regard to the Trojan War, mob power is an anachronism: Euripides was speaking about his own time. His later plays reflect Thucydides' evaluation of a general deterioration of morals that occurred in Athens in the course of the Peloponnesian War. Words acquired new meanings; power and success were worth more than justice or truth.[5] Euripides' Iphigenia, with her noble display of self-sacrifice for the sake of Greece, seems a Homeric hero lost in a Thucydidean world, seeking honor when the people about her do not know the meaning of the word.[6]

This is also Cacoyannis's perspective. He reproduces the corruption of people and political leaders he himself had known in modern Athens. To him, the contemporary situation had resonances from his country's antiquity, just as to Euripides the confrontation between the mythical brothers Menelaus and Agamemnon exemplified the struggle for power with which he was familiar at his own time. Conflicts and indecision such as theirs led to an oligarchic takeover in Athens in 411–410 B.C., which in turn brought about a number of murders to consolidate the new power. Similar things happened in Cacoyannis's Athens, when the conflict between various leaders allowed someone else to take advantage of the situation and seize power for himself. In 1967, vacillations in leadership led to a general disillusionment with the government and to the military coup by Giorgos Papadopoulos. When Menelaus accuses Agamemnon of abandoning the people who helped him after he consolidated his power, Cacoyannis sees in this a parallel to Papadopoulos's gradual rise and subsequent abandoning of the constituency that had helped him obtain his position of leadership. Euripides and Cacoyannis show us that this is the lesson history teaches: Leaders make and break alliances with the people for the sake of political expediency.

4. Choice, particularly moral choice, was important in tragedy and was determined by character; see Aristotle, Poetics 1450b17–18.

5. See Thucydides, The Peloponnesian War 3.82–84.

6. As other scholars have done, Thomas Rosenmeyer, "Wahlakt und Entscheidungsprozess in der antiken Tragödie," Poetica, 10 (1978), 1–24, explains Iphigenia's change of mind in terms of heroism. He sees Iphigenia as impelled by desire for glory, pursuing the Homeric ideal of "immortal fame" (Iliad 9.413).

Cacoyannis humanizes Euripides by eliminating the ancient gods and centering good and evil in humans, with no divine element as either source or judge. Without any supernatural framework, and in the absence of fatalism, man is now wholly responsible for his actions. Euripides shows some human alliances as a way of combating irrational gods, but Cacoyannis puts man in charge of his fate, although he is often victimized by his own weakness. He adds a calculating and obviously corrupt Calchas in league with a self-serving Odysseus. Neither Calchas nor Odysseus had appeared in Euripides' play. Cacoyannis's Calchas takes on the arbitrary and perverse qualities of Euripidean gods, who exercise their irrational power to cause human suffering. In this Calchas we may also see Cacoyannis's criticism of the Greek Orthodox Church, which sometimes made morally questionable decisions. The church allied itself with the colonels' junta because it approved of the conservative values of the military and wanted to be protected from Communism. Cacoyannis may also have had in mind some of the disastrous decisions made by Bishop Makarios on Cyprus.[7]

There are other humanizing factors in the film. The army's struggle is not simply for honor, vengeance, or some other abstract ideal. In his earlier film *The Trojan Women*, getting Helen back from the Trojans was simply a pretext for the Greeks; their real motive had been gold. In *Iphigenia*, Cacoyannis echoes this when Agamemnon says that Helen gave them an excuse to go to war but that Troy's gold was the real reason. The economic basis of power was the major criticism leveled by Andreas Papandreou against the "palace, the Junta, the economic oligarchy, and the American CIA."[8] This illustrates what history confirms: Economically comfortable people are easily ruled.

Cacoyannis presents an Achilles more sympathetic to Clytemnestra's and Iphigenia's predicament than Euripides' had been. Cacoyannis introduces a charming Achilles, played by a young, handsome actor, instead

---

7. Keith R. Legg and John M. Roberts, *Modern Greece: A Civilization on the Periphery* (Boulder, Colo.: Westview, 1997), 104: "The church has generally been more comfortable with conservative parties because of its fears of educational and language reforms. In the postwar period, the fear of communism—especially considering the position of Orthodox Christianity in communist countries—surely made the church a natural ally of right-wing parties. . . . The traditional values espoused by the military leadership were far more congenial to church leaders than to center and center-left politicians." The Greek Orthodox Church, however, has occasionally made glorious gestures, such as backing the revolution of 1821. On March 25 of that year, Bishop Germanos, Metropolitan of Patras, raised the flag of Greece at Agia Lavra, signaling the beginning of the revolution.

8. D. George Kousoulas, *Modern Greece: Profile of a Nation* (New York: Scribner, 1974), 275.

of the egotistical prig we find in Euripides. Achilles' eyes meet Iphigenia's slowly, and it is love at first sight. Kenneth MacKinnon describes the way they look at each other as "oddly reminiscent of Tony's first glimpse of Maria in Robert Wise's *West Side Story*."[9] Cacoyannis seems to think that a popular film needs a love interest. His Achilles takes Clytemnestra and Iphigenia more seriously than Euripides' Achilles does. This Achilles is certainly more willing to risk his life for Iphigenia. He is a hero capable of making her change her mind, not least for his sake; he looks at her first with compassion, later with admiration. His first direct words to her are: "Don't be afraid, I'll defend you." In Euripides, he had only addressed her directly after her decision to accept death with dignity, and he begins by calling her "child of Agamemnon" (1404). In the film we see him arguing with his men on her behalf and even being driven off by them with stones for his effort. Euripides had played this down; his Achilles only reports it (1349–1357). Cacoyannis's Achilles acts heroically, and what was verbal in Euripides has become visual.

Agamemnon also appears softened from his Euripidean counterpart. In Euripides, Agamemnon waffles over his choices, as does Menelaus, and they both unveil each other's weakness, the one's for power, the other's for a woman (317–414). Neither has the people's good at heart, or his family's. Euripides unmasks the men and shows them changing their position, reversing their roles as to which of them is in favor of the sacrifice. Cacoyannis has also made Menelaus more sympathetic, as when he shows Menelaus swayed by family loyalty after his argument with his brother, whose hand he takes in a gesture of emotional closeness. Cacoyannis's Agamemnon is weak, but we never doubt that he is a loving father.[10] His weakness is visible as he wavers between sacrificing his child and giving up the expedition; he is finally resolved when the army hails him as leader and sings a song of victory at the instigation of Odysseus. Agamemnon then takes a deep breath, an indication not so much of relief as of defeat and complicity. Another filmic effect that conveys Agamemnon's weakness and hesitation appears in what we might call a visual and aural close-up. We see and hear Agamemnon scratching his nails across a clay jar as he waits for the arrival of his daughter; we hear his labored breathing and see his tortured eyes. With such physical indications Cacoyannis conveys to us Agamemnon's emotional torment.

9. MacKinnon, *Greek Tragedy into Film*, 90.

10. There are many interpretations of Agamemnon, from father and general to wholly corrupt politician. For a summary of scholarly views of his motives see Herbert Siegel, "Agamemnon in Euripides' 'Iphigenia at Aulis'," *Hermes*, 109 (1981), 257–265.

In both play and film, Iphigenia changes her mind. At the beginning she says that she would be a fool to want to die, at the end that she embraces death for the good of the people. Her father gave her no more than rhetorical reasons for the sacrifice, but she idealistically embraces this rhetoric. Rather than violating Aristotle's principles about tragic characters—according to *Poetics* 1454a26–33, her change of mind is too abrupt—she follows his ethics by obeying the concept of *philia* ("devotion, love") and the duties it entails.[11] Aristotle complained that Euripides threw her into contradiction, giving a young girl mature patterns of thought. Here Aristotle's misogyny is evident, denying a woman the freedom to think. Today we are more likely to see Iphigenia's embrace of pan-Hellenism as essentially tragic. Tragic heroes seize as their own the choice the gods seem to have made for them.

Cacoyannis has made Iphigenia's death more believable by emphasizing her gradual realization that she has no choice about living or dying but that she does have a choice over the manner of her death. He has eliminated the Euripidean Iphigenia's chilling comment to Achilles that "one man's life is worth more than ten thousand women's" (1394). In the film, her dignity is unmistakable; it is that of a brave child. (Tatiana Papamoskou, the extraordinary actress playing her, was only twelve years old.) At the last minute she tries to escape again when she realizes that the winds are rising, but she is caught by a fiendish-looking Calchas. Her terrified scream is not a final heroic moment, but it does not diminish her bravery. Her humanity intensifies her credibility and deepens our sympathy for her. Cacoyannis's Iphigenia has much in common with Carl Theodor Dreyer's heroine in *The Passion of Joan of Arc* (1928). Both protagonists are young girls surrounded by the corrupt or the weak. Their vulnerability, innocence, and moral choices contrast with the sordid nature of the people at whose hands they are forced to die. Both choose a heroic death. But Cacoyannis's Iphigenia is also similar to Shakespeare's Juliet in the combination of adult and child. When she contemplates suicide, Juliet combines the determination of a woman in love with a child's fear of death and the dark (*Romeo and Juliet*, act 4, scene 3).

In the film's prologue and in Calchas' private interchanges with Odysseus, Cacoyannis makes it clear that the seer has personally contrived the oracle, falsely claiming that the goddess Artemis demands Iphigenia's

11. On this see my "Iphigenia's *Philia*: Motivation in Euripides' *Iphigenia at Aulis*," *Quaderni Urbinati di Cultura Classica*, new ser., 34 (1990), 69–84. The only value in a morally unstructured universe is *philia*, the tie linking one person to another, as Euripides' Heracles says: "Whoever prefers wealth or power over faithful friends thinks poorly" (*Heracles* 1425–1426).

death. Odysseus tells Calchas to hurry the sacrifice because the winds are already rising. This is a radical change from Euripides: Artemis was to send winds only after Iphigenia's death. It is clear that Cacoyannis's Agamemnon knows that Calchas has invented the oracle and is fully aware of the priest's corruption. When Iphigenia approaches him to ask him to spare her life, he says that it is too late, that the army has been incited to frenzy and demands the sacrifice. To deny them means death—hers, his, and his family's.

At the end of the film, when Agamemnon sees the wind rising and runs up the steps toward the altar and Calchas, he really is too late, as we know from his eyes, in which we see his defeat more effectively than words could convey. There is no messenger speech telling us about the sacrifice, as there had to be in Euripides; in the film we understand from her father's eyes that Iphigenia is now dead. Eyes are the vehicle Cacoyannis uses to convey suffering, pity, love, hate, horror, defeat, and finally death. They are indeed the windows of the soul, through which the ancient Greeks had expressed the concept of the self.

The director's eye is the camera, with which the audience also sees and understands. Throughout the film Cacoyannis makes reference to eyes. Who sees and who does not see relates to the issue of power; more often than not, seeing is the sole power of the female, as in the confrontations between Agamemnon and Clytemnestra. Looks emphasize the differences between the sexes. There is a distinct difference between the way Cacoyannis presents males and females. Men can be static and are shown from behind; they often avoid the eyes of a female. Women move and are seen from the front; female eyes stare, blaze, blame, or threaten. Iphigenia pierces her father with her eyes as she is crowned and sprinkled with water in preparation for death; Agamemnon avoids her gaze here as he did earlier when she first arrived. He only stares at her after she is dead and her movements have ceased. Clytemnestra's gaze, particularly at the end, is like the destructive gaze of the Gorgon, which turned people to stone. Modest women should avert their eyes; women who are transformed by their pain transfix their abusers with their silent stare.

One of the most significant modern expressions in *Iphigenia* is Clytemnestra's term of endearment for her daughter: *matia mou* ("my eyes"). The words convey the ultimate human value, a parent's love for a child. The same words had occurred in *Attila '74*, with weeping parents mourning their children. To viewers of both films, the timeless theme of Euripides becomes perhaps more poignant here than anywhere else.

In *Iphigenia*, Cacoyannis shows heroes (Iphigenia, Achilles), mixed characters (Agamemnon, Menelaus), and villains (Calchas, Odysseus, the army). There are also those who are only victims (Clytemnestra, the old servant). This is in contrast to Euripides, who makes all except Iphigenia partially blameworthy. Some critics see even her as calculating; they interpret literally Achilles' words at line 1409 that Iphigenia has aligned her will with what she sees as clear necessity.[12] Euripides has no heroes except Iphigenia and no out-and-out villains. Menelaus and Agamemnon are corrupt only up to a point.

Cacoyannis's treatment, particularly in his prologue and ending, and in the chase sequence in the middle of the film, resolves a number of the ambiguities inherent in Euripides' text, but it presents us with some new ones. We have an open-ended drama and not the compact and complete imitation of an action that Aristotle demanded (*Poetics* 1459a17–20). Cacoyannis's prologue suggests the major themes of the entire film. He shows us the Greek fleet and the restless army, overcome with heat and impatient in its desire to sail to Troy. From the very beginning, Cacoyannis makes us conscious of the army and of the power that an anonymous mass can exert over its leaders. Given the limitations of the ancient stage, Euripides could only suggest, whereas Cacoyannis can be visually far more explicit. So we can understand why Agamemnon panders to his men by leading them on a slaughter of animals tended by Calchas and his followers. He tries to prevent the killing of a sacred deer but is too late. We see the deer flee, trying to escape through the woods. We see the woods through the deer's eyes, sharing the victim's perspective. The animal's death foretells Iphigenia's. Later, when Iphigenia is hunted down, we again see as if through her eyes.[13] We share her perspective, literally and figuratively. The parallel and its meaning are clear.

Close-ups of eyes and shared perspectives convey the major issues of the film. Over the dying deer, his sacred property, Calchas looks at Agamemnon. The close-up of his eyes suggests his future course of action, his power play against Agamemnon. After the death of the deer,

12. One of the earliest negative assessments of Iphigenia was by Bruno Snell, "From Tragedy to Philosophy: *Iphigenia in Aulis*," in *Greek Tragedy: Modern Essays in Criticism*, ed. Erich Segal (New York: Harper and Row, 1983, also published in *Oxford Readings in Greek Tragedy* [Oxford: Oxford University Press, 1983]), 396–405; this is a slightly abridged English version of "Euripides' aulische Iphigenie," in *Aischylos und das Handeln im Drama* (Leipzig: Dieterich, 1928 [Philologus Supplementband 20, no. 1]), 148–160. Snell suggests that Euripides may be questioning the entire heroic code. Cf. Herbert Siegel, "Self-Delusion and the *Volte-Face* of Iphigenia in Euripides' 'Iphigenia at Aulis'," *Hermes*, 108 (1980), 300–321.

13. We may compare the hunt in Jean Renoir's film *Rules of the Game* (1939). The pilot Jurieux is caught in a similar game that takes place among the humans and dies a casual sacrifice in a sport he took seriously. The film, coming shortly after Renoir's *Grand Illusion* (1937), warns against war as the ultimate game. The duck hunt in Bernardo Bertolucci's *1900* (1977) is a brief homage to Renoir's film.

·

100

CLASSICAL

MYTH &

CULTURE

IN THE

CINEMA

Cacoyannis returns to the fleet. One of the ships' masts is made to resemble a death's head, and then the film's title appears over a blood-red sea. Cutting and close-ups make for an ominous and immediately gripping opening sequence.

The film comes to an end with the sunset and the ships sailing for Troy, but the future is in Clytemnestra's eyes. We see her watching the Greek fleet sailing off; her face reveals her ineffable grief over the loss of her daughter but also threatens the revenge to come when her husband, murderer of her child, returns from the Trojan War. The sunset colors the sea a red as bloody as that at the beginning. Then Clytemnestra's gaze pierces us, for she looks straight into the camera, her black hair blowing across her face. Cacoyannis, who does not believe in the use of masks in realistic films, captures Clytemnestra's suffering and brooding desire for revenge in this powerful prolonged close-up. The wind now stirs both us and Clytemnestra; just as she appears to us, it is primordial, irresistible, implacable. The wind and Clytemnestra combine to represent elemental forces. Then, through a cut to a close-up of her point of view, we see her hair blow across the screen, obscuring our view of the fleet. We now have become Clytemnestra, just as earlier we had been the deer and Iphigenia. This ending is one of doom brooding and waiting. The true end of the story will occur after Agamemnon's return home. Iphigenia is dead, but her mother lives for vengeance. She, too, after killing Agamemnon, will be killed, in what threatens to become an endless cycle of vengeance and bloodshed. Even a victim of violence can become a perpetrator, then again a victim in retaliation for this violence. This is the plot of Euripides' *Electra*, a tragedy Cacoyannis had already filmed.

Of all the choices and changes that Cacoyannis made for his film, perhaps the most significant is to have cast Irene Papas as Clytemnestra. Cacoyannis and Papas have a deep political and philosophical rapport, which explains the artistic success of their collaboration. They provide us with as immediate an experience of ancient tragedy as is possible today. Their own political experiences lend force and nuance to their work, although the substance remains Euripides'. As Euripides had done long ago, Cacoyannis and Papas show us, in a modern artistic medium, human beings bending to forces beyond their control, compelled to make tragic choices. Irene Papas's Clytemnestra becomes a force of nature, but we do not forget Iphigenia. Mother and daughter together come close to embodying the core of human existence itself.

I close on a personal note. The works of classical literature are vitally modern and should be approached accordingly. For this reason I regularly incorporate film screenings into my courses on Greek mythology and literature and on classical civilization. In 1990, my students read Euripides'

Iphigenia in Aulis and watched and discussed Cacoyannis's *Iphigenia* in a course on Greek tragedy and film. For their final project, the students put on a performance of Euripides' play. Several of them were going off to fight in the Gulf War. The play was staged outdoors, and jets flew over our heads during the performance. We, the audience, saw our children being sent off to fight a war that did not directly concern many of us but that politicians in a faraway capital had set in motion for reasons of power. We were all Clytemnestra then.

V

Iphigenia: A Visual Essay

Michael Cacoyannis

EDITOR'S NOTE: As a visual accompaniment to his discussion, on preceding pages, of his views of filming ancient
plays, Mr. Cacoyannis chose fifteen images from his *Iphigenia*
which illustrate his approach to a realistic modern adaptation
of a classical play to the cinema. As the moving image on the
screen cannot do, a film still affords the opportunity to study
or contemplate at some length a particular moment. Black-and-
white stills of a color film bring out the textures underlying its
visual composition, as they do here. The following images
should increase both insight and pleasure on the viewer's part.

1. After weeks of waiting on the beaches of Aulis, the mood of the soldiers becomes threatening. Men faint, exhausted by long exposure to the sun.

2. The army comes dangerously close to rioting

3. At the generals' meeting, a priest hands Calchas, the High Priest and Agamemnon's enemy, a tablet containing the oracle demanding Iphigenia's sacrifice.

4. Wearing their war masks, Agamemnon and Menelaus face the other generals, who accuse them of indecision

5. In the presence of Odysseus, Calchas confronts Agamemnon with the oracle.

6. Against Agamemnon's wishes, Clytemnestra accompanies Iphigenia to Aulis, believing her husband's lies about Iphigenia's marriage to Achilles

7. Clytemnestra arrives at the army camp.

8. Clytemnestra, mystified by Agamemnon's evasiveness, discusses with him their daughter's wedding

9. Torn between fury toward Agamemnon and fear for Iphigenia. Clytemnestra screams in anguish and defiance after her meeting with Achilles has revealed Agamemnon's plot.

10. Iphigenia pleads with Agamemnon for her life, but her father is unable to extricate himself from his

11. Abandoned by all, mother and daughter cling to each other.

12. An angry Achilles swears to avenge his honor by defending Iphigenia. Seeing her for the first time, Achilles is moved by her beauty and courage.

13. After Iphigenia has decided to die with honor, Clytemnestra in a rage accuses the army of "unholy murder."

14. The army is assembled for the sacrifice.

15. Crowned with a wreath of flowers, Iphigenia walks to her death.

VI

Tragic Features in
John Ford's *The Searchers*

Martin M. Winkler

One of the chief reasons for the lasting appeal of Greek tragedy lies in its mythical nature. With their archetypal qualities, myths are the foundation of tragedy. In modern societies, too, myths have preserved much of their appeal, although today they often appear in a diluted or not readily apparent form. In American culture, the mythology of the West has given twentieth-century literature and art one of its enduring new archetypes: that of the westerner. In ways comparable to the Greek tragedians' use of received mythology for social, political, and moral reflection on their day and age, the myths of the West have frequently been used for similar purposes. In the words of director Sam Peckinpah: "The Western is a universal frame within which it is possible to comment on today."[1]

The mythology of the western hero bears obvious parallels to classical hero myths; such major themes as the quest, arms and violence, and even immortality, a crucial aspect of archaic and other mythologies, recur prominently in the comparatively recent myths surrounding the westerner.[2] The greatest significance and the highest emotional and intellectual appeal which can derive from the figure of the westerner are to be found in films that merit our attention as works of art. As in the classical cultures, the

---

1. The quotation is taken from Paul Seydor, *Peckinpah: The Western Films: A Reconsideration* (Urbana: University of Illinois Press, 1997), 362.

2. I have traced parallels between classical mythological heroes and the western hero in "Classical Mythology and the Western Film," *Comparative Literature Studies*, 22 (1985), 516–540, and in "Homeric *kleos* and the Western Film," *Syllecta Classica*, 7 (1996), 43–54. On the history and mythology of the western and its origins see especially Henry Nash Smith, *Virgin Land: The American West as Symbol and Myth* (1950; rpt. Cambridge: Harvard University Press, 1978), 51–120.

archetypes underlying mythology manifest themselves to best effect when they have been reworked into the unity of a literary—or literate—work. The principal genres in which this process took place in ancient Greece are epic and drama; in the *Poetics*, Aristotle makes no generic distinction between these two.[3] The popular stories of myth transcend their non-literary origins when they are molded into the masterpieces of Homer and Hesiod, of Aeschylus, Sophocles, Euripides, and of a number of other authors whose works have not survived. A parallel process obtains for the myth of the American West. Well-known plots and figures reappear in the cinema, particularly in the films of such acknowledged masters of the genre as John Ford, Howard Hawks, Anthony Mann, and Sam Peckinpah.

The best western films can, and often do, exhibit the features of tragedy which Aristotle discussed well over two thousand years before the history and mythology of the American West came into existence. I will outline some of the chief aspects of tragedy in connection with the western film and then turn to a particular film, John Ford's *The Searchers* (1956).

1. Tragedy and the Western

In his *Poetics*, Aristotle takes as his point of departure the concept of mimesis. Poetry, drama, and music are all forms of representation or imitation, and so is the cinema.[4] To Aristotle, tragedy is a representation of action and life. He defines it as follows:

> Tragedy, then, is a representation of an action which is serious, complete, and of a certain magnitude—in language which is garnished in various forms in its different parts—in the mode of dramatic enactment, not narrative—and through the arousal of pity [*eleos*] and fear [*phobos*] effecting the *katharsis* of such emotions.[5]

3. Aristotle discusses the links between epic and tragedy in chapters 4, 5, 23, 24, and 26 of the *Poetics*. On tragedy in Homer see, for example, James M. Redfield, *Nature and Culture in the "Iliad": The Tragedy of Hector*, 2nd ed. (Durham, N.C.: Duke University Press, 1994). Aeschylus, who wrote a trilogy about Achilles which has not come down to us, considered his tragedies to be "slices from the large meals of Homer" (Athenaeus, *The Deipnosophists* 8.347e).
4. *Poetics*, chapter 3 (1448a19–b3). On classical mimesis see, for example, Stephen Halliwell, *Aristotle's Poetics* (1986; rpt. Chicago: University of Chicago Press, 1998), 109–137; on mimesis and film see Gerald Mast, *Film/Cinema/Movie* (1977; rpt. Chicago: University of Chicago Press, 1983), 38–61.
5. *Poetics* 6.2 (1449b24–28); the translation is from Halliwell, *The* Poetics *of Aristotle: Translation and Commentary* (Chapel Hill: University of North Carolina Press, 1987), 37.

120

CLASSICAL

MYTH &

CULTURE

IN THE

CINEMA

Representation naturally resides in and is carried out by the actors appearing on the stage, most importantly by the tragic protagonist, who, according to Aristotle, should be neither wholly good nor wholly evil but rather someone with whom we may identify despite the extremity of his situation or fate: "Such a man is one who is not preeminent in virtue and justice, and one who falls into affliction not because of evil and wickedness, but because of a certain fallibility (*hamartia*)."[6] The spectator is affected by his realization that what takes place on stage may happen to himself: "There, but for the grace of God, go I." From such an understanding derives a heightened awareness of the frailty of human life, the fickleness and unpredictability of fortune, and ultimately a greater consciousness of the bond that holds mankind together: "pity is felt towards one whose affliction is undeserved, fear towards one who is like ourselves."[7]

Such pity and fear are linked to the suffering and violence which the principal characters, and often the chorus as well, must undergo. According to Aristotle, violence and suffering inflicted by and upon family members in particular increase the viewer's emotional involvement.[8] Pity and fear, previously latent emotions, are thus stirred up and accumulate in the spectator. This intense strain is broken at the drama's climax; in Aristotle's words, the viewer is purged of his heightened sensations of pity and fear by means of catharsis. Originally a term used in ancient Greek medicine, *catharsis*—traditionally rendered in English as either "purification"or "purgation"—restores emotional balance and leads to a temporary psychological calm, even numbness. The decrease in emotional excitement, which catharsis effects, brings about a feeling of pleasurable relief.[9] Psychologically and emotionally the spectator, who has become one with the protagonist, is now released from this identification. To employ a phrase from Aeschylus, the protagonist's suffering (*pathos*) arouses pity and fear; this in turn brings about a learning process (*mathos*) in the viewer.[10] Tragic mimesis and catharsis provide for an increase in knowledge and moral insight.

In order for the viewer's learning process to be effective, the tragic protagonist is placed in a situation where he must decide on a course of

---

6. *Poetics* 13.3 (1453a7–10); quoted from Halliwell, *The* Poetics *of Aristotle*, 44.

7. *Poetics* 13.2 (1453a5–6); quoted from Halliwell, *The* Poetics *of Aristotle*, 44. On tragedy's timeless quality see, for example, Albin Lesky, *Die griechische Tragödie*, 5th ed. (Stuttgart: Kröner, 1984), 22–23.

8. *Poetics*, chapter 14 (1453b1–1454a15).

9. For a modern examination of the evidence and the controversies surrounding Aristotelian catharsis see Halliwell, *Aristotle's Poetics*, 168–201 and 350–356.

10. Aeschylus, *Agamemnon* 177: *pathêi mathos* ("learning through suffering"); see also lines 249–250.

action. His ethical dilemma arises from the fact that he becomes guilty whichever decision he makes; Aeschylus especially confronts his characters "with dilemmas where there is a conflict of duties such that while a choice is morally imperative, none is morally possible."[11] At the same time, however, the protagonist is innocent on another level. Oedipus, to cite only the most famous example, is objectively guilty of parricide and incest but is subjectively innocent because of, for example, an absence of evil intentions. Nevertheless he accepts the responsibility for his deeds. The simultaneous presence of guilt and innocence in the hero is one of the chief characteristics of Greek tragedy, one of its most complex and fascinating features.

This question of innocence and guilt is also important for western films, since they employ mythical archetypes for its story patterns. Standard westerns present us with a protagonist who is excessively good and strong; being one-dimensional, he remains outside serious consideration as a figure of art. But when the westerner, like the hero on the tragic stage, becomes morally questionable, the genre transcends the limits of popular entertainment.[12] As Robert Warshow has observed in his now classic essay on the westerner:

> The truth is that the westerner comes into the field of serious art only when his moral code, without ceasing to be compelling, is seen also to be imperfect. The westerner at his best exhibits a moral ambiguity which darkens his image and saves him from absurdity; this ambiguity arises from the fact that, whatever his justifications, he is a killer of men.[13]

The westerner must both act and react: act in order to preserve his status as hero, react—usually to injustice and violence—to preserve his moral

11. Benjamin Apthorp Gould Fuller, "The Conflict of Moral Obligation in the Trilogy of Aeschylus," *Harvard Theological Review*, 8 (1915), 459–479; quotation at 460. Richmond Lattimore, *Story Patterns in Greek Tragedy* (Ann Arbor: University of Michigan Press, 1964; rpt. 1969), 29–49, gives a detailed discussion.

12. On formula and genre in American literature and film see in particular John G. Cawelti, *Adventure, Mystery, and Romance: Formula Stories as Art and Popular Culture* (Chicago: University of Chicago Press, 1976), especially 192–259, and *The Six-Gun Mystique Sequel* (Bowling Green, Ky.: Bowling Green State University Popular Press, 1999), especially 11–56; also Stanley J. Solomon, *Beyond Formula: American Film Genres* (Chicago: Harcourt Brace Jovanovich, 1976), 12–29. See also Joseph W. Reed, *Three American Originals: John Ford, William Faulkner, and Charles Ives* (Middletown, Conn.: Wesleyan University Press, 1984; rpt. 1987), 143–149.

13. Robert Warshow, "The Westerner," in *The Immediate Experience: Movies, Comics, Theatre and Other Aspects of Popular Culture* (1962; rpt. New York: Atheneum, 1979), 135–154; quotation at 142. Warshow's essay first appeared in *Partisan Review*, 21 (1954), 190–203.

integrity. Thus forced into action, he is often confronted with a situation that compels him to make a choice. In those films which leave behind the stereotypical "good guy vs. bad guy" format in favor of a more complex and psychologically convincing plot, the westerner may face conflicting alliances and responsibilities; in choosing a course of action, he is confronted with a problem comparable to that of the tragic protagonist. A well-known example is Fred Zinnemann's *High Noon* (1952), in which the hero is caught in a triple bind: responsibility to his wife, to and for the citizens of his town, and to himself. (He must not abandon his code of honor.) Another example is Victor Fleming's *The Virginian* (1929), an archetypal western based on the novel by Owen Wister. Here the villain has lured the eponymous hero's close friend into stealing cattle; the Virginian, leader of the posse pursuing the thieves, must himself bring about the death of his friend when the latter has been caught. Warshow's observations on the "seriousness of the West" as exemplified in this film serve well to illustrate the similarities between the westerner and the hero of Greek tragedy:

> The Virginian is thus in a tragic dilemma where one moral absolute conflicts with another and the choice of either must leave a moral stain. . . . the movie is a tragedy, for though the hero escapes with his life, he has been forced to confront the ultimate limits of his moral ideas.

The tragic quality of the serious western film gives this genre its "mature sense of limitation and unavoidable guilt." As do the heroes of drama both ancient and modern, the hero of the western affects us by an appeal to our sense of compassion; in Warshow's words: "what we finally respond to is not his victory but his defeat."[14] Ultimately, the westerner is a modern reincarnation of the archetypal mythic and tragic hero; hence largely his universal appeal.[15]

The complexity of the westerner, in which he is again comparable to some of the classical tragic heroes, may be illustrated by the duality of his nature, which combines rationality, experience, ingenuity, and love

14. The quotations are from Warshow, "The Westerner," 142–143.
15. Warshow, "The Westerner," 154: "The Western hero is necessarily an archaic figure." On the universality of the westerner, exemplified by the eponymous hero of George Stevens's *Shane* (1953), see Warshow, 150–151. The film's review in the *Motion Picture Herald* saw in it "the inevitability of the ancient Greek tragedy"; quoted from Michael Coyne, *The Crowded Prairie: American National Identity in the Hollywood Western* (London: Tauris, 1997), 75. Peter A. French, *Cowboy Metaphysics: Ethics and Death in Westerns* (Lanham, Md.: Rowman and Littlefield, 1997), examines the western as a popular morality play and has frequent recourse to ancient tragedy and to Aristotle.

122

CLASSICAL

MYTH &

CULTURE

IN THE

CINEMA

for peace with violence and destruction. On the Greek stage, it is particularly an authority figure such as the king, ruler of his city-state, who is caught between the demands of order, peace, and justice to ensure the stability and survival of the city and, on the other hand, the urges, often irrational and violent, to impose his views on others and to force them into submission. Even with the best intentions his power can lead him into suspicion, arrogance, oppression of dissenters, and a violent crushing of sometimes only imagined opposition. Examples are Sophocles' Oedipus and Creon in *Oedipus the King* and Euripides' Pentheus in the *Bacchae*. In the western film we find a corresponding figure in the harsh patriarch who rules with an iron fist over his cattle empire; a good example, to mention only one, is found in Edward Dmytryk's *Broken Lance* (1954), a film with overtones of Shakespeare's *King Lear*. The dual nature of the westerner usually shows itself in his being paired with a badman who is in many ways the hero's alter ego. The hero and his opponent often represent two sides of the same coin; their antagonism, sometimes postponed by an uneasy temporary alliance, finally erupts in a violent showdown at the film's climax. Direct echoes of Greek tragedy by way of intrafamilial and Oedipal conflicts appear in King Vidor's *Duel in the Sun* (1946) and Howard Hawks's *Red River* (1948). Many of Anthony Mann's films reveal this director's preoccupation with both Greek and Elizabethan tragedy: his film *Winchester 73* (1950) shows the hero's revenge on his brother who had killed their father, and *The Man from Laramie* (1955), an even more accomplished work, further deepens the kinds of conflict with which the earlier film had dealt.[16] The revenge theme in the western film derives in no small degree from a literary tradition, that of Jacobean drama, which in turn ultimately derives from classical Greek and Roman tragedy. Screenwriter Philip Yordan aimed at tragedy in several of the westerns he wrote:

> I have . . . attempted to discover again the purity of the heroes of classical tragedy. I have always wanted to re-create a tragic mythology, giving a large role to destiny, solitude, nobility. At the same time I've tried to join this type of hero to typically American characters.[17]

16. See Christopher Wicking and Barrie Pattison, "Interviews with Anthony Mann," *Screen*, 10 no. 4 (1969), 32–54, especially 41–42; and Jim Kitses, *Horizons West: Anthony Mann, Budd Boetticher, Sam Peckinpah: Studies of Authorship within the Western* (1969; rpt. Bloomington: Indiana University Press, 1980), 72–73 (also 46–59 and 73–77). At the time of his death Mann planned to film *King Lear* as a western (Kitses, 80). Borden Chase, one of the most distinguished western novelists and screenwriters, reverses his *Winchester 73* theme in his script for John Sturges's *Backlash* (1956) with the figure of a guilty father instead of a guilty son.

17. Quoted from *The BFI Companion to the Western*, ed. Edward Buscombe (London: Deutsch/British Film Institute, 1988; rpt. 1996), 397. The most remarkable of the

124

CLASSICAL

MYTH &

CULTURE

IN THE

CINEMA

The use of the American West as a setting for tragedy appears to be an integral feature of American culture, going back at least as far as James Fenimore Cooper's *The Prairie* (1827). In this novel, the tragedy centers on Ishmael Bush, a patriarchal authority figure who metes out harsh and bloody justice to his brother-in-law, who had killed Bush's son.[18] Contemporary to the actual settlement of the West, tragic archetypes were already inspiring the imagination of popular novelists. This tradition continued in the twentieth century with, for example, the western novels of Max Brand. More recently, Frederick Manfred's novel *King of Spades* (1966) presents a thinly disguised retelling of the Oedipus myth set in the West. With the cinema superseding literature as the chief medium of popular American culture, it is not surprising that one of the foremost examples of the tragic hero can be encountered in what is generally acknowledged to be the most important work by John Ford, America's greatest filmmaker. To this film I now turn. Since the tragic nature of *The Searchers* is most clearly present in Ford's film but largely missing from its source, the 1954 novel by Alan LeMay, I proceed from the assumption that Ford, as director, is to be credited for *The Searchers* being the enduring work of popular art that it is.[19] This not only is in keeping with the auteur theory of cinema but also parallels the practice of ancient and later tragedians of using received material which they then turned into their lasting works of art.[20]

---

films written or cowritten by Yordan are Nicholas Ray's *Johnny Guitar* (1953), Mann's *The Man from Laramie*, Henry King's *The Bravados* (1958), and Andre de Toth's *Day of the Outlaw* (1959). On revenge tragedy see Anne Pippin Burnett, *Revenge in Attic and Later Tragedy* (Berkeley: University of California Press, 1998).

18. On *The Prairie* see D. H. Lawrence, *Studies in Classic American Literature* (1923; rpt. Harmondsworth: Penguin, 1981), 62–63; Smith, *Virgin Land*, 221–222; and Cawelti, *Adventure, Mystery, and Romance*, 201–202. See also Eric Rohmer, "Rediscovering America," tr. Liz Heron, in *Cahiers du Cinéma: The 1950s*, ed. Jim Hillier (Cambridge: Harvard University Press, 1985), 88–93, especially 90–91.

19. Some of the differences between the novel and the film are discussed by James Van Dyck Card, "The 'Searchers' by Alan LeMay and by John Ford," *Literature/Film Quarterly*, 16 (1988), 2–9. The screenplay by Frank Nugent, Ford's most congenial collaborator, falls short of conveying much of the starkness and emotional power of the film, serving Ford for no more than a rough guide. For a discussion of some of the significant changes from script to finished film, on which Ford decided during the actual filming and which illustrate his creative procedure, see Arthur M. Eckstein, "Darkening Ethan: John Ford's *The Searchers* (1956) from Novel to Screenplay to Screen," *Cinema Journal*, 38 no. 1 (1998), 3–24.

20. On the continuing importance of this theory, first articulated by François Truffaut, and on the larger question of authorship in film see, for example, Paisley Livingston, "Cinematic Authorship," and Berys Gaut, "Film Authorship and Collaboration," both in *Film Theory and Philosophy*, ed. Richard Allen and Murray Smith (Oxford: Clarendon Press, 1997), 132–148 and 149–172.

2. The Tragic Hero

In one of his influential articles, classical scholar Jean-Pierre Vernant asks
the following questions about the tragic hero:

> What is this being that tragedy describes as a *deinos*, an incomprehensible
> and baffling monster, both an agent and one acted upon, guilty and inno-
> cent, lucid and blind, whose industrious mind can dominate the whole of
> nature yet who is incapable of governing himself? What is the relation-
> ship of this man to the actions upon which we see him deliberate on the
> stage and for which he takes the initiative and responsibility but whose
> real meaning is beyond him and escapes him so that it is not so much the
> agent who explains the action but rather the action that, revealing its true
> significance after the event, recoils upon the agent and discloses what he
> is and what he has really, unwittingly, done? Finally, what is this man's
> place in a world that is at once social, natural, divine, and ambiguous, rent
> by contradictions . . . ?[21]

We may apply these questions to Ethan Edwards, the central character in
The Searchers, with regard to the film's tragic nature.[22]

21. Jean-Pierre Vernant, "Tensions and Ambiguities in Greek Tragedy," in Vernant
and Pierre Vidal-Naquet, *Myth and Tragedy in Ancient Greece*, tr. Janet Lloyd (1981;
rpt. New York: Zone Books, 1990), 29–48 and 417–422 (notes); quotation at 32.

22. The following are among the standard critical sources on John Ford; page references
are to *The Searchers*: John Baxter, *The Cinema of John Ford* (New York: Barnes, 1971),
144–152; J. A. Place, *The Western Films of John Ford* (Secaucus, N.J.: Citadel Press, 1974),
160–173; Joseph McBride and Michael Wilmington, *John Ford* (1974; rpt. New York: Da
Capo, 1975), 147–163; Andrew Sarris, *The John Ford Movie Mystery* (Bloomington:
Indiana University Press, 1976), 170–175; Peter Stowell, *John Ford* (Boston: Twayne,
1986), 122–140; Tag Gallagher, *John Ford: The Man and His Films* (Berkeley: University
of California Press, 1986), 324–338; Ronald L. Davis, *John Ford: Hollywood's Old Master*
(Norman: University of Oklahoma Press, 1995), 270–279; Scott Eyman, *Print the Legend:
The Life and Times of John Ford* (New York: Simon and Schuster, 1999), 442–450. Rich-
ard Slotkin, *Gunfighter Nation: The Myth of the Frontier in Twentieth-Century America*
(1992; rpt. Norman: University of Oklahoma Press, 1998), 461–473 and 737–738 (notes),
Coyne, *The Crowded Prairie*, 76–78 and 203 (notes), and Sam B. Gurgis, *Hollywood
Renaissance: The Cinema of Democracy in the Era of Ford, Capra, and Kazan* (Cambridge:
Cambridge University Press, 1998), 25–55 and 231–233 (notes), place *The Searchers* in
the context of contemporary American politics and society. Not all of Slotkin's and Gurgis's
observations are accurate or convincing. The chapter on *The Searchers* in Garry Wills,
John Wayne's America: The Politics of Celebrity (1997; rpt. New York: Simon and
Schuster, 1998), 251–261 and 346–347 (notes), briefly touches on Homer (as in its title,
"The Fury of Ethan"), Greek tragedy, and Aristotle but does so with a superficial brevity
surprising in an author with Wills's classical background. The chapter also contains a
number of elementary factual errors about *The Searchers*. Harry Carey, Jr., *Company of
Heroes: My Life as an Actor in the John Ford Stock Company* (Metuchen, N.J.: Scarecrow Press, 1994), 157–174, provides a look behind the scenes during the making of the
film by one of its principal actors. Douglas Pye, "Writing and Reputation: *The Searchers*

126

CLASSICAL

MYTH &

CULTURE

IN THE

CINEMA

Three years after the end of the Civil War, in which he had fought for the Confederacy, Ethan returns to his brother's homestead in the Texas wilderness, and, as if precipitated by his unexpected return, a series of catastrophes begins. Hostile Comanche Indians under their war chief Scar massacre Ethan's brother, sister-in-law, and nephew and abduct Ethan's two young nieces. Ethan, after many years still secretly in love with his brother's wife, embarks upon a desperate search for the girls, accompanied by Martin Pawley, a young man of partly Indian origin, whom the Edwardses had reared as their own son. When Ethan discovers the raped and mutilated body of his older niece Lucy, his determination to save Debbie, the younger girl, who could be his own daughter, grows even stronger. His search, however, remains unsuccessful for several years. His anguish and despair over Debbie then gradually change into a murderous obsession to kill her once he realizes that she has grown up and must have become one of Scar's wives.

Ethan is the psychologically most complex and ambivalent figure in the history of the western film. That Ford cast John Wayne, the archetypal icon of the westerner, in the part of a man "not conspicuous for virtue and justice" only enhances the film's dramatic power. In keeping with the heroic and tragic tradition, Ethan is first and foremost a man of action. After the end of the Civil War he has resorted to marauding; he possesses freshly minted dollars, and his description appears on several Wanted posters. Although fallen on hard times, he remains a figure of authority and does not hesitate to assert himself: "I'm giving the orders." The Confederate uniform coat which he still wears points to his former rank as officer and to his inability to adjust to a peaceful life. His own words characterize him well: "I still got my sabre . . . didn't turn it into no plowshare, neither." Violence is the key to Ethan's character; it exposes his increasing madness and viciousness in the course of the film. There is also a pronounced streak of racial bigotry toward Indians in Ethan. This reveals itself, for instance, in his gruff, even hostile, treatment of Martin, whom he has no scruples to use as bait for a trap. His ugly and crazed laugh at Martin's Indian bride underscores his hatred and contempt of Indians. In all likelihood, Ethan is such a racist because he is aware, without conscious knowledge, that he is in many ways like an Indian himself: savage, violent, and without a permanent home. Not only is Ethan well versed in Indian languages, customs, and religion but he also knows much about Indian strategy and psychology. He understands the diversionary

---

1956–1976," in *Writing and Cinema*, ed. Jonathan Bignell (London: Longman, 1999), 195–209, summarizes the main critical views of the film.

tactics of Scar's raid and realizes that his only chance in catching up with Scar lies in a perseverance greater than the Indians'. A visual clue to the Indian aspects of his nature is the scabbard in which he keeps his rifle; it has long fringes and looks Indian-made. Ethan is a man who exists on the borderline between savagery and civilization.

That Ethan is by no means the usual clean-cut (and clean-shaven) western hero becomes overwhelmingly clear in the course of the film. Early on, he defiles a dead Indian's body by shooting the corpse's eyes out, an indication that his hatred of Indians goes even beyond death. Ethan's reason for this is his knowledge that, in the Indians' belief, such loss of sight will prevent their souls from entering the spirit land and condemn them "to wander forever between the winds." As startling and morally questionable as the defilement of a dead enemy's body is, it is nevertheless within the heroic tradition. In the *Iliad*, Achilles defiles Hector's corpse and, denying it proper burial, intends to prevent Hector's shade from entering the underworld; this is Achilles' ultimate revenge.[23] That Ethan, like Achilles, goes beyond the limits of heroic behavior becomes evident on several other occasions. At a skirmish with Scar's warriors by the riverside he attempts to shoot Indians whose backs are turned in retreat; later on, he sets a trap for the treacherous white trader Futterman and his two henchmen, killing all three by shooting them in the back. A close-up of Ethan's rifle at this point emphasizes that this act is in direct violation of the traditional code of honor usually upheld in the American western film.

I have earlier remarked on the duality of the western hero in terms of his close association with his antagonist, an association that points to the morality-play quality of the western film: the struggle between good and evil. A significant variation of this theme occurs in *The Searchers* in the figures of Ethan and Scar. Just as Ethan, despite his negative traits, is a superior westerner, Scar is a skillful leader. Both are heroes in their different ways. On two significant occasions in the film Ford emphasizes Scar's heroic nature by showing him putting on his war bonnet. The fact that both times Ethan then shoots Scar's horse from under him foreshadows the latter's eventual defeat and death. Before the skirmish at the river begins, Ford cuts from a close-up of Ethan directly to one of Scar, underscoring the tension between the two. A similar series of fast cuts occurs when Ethan, Martin, and Scar finally meet face to face in front of Scar's tent. Ford cuts from Scar to Ethan, back to Scar, and to Martin. In keeping with the heroic tradition, a verbal duel between Ethan and Scar

---

23. See Charles Segal, *The Theme of the Mutilation of the Corpse in the "Iliad"* (Leiden: Brill, 1971).

128

CLASSICAL

MYTH &

CULTURE

IN THE

CINEMA

ensues, in which Ethan insults Scar, while Scar acknowledges Ethan's prowess and tenacity. The verbal parallelism in their exchange on language at this moment reinforces Ethan and Scar's closeness to each other. (Ethan: "Scar, eh? Plain to see how you got your name." Then: "You speak pretty good American—someone teach you?" Moments later, Scar has the last word on Ethan: "You speak good Comanch'—someone teach you?") Both men bear wounds, Scar physically, Ethan in his soul: "Scar, as the name suggests, is Ethan's mark of Cain."[24] That the part of Scar is played by a white actor takes on added meaning in this context.[25]

3. Journey into Madness

The motif of the search or quest is one of the basic themes of mythology; Jason and the Argonauts in classical and Parsifal's search for the Grail in medieval literature are prominent examples. Frequently in the mythological tradition of such travels, the hero's ultimate goal is the attainment of self-knowledge and the ideal of achieving moral goodness. For Ethan, however, the quest for his niece over several years is a journey not so much of glorious heroism as one of obsession and defeat, which will eventually drive him to the brink of madness. His fall into savagery during his search parallels and intensifies his social decline from army officer to renegade. In this as in other films by Ford, "the sense of duty that sustains his individuals also commonly leads them astray into aberrations or death."[26] In this regard Ethan resembles less the mythological hero of epic or the chivalrous knight of romance than the tragic sufferer of the Greek stage. Ethan's increasing obsession with finding his niece and avenging his family's destruction upon Scar, coupled with his racism toward the Indians, represents the film's true tragic theme. What Vernant observes about Eteocles in Aeschylus' *Seven against Thebes* may, with some adjustments, describe Ethan as well:

> The murderous madness that henceforth characterizes his *ethos* is not simply a human emotion; it is a daemonic power in every way beyond him. It envelops him in the black cloud of *ate*, penetrating him . . . from within, in a form of *mania*, a *lussa*, a delirium that breeds criminal acts of *hubris*.[27]

24. Stowell, *John Ford*, 135.
25. See McBride and Wilmington, *John Ford*, 152.
26. Gallagher, *John Ford*, 274.
27. Vernant, "Tensions and Ambiguity in Greek Tragedy," 35. The Greek terms mean "personality," "ruinous delusion," "madness," "rabid wrath," and "arrogance."

As H. A. Mason has noted: "The greatest poets have always found the greatest pathos by taking away from the hero's mind what we call the rational faculty and giving him a greater hold over us by making him *mad*."[28] It attests to the subtlety with which Ford structures the development of his narrative that the theme of Ethan's obsession is made explicit only intermittently and unobtrusively, and a casual viewer might overlook it. Nevertheless, its dramatic force increases steadily until it culminates in Ethan's last confrontation with Scar, by then dead. Added momentum derives from the underlying subject of miscegenation and sexual jealousy and frustration. The catalyst for this is Ethan's secret and hopeless love for his brother's wife. Ford introduces this topic as the starting point for the film.

The Searchers begins with the camera following Martha Edwards, Ethan's sister-in-law, as she opens the door of her house and walks out onto the porch, having noticed a horseman approaching. This moment contains the first indication of a close emotional bond between herself and Ethan, the man arriving, because cinematic tradition induces a viewer to assume that this woman is expecting the return of her husband. Martha is the first to greet Ethan, who responds by gently kissing her on the forehead. He later lifts up little Debbie as if she were his own daughter. Next morning, when Ethan prepares to leave with a posse of Texas Rangers led by the Reverend Clayton in order to retrieve the settlers' stolen cattle, Martha, gone to fetch Ethan's coat and thinking herself alone, tenderly strokes it. This gesture, however, is observed by Clayton, who discreetly turns his gaze away. His eyes speak volumes.[29] At the end of this moving and justly famous scene, Martha and Debbie wave and look after Ethan riding off, just as a departing man's wife and daughter would do. This is Martha's last glimpse of Ethan. With utter economy Ford here suggests a deep-seated but hopeless love between them. It is most likely because of this love that Ethan left his home years ago, joined the Confederate army, and stayed away for three years even after the war had ended. Ethan, the would-be husband of Martha, by extension becomes the would-be father of her children. This partly accounts for his unceasing pursuit of Scar, who had raped and killed the woman Ethan had chastely loved from afar. That Scar raped Martha before killing her may be inferred from the scene in

28. H. A. Mason, *The Tragic Plane* (Oxford: Clarendon Press, 1985), 146.

29. On this brief moment see Andrew Sarris, *The American Cinema: Directors and Directions: 1929–1968* (1968; rpt. New York: Da Capo, 1996), 47, and *The John Ford Movie Mystery*, 172; see also Baxter, *The Cinema of John Ford*, 150, and Ford's own remarks in Peter Bogdanovich, *John Ford*, rev. ed. (Berkeley: University of California Press, 1978), 93–94.

130

CLASSICAL

MYTH &

CULTURE

IN THE

CINEMA

which Ethan finds the bodies of Martha, his brother, and his nephew. Later Ethan will discover Lucy in a canyon where she had been abandoned after being raped and killed and probably mutilated as well; he buries her in the cloak that Martha had brought him before his departure. From now on his obsession to kill Scar and in this way to avenge Martha's dishonor becomes an overpowering force, which will relentlessly drive him on. Ethan knows that Scar has defiled and destroyed what has been unattainable and most sacred to himself. This is another bond between Ethan and Scar, perhaps the strongest one. At the outset of the search, Ethan is motivated by two powerful impulses: avenging Martha and rescuing Debbie, who could be his own daughter. A third driving force will eventually overshadow both of these.

Ford develops Ethan's journey into obsession and madness in psychologically convincing and, to the spectator, increasingly involving stages. First doubts about Ethan's mental state arise both in Martin Pawley and in the viewer when Ethan, reluctantly agreeing to take Martin and Brad Jorgensen, Lucy's boyfriend, with him on the search, asserts his authority over the two young men. This prompts Martin's question: "Just one reason we're here, ain't it? To find Debbie and Lucy?" Ethan does not reply, and suspicion begins to grow in Martin's mind, as it does in the spectator's, about Ethan's true motivation. Things are spelled out more clearly later when Ethan decides to turn back for the winter and to continue his search in the spring: "She's alive, she's safe for a while. They'll . . . keep her to raise as one of their own until—until she's of an age to . . ." He breaks off, but it is clear that Ethan is thinking of Martha's violation by Scar and of Debbie's future fate. That Scar will eventually force his captive into sexual relations with him represents, to Ethan's mind, a fate both worse than and worthy of death; that Scar will have had intercourse with both mother and daughter is a thought unbearable to him. This brief scene in the film marks the turning point in Ethan's character. From now on he is bent on revenge and destruction and will seek the deaths of Scar, Debbie, and of Indians in general. Ethan's suppressed intensity effectively contrasts with the quiet beauty of nature: a peaceful winter forest, gently falling snow, and complete silence. While nature is pure and calm, a violent rage is stirring in man.

The first open revelation of this occurs at the beginning of the film's cavalry sequence, which also takes place in winter. Ethan and Martin have come upon a herd of buffalo, and Ethan begins to shoot as many of them as he can. When Martin tries to prevent such meaningless slaughter, Ethan for the first time explicitly reveals his obsession. Brutally knocking Martin down, he exclaims: "Hunger, empty bellies . . . at least *they* won't feed any Comanch' this winter." Then, at the cavalry fort, the searchers find some mad white women and girls of Debbie's age who had lived among Indians and have now been "liberated" by the army. It is of crucial importance for a correct understanding of the film to realize that their madness is not caused by mistreatment at the hands of "the savages" but rather by the brutality of the cavalry. One of them immediately breaks into a series of horrible screams at the sight of an army sergeant and doctor entering with Ethan and Martin.[30] Nevertheless, Ethan blames the Indians for the girls' fate: "They ain't white—anymore. They're Comanch'." The camera then moves in to a close-up of Ethan's face, and a different kind of madness is clearly written on his features. The extreme rarity of such a camera movement attests to its utmost significance; it reveals Ethan's murderous obsession. The moment is emphasized by the predominant dark colors of this scene, and Ethan's face is partly obscured by shadow.

With the inexorable logic of paranoia, Ethan later attempts to shoot Debbie once he has caught up with her. Ironically, she has come to warn him and Martin against an impending attack by Scar. Martin shields Debbie with his body as Ethan, gun drawn, approaches. But an Indian's arrow, which wounds Ethan in the shoulder, prevents the murder. The impending intrafamilial bloodshed is thus avoided at the last moment. Ford visually emphasizes the nefarious nature of Ethan's attempt on his niece's life when Ethan draws his gun in a sweeping, circular movement; this is

30. This is a point missed in most critical studies of *The Searchers*, which attribute the girls' madness to their experiences among the Indians and then have to explain the fact that Debbie has not been driven mad by her life among these same Indians. A prominent recent example of this view is Douglas Pye, "Double Vision: Miscegenation and Point of View in *The Searchers*," in *The Book of Westerns*, ed. Ian Cameron and Douglas Pye (New York: Continuum, 1996, also published as *The Movie Book of the Western* [London: Studio Vista, 1996]), 229–235. Pye's is a thoughtful and serious essay, but it is wrong on the subject of madness and miscegenation and hence reaches false conclusions. A view similar to Pye's occurs in Slotkin, *Gunfighter Nation*, 468–470. Anyone doubting that the savagery of white rather than Indian society and, related to this, Ethan's racism are the issue of the cavalry sequence should consider that this army is none other than George Armstrong Custer's Seventh Cavalry, clearly identified by the number seven on its pennants and by its well-known tune "Garry Owen" on the soundtrack. On the significance of Max Steiner's musical scoring of the cavalry sequence see William Darby and Jack Du Bois, *American Film Music: Major Composers, Techniques, Trends, 1915–1990* (Jefferson, N. C.: McFarland, 1990), 53–55, especially 53. More important, Ford filmed but then excised from this sequence a scene in which Ethan and Martin meet a swaggering and brutal Custer face to face; see on this Eckstein, "Darkening Ethan," 9–11. In production notes for *The Searchers* Ford described Custer as "inept . . . arrogant . . . a phony . . . a glory-hunter" (quoted from Eckstein, 22 note 46). This view is consistent with Ford's film *Fort Apache* (1948), a thinly disguised story about Custer's incompetence and eventual defeat at the Little Bighorn.

132

CLASSICAL

MYTH &

CULTURE

IN THE

CINEMA

the same manner in which he had earlier shot out the dead Indian's eyes. The identity of the gesture indicates an identical inhumanity underlying both acts and points to the fact that, to Ethan, Debbie is no longer white. His rejection of her is made chillingly explicit in two verbal exchanges he has with Martin in later scenes in the film. In his last will and testament he renounces her as not being his "blood kin" because "she's been living with a buck." More explicitly, before the whites' final attack on Scar, Martin pleads with Ethan and the Rangers not to destroy the entire Indian camp, as they are planning to do. Ethan now admits to him his hope that Debbie will not survive the indiscriminate slaughter and adds: "Living with Comanches ain't being alive." These words and the Rangers' scorched-earth tactics will have reminded viewers at the time of the film's initial release of parallels with recent history.

4. Pity and Fear

Ford reveals Ethan's madness through extreme close-ups of his face. While he usually shows us both the people and the environment in which they act—Ford is well known for his medium-long shots indoors and extreme long shots outdoors, which dwarf the human figures—there are some highly significant moments when the camera and with it the viewer move in for a closer look. The close-ups of Ethan powerfully depict the turmoil inside him. As Béla Balász has emphasized: "Close-ups are often dramatic revelations of what is really happening under the surface of appearances."[31] Ford prepares the viewer for the impact of these close-ups early in the film, when he shows Ethan in a medium shot after he has realized what strategy lies behind the Indians' theft of the white settlers' cattle. Knowing that it is too late to bring help, he allows his horse to rest while the others return in futile haste. To judge from his words and actions during this scene, Ethan is calm and self-controlled, but when we see him more closely, mechanically rubbing down his horse and staring vacantly into the distance, the expression on his face tells us differently: "He is contemplating the unthinkable."[32] Watching Ethan's partly shadowed face,

---

31. Béla Balász, *Theory of the Film: Character and Growth of a New Art*, tr. Edith Bone (1952; rpt. New York: Ayer, 1997), 56. Cf. Soviet theorist and director Sergei Eisenstein on the function of the close-up: it is "not so much to *show* or to *present* as to *signify*, to *give meaning*, to *designate*"; quoted from Eisenstein, *Film Form: Essays in Film Theory*, tr. and ed. Jay Leyda (1949; rpt. San Diego: Harcourt Brace Jovanovich, 1977), 238.

32. McBride and Wilmington, *John Ford*, 160. Stowell, *John Ford*, 139, characterizes Ethan's expression at this moment as "powerfully tragic."

we can see in our minds exactly what he sees with his mind's eye: the rape and slaughter taking place some forty miles away at his brother's home. Ford forcefully communicates to us Ethan's feelings of helplessness, anxiety, grief, and despair. With this brief shot he makes the filming of the actual carnage unnecessary. At this moment the spectator begins to be drawn irresistibly into the tragedy about to unfold. A full close-up of Ethan then logically occurs when he comes upon the aftermath of the slaughter. When Ethan forcibly restrains Martin from rushing into the shed where the dead bodies of his foster parents have been thrown and when, later, after finding Lucy, he behaves in a manner strange and inexplicable to Martin, the viewers can themselves picture what Ethan has seen and can feel with him. Ethan's discoveries of the bodies of Martha and Lucy are not presented to us in gruesome detail; instead, Ford eschews any trace of luridness by only showing us the effect on Ethan of the emotional shock of these grisly moments. Ford's discreet handling of such instances of high emotional strain, obliquely depicting the results of savage violence against helpless victims, is in a direct line of tradition from Greek tragedy, in which acts of violence took place offstage and were reported by a messenger or eyewitness. On the Greek tragic stage and in artistic cinema, the spectators' task is to fill in the terrifying details themselves; in this way playwright and film director ensure their audience's emotional involvement and call forth their feelings of pity and fear.

These emotions rise in the viewer at several crucial moments in *The Searchers*. At the beginning, we fear for the survival of Ethan's relatives while they are being stalked by an unseen and terrifying enemy; the greater is our shock when we first see Scar, his shadow falling over the crouching figure of little Debbie and his face decorated with war paint. Next we fear for the fate of the two abducted girls and hope that Ethan will find them; later, after we have become aware of Ethan's obsession, we begin to hope that he will *not* find Debbie. More extended scenes of pity and fear in *The Searchers* appear in the cavalry sequence. Ethan and Martin come upon the aftermath of the cavalry's massacre of an entire Indian village, with tepees burning and bloody corpses of humans and animals lying about and left to freeze in the winter cold, a scene of documentary realism.[33] Shortly thereafter, the searchers witness the white

33. The documentary-like realism in this scene becomes evident if we compare it with photographs of the massacre at Wounded Knee; see photos 66–75 in Richard E. Jensen, R. Eli Paul, and John E. Carter, *Eyewitness at Wounded Knee* (Lincoln: University of Nebraska Press, 1991), 105–114. Eckstein, "Darkening Ethan," 21–22 note 44, adduces George Armstrong Custer's massacre of the Cheyennes at the Washita River in Oklahoma in November 1868. Cf. Slotkin, *Gunfighter Nation*, 467–468 and 737 note 52.

134

CLASSICAL

MYTH &

CULTURE

IN THE

CINEMA

man's "civilizing" influence when they interrogate the mad women. The visual contrast of the cavalry sequence to the rest of the film enhances our sympathy for the victims, particularly women and children. With the exception of the brief scene of dialogue in which Ethan decides to break off the search, the cavalry sequence is the only part of the film taking place in winter; with the same exception, it is also the only sequence of location filming outside Monument Valley. The predominant colors of the cavalry sequence are red (blood shed, fires burning), white (the snow covering the land and the dead like a shroud), and blue (the cavalry uniforms), hardly an accidental scheme. The violence in the cavalry sequence, underscored by its cold colors, which contrast with the warm brown-red of Monument Valley, foreshadows Ethan's coldblooded attempt on his niece's life.

As the preceding comments have already indicated, the tragic quality of *The Searchers* is founded on its natural setting. The landscape, one of the basic aspects of meaning in the western genre, is Monument Valley, the western country par excellence, whose iconography is most closely associated with the cinema of John Ford.[34] The valley's cyclopean rocks form the perfect background to the film's human actions and impart to them an overwhelming sense of doom. Towering cliffs dwarf the protagonists and implacably look down upon the deeds and sufferings of the people living or moving among them. This landscape, in which both whites and Indians are carving out their existence, points to the duality of both races' ways of life, a rudimentary social organization enveloped by savagery. It is not by accident that Ethan is photographed with a sheer wall of rock rising up behind him at the moment he commits his first inhuman act, blinding the dead Indian. This is a side of Ford's filmmaking well-known in Hollywood, as the following words of his fellow western director John Sturges indicate: "He [Ford] used big, big things behind people, and he shot up at them to make them look menacing by taking on the character of the mountains behind that were menacing."[35] In Ford's westerns, Monument Valley does not function as mere pictorialism but rather pos-

34. On landscape in the western see Warshow, "The Westerner," 139; Philip French, *Westerns: Aspects of a Movie Genre*, 2nd ed. (London: Secker and Warburg, 1977), 100–113; Cawelti, *The Six-Gun Mystique Sequel*, 23–27; Solomon, *Beyond Formula*, 12–17; and Clive Bush, "Landscape," in *BFI Companion to the Western*, 167–170. In general see Smith, *Virgin Land*. For the literary roots of the meaning of the western landscape see Bush, 169.

35. The quotation is taken from Sturges's audio commentary on the Criterion Collection laserdisc edition of his 1954 film *Bad Day at Black Rock* (Santa Monica, Calif.: Voyager, 1991).

sesses thematic meaning as his "moral universe."[36] He himself observed about Monument Valley: "the real star of my Westerns has always been the land." Ford also implies moral regeneration arising from the western landscape in an almost cathartic experience: "When I come back from making a Western on location, I feel a better man for it."[37] Thus Ethan's journey into madness takes on an almost unbearable poignancy: a sense of both timelessness and doom permeates *The Searchers*. When Ethan and Martin are pursued by Scar and his warriors, we see them fleeing toward a cave, just as later Debbie, fleeing from Ethan, will run toward a cave of similar appearance. In both instances the camera observes the fugitives from inside. The impression is that of nature implacably watching the acts of men. But nature is not always hostile; the camera placement suggests its readiness to receive, shelter, and protect. Martin, for instance, finds lifesaving water dripping from the barren rock when he and Ethan are secure in the cave. Nature's ambivalence mirrors the ambiguous nature of man.

5. Recognition and Reversal

The effects of classical tragedy are heightened by the complexity of its plot. Aristotle calls those plays complex whose plots contain *anagnorisis* and *peripeteia*. The former term denotes the discovery of someone's identity, while peripety, a reversal of fortune, occurs as a result of actions and sufferings whose implications, unknown before but then revealed through *anagnorisis*, lead to the hero's tragic fall.[38] Both recognition and peripety

---

36. French, *Westerns*, 104; on Ford and Monument Valley see also McBride and Wilmington, *John Ford*, 36–37 ("Monument Valley is a moral battleground"), and Jean-Louis Leutrat and Suzanne Liandrat-Guigues, "John Ford and Monument Valley," in *Back in the Saddle Again: New Essays on the Western*, ed. Edward Buscombe and Roberta E. Pearson (London: British Film Institute, 1998), 160–169. The latter discuss the 1925 film *The Vanishing American*, directed by George B. Seitz from a novel by Zane Grey, which was inspired by Grey's travels to Monument Valley and intended to be the companion of a film. Intertitles of this film, which begins and ends with views of Monument Valley, describe it as "a stately valley of great monuments of stone," replete with "the hush of the ages, for men come and live their hour and go away, but the mighty stage remains" (quoted from Leutrat and Liandrat-Guigues, 168). One year before *The Searchers*, the film was remade from a screenplay by LeMay. This version of *The Vanishing American*, directed by Joe Kane, differs from the silent one in that it allows its Indian hero to marry his white sweetheart; in the original version he had been killed off to avoid miscegenation.

37. Bill Libby, "The Old Wrangler Rides Again," *Cosmopolitan* (March 1964), 12–21; quotations at 21 and 14.

38. On *anagnorisis* and peripety see *Poetics*, chapters 10–11 (1452a12–b13).

represent a passage from ignorance to knowledge and self-awareness and complement the workings of catharsis. Forms of recognition and peripety often recur in the later dramatic tradition and occasionally in the medium of film.

136

CLASSICAL

MYTH &

CULTURE

IN THE

CINEMA

Recognition and reversal occur in two key scenes in *The Searchers*. The former takes place in three separate stages during a council of Ethan, Martin, and Scar in the chief's tent. Scar calls upon one of his wives to show Ethan and Martin some of the scalps he has taken to avenge his sons killed by whites. Ethan recognizes, as he will later tell Martin, one of the scalps to be that of Martin's mother; evidently, Scar has been the white settlers' nemesis for longer than they themselves had realized. This first recognition leads directly to another. Scar now draws attention to the medal he is wearing among other decorations on his chest; Ethan recognizes it as the one he gave as a present to little Debbie upon his return home after the Civil War. This is the first tangible proof for Ethan, besides the circumstantial evidence he has come upon so far, that it is indeed Scar who has kidnapped Debbie. A rapid tracking shot underscores the importance of the moment, the camera moving in to a close-up of the medal from Ethan's point of view. This particular piece of camera work serves a double purpose. It closely links Ethan and Scar and also prepares Ethan and the viewer for their first glimpse of Debbie after her kidnapping. Ethan and Martin now look up simultaneously at Scar's young wife holding the scalps in front of them; both immediately recognize Debbie in her. Their long and arduous search has finally come to an end, although they are at the moment powerless to take her away from Scar.

Peripety is linked to catharsis in what must be the most gripping and emotionally draining sequence in the entire film. Before the Rangers' and Ethan's final attack on Scar's village, Martin has crept into Scar's tepee to save Debbie from the indiscriminate slaughter that is imminent. Surprised by Scar, Martin shoots and kills him. After the Rangers' massacre of the village, Ethan, bent on murder and revenge, finds the chief dead in his tent. Ford denies Ethan the western hero's most basic exploit, the showdown with his enemy. Scar's death is intentionally anticlimactic, a deliberate revision of the traditional code of combat which goes back to the duel of Achilles and Hector in the *Iliad*. Ethan, denied heroic stature, now defiles a corpse for the second time: he scalps Scar. While Ford does not show the actual scalping on the screen, he cuts away only at the last possible moment, thereby emphasizing both its terror and its significance. Although probably introduced by whites, the custom of scalping is associated almost exclusively with the Indians as a symbol of their savagery. According to this convention, a white man, unless presented as wholly dehumanized, would not commit such an act. Ethan's deed represents the moral nadir down to which his obsession has brought him. This is the moment of his greatest self-abasement as a human. Ford emphasizes Ethan's savagery when he shows him riding out of Scar's tent, holding the dripping scalp in his hand. Ethan appears like a gruesome angel of death, and Ford gives us another close-up of his face. Once outside the tepee, Ethan sees Debbie, who turns and flees in terror, pursued by her uncle.

The viewer's emotions of pity and fear begin to reach their peak at this moment, enhanced by the fact that Martin, who had saved Debbie's life once before, now is helpless in the face of Ethan's frenzy. When Martin tries to stop him, Ethan simply knocks him down. Ethan finally catches up with Debbie at the entrance to a cave. The exhausted girl, fallen to the ground, recoils in horror from her pursuer, who has dismounted and is approaching. But now a surprising reversal of the girl's—and the viewer's —expectations occurs. Instead of killing her, Ethan picks her up in his arms, just as he had done on first seeing her after his return home, and takes her back to white society. The explanation for this dramatic peripety must be that all the hatred, violence, and obsession, accumulated in Ethan during the years spent in pursuit of Scar and Debbie, have drained from him after his meanest act, the scalping of Scar. The brief period of time elapsed between his knocking down Martin and catching up with Debbie has brought Ethan back to his senses. Finally acknowledging the ties of blood kinship he has denied for so long, Ethan is at last saved from what seemed up to now an inevitable fall into savagery and inhumanity. The draining of violence from Ethan parallels the viewer's cathartic experience. The scene just described is the best proof for the film's tragic nature.[39]

6. Changes of Mind

Ethan's change of mind has elicited much negative comment from critics for being too abrupt. Although Ford intended it to come as a surprise, it is neither merely a coup de théâtre nor a cheap means to ensure a happy

39. Sarris, *The John Ford Movie Mystery*, 173: "a man picks up a girl in his arms and is miraculously delivered of all the racist, revenge-seeking furies that have seared his soul." Cf. Lattimore, *Story Patterns in Greek Tragedy*, 8, on *anagnorisis* and peripety: "And this is the moment of truth or revelation or recognition when the hero in drama sees the shape of the action in which he is involved." As Ford himself has said about the protagonists of his films: "the tragic moment . . . permits them to define themselves, to become conscious of what they are. . . . to exalt man 'in depth,' this is the dramatic device I like"; quoted from Gallagher, *John Ford*, 302, from an interview with Jean Mitry, first published in French in *Cahiers du Cinéma*, 45 (March 1955), 6.

138

CLASSICAL

MYTH &

CULTURE

IN THE

CINEMA

ending for a mainstream Hollywood genre film ("John Wayne would never shoot a girl!"). Rather, Debbie's earlier change of mind about the Indians with whom she has been living sets the stage for Ethan's. Warning Martin against Scar, Debbie urged him to "go away" and leave her with the Comanches: "These are my people." But when Martin wakes her up in Scar's tepee to save her from the Rangers' attack, she immediately consents. Her change of mind, likewise surprising, has likewise been criticized as a major dramatic weakness.[40]

Such charges, however, lose conviction if we place the two moments concerned into the tradition of Greek and specifically Euripidean tragedy. The one play that has received the most extensive criticism since antiquity is Euripides' *Iphigenia in Aulis*. Its heroine first pleads with her father for her life, then suddenly accepts and even seeks out her sacrificial death.[41] Nor is hers the only abrupt change in the play. Earlier, her uncle Menelaus had unexpectedly changed his mind about her death, and her father Agamemnon had changed his more than once. If we adduce another famous instance of a change of mind from Shakespearean drama, Prince Hal's rejection of his old friend Falstaff after Hal has been crowned king—"I know thee not, old man" (2 *Henry IV*, act 5, scene 5), a denial that leads to Falstaff's death—then we see that Ford kept well within the bounds of the dramatic tradition.

While there exist obvious thematic differences between Euripides' play and Ford's film, and while it is clear that Ford was not consciously imitating Euripides, the theme of intrafamilial murder and changes of mind occurring in connection with such an act are present in both works and may be considered together, notwithstanding the fact that Iphigenia is a much

40. For example, Pye, "Double Vision," 235. Cf. Gallagher, *John Ford*, 335–336 (note). Eckstein, "Darkening Ethan," 14, adduces the film's screenplay to explain the change.

41. Aristotle, *Poetics* 15.5 (1454a32–33): "the girl who beseeches bears no resemblance to the later girl" (quoted from Halliwell, *The Poetics of Aristotle*, 48); H. D. F. Kitto, *Greek Tragedy: A Literary Study*, 3rd ed. (1961; rpt. London: Routledge, 1990), 362: "a thoroughly second-rate play [whose] whole idea was second-rate"—an extreme and untenable verdict. A modern defense of Aristotle's charge of inconsistency in Iphigenia's character is Hermann Funke, "Aristoteles zu Euripides' Iphigeneia in Aulis," *Hermes*, 92 (1964), 284–299; against his view see especially Albin Lesky, *Die tragische Dichtung der Hellenen*, 3rd ed. (Göttingen: Vandenhoeck und Ruprecht, 1972), 483–484; Herbert Siegel, "Self-Delusion and the *Volte-Face* of Iphigenia in Euripides' 'Iphigenia at Aulis'," *Hermes*, 108 (1980), 300–321; and Heinz Neitzel, "Iphigeniens Opfertod: Betrachtungen zur 'Iphigenie in Aulis' von Euripides," *Würzburger Jahrbücher für die Altertumswissenschaft*, 6 (1980), 61–70. The most extensive recent discussion of the play is John Gibert, *Change of Mind in Greek Tragedy* (Göttingen: Vandenhoeck und Ruprecht, 1995), 202–254. On Iphigenia's character and her sacrifice see further Walter Stockert, *Euripides, Iphigenie in Aulis*, vol. 1: *Einleitung und Text* (Vienna: Verlag der Österreichischen Akademie der Wissenschaften, 1992), 26–37 and 59–61.

more prominent character in her story than Debbie is in hers. In the *Iphigenia in Aulis* we have a situation of father–daughter killing, in which both change their minds; in *The Searchers* it is that of an uncle–niece killing, in which both also change their minds. The definition of such changes of mind given by Bernard Knox in regard to Greek tragedy—"the dramatic presentation and formulation of a new decision or attitude which supplants and reverses a previously determined course of action"—applies equally to Ford's film.[42]

Some additional parallels may help obviate critics' concerns about *The Searchers*. As Menelaus' change of mind prepares us for Iphigenia's, so Debbie's prepares us for Ethan's. All four "arise from the intrinsic structure of events," to quote Aristotle.[43] Both Iphigenia's and Debbie's changes of mind are instances of spontaneous action in highly dramatic circumstances that do not allow for any deliberation.[44] The same is true for Ethan's change of mind. Swiftness of action in crucial scenes makes important reversals more easily acceptable to audiences than they would be otherwise. An extreme example of no less than four changes of mind within twenty lines occurs in Euripides, when Medea is torn between killing and saving her children (*Medea* 1043–1063). The pressure under which dramatic characters act is made palpable to the sympathetic spectator, and their surprising changes of mind are important for the effect of tragic catharsis on the viewer.[45] As regards *The Searchers*, Debbie has been living for years surrounded by threats of imminent death, both as a member of an Indian war party constantly campaigning and as a target of the whites' pursuit. Her acceptance of Martin and its concomitant rejection of the Indians is an instance of that sudden eruption of the elemental will to live that is fundamental to every living being in situations of mortal danger; the same instinct had prompted Iphigenia to plead with Agamemnon for her life.[46] As Bruno Snell observed about the Greeks in

42. Bernard Knox, "Second Thoughts in Greek Tragedy," in *Word and Action: Essays on the Ancient Theater* (Baltimore: Johns Hopkins University Press, 1979), 231–249; rpt. from *Greek, Roman and Byzantine Studies*, 7 no. 3 (1966); quotation from 246 note 1. On this article see Gibert, *Change of Mind in Greek Tragedy*, 255–262.

43. Aristotle, *Poetics* 14.1 (1453b2), in the context of *eleos* and *phobos*; quoted from Halliwell, *The Poetics of Aristotle*, 45. Cf. David Sansone, "Iphigeneia Changes Her Mind," *Illinois Classical Studies*, 16 (1991), 161–172, especially 168–169. Knox, "Second Thoughts," 243–244: "Iphigenia's change of mind has been well prepared for in Euripides' play—it comes as the climax of a series of swift and sudden changes of decision which is unparalleled in ancient drama."

44. Cf. Neitzel, "Iphigeniens Opfertod," 69–70.

45. So (all too briefly) Stockert, *Euripides, Iphigenie in Aulis*, 60.

46. Here I follow Funke, "Aristoteles zu Euripides' Iphigeneia in Aulis," 298: "der Ausbruch elementaren Lebenswillens, der natürlichsten Anlage in jedem Lebewesen."

140

CLASSICAL

MYTH &

CULTURE

IN THE

CINEMA

general: "The tragic arose from an awareness of the necessity of making decisions and reached its full development as the decisions engendered a growing sense of urgency and perplexity"—to which we could add: a sense of urgency and perplexity present not only in the dramatic character but also in the spectator.[47] How else could audiences get emotionally involved, either then or now?

In connection with Euripides' *Hippolytus*, Albin Lesky concluded that changes in character are always abrupt in this author's plays and occur without any intermediate stages but are nevertheless well motivated psychologically.[48] The same is true for *The Searchers*. Repeated emphasis on the blood relation between Debbie and Ethan made his change of mind understandable, as we have seen; equally, the close ties between Debbie and Martin, which were formed during her infancy and his childhood, for them fulfill the function of blood kinship. This becomes evident from their dialogue when they first meet outside Scar's camp. Martin, unsure if she will recognize him, tries to jog her memory: "Debbie, don't you remember? I'm Martin, Martin your brother. Remember?—Debbie, remember back." And she *has* recognized him: "I remember—from always." Her simple words speak volumes.

Snell noted about Agamemnon and Menelaus in *Iphigenia* that their "sudden exchange of roles reveals Euripides' deft and ingenious grasp of what was dramatically effective." Again, true for Ford as well. Nevertheless, in *Iphigenia* "the course of events is intelligible within the context of the play itself, but from an external perspective much of it must seem rather odd."[49] Almost the same has been said about *The Searchers*. But even if not everything in its plot develops as smoothly as fastidious critics demand, a comparison with Euripides—and, for that matter, with Shakespeare or others—reveals that great artists are not always out for perfection and that its absence need not seriously impair or invalidate their work. Ford said during the filming of *Cheyenne Autumn* (1964), his last western: "I don't *want* it to look perfect."[50] *The Searchers* also does not always look perfect, and we see its characters as humans are, not as they

---

47. Bruno Snell, "From Tragedy to Philosophy: *Iphigenia in Aulis*," in *Greek Tragedy: Modern Essays in Criticism*, ed. Erich Segal (New York: Harper and Row, 1983, also published as *Oxford Readings in Greek Tragedy* [Oxford: Oxford University Press, 1983]), 396–405; quotation at 396. This is a slightly abridged English version of "Euripides' aulische Iphigenie," in *Aischylos und das Handeln im Drama* (Leipzig: Dieterich, 1928 [Philologus Supplementband 20 no. 1]), 148–160. Snell, 399, also speaks of Iphigenia's "uncertainty of inexperience," another point of comparison with Debbie.

48. Lesky, *Die tragische Dichtung der Hellenen*, 317 (on the nurse).

49. Snell, "From Tragedy to Philosophy," 398 and 399.

50. Quoted from Bogdanovich, *John Ford*, 8.

should be. This, too, conforms to Aristotelian precepts in the *Poetics*. Aristotle also quotes a saying, attributed to Sophocles, that Sophocles painted people as they ought to be but that Euripides painted them as they are.[51]

7. The Ending of the Film

That Ford eschews a violent climax—such as Ethan killing Debbie and later paying with his own life for this—might at first speak against the tragic quality of the film. But "happy endings" are an important part of the tradition of ancient tragedy. All three Athenian dramatists wrote plays in which murder and bloodshed were avoided. In the *Eumenides*, the conclusion of Aeschylus' *Oresteia*, the Furies are placated and Orestes is absolved from the blood guilt of killing his mother; the eponymous hero of Sophocles' *Philoctetes* forbears from killing his archenemy Odysseus and agrees to help the Greeks before Troy; in Euripides' *Iphigenia among the Taurians*, Orestes is saved from immolation upon the altar of Artemis at the hands of his sister, the goddess's priestess; Euripides' lost play *Antigone* ended with the wedding of Haemon and Antigone, who does not die as she does in Sophocles' *Antigone*; Euripides' *Ion* and *Helen* end happily as well. In chapter 14 of the *Poetics*, Aristotle even prefers an avoidance of intrafamilial killing.[52] For the protagonist of the western film, we have Robert Warshow's observation that "his story need not end with his death (and usually does not)."[53]

Even so, Ford avoids any superficial dénouement. Debbie is restored to civilization when Ethan takes her to the Jorgensens, who will, presumably, keep her as a member of their family. But Ethan himself remains an outcast from society, homeless and alone. In the film's famous last scene, after everybody else has gone inside, Ethan is left behind on the doorstep. His look follows the others; he then turns away and slowly begins to walk back into the desert wilderness while the door closes upon him. Thematically, and cinematically, through its camera setup, this parallels the film's opening scene, providing a perfect example of ring composition and emphasizing the Aristotelian unities of time, place, and action. In addition, the ending summarizes the protagonist's state of mind: Ethan,

---

51. Aristotle, *Poetics*, chapter 25, especially 25.6 (1460b33–36).
52. On this aspect of Greek tragedy see also Lattimore, *Story Patterns in Greek Tragedy*, 13 and 76–77 note 39.
53. Warshow, "The Westerner," 143.

142

CLASSICAL

MYTH &

CULTURE

IN THE

CINEMA

drained of emotions and beyond violence, resigns himself to the status of an outcast and loner. While Ethan is not punished by death, his survival hardly constitutes a complete redemption. In a reversal of the case of Oedipus, who is guilty in deed but innocent in intention, Ethan has been guilty in intention—that of killing his niece—and innocent of the deed, but he is by no means absolved from guilt, as his status of social outcast attests. And just as Oedipus exiled himself from Thebes, Ethan takes upon himself a voluntary exile to the wilderness. Vernant's comments on Sophocles' *Oedipus the King* emphasize the duality inherent in the tragic protagonist thus exiled: "the tragedy is based on the idea that the same man . . . on whom the prosperity of the earth, of the herds, and of the women depends . . . is at the same time considered to be something dreadfully dangerous, a sort of incarnation of *hubris*, which must be expelled."[54] The task of finding his niece accomplished, Ethan has become superfluous to a society that, from now on, will live in peace, no longer threatened by Indian raids and no longer needing the archaic man of violence for its protection. When Ethan hugs his right arm with his left hand before turning away, this gesture indicates both his loneliness and the fact that he has outlived his usefulness to society. It attests to Ford's mastery that these last moments in the film are completely wordless (except for the title song returning on the soundtrack). Nobody explains anything; the implications are nevertheless overwhelmingly clear. The subtlety of this closure to the film even surpasses that in the scene where Ford revealed Martha's love for Ethan. Ethan now receives the reward for his sacrilegious obsession; as critics have observed, he, too, will "wander forever between the winds," refused entry into the land of home and family, peace and civilization.[55] Like a new Ahasver, he is condemned to roam restlessly and aimlessly. In this context the names of the Edwards brothers, Ethan and Aaron, take on added meaning through their biblical connotations: Aaron is the brother of Moses, the wanderer in the desert who may not enter the Promised Land. It is worth noting that the two names are changed from those the brothers carried in LeMay's novel. Both

54. Vernant, "Greek Tragedy: Problems of Interpretation," in *The Languages of Criticism and the Sciences of Man*, ed. Richard Macksey and Eugenio Donato (Baltimore: Johns Hopkins University Press, 1970), 273–295; quotation at 277. Jaan Puhvel, *Comparative Mythology* (Baltimore: Johns Hopkins University Press, 1987; rpt. 1989), 242, makes a similar point about the Indo-European tradition of heroic myth: "The warrior . . . had an ambivalent role as single champion or part of a self-centered corps or coterie, both a society's external defender and its potential internal menace."

55. Thus McBride and Wilmington, *John Ford*, 163. On the filming of the ending see Carey, *Company of Heroes*, 173–174.

Ethan and his alter ego Scar represent necessary steps in the historical evolution of the country from savagery to civilization. They must live violent lives to prepare the way for future peace and justice, but they themselves have no part in this. It is the westerner's task to aid in the transformation of nature from cruel and barren wilderness to a blossoming garden made fertile and tended by man, but he is not meant to participate in the result.[56] In *The Searchers*, the movement from violence to order is represented primarily in the figure of Ethan; his tragedy lies in the fact that he helps bring about this development but, belonging only to the archaic side, is himself unable to make the transition. When he tells Debbie, "Let's go home," he can take her home and hand her over to others, but he cannot go home himself. Ethan, like other Fordian heroes, takes up "with resignation his burden as scapegoat and saviour. These transitional figures accept the stigma of all heroes since the beginning of society, and their characters often have mythical or Biblical overtones."[57] Our emotional involvement in the visual poetry of the film's final moments derives from our awareness of this; the ending also bears out Warshow's observation that we primarily respond to the hero's defeat. The theme of violence and disorder giving way to culture, law, and a stable society is perhaps the most fundamental subject in the history of Western literature. Among its earliest ancient examples is the *Theogony*, Hesiod's epic on the creation of the world and the gods, in which the movement from *chaos* to *kosmos*, from disorder to the order of the universe as ruled by divine justice, is embodied in the myth of the three generations of gods who successively rule over the world. The motif of the heroic journey or quest and that of savage wilderness changing to a civilization ordered by law are fundamental to Western culture and myth.[58]

56. On this pervasive theme in American intellectual history see Smith, *Virgin Land*, 121–260, especially 123–132 and 250–260, the latter passage on Frederick Jackson Turner's 1893 frontier hypothesis ("The Significance of the Frontier in American History"). In this landmark essay Turner called the frontier "the meeting point between savagery and civilization." Its strongest restatements in the cinema of John Ford occur in *The Searchers* and in *The Man Who Shot Liberty Valance* (1962). On the connections between these two films and Ford's *My Darling Clementine* (1946) see Peter Wollen, *Signs and Meaning in the Cinema*, 4th ed. (London: British Film Institute, 1998), 66–70.

57. Baxter, *The Cinema of John Ford*, 21. (Appropriately, when he first sees Ethan after his return from the war, Clayton calls him "the prodigal brother.") In antiquity the hero's acceptance of his burden finds its most moving expression in Virgil's description of Aeneas taking up his shield (*Aeneid* 8.729–731); in his discussion of these lines Jasper Griffin, *Virgil* (New York: Oxford University Press, 1986), 67, speaks of "the pathos of the pioneer who must work for a result which he will never see."

58. Cf. Northrop Frye, *Anatomy of Criticism: Four Essays* (Princeton: Princeton University Press, 1957; rpt. 1990), 186–206, especially 192–195.

8. Choric Commentators

144

CLASSICAL

MYTH &

CULTURE

IN THE

CINEMA

One of the most distinctive features of Greek drama is the chorus. Far from being a mere adornment to the action of the play, choral songs form an integral part of both tragedy and comedy; indeed, as far as we know, Greek drama may have developed from originally static choral recitations. The tragic chorus finds its chief function in commenting on the protagonist's words and deeds. Voicing the author's thoughts and opinions, the chorus provides an important link to the audience. Its integration into the plot can range from detached observation to active participation. While in the history of theater the chorus has not preserved its importance beyond the ancient stage, traces of its function are still to be found in later developments of tragedy. Shakespearean drama with its fools and clowns immediately comes to mind. Continuing this tradition, comment on the action in the cinema is frequently assigned not to a group of observers but to one or more individual characters often closely associated with the hero. In artistically meaningful films, a character's comments on the protagonist's deeds or attitudes may provide as close a bond to the audience as did the chorus on the classical stage. Not surprisingly, characters of a choric nature also appear in *The Searchers*.

One of these is old Mose Harper, a divine fool in an almost Shakespearean sense, reminiscent of the fool in *King Lear*.[59] Mose does not play a major part in the film, being on screen for only a comparatively short time; nevertheless, he is present during some of the film's key scenes. Mose is one of Ford's most memorable creations, providing the richness of detail and characterization unique to the characters who people his best films. In this way, even marginal figures may become essential. Mose is important on different levels. For one, he provides comic relief from the film's stark tragedy.[60] Under a less accomplished director than Ford, these comic

59. Cf. Baxter, *The Cinema of John Ford*, 19.

60. Evidence of Ford's narrative mastery in this film is his seamless integration of two comic subplots into the main tragic plot. This, too, is in keeping with Greek tragedy, which could contain comic elements; see Bernd Seidensticker, *Palintonos Harmonia: Studien zu komischen Elementen in der griechischen Tragödie* (Göttingen: Vandenhoeck und Ruprecht, 1982). While humor is present even in its serious moments, the film in its second half switches back and forth between tragedy and comedy with effortless grace. As Ford said before beginning work on *The Searchers*: "I should like to do a tragedy, the most serious in the world, that turned into the ridiculous"; quoted from Michael Goodwin, "John Ford: A Poet Who Shot Great Movies," *Moving Image*, 1 no. 3 (December 1981), 59–63; quotation at 62. See also Andrew Sinclair, *John Ford* (New York: Dial Press/Wade, 1979), 213–214, on Ford's interest in tragedy and on his place in the history of tragedy as a popular art form, and cf. Solomon, *Beyond Formula*, 46. The two comic strands in the film involve Martin's inadvertent acquisition of an Indian girl as a bride; this reverts to

touches could easily destroy the film's dramatic equilibrium; as it is, the viewer's apprehension of impending tragedy even increases. More important, Mose is also an experienced westerner. He immediately grasps the reason why Ethan blinds the dead Indian, and on two occasions he gives Ethan decisive information about Debbie after Ethan has lost all traces of her. For this, Mose endures great physical exhaustion. The bald and emaciated old man ends as a figure of pity and woe. Ford uses Christian imagery to emphasize his long suffering when, toward the end of the film, Mose is supported by a soldier on either side of him, his arms outstretched in a Christlike pose. In contrast to the greed of Futterman, the corrupt trader who sold Ethan information about Debbie, Mose has no desire for material rewards: "Don't want no money . . . just a roof over old Mose's head, and a rocking chair by the fire." His awareness of old age and encroaching death and his selfless loyalty endow him with quiet dignity. It is fitting that the old man will find a permanent home with the Jorgensens. Mose, as his name implies, has been a homeless wanderer for most of his life; in this he, too, is an alter ego of Ethan. This is reinforced by the slight touches of childishness and harmless madness in Mose, of which he is himself aware. But since he is a gentle and innocent soul, his end will be different from Ethan's.

More directly than Mose Harper, the figure of Mrs. Jorgensen serves as a choric commentator. Not only is she the archetypal hardy pioneer woman, but she also embodies pragmatism and common sense in the face of the men's more emotional and irrational reactions to the tragic events in their lives. She is an example of what Ford described as "the home women who helped break the land, bear and raise children and make a home for their families. These were hard times for women and they acquitted themselves nobly."[61] After the Edwards family's funeral, Mrs. Jorgensen's is the voice of restraint, which counsels against meaningless and ruinous revenge. She implores Ethan to refrain from drawing

---

stark tragedy when Ethan later finds her killed by the cavalry. In the courtship of Laurie Jorgensen by Charlie McCorry, an archetypal redneck, and in his subsequent brawl over Laurie with Martin, the comedy in the film comes close to farce. Cf. McBride and Wilmington, *John Ford*, 32: "In [Ford's] greatest works, the plot line oscillates freely between the tragic and the ridiculous, with the comic elements providing a continuous commentary on the meaning of the drama." As Sarris, *The John Ford Movie Mystery*, 174, has noted on the humor in *The Searchers*: "If Ford had been more solemn, *The Searchers* would have been less sublime." There is even a fair share of ridicule of the military in the film. Whereas the army had been characterized as indiscriminate butchers of Indians in the cavalry sequence, its second appearance—indeed, interference—at the film's close gives Ford occasion to satirize it for nepotism, bureaucracy, and incompetence.

61. Libby, "The Old Wrangler Rides Again," 17.

146

CLASSICAL

MYTH &

CULTURE

IN THE

CINEMA

Martin and her son Brad into a useless crusade against the Indians: "If the girls are dead, don't let the boys waste their lives in vengeance—promise me, Ethan!" She receives no reply. As usual, the voice of reason goes unheeded, and Mrs. Jorgensen's urgent plea foreshadows her son's death: When he learns about Lucy's fate, Brad impulsively rushes off to the Indian camp to avenge her but falls into Scar's trap. When we next see his mother again, more than a year later in narrative time, she has come to terms with her son's fate, with the harshness of the settlers' existence, and with the hostility of the land in which the pioneers are struggling to survive. In one of the film's key scenes—this is after Ethan and Martin's temporary return from their search—Mr. Jorgensen submits to his grief over Brad's death: "Oh, Ethan, this country . . . it's this country killed my boy." His quiet despair contrasts with his wife's stoic acceptance of her son's death. She characterizes the pioneers' life on the edge of civilization as being "way out on a limb, this year and next, maybe for a hundred more, but I don't think it'll be forever. Someday this country is gonna be a fine, good place to be. Maybe it needs our bones in the ground before that time can come." Her awareness of the necessity for sacrifices gives her the strength to endure. Savagery and violence will eventually be overcome, and there is hope for peace in the future. Her words perfectly summarize the underlying theme of *The Searchers* and of most of Ford's other westerns: the evolution from savagery to civilization, the change in the land from wilderness to garden. Her words point to her own generation's part in this process and to the knowledge that she and the other settlers will not live to see the task completed. They also foreshadow Ethan's eventual fate. Significantly, the setting of this short scene, memorable for its peace and quiet, is the Jorgensens' porch at evening. In a touch typical for his reversals from seriousness to humor or vice versa, Ford circumvents melodramatic emotionalism at this point by having Mr. Jorgensen explain to Ethan his wife's surprising eloquence: "She was a school teacher, you know."

The Jorgensens' is the kind of home which Ethan can visit for a time but to which he cannot belong. Affirmation of hope for the future contrasts with the increasing disappointment of this hope that characterizes the later films of John Ford.[62] *The Searchers* thus takes on added significance if considered in the context of Ford's entire body of work. But even when examined on its own terms, the film represents his foremost achieve-

---

62. On this see, for example, Robin Wood, "Shall We Gather at the River? The Late Films of John Ford," *Film Comment*, 7 no. 3 (1971), 8–17; rpt. in *Theories of Authorship: A Reader*, ed. John Caughie (London: Routledge and Kegan Paul, 1981; rpt. 1988), 83–101.

ment. In no small degree this is due to the fact that Ford makes powerful use of mythic and dramatic archetypes and successfully translates them into a modern medium. In his questions quoted at the beginning of this discussion, Vernant emphasizes the ambiguities inherent in the tragic hero and his environs. Ethan is a modern example of such a tragic *deinos*. Ford once described *The Searchers* as "the tragedy of a loner."[63] Although he used the term loosely, his remark came far closer to the film's true nature than he himself may have realized.

63. Quoted from Bogdanovich, *John Ford*, 92.

VII

An American Tragedy: *Chinatown*

Mary-Kay Gamel

History is what hurts.
—Fredric Jameson

Since the late twentieth century, generic distinctions in the arts seem to have been rapidly breaking down, as old genres merge and new ones arise.[1] Contemporary literary studies often dismiss genre criticism. In film, however, genre remains a widely used system of classification for producers, critics, and consumers. Every video store, for example, displays its wares as "drama," "comedy," "action," and so on.[2] For classical antiquity, the idea of genre is so central to the production, presentation, discussion, and evaluation of texts that a systematic discussion of genre in those texts and in film is appropriate. But to date, most dis-

---

1. Heather Dubrow, *Genre* (London: Methuen, 1982), gives an overview of genre criticism in literature, including references to the work of contemporary critics. My essay is informed especially by Fredric Jameson, "Magical Narratives: On the Dialectical Use of Genre Criticism," in *The Political Unconscious: Narrative as a Socially Symbolic Act* (Ithaca, N.Y.: Cornell University Press, 1981), 103–150. My epigraph is from "On Interpretation: Literature As a Socially Symbolic Act," in *The Political Unconscious*, 17–102; quotation at 102. I am grateful to David Kirk and Kenneth McKenzie of the McHenry Library at the University of California, Santa Cruz; to H. Marshall Leicester for access to his collection of film noir; and to Daniel L. Selden and Peter Richardson for their valuable suggestions. I owe special thanks, as always, to Thomas A. Vogler.

2. For genre in film see *Film Genre Reader II*, ed. Barry Keith Grant (Austin: University of Texas Press, 1995), and the thorough discussion by Rick Altman, *Film/Genre* (London: British Film Institute, 1999).

cussions of classical texts and film have focused on content rather than on formal or generic aspects.[3]

Greek drama and film share obvious formal, thematic, and affective features. Like drama, film is the product not of an individual but of the combined talents of author, director, actors, designers, and musicians. Material aspects are crucial to both. The financial support of a producer and the economic, social, historical, and ideological circumstances of production shape the characteristics of individual artifacts.[4] In both cases a large audience, comprising all classes of society, expresses strong responses to what it sees.[5] Yet most discussions of Greek tragedy and cinema limit themselves to comparing filmic treatments of ancient dramas to the original scripts.[6] The lack of other work in this area may be attributed

3. Examples of content-based discussions are Maria Wyke, *Projecting the Past: Ancient Rome, Cinema and History* (New York: Routledge, 1997), and Jon Solomon, *The Ancient World in the Cinema*, 2nd ed. (New Haven: Yale University Press, 2000). Derek Elley, *The Epic Film: Myth and History* (London: Routledge and Kegan Paul, 1984), examines films depicting periods up to the end of the Dark Ages. Mary Whitlock Blundell and Kirk Ormand, "Western Values, or the Peoples Homer: *Unforgiven* as a Reading of the *Iliad*," *Poetics Today*, 18 (1997), 533–569, examine genre, plot, and ideology in Clint Eastwood's 1992 film and in Homer.

4. Recent studies that place tragedy in its sociopolitical and institutional context include *Greek Tragedy and Political Theory*, ed. J. Peter Euben (Berkeley: University of California Press, 1986), and *Nothing to Do with Dionysos? Athenian Drama in Its Social Context* (Princeton: Princeton University Press, 1990), ed. John J. Winkler and Froma Zeitlin. On the historical and political contexts of American films see John Baxter, *Hollywood in the Thirties* (1968; rpt. New York: Barnes, 1980); Charles Higham and Joel Greenberg, *Hollywood in the Forties* (New York: Barnes, 1968; rpt. 1970); Peter Biskind, *Seeing Is Believing: How Hollywood Taught Us to Stop Worrying and Love the Fifties* (New York: Pantheon, 1983) and *Easy Riders, Raging Bulls: How the Sex-Drugs-and-Rock-'n'-Roll Generation Saved Hollywood* (New York: Simon and Schuster, 1998; rpt. 1999). Thomas Schatz, *Hollywood Genres: Formulas, Filmmaking, and the Studio System* (New York: McGraw-Hill, 1981), analyzes the relation of the studio to genre; Schatz, *The Genius of the System: Hollywood Filmmaking in the Studio Era* (1988; rpt. New York: Holt, 1996), examines how the studio system shaped film production. See also Altman, *Film/Genre*, 44–48 and 115–121.

5. Plato, *Gorgias* 502b–c and *Laws* 658d, and Aristotle, *Poetics* 1462a2–4, express dismay at tragedy's appeal to a mass audience. On the Athenian audience see primarily Arthur Pickard-Cambridge, *The Dramatic Festivals of Athens*, 2nd ed., rev. John Gould and D. M. Lucas (Oxford: Clarendon Press, 1968; rpt. 1991), 263–278, and Eric Csapo and William J. Slater, *The Context of Ancient Drama* (Ann Arbor: University of Michigan Press, 1995), 286–305. Patrick Brantlinger, *Bread and Circuses: Theories of Mass Culture as Social Decay* (Ithaca, N.Y.: Cornell University Press, 1983; rpt. 1985), provides a general discussion of mass culture, including tragedy.

6. Kenneth MacKinnon, *Greek Tragedy into Film* (Rutherford, N.J.: Fairleigh Dickinson University Press, 1986), and Marianne McDonald, *Euripides in Cinema: The Heart Made Visible* (1983; rpt. Boston: The Greek Institute, 1991), deal with filmed versions of Athenian tragic scripts. Martin M. Winkler, "Classical Mythology and the Western Film,"

150

CLASSICAL

MYTH &

CULTURE

IN THE

CINEMA

to various factors, among them the tendency to regard ancient dramas as literary texts rather than performance texts, as "high culture" not to be compared to the "low culture" of film, and to the dominance of narrative and textual over dramatic models in film theory.[7]

One critical study does attempt a more complex comparison between ancient drama and film. In "Genre Film: A Classical Experience," Thomas Sobchack ascribes to all genre films a "classical" status established by three elements.[8] First is form. The genre film's "sole existence is to make concrete and perceivable the configurations inherent in its ideal form" (103). Genre films always imitate past models, since they "are made in imitation not of life but of other films. . . . A genre film . . . is capable of creating the classical experience because of this insistence on the familiar" (104–105). The third "classical" element is ahistoricity: "The contemporary and the particular are inimical to the prevailing idea in classical thought that knowledge is found in the general conclusions that have stood the test of time" (102). The setting of genre films is "an ideal plane, a utopia, as far removed from our world as was the world of kings and nobles and Olympian gods from the lives of the Athenians who attended the plays" (108).

Sobchack acknowledges that formal aspects have social implications but insists that "the genre film, like all classical art, is basically conservative, both aesthetically and politically" (112). Such "classical" films do not provoke the audience to think about or take action on the questions they raise; rather, "given the appropriate ending, these emotions [of pity and fear, evoked by tragedy] are dissipated, leaving viewers in a state of calm" (109). Genre films are comforting fodder for "ordinary people . . . fated to a life in society in which they are relatively powerless to change the course of things" (112).

Sobchack bases his sweeping conclusions about "classical" art on very narrow evidence. He discusses no ancient script, referring only to the "story" of Oedipus or Odysseus. Aristotle and Northrop Frye, a neo-Aristotelian, are his only theoretical models. Other scholars have discussed

---

Comparative Literature Studies, 22 (1985), 516–540, outlines epic and tragic patterns in the western.

7. Literature on the relationship between film and theater is extensive. Roy Armes, *Action and Image: Dramatic Structure in Cinema* (Manchester: Manchester University Press, 1994), discusses films as examples of drama.

8. Sobchack's article first appeared in *Literature/Film Quarterly*, 3 (1975), 196–204; reprinted in *Film Genre Reader II*, 102–113. Further page references are to this reprint and appear in the text. Sobchack and other film theorists use "genre" in a quite different sense from that of Aristotle and literary critics. In film contexts, the word is often adjectival, meaning "formulaic."

the relationships among genre, ideology, and cultural products much more thoughtfully.[9] I have dwelt on Sobchack's article because his uncritical acceptance of Aristotelian categories and his quietistic social views echo conservative defenses of the established literary canon because of its "timeless" or "universal" values. A careful examination of ancient dramas in their original context, however, contradicts these views. Athenian audiences did not seek comfort and "calm"; rather, they scrutinized the plays produced in the dramatic competition for their immediate topical meanings and responded actively to what they saw. Aristophanes' plays *Frogs* and *Thesmophoriazusae*, for example, include debates about tragedy's moral and political meaning and its effect.[10]

To test the validity of Sobchack's view of "classical art" in regard to Greek drama I will examine a film that shares conspicuous formal and thematic characteristics with Greek tragedy: *Chinatown* (1974), written by Robert Towne and directed by Roman Polanski. In making this comparison I am not trying to honor an especially worthy film by comparing it to past "masterpieces." Intertextuality works both ways, and any consideration of the connections between ancient drama and modern film requires our reassessment of the former as much as our evaluation of the latter. Understanding *Chinatown* in terms of tragedy also raises questions about tragedy as a "classic" genre.

1. *Chinatown* and Greek Tragedy

The film's plot: In 1937 Los Angeles, private detective Jake Gittes is hired by a woman who calls herself Evelyn Mulwray to ascertain whether her husband Hollis, city commissioner of Water and Power, is having an affair. Gittes follows Mulwray and takes photos of him with a young girl. After these photos appear in a newspaper article, the real Mrs. Mulwray sues Gittes. Soon after Gittes sets out to discover who arranged the deception, Mulwray is found dead. Gittes gradually discovers that Mulwray's

9. For discussions specifically of film see Stephen Neale, *Genre* (London: British Film Institute, 1980; rpt. 1996); Barbara Klinger, "'Cinema/Ideology/Criticism' Revisited: The Progressive Genre," in *Film Genre Reader II*, 74–90 (originally published in slightly different form and with a slightly different title in *Screen*, 25 [1984], 30–44); Schatz, *Hollywood Genres*, 6–41; Altman, *Film/Genre*, 26–28 and 222–225; and Deborah Knight, "Aristotelians on *Speed*: Paradoxes of Genre in the Context of Cinema," in *Film Theory and Philosophy*, ed. Richard Allen and Murray Smith (Oxford: Clarendon Press, 1997), 343–365.

10. On Athenian audience reactions see Pickard-Cambridge, *Dramatic Festivals of Athens*, 272–278.

152

CLASSICAL

MYTH &

CULTURE

IN THE

CINEMA

death is part of a huge scheme masterminded by Noah Cross, Evelyn Mulwray's father and Hollis Mulwray's former business partner. Cross is secretly buying land in the San Fernando Valley and promoting the construction of a new dam that the citizens of Los Angeles think will serve their city. The dam will actually irrigate Cross's land, which he will then be able to sell at huge profit. The young girl is not Mulwray's mistress but Evelyn's daughter and sister Katherine, the product of Evelyn's incest with her father. She and Hollis have brought Katherine up in Mexico, hidden from Cross. Gittes's efforts to solve Hollis Mulwray's murder, help Evelyn, and thwart Cross result instead in Evelyn's death and Cross's triumph.

Chinatown has the intensity and economy of Greek tragedy. The plot is concentrated. The events all take place within a few days, and the passage of time is carefully marked. Scenes are shot in various locations, but Los Angeles, the overall setting, is constantly present verbally and visually. The film thus conforms to Aristotle's prescription for temporal and spatial unity (*Poetics* 1450b24–35). The number of characters is limited, and every character introduced, even the most minor, plays a crucial role. The action is punctuated by physical violence and culminates in a shocking death. But violence is used sparingly and is closely connected to the film's semiotic pattern. As such, it has the same function as it does in Greek tragedy: to underline the importance of the issues at stake. Family members use violence on one another, the kind of event Aristotle thinks most arouses pity and fear in the audience (*Poetics* 1453b19–26). The dialogue, while apparently naturalistic, is tightly knit; every line, every exchange either advances the plot or touches on its themes. Every shot, carefully planned, contains meaningful elements.

The names of several characters are as significant as those of Oedipus ("Swollen Foot"), Hippolytus ("Destroyed by Horses"), and Orestes ("Snakelike"). Gittes's name is pointedly different from those of other hard-boiled detectives, which tend to be either phallic (Sam Spade, Mike Hammer) or poetic (Philip Marlowe). Noah Cross purposefully mispronounces it "gits," suggesting that Gittes "gits his" and then "gits out." Lou Escobar, the police lieutenant who worked with Gittes in the past, may be a new broom trying to sweep clean (Spanish *escobar*, "to sweep"), but Claude Mulvehill, Noah Cross's hired thug, is a clod, and Escobar's fellow cop Loach (whose shot kills Evelyn) is louche, a low roach. Evelyn's name suggests that she may be evil, an Eve tempting man to sin. Most significant of all is that of Noah Cross, a patriarch who controls the waters and is master of the double cross.

Oedipus the King is often considered the first detective story, and the protagonist and structure of *Chinatown* resemble those of Sophocles' play in striking ways.[11] Like Oedipus, Gittes at first seems intelligent, powerful, in control. He dresses nattily; meeting him again, Escobar notes: "looks like you've done all right for yourself." He has a nice office and employs his own "operatives" and a cute secretary. (Her name is Sophie; like the flute girl in Plato's *Symposium*, she is sent out of the room when male wisdom needs to be heard.) Like Oedipus, Gittes sets out on an investigation confident of results. He gets information even from unwilling sources. He lectures his employees Walsh and Duffy on "finesse" and delivers snappy verbal comeuppances to those he considers his inferiors. He pursues his investigation with determination and uses professional tricks, such as leaving a watch under a parked car's wheel to time a suspect's movements and breaking the taillight on Evelyn's car to be able to follow her at night without being spotted. He thinks and acts quickly. Gittes endures not only lies and threats but also violence—he dodges bullets, he is beaten up, his nose is slit—and like Oedipus he seems heroic when he courageously continues his investigation.

Gittes also fits Aristotle's prescription for a protagonist who is morally "between the extremes" (*Poetics* 1453a7). As John Cawelti has observed:

> One of the most deeply symbolic clichés of the traditional hard-boiled formula is the hero's refusal to do divorce business. . . . By this choice the traditional private eye of the myth established both his personal sense of honor and his transcendent vocation.[12]

Since divorce work is his "meetiyay," Gittes resembles the unscrupulous "bedroom dick" Mike Hammer of Robert Aldrich's *Kiss Me Deadly* (1955). Gittes is generous to working-class Curly but decides to overcharge Mrs. Mulwray as soon as he finds out her husband's high position at Water and Power. He reacts indignantly when accused of trading on scandal: "I make an honest living! People only come to me when they're in a desperate situation—I help 'em out." But while nobly shielding Evelyn Mulwray

11. Robert Warshow, "The Gangster as Tragic Hero," in *The Immediate Experience: Movies, Comics, Theatre and Other Aspects of Popular Culture* (1962; rpt. New York: Atheneum, 1979), 127–133, argues that the gangster film is a tragic form. His essay first appeared in *Partisan Review*, 15 (1948), 240–244. On *Oedipus the King* and *Chinatown* see Deborah Linderman, "Oedipus in Chinatown," *enclitic*, 5.2/6.1 (1981–1982), 190–203, and John Belton, "Language, Oedipus, and *Chinatown*," *Modern Language Notes*, 106 (1991), 933–950.

12. John G. Cawelti, "*Chinatown* and Generic Transformation in Recent American Films," in *Film Theory and Criticism: Introductory Readings*, 4th ed., ed. Gerald Mast, Marshall Cohen, and Leo Braudy (New York: Oxford University Press, 1992), 498–511; quotation at 502. The essay first appeared in *Film Theory and Criticism*, 2nd ed., ed. Mast and Cohen (New York: Oxford University Press, 1979), 559–579.

154

CLASSICAL

MYTH &

CULTURE

IN THE

CINEMA

from reporters' questions and flashbulbs he tries to get publicity for himself ("Gittes—two t's and an e!"). He negotiates simultaneous contracts for large sums with both Evelyn and Noah Cross, despite obvious signs that they are at odds with one another. His primary motive for continuing the investigation, it seems, is not desire for the truth but worry about losing his reputation as a businessman: "I'm not supposed to be the one caught with my pants down."

Gittes's understanding, like that of Oedipus, is deeply flawed. Noah Cross tells him: "You may think you know what you're dealing with here, but believe me, you don't." Gittes ignores important clues and fails to draw obvious conclusions—for example, that Hollis is spending his nights on his own investigation and not with a mistress or that following a tip might endanger the informant who gave it. Like Oedipus, Gittes is easily angered and impulsively jumps to wrong conclusions, accusing first Yelburton, Hollis Mulwray's successor, and then Evelyn of Mulwray's murder. His misplaced self-confidence even leads him to stage a showdown with Noah Cross, but Cross, who has brought along a gunman, forces Gittes to take him to Katherine. This botched confrontation inverts the typical scene in the hard-boiled plot in which the hero confronts, hears the confession of, and sometimes executes the criminal. In other films, characters from whom information is demanded protect others by refusing to divulge it, even at the price of a beating, as in Samuel Fuller's *Pickup on South Street* (1953), or death, as in Howard Hawks's *The Big Sleep* (1946). As a result of Gittes's combination of overconfidence and cowardice, those he despises, like Mulvehill and Loach, triumph over him. Thus, after his nose is slit, the wound does not disappear as do most film injuries but stays in prominent view for the entire film. This wound, covered with a comic bandage or revealing its stitches, is a sign not of courage but of the hero's vulnerability, comparable to Oedipus' pierced ankles.

Gittes's investigation, like that of Oedipus, results in his finding himself part of the problem rather than the solution, the murderer of the king whose murderer he seeks, as Tiresias says (*Oedipus the King* 362). In both, fate seems to be directing the course of human action. Despite all his efforts to avoid it, Oedipus fulfills the destiny predicted for him; in the past, Gittes says, he "was trying to keep somebody from getting hurt and ended up making sure that she was hurt," and he does exactly the same this time. The film's dénouement can be described in the Aristotelian terms of "reversal" and "recognition" (*peripeteia, anagnorisis*; *Poetics* 1452a12–b8). Evelyn's revelation of the incest with her father is the film's *peripeteia*, which causes Jake to try to help her instead of blocking her, and her death causes his *anagnorisis*, recognition not only of Noah Cross's schemes but also of his own failure, lack of understanding, and ironic complicity in the outcome. (I am using the term *anagnorisis* not in the strict Aristotelian sense—recognition of the identity of persons previously unknown—but in the more general sense of intellectual and moral understanding.) This recognition comes, however, too late to avert disaster, as it does to Greek protagonists such as Oedipus, Hippolytus, Theseus, Heracles, and Creon. As Escobar says: "You never learn, do you, Jake?" The film is bracketed by suggestions that knowledge only serves to increase pain. "You're better off not knowing," says Gittes to the fake Mrs. Mulwray at the beginning, and the film's last line is "Forget it, Jake, it's Chinatown."

Chinatown displays a complex of visual imagery that is comparable to the verbal imagery of many Greek tragedies.[13] Oedipus, who has put too much trust in his intellectual understanding, blinds himself when that understanding fails him. Gittes, too, seems to be an expert manipulator of specular technology (binoculars, camera, magnifying glass), but his and others' imperfect knowledge is consistently represented by visual images of flawed sight: eyeglasses with a broken lens, the broken taillight on Evelyn's car. When the dead Mulwray is dragged from the reservoir, his glasses are gone, and he is popeyed as if in amazement at what he has seen. The punishment of Curly's wife for "seeing" another man is a large black eye. Evelyn describes a flaw in the iris of her left eye as "a sort of birthmark," and Loach's bullet blasts through this eye. As Katherine screams at the sight of her dead mother, Noah Cross covers his daughter-granddaughter's eyes, suggesting that he will be able to control and abuse her as he did Evelyn. By contrast, Cross's bifocals become a sign not of feeble old age but of duplicity of vision: the ability to see Evelyn both as daughter and lover, to see private profit in the public domain. Similarly, his walking stick suggests not an old man's cane but the phallic power of a patriarch's staff. The famous riddle of the Sphinx was: "What walks on four legs at dawn, two at noon, and three at nightfall?" The correct answer is man, who crawls, walks, and then uses a cane. Cross, like Oedipus, confounds such "natural" distinctions.

Many times mechanical means that should aid vision obstruct it instead. When Gittes perches on a roof to get photographs of Hollis with his supposed girlfriend, the shot moves away from the couple below to

---

13. On the complex verbal imagery in the *Oresteia*, for example, see Anne Lebeck, *The Oresteia: A Study in Language and Structure* (Cambridge: Harvard University Press, 1971), and Pierre Vidal-Naquet, "Hunting and Sacrifice in Aeschylus' *Oresteia*," in Jean-Pierre Vernant and Pierre Vidal-Naquet, *Myth and Tragedy in Ancient Greece*, tr. Janet Lloyd (1981; rpt. New York: Zone Books, 1990), 141–159. On Aeschylean visual imagery in performance see Oliver Taplin, *The Stagecraft of Aeschylus: The Dramatic Use of Exits and Entrances in Greek Tragedy* (Oxford: Clarendon Press, 1977).

156

CLASSICAL

MYTH &

CULTURE

IN THE

CINEMA

focus on his face obscured by his camera. The reversed image of Mulwray and Katherine in his camera lens, like the images in Gittes's car mirror as he follows Hollis, indicates that he is getting things backward. As Gittes drives up to the reservoir, Polanski's camera, positioned behind Jake's right shoulder, shows a closed gate framed in the windshield of his car. The image suggests that the windshield, too, is a barrier rather than a visual conduit. The photographs Gittes takes of Hollis with Katherine are interpreted incorrectly—by the newspapers as proof of a "love nest," by Escobar as proof that Gittes is guilty of extortion. The self-reflexive motif of photography as inadequate mimesis that must be interpreted and supplemented owes much to Michelangelo Antonioni's influential *Blow-Up* (1966). The constant presence of Venetian blinds is both a visual homage to 1930s noir films and another barrier to sight.

Polanski's ironic use of cinematic techniques further reinforces the film's theme of flawed sight.[14] The film uses continuity editing, featuring long takes, which establishes visually clear relationships between characters and surroundings. This "classical" style, rather than that of montage or discontinuity editing, which calls attention to the director's manipulation of the image, suggests that the viewer is getting the whole, undistorted picture.[15] So do Polanski's use of undiffused light, which creates hard edges, and of deep focus, which renders visible all objects in the frame. But here, as in *Oedipus the King*, seeing does not lead to understanding. Instead, these techniques underline the inadequacy and deceptiveness of sight, reminding viewers that their sight, the primary means of understanding motion pictures, is really only partial and controlled by someone else. The close-up, for example, normally used to mark an object as especially important, occurs in a deceptive manner when a manicure kit in Mulwray's office drawer and documents in the wallet of the fake Mrs. Mulwray are clues that lead nowhere.

As in *Oedipus the King*, the protagonist's point of view—his "private eye"—dominates the film. Not only does Gittes appear in every scene, but the camera is frequently placed near his shoulder so that the audience

14. Cinematographer John A. Alonzo describes his technique in "Shooting *Chinatown*," *American Cinematographer*, 56 (1975), 526–529, 564–565, 572–573, and 585–591. On the relationship between the film's themes and cinematic techniques see William J. Palmer, *The Films of the Seventies: A Social History* (Metuchen, N.J.: Scarecrow Press, 1987), 117–178; Virginia Wright Wexman, *Roman Polanski* (Boston: Twayne, 1985), 91–106 ("*Chinatown*: The Generic Synthesis"); and Michael Eaton, *Chinatown* (London: British Film Institute, 1997), 56–57.

15. On the distinction between these editing techniques see David Bordwell and Kristin Thompson, *Film Art: An Introduction*, 6th ed. (New York: McGraw-Hill, 2001), 262–290.

sees from his point of view. The film's only dissolve occurs when angry farmers knock Gittes unconscious. When Gittes focuses binoculars on Mulwray and a Mexican boy talking, they are shown in a double iris shot so that the audience is looking through the binoculars with Gittes. Gittes is frequently shown making his observations from a high position—a bluff over the sea, the bank of the Los Angeles River, a roof overlooking Katherine's apartment. Such a position might suggest that his vision is godlike, Olympian. But at the apartment he dislodges a roof tile and has to jump back to keep from being seen. The result of giving the viewer Gittes's point of view is to implicate the audience in his fallibility.

In Francis Ford Coppola's *The Conversation* (1977), an eavesdropping expert learns that words must be complemented by visual information. *Chinatown* offers the converse of this lesson. Gittes's binoculars let him see Mulwray talking to the Mexican boy, but he cannot hear their words, and Walsh takes pictures of Cross and Mulwray arguing but hears only words that he understands as "apple core." When spying on Katherine, Gittes does not hear that she is speaking Spanish with Hollis at the supposed love nest and with Evelyn at the safe house, where Gittes sees them through a closed window. Gittes disregards verbal clues such as Cross's evading his question about the argument Cross had had with Mulwray, Evelyn's stammering whenever her father is mentioned, and the Japanese gardener's "Velly bad for glass." These words are a double clue, to both the salt water in the Mulwrays' pond and the glasses lost there. Flawed sight as a metaphor for the difficulty of knowledge and the need for other kinds of knowledge than intellectual understanding are Sophoclean themes. As Tiresias says to Oedipus: "you are blind in mind and ears as well as in your eyes" (*Oedipus the King* 371).[16] The plays of Euripides often emphasize the need to integrate verbal with visual evidence, the two modes of understanding fundamental to theatrical experience, for example in the contrast in *Electra* between the criminal Clytemnestra as described by Electra and the contrite, compassionate mother who later comes on stage. When featured in drama and film, such epistemological themes raise important metatheatrical and metacinematic issues about the validity of the understanding these media seem to provide. Dramas and films that call attention to their own status as media suggest that simple mimesis is impossible, that all experience is mediated.

Chinatown does not simply indict Gittes as an individual. Its central theme is the complexity and obscurity of human experience, which makes understanding difficult or impossible. Chinatown, where "you

16. David Seale, *Vision and Stagecraft in Sophocles* (Chicago: University of Chicago Press, 1982), is one of many analyses of Sophocles' use of verbal imagery involving sight.

158

CLASSICAL

MYTH &

CULTURE

IN THE

CINEMA

can't always tell what's going on," is a metaphor for the reality experienced by the film's characters and audience. Like Oedipus, who thinks he has escaped from danger by fleeing Corinth, Gittes thinks he's "outta Chinatown," but he, Escobar, Evelyn, Cross, and Katherine are all inevitably drawn back to the crossroads and must play out the catastrophe. The world of *Chinatown* is not only more complex and enigmatic but also more evil than Gittes could ever have imagined. What his investigation discovers is greed and corruption so pervasive, a corporate conspiracy so immense, that no individual can get to the bottom of it or do anything about it, and almost anybody may be complicit in it. Whether Yelburton or Loach are part of Cross's scheme is never established; the film's conclusion and even repeated viewings refuse the audience complete knowledge. But there are constant suggestions that public officials have been bought. "Who's paying you?" Hollis is asked. Visitors to Noah Cross's ranch "paid five thousand dollars each towards the sheriff's re-election," and the hood Mulvehill is a corrupt former sheriff. When Gittes says that he'll sue "the big boys who are making the payoffs," his employee Duffy scoffs: "People like that are liable to be having dinner with the judges trying the suit." Escobar seems to be a good cop, but when asked if he is honest, Gittes responds: "As far as it goes—of course, he has to swim in the same water we all do." When Gittes pleads with Evelyn to let the police handle her father, she screams: "He owns the police!" The end of the film reverses the conclusion of *Oedipus the King*: Noah Cross, the father who has had his "son" Hollis killed and has caused his daughter's death, is not driven out by the revelation of his guilt but remains firmly in power.

In this complex, corrupt world causality is intricate, involving institutions as well as individuals. The family, which Aristotle, whose focus was on natural forms, did not consider a political institution, causes abuse, pain, and violence. The founding of a city is treated with the same ambivalence which Aeschylus exhibited in *The Eumenides* and Euripides in *Medea* and *The Bacchae*. As incestuous paterfamilias, murderer, and scheming city "father," Noah Cross combines individual and institutional transgressions. His scheme will make him millions on real estate, yet his motive is ultimately not money but power. When Gittes asks: "What can you buy that you can't already afford?" Cross answers: "The future, Mr. Gits! The future!" Cross is presented not as a monstrous aberration but as an example of human nature at its most basic. When Gittes confronts him with his incest he replies: "I don't blame myself. Most people never have to face the fact that at the right time and the right place they're capable of *anything*." Cross's and Mulwray's partnership ("Hollis Mulwray and I were a lot closer than Evelyn realized"), Cross's and Evelyn's sexual involvement, even the similarity in the names Mulwray and Mulvehill, all indicate that no one is innocent.[17]

Hence history is presented as cyclical. Progress is impossible, and people are fated to repeat past actions, however evil or disastrous. In the past, Cross had convinced Mulwray to build a dam that later collapsed and killed several hundred people. Mulwray now opposes plans for the new dam, swearing: "I won't make the same mistake twice," but his disgrace and death clear the way for this dam to be built. Like Mulvehill, Gittes has been a police officer. While serving in Chinatown, he had been told to "do as little as possible," and these are his last words in the film, whispered to himself as he stares at Evelyn's body. Jake again makes the mistake of hurting someone he was trying to help, and Noah Cross is free to commit incest again.

The setting for the film's plot is literally elemental. Cross is able to control not only individuals and institutions but also land and water. The action takes place during a drought exacerbated by a heat wave: "LOS ANGELES IS DYING OF THIRST," proclaims a handbill, and the mayor warns that the city is caught "between the desert and the Pacific Ocean." The film's imagery emphasizes the dry–wet dichotomy. Polanski shot it with a subtle brown-beige filter, which gives it a period look and also increases the sense of heat. Set against this are constant images of water—lake, reservoirs, channels, surf, Mulwray's tidepool "where life begins," the spouting radiator of Gittes's crashed car, even glasses of iced tea—and verbal references to it: "Water again!" exclaims Gittes; Curly is a fisherman; Hollis has "water on the brain"; and the retirement home is called Mar Vista. This name is a bilingual clue that combines the themes of water and sight and suggests that Cross's scheme will disfigure the landscape. Liquid sound effects of water thundering down runoff channels, splashing gently as Evelyn offers Gittes a drink, dripping ominously into a sink as Gittes discovers the body of the woman who gave him the Mar Vista clue are aural indications that water is the key to the whole mystery. In this film water is a complex symbol that can represent either refreshment and safety or danger, as when it drowns Mulwray or almost sweeps Gittes away.

This elemental imagery evokes mythical themes and imbues the film with allegorical meanings.[18] Los Angeles is a Waste Land, a sterile kingdom with a drowned man and a wounded king, waiting for the water of redemption. But no redeemer comes, and the wound is not healed. Cross

17. Cf. Eaton, *Chinatown*, 64–65.

18. See Cawelti, "*Chinatown* and Generic Transformation," 503; Garrett Stewart, "The Long Goodbye from *Chinatown*," *Film Quarterly*, 28 (1974), 25–32; Eaton, *Chinatown*, 40–43.

160

CLASSICAL

MYTH &

CULTURE

IN THE

CINEMA

is an Old Testament patriarch who will not give up his power to the new generation. The casting of John Huston as Noah Cross had significant intertextual overtones, since in 1966 Huston had portrayed a folksy, comic Noah in his own film *The Bible*. Hollis thinks that "the public should own the water," but Cross keeps private what should be public: the water, the land, and his daughters. His sexual and political behavior are both incestuous, and its final result is sterility. Evelyn hates him and dies trying to keep Katherine from him. His agents dump water, poison wells, and blow up water tanks. "Pretty funny irrigation," observes the owner of an orange grove as fertile agricultural land is transformed into an arid city.

In this context Christian references become ironic. Cross is a double-crosser, an antichrist who crucifies others, a fisher of men who picks bad rather than good. "You have a nasty reputation," he says to Gittes; "I like that." As Cross and Gittes eat lunch, the camera focuses on a fish's eye staring up from the plate, and Cross comments: "I believe fish should be served with the head." A fish seen in silhouette and resembling the ICHTHYS symbol appears on the flag of the Albacore Club, which Cross owns, but here the fish symbolizes not Christian benevolence but elemental rapacity. Cross dispenses alms to the residents of Mar Vista not as an act of charity but to increase his power. In the argument between Mulwray and Cross, Walsh hears "apple core" for "Albacore," suggesting that Los Angeles is another Eden destroyed by greed, but for this original sin there is no redemption. As in the films of Sam Peckinpah, Mexico, represented by the boy on the white horse and as refuge for Katherine, seems to symbolize a place and time of innocence and beauty, an early, still unspoiled California. But Noah Cross dresses like a Spanish grandee and lives in a Spanish-style ranch house, so that symbol, too, is tainted.

Chinatown resembles Greek tragedy, then, with its extremely condensed, intense format used to raise significant issues in individual, familial, political, even cosmic terms, with individual characters representing human experience in general, with its heightened contrasts and choices between extreme alternatives. The film's emphasis on stasis and hierarchy in both plot and character, suggesting that progress is impossible and that an individual's power to act is constrained by other, stronger people or even by extrahuman forces, seems to support Sobchack's thesis that creating "classical" art depends on imitating past models. Hence even Polanski's casting himself as a hood, making himself the hireling of John Huston, director of such film "classics" as *The Maltese Falcon* (1941) and *The Treasure of the Sierra Madre* (1948), may be regarded as his admission that a contemporary director can only follow the old masters.[19]

19. This is the view of Stewart, "Long Goodbye from *Chinatown*," 30–32.

2. Cinema and History in *Chinatown*

Robert Towne, who was educated at Pomona College, a traditional liberal arts school, may have been consciously following Aristotelian ideas. But even if he did not, Aristotle's influence on playwrights and screenwriters, often at second- or thirdhand, has long been pervasive in Hollywood.[20] Yet my point in connecting *Chinatown* and Greek tragedy is not to demonstrate conscious imitation or influence. Towne drew on the novels of Dashiell Hammett, Raymond Chandler, and John Fante, and director Polanski on American black-and-white films of the 1930s and 1940s such as *The Maltese Falcon*, Orson Welles's *Citizen Kane* (1941), and *The Big Sleep*. Nor am I suggesting that the "classical" features of *Chinatown* support a theory of recurring archetypes, such as Joseph Campbell's, based on C. G. Jung's, or of conscious use of an Aristotelian or neo-Aristotelian model of the organic development of genres, such as Northrop Frye's.[21] For all its emphasis on repetition, inevitability, and closure, *Chinatown* is not a closed text that imitates the ideal form of past models and avoids contemporary reference and relevance. In fact—and this is my central point—it is the "classical" elements in the film that most clearly establish its connections to the historical, political, and aesthetic circumstances of its own production.

My comparison up to this point, based on formal and thematic similarities between *Chinatown* and tragedy, employs the very approach for which I have criticized Sobchack. Hans Robert Jauss has said that

> even the most highly developed practice of comparison tells us neither what should enter into the comparison (and what not), nor to what end. The relevance and thereby the selection of the comparison cannot be drawn directly from the compared elements themselves; even when in the end significance apparently "springs out" on its own, it nonetheless presupposes hermeneutically a preconception . . . however often unadmitted.[22]

20. Two recent examples of popular guides to screenwriting that use Aristotelian principles and discuss *Chinatown* (on the pages indicated) are Thomas Pope, *Good Scripts, Bad Scripts: Learning the Craft of Screenwriting through the Twenty-Five Best and Worst Films in History* (New York: Three Rivers, 1998), 183–192, and Linda J. Cowgill, *Secrets of Screenplay Structure: How to Recognize and Emulate the Structural Frameworks of Great Films* (Los Angeles: Lone Eagle, 1999), 87–94.

21. Cf. Northrop Frye, *Anatomy of Criticism: Four Essays* (Princeton: Princeton University Press, 1957; rpt. 1990).

22. Hans Robert Jauss, *Toward an Aesthetic of Reception*, tr. Timothy Bahti (Minneapolis: University of Minnesota Press, 1982), 110. Further page references appear in the text.

162

CLASSICAL

MYTH &

CULTURE

IN THE

CINEMA

Formal or "timeless" comparison appears to be "a high-level dialogue between illustrious spirits, with the philologist only needing to eavesdrop in order to understand" (112–113). But this apparently objective procedure ignores the historical processes of "preservation, suppression, and omission" that are part of all "formations of tradition" and the process of "approval as well as disapproval in which the judgment of the particular present either takes over or gives up past experience, either renews it or rejects it" (112). To avoid the reductiveness inherent in the timeless comparison, Jauss argues, an interpreter must locate individual works in their historical contexts and also discover "the contemporary horizon of interest of the interpreter who is comparatively questioning them" (113).

The preconception motivating Sobchack's comparison of genre film and Greek tragedy is that the established order, social and aesthetic, must not be questioned; hence he approves of progenitors and disapproves of antigenre films. By contrast, a classical scholar's chief horizon of interest might be the continued value of ancient themes or forms. But there are many other possible horizons. For example, *Chinatown* has strong thematic connections with film noir, a group of American films made from the 1940s to the early 1960s.[23] Since these films cut across many of the traditional film genres, critics are divided about whether to define film noir by theme (crime, corruption, deception), by visual style (high-contrast lighting, complex composition, symbolic use of camera angles), or by mood (pessimism, alienation, dread).[24] In his fallibility and moral ambiguity Gittes resembles Walter Neff in Billy Wilder's *Double Indemnity* (1944). The dark past from which he cannot escape recalls Jeff Bailey in Jacques Tourneur's *Out of the Past* (1947). Despite his tough appearance, he is vulnerable, as are the main characters in Robert Siodmak's *The Killers* (1946) and *Criss Cross* (1949). In the last-mentioned film, a cast on the protagonist's broken arm functions like the bandage on Jake's nose. The escalation from an individual crime to a political network recalls Fuller's *Pickup on South Street* and *Under-*

23. The bibliography on film noir is extensive. Basic sources include Foster Hirsch, *The Dark Side of the Screen: Film Noir* (1981; rpt. New York: Da Capo, 1983); Frank Krutnik, *In a Lonely Street: Film Noir, Genre, Masculinity* (London: Routledge, 1991); and *Film Noir: An Encyclopedic Reference to the American Style*, ed. Alain Silver and Elizabeth Ward; 3rd ed., rev. James Ursini (Woodstock, N.Y.: Overlook, 1992). *Film Noir Reader 2*, ed. Silver and Ursini (New York: Limelight, 1999), reprints some influential essays. See also Michael L. Stephens, *Film Noir: A Comprehensive, Illustrated Reference to Movies, Terms and Persons* (Jefferson, S.C.: McFarland, 1995).

24. On this see James Naremore, *More Than Night: Film Noir in Its Contexts* (Berkeley: University of California Press, 1998).

world U.S.A. (1961). In *Chinatown*, the alienation of the characters, an increasingly tense and threatening mood, the sense of inevitability, and the film's pessimistic conclusion are all reminiscent of earlier films. So are some of its stylistic features: framing devices (windows, mirrors, windshields, hats, veils), lighting, a complex mise-en-scène, and the musical score. From the very beginning, the thirties-style opening credits— black and white in the standard aspect ratio of 1.33:1, after which the film goes to color and the image expands to widescreen format—send a clear message to the viewer.[25]

The original films noirs also display many of the formal and thematic similarities to Athenian tragedy I have noted in *Chinatown*. Noir acting tends to be somewhat nonnaturalistic, and the cinematography renders it still more so. Extreme close-ups, for example, in which an actor's face fills the screen, produce an effect of alienation rather than intimacy. "The performers most closely identified with the genre have masklike faces, their features frozen not in mid- but in pre-expression. The noir actor is an icon . . . embodying a type."[26] Many noir films use low-key lighting, in which the ratio of key light to fill light creates sharp black-and-white contrasts. Such lighting also renders characters and situations more abstract and suggests that strong, fundamental issues are at stake—that characters must choose between extreme alternatives.

As noted, *Chinatown* employs a "classical" film style rather than the expressionistic techniques characteristic of film noir. Polanski was very conscious of the implications of the mixture of styles and periods he was creating:

> I saw *Chinatown* not as a "retro" piece or conscious imitation of classic movies shot in black and white, but as a film about the thirties seen through the camera eye of the seventies. . . . I wanted the style of the period conveyed by a scrupulously accurate reconstruction of decor, costume, and idiom—not by a deliberate imitation, in 1973, of thirties film techniques.[27]

25. Naremore, *More Than Night*, 196–277, discusses later films influenced by, similar to, and parodying film noir, including *Chinatown* (205–212).

26. Hirsch, *Dark Side of the Screen*, 146.

27. Quoted from Roman Polanski, *Roman by Polanski* (New York: Morrow, 1984), 349. Jameson, "Postmodernism and Consumer Society," in *The Anti-Aesthetic: Essays on Postmodern Culture*, ed. Hal Foster (1983; rpt. New York: New Press, 1998), 111–125, ignores the irony in *Chinatown* and groups it with nostalgia films that "set out to recapture all the atmosphere and stylistic particularities" (116) of past eras and categorizes such films as symptomatic of a society "incapable of dealing with time and history" (117). Naremore, *More Than Night*, 210–212, criticizes this view. Stephen Paul Miller, *The Seventies Now* (Durham, N.C.: Duke University Press, 1999), 65–106, "micro-periodizes" some 1970s films but not *Chinatown*.

164

CLASSICAL

MYTH &

CULTURE

IN THE

CINEMA

This is why he shot the film in color and Panavision. Classic noir films have almost exclusively urban settings. The occasional rural setting suggests an ideal the doomed protagonist cannot reach, as in the finale of Huston's *The Asphalt Jungle* (1950). But landscapes fill the wide screen of *Chinatown*. The "pan and scan" technique used on television and video to reduce widescreen film images destroys this important aspect. Its combination of period setting and echoes of film noir with "classical" film techniques keeps *Chinatown* from being a simple imitation or exercise in nostalgia. Such complexity creates opportunities for tragic irony. The wide screen suggests that escape is possible, the landscapes that nature cannot be contained by Cross's schemes. But these expectations are consistently disappointed. For example, the wide screen appears to offer complete vision, but again and again characters walking into the frame catch Gittes by surprise. In the last scene, the lush sunlit landscapes narrow to dark city streets—the Los Angeles that Cross is creating—and a white car is framed in black night speckled only by neon and blood.

Chinatown also swerves emphatically away from certain noir themes. Many noir films prize the protagonist's individualism and self-reliance, which keep him free from corruption. But Gittes's inability to join with others is a failing. Repeatedly he misses opportunities to make common cause with people who could give him information and help, such as Evelyn, Escobar, and the orange growers. He remains a private I. Asked at one point whether he is alone, he quips: "Isn't everyone?" He lumps others into categories and derides them. He makes a joke out of discrimination against Jews, calls a hood a "midget" and in return has his nose slit, calls an orange grower a "dumb Okie" and is knocked out. He tells a vulgar joke about a man who practices coitus interruptus "like the Chinese" with his wife, only to have her exclaim: "What's the matter with you? You're screwing like a Chinaman!" Jake likes this joke because it shows both that Asians are bizarre and that women are untrustworthy— a lesson he has already "learned" from his profession, as the opening sequence about Curly's unfaithful wife shows. The joke also indicates, quite early in the film, that expected sexual and dramatic climaxes may be deferred or avoided altogether.

In the original films noirs Chinese motifs and characters have a very different meaning. In *The Big Sleep*, for example, Chinese furniture and art is used to signal drugs, criminality, and sexual perversity. In Orson Welles's *The Lady from Shanghai* (1948), the eponymous heroine has lived in China, speaks Chinese, and has a Chinese servant, all indications that she is deceptive and deadly. But in *Chinatown* the Chinese servants and the references to Chinatown say nothing about Asians. They signal

Gittes's prejudices and inability to see with any eyes but his own, and his vision, as we have seen, is inadequate.[28]

Evelyn Mulwray seems a perfect noir "black widow," the mysterious femme fatale who uses her sexuality to entrap men and is finally revealed as a killer.[29] As if he had seen these noir portrayals, Gittes shows his "finesse" by doubting and suspecting Evelyn from the start, accusing her of lying and murder. But Evelyn is complex, not just deceptive. She is smart enough and strong enough to defy her father and to rescue Gittes twice. Her plan for escape would have worked if Gittes had not been so foolish as to create a showdown with Cross. Evelyn is both sensual and nurturing, strong and vulnerable, untrusting rather than untrustworthy. Although sexually unfaithful to her husband, she speaks of him with deep emotion and tries to find his murderer. Gittes's preconceptions about women—for example, that the only relationship possible between them is sexual rivalry over a man—make him unable to understand her. The female and Asian as Other intersect in the figure of Mrs. Mulwray: Faye Dunaway is made up and lit so as to make her look as Asian as possible. As Gittes tells the "Chinese" joke to his operatives, she makes her first appearance, elegant and unsmiling, from behind him. This is the first time Jake is revealed "not only as someone who cannot see correctly but as someone who doesn't know how to listen."[30]

On a few occasions love is proffered as a response to the bleakness of this world. "Do you love your husband?" Gittes asks the fake Mrs. Mulwray. "Of course." "Then go home and forget the whole thing." After rescuing Jake from danger at Mar Vista, Evelyn takes him home and nurses his wound, and they end up making love. These scenes contain the only moments of tenderness and relaxation in the entire film, but Gittes and Evelyn are too scarred and too scared to love. In bed she asks him about himself, but he brushes her off. When she must leave abruptly, she begs him to stay: "I need you here. Trust me this much." Instead, he follows her and breaks the security of Katherine's hiding place. In a long scene in her car she tells him, with great difficulty, that Katherine is her sister. This crucial scene epitomizes Gittes's inability to go beyond appearances ("That's not what it looks like"), his acceptance of easy answers, such as

28. On Asian motifs in film noir, see Naremore, *More Than Night*, 225–229. For a different view see Karen Lynch, "Orientation via Orientalism: Chinatown in Detective Narratives," *Popular Culture Review*, 11 (2000), 13–29. In Towne's screenplay, Mrs. Mulwray's servants have Hispanic names. It was presumably Polanski who increased the Asian presence in *Chinatown*.

29. In general, see *Women in Film Noir*, ed. E. Ann Kaplan, rev. ed. (London: British Film Institute, 1998).

30. Eaton, *Chinatown*, 31.

166

CLASSICAL

MYTH &

CULTURE

IN THE

CINEMA

her too-quick agreement to his suggestion that she is maintaining secrecy because of her sister's affair with her husband, and his distrust of genuine, complex emotions. When she speaks of her husband and weeps, Gittes pulls away and gets out of the car; she asks him to come home with her. With the car window separating them, his lower face in shadow, he replies: "I'm tired, *Mrs. Mulwray,*" implying that she is interested in him only for sex. Evelyn's death is explicitly foreshadowed in this scene. "I don't want to hurt you," says Gittes, and in pain she drops her head forward onto the steering wheel, sounding the horn. In the final scene, the car in which she is rescuing Katherine speeds directly away from the camera down the dark Chinatown street. After Loach fires, the moan of the horn is the signal that his bullet has found its mark. The two scenes indicate that Gittes's inability to make connections with others destroys Evelyn, hurts himself, and keeps Noah Cross in power.

The film's critique of individualism and traditional masculine behavior, its sympathetic treatment of a complex female character, and its revision of Asian motifs all reflect the social values of the time of its production.[31] The explicit political focus of *Chinatown* also marks it as a film of the 1970s, distinguishing it from the concentration on individual and domestic problems usually found in film noir. The conspiracy is depicted in much more specific terms than those in *Pickup on South Street* or in Fritz Lang's *The Big Heat* (1953). Noah Cross's greed and lust for power may be primeval, but in *Chinatown* capitalism justifies and institutionalizes individual rapacity. Depicting 1937 with modern film technology and sociopolitical attitudes, however, does not take *Chinatown* out of history into some timeless place. Instead, it puts 1937 and 1974 in a dialectical relationship that evokes both continuities (capitalism, corruption) and discontinuities (gender roles, attitudes toward race). Thus the film establishes a complex relationship between present and past, just as it does between sight and knowledge. Considered as a historical document, moreover, *Chinatown* suggests that "history" is not some abstract, permanent truth but rather an ever-changing series of attempts to confer meaning on immediate events.

3. History and Tragedy

To counteract the "timeless comparison" that Jauss dismisses, Fredric Jameson suggests that immanent formal analysis of an individual text be

31. Cf. Robert Towne, *Chinatown, The Last Detail: Screenplays* (New York: Grove Press, 1997), xii, and Glenn Man, *Radical Visions: American Film Renaissance, 1967–1976* (Westport, Conn.: Greenwood, 1994), 138–148.

coordinated with "the twin diachronic perspective of the history of forms and the evolution of social life." But another variable should also be considered, he argues: "history itself, as an absent cause."[32] The causes of *Chinatown* are not all that absent. On a biographical level, this was the first film Polanski made in America after his wife Sharon Tate had been brutally murdered in Los Angeles. Writing in his autobiography of his anger, guilt, and pessimism after the murder, Polanski called Los Angeles the most beautiful city in the world, "provided it's seen by night and from a distance."[33] On the historical level, the engineer in charge of the Owens Valley water project, the historical event on which the film's plot is based, was William Mulholland. Unlike the film's similarly named Mulwray, Mulholland was the prime mover of the project; he is memorialized as a founding father of modern California.[34] More immediately, 1974 was the year in which a president of the United States resigned for the first time, forced to do so by revelations about involvement in criminal activity, misuse of funds, and a massive cover-up conspiracy. In the same year the United States was still enmeshed in a politically and morally questionable war in Vietnam, whose huge cost in money and lives had deeply divided the country. The inability of American leaders to comprehend a culture completely different from their own and to learn from the past led to a repetition of many of the mistakes the French colonial powers had made. The guerrilla war waged by the Asian enemy resembled the "Chinese" sexual technique of Gittes's joke; since this *bellum interruptum* did not fit Western ideas of confrontation, it seemed mysterious and interminable to the American public. Gittes's mixture of altruism and selfishness, his misplaced heroics, and his inability to get beyond his own limited perspective make him a figure representative of American involvement in Vietnam. The literary and cinematic genre of American history has traditionally been romance. *Chinatown* rewrites it as tragedy but deprives us of Aristotelian catharsis.

In Athenian tragedy, the playwrights' use of myth is often regarded to have been a technique of avoiding topical political and ideological mean-

32. The quotations are from Jameson, "Magical Narratives," 105 and 146.

33. Polanski, *Roman by Polanski*, 348.

34. Towne used Carey McWilliams, *Southern California Country: An Island on the Land* (New York: Duell, Sloan and Pearce, 1946), as his source. William L. Kahrl, *Water and Power: The Conflict over Los Angeles' Water Supply in the Owens Valley* (Berkeley: University of California Press, 1982), provides a full discussion of the project. Mike Davis, *City of Quartz: Excavating the Future in Los Angeles* (1990; rpt. New York: Vintage, 1992), 114, calls history in *Chinatown* "more syncretic than fictional." See also Eaton, *Chinatown*, 22–26. See now also Catherine Mulholland, *William Mulholland and the Rise of Los Angeles* (Berkeley: University of California Press, 2000).

ings. But myth allowed them to deal with significant issues in complex ways, and they had considerable leeway in shaping their treatment of traditional material to suit their ends. The mythical settings of tragedy establish an ironic relationship between present and past; between Athens and, for example, Thebes, between the Peloponnesian War and the Trojan War, between audience and characters. So does the period setting of *Chinatown*. Jean-Pierre Vernant, following German scholar Walter Nestle, has observed that

> tragedy is born when myth starts to be considered from the point of view of a citizen. But it is not only the world of myth which loses its consistency and dissolves in this focus. By the same token the world of the city is called into question and its fundamental values are challenged by the ensuing debate.[35]

Artistic products that deal directly with contemporary issues can be, or at least can be seen to be, reductive and tendentious. As long as it continued, films on the Vietnam War would have been regarded as tracts, as was *The Green Berets* (1968), directed by a right-wing John Wayne. But after the fall of Saigon filmmakers could use history as myth, and films about the war poured out.[36]

As I argued earlier, a comparison of ancient drama with contemporary film expands our understanding of both. The abundant amount of films means that any individual film must be considered in the context of others—in a generic tradition and in a historical context—rather than in isolation. And that abundance can remind us that the surviving Greek tragedies are only a small fraction of the total body of the works produced. Our judgments of surviving plays need to be tempered by whatever information we can obtain about lost works. Moreover, resources mainly unavailable for ancient drama, such as production records and contemporary responses, make us aware of the multiplicity of factors that influence a work's meaning and help us reject positivistic and univocal interpretations. Not least, film reminds us that drama is performance. For Aristotle, as for many modern academics, drama means only the literary text: "Tragedy fulfills its function even without a public performance and actors. . . . when it is merely read the tragic force is clearly manifested" (*Poetics* 1450b19–20 and 1462a11–13). A film critic who followed this approach would ignore the finished film and discuss only its screenplay.

35. Vernant, "Tensions and Ambiguity in Greek Tragedy," in Vernant and Vidal-Naquet, *Myth and Tragedy in Ancient Greece*, 29–48; quotation at 33.

36. On the Vietnam War in film see *From Hanoi to Hollywood: The Vietnam War in American Film*, ed. Linda Dittmar and Gene Michaud (New Brunswick, N.J.: Rutgers University Press, 1990).

168

CLASSICAL

MYTH &

CULTURE

IN THE

CINEMA

Contemporary performance criticism of ancient drama, by contrast, examines how all aspects of performance affect a script's meaning.[37]

The "classical" features of *Chinatown* I evoked in the first part of this essay must not be reduced to items in a flat Aristotelian checklist. Characters' moral ambiguity and a dynamic interplay between character and plot appeal to both the audience's intellect and their emotions. A complex web of causality precludes resolution into binary oppositions such as guilt versus innocence or free will versus predestination. The film's "classical" features are precisely those that prohibit closure. Yet the question of Cross's incest with Evelyn shows how attractive an easy resolution can be. Jake asks Evelyn: "He raped you?" She shakes her head—not an unambiguous "no" but certainly not a clear "yes." Towne did not intend the incest to be regarded as rape. His screenplay contains the following dialogue for Evelyn, which was omitted from the film: "he had a breakdown . . . the dam broke . . . my mother died . . . he became a little boy . . . I was fifteen . . . he'd ask me what to eat for breakfast, what clothes to wear! It happened . . . then I ran away."[38] Yet over the years many critics have insisted that Cross raped his daughter. By defending Evelyn's virtue they reduce her agency, her character, and the moral complexity of the situation. Here again we see the influence of history. In the twenty-five years since *Chinatown* appeared, in parent–child incest the adult has come to be regarded as completely responsible. In the 1990s, a screenwriter would probably treat this incest as rape. In Towne's rather sardonic words: "Today, of course, Evelyn Mulwray would go on 'Oprah' as an abused child, talk about what a bad scene it was banging her pappy, launch a huge lawsuit against Noah Cross, his partners and corporations, and probably the DWP."[39]

Polanski did not want to induce in his audiences the "calm" that easy answers provide. Towne's original script called for Evelyn to kill her father and escape to Mexico with her daughter, but Polanski insisted:

> if *Chinatown* was to be special, not just another thriller where the good guys triumph in the final reel, Evelyn had to die. Its dramatic impact would be lost unless audiences left their seats with a sense of outrage at the injustice of it all.[40]

37. Oliver Taplin, *Greek Tragedy in Action* (Berkeley: University of California Press, 1978; rpt. 1979), and David Wiles, *Tragedy in Athens: Performance Space and Theatrical Meaning* (Cambridge: Cambridge University Press, 1997; rpt. 1999), offer different kinds of performance criticism of ancient Athenian drama.

38. Towne, *Chinatown*, 129.

39. Towne, *Chinatown*, xiii.

40. Polanski, *Roman by Polanski*, 348. On Towne's reaction to Polanski's ending see Pope, *Good Scripts, Bad Scripts*, 192. Reviewers' reactions suggest that Polanski's viola-

170

CLASSICAL

MYTH &

CULTURE

IN THE

CINEMA

The conclusion, like that of many Athenian tragedies, gives no resolution to the questions it has raised about understanding, responsibility, and justice. In the very last shot of the film, as the residents of Chinatown gather to witness the disaster, Duffy and Walsh pull Gittes away down the dark street. The camera rises for the film's only crane shot, offering the audience the "Olympian" position of distance and superiority to Gittes that he took to others early in the film. But here again such distance quite literally keeps us from seeing clearly as Gittes disappears into the darkness of both Chinatown and *Chinatown*. The film insists that audience members create their own meaning. This is perhaps its most "classical" feature.

Pace Aristotle, genres, including tragedy, are located in history. Tzvetan Todorov observes:

> The existence of certain genres in a society and their absence in another reveal a central ideology, and enable us to establish it with considerable certainty. It is not chance that the epic is possible during one era, the novel during another.

Jameson concurs that the presence or absence of a particular genre at a particular historical moment "alerts us to the historical ground . . . in which the original structure was meaningful."[41] Scholarly discussions of the historical context of Athenian tragedy have often focused on the state's sponsorship of the dramatic festivals and have linked it to the democratic form of government in Athens.[42] The tragic qualities of film noir have frequently been traced to American postwar guilt and readjustment anxieties, especially in regard to gender roles. Other important American films of the same period as *Chinatown*, such as Francis Ford Coppola's *The Godfather* (1972) and *The Godfather, Part II* (1974), Sidney Lumet's *Dog Day Afternoon* (1975), and Martin Scorsese's *Taxi Driver* (1976) share *Chinatown*'s tragic characteristics and its lack of resolution. By contrast, Curtis Hanson's *L. A. Confidential* (1997), which

tion of generic conventions succeeded in provoking his audiences. For a list of reviews see Gretchen Bisplinghoff and Virginia Wright Wexman, *Roman Polanski: A Guide to References and Resources* (Boston: Hall, 1979), 78–92.

41. Tzvetan Todorov, "The Origin of Genres," *New Literary History*, 8 (1976), 159–170; quotation at 164; Jameson, "Magical Narratives," 146. Todorov's essay is reprinted in his *Genres in Discourse*, tr. Catherine Porter (Cambridge: Cambridge University Press, 1990; rpt. 1993), 13–26.

42. See, for example, Gerald F. Else, *The Origin and Early Form of Greek Tragedy* (Cambridge: Harvard University Press, 1965; rpt. 1972), and Simon Goldhill, "The Great Dionysia and Civic Ideology," in *Nothing to Do with Dionysos?* 97–129.

superficially resembles *Chinatown*, is a simplistic melodrama with a preposterous happy ending.[43]

What were the historical grounds in the United States of the early 1970s
and in the Athens of the late fifth century B.C. that made tragedy as a genre
meaningful to artists and audiences? Among other possible answers is the
following parallel. Each of these states had taken the lead in glorious wars
that brought about the defeat of foreign powers considered formidable
and evil, the Persian Empire in the case of Athens and Nazi Germany, Italy,
and Japan in the case of the United States. Both Athens and the United
States then became embroiled in a war that divided the populace, toppled
leaders, and shook the moral foundation of the state itself. These are historical grounds when human nature can seem corrupt and human vision
flawed, when even good intentions lead only to disaster.

In these circumstances, genres that provide a frame for self-scrutiny
are likely to flourish. But tragedy is more than a structure for examination and judgment. Its combination of history and myth transcends particular individuals and societies. If the cosmos itself is seen as being
guided by inscrutable, possibly malevolent forces, human agency is
not completely responsible for the course of events. Tragedy, which provides a framework for self-scrutiny, judgment, and outrage, also offers
consolation.

43. See Naremore, *More Than Night*, 275–276.

VIII

Tricksters and Typists:
9 to 5 as Aristophanic Comedy

James R. Baron

Nothing in this chapter is intended to put forth any claim that the creators of the film *9 to 5* consciously copied or imitated Aristophanes' comedies in general or his *Lysistrata* in particular. Some of the evidence presented here may suggest such a hypothesis to bolder scholars, but there is no proof of any direct connection in the form of identifiable quotations, unquestionable borrowings, or clear, if indirect, references. Nevertheless, it would not surprise me to learn that the scriptwriters had some knowledge of or contact with Aristophanes' plays, perhaps even with contemporary scholarship about them. Rather, what is important is the pure comparison of shared formal features and main characters and the common relationship of the latter to the lovable scoundrels of the trickster tales that are a well-documented feature of many cultures, including that of Hollywood.

This essay consists of two rather distinct parts. The first will focus on formal and stylistic aspects of the film in order to demonstrate that *9 to 5* matches not one particular ancient play but the typical features of Old Greek Comedy that scholars have inferred from the surviving plays of Aristophanes and, indeed, that the film matches them at least as well as many of the plays of Aristophanes do themselves, varied in nature as these are.[1] The second part attempts to demonstrate that the three main female

---

1. K. J. Dover, *Aristophanic Comedy* (Berkeley: University of California Press, 1972), 66–77, and Francis Macdonald Cornford, *The Origin of Attic Comedy* (1914; rpt. Ann Arbor: University of Michigan Press, 1993), 27–77, present two very different approaches to the analysis of Aristophanes' basic structural design. Although the theories of the Cambridge School, including Cornford's, have been out of fashion with the majority of classical scholars for some time because of their narrow focus on fertility ritual as a source of Attic drama, their great influence on creative writers and artists earlier in this century continues to produce echoes in literature and film. Aristophanes' *Acharnians* and *Birds*

characters of *9 to 5* are not just typical Aristophanic heroes but correspond closely to the three principal characters of *Lysistrata*.

1. *9 to 5* and the Comedy of Aristophanes

In the critical study of film genres, as with that of the categories of ancient drama, the actual products seldom fit perfectly into the schemata scholars devise; this is certainly the case with *9 to 5* (1980).[2] Although the shenanigans of the film's three heroines are as zany as those of the heroines of classic screwball comedies, romance plays no part in the plot, whereas it is essential to its resolution in the screwball genre. *9 to 5* steals several stock scenes from the tradition of clowning and slapstick; nevertheless, these are by no means the essence of the film but hold the same place they occupy in the plays of Aristophanes, as shall become clear. *9 to 5* is not predominantly an ironic comedy, either. Viewers do not experience the thrill of superior knowledge of an omniscient spectator, as with the plays of Plautus and his imitators, nor do they perceive the ironic form of complex sociopolitical commentary discussed by Gerald Mast when he classifies such diverse films as Ingmar Bergman's *Smiles of a Summer Night* (1955) and Stanley Kubrick's *Dr. Strangelove* (1963) as ironic.[3] Finally, it would certainly be difficult to fit *9 to 5* into the branches of the "dialogue" or "literary" traditions of film comedy derived from the high comic stage. *9 to 5* is a film that has some elements of most of these types, but they are blended in much the same measures as were the comedies of Aristophanes from the late fifth and early fourth centuries B.C., which also

---

are the plays that best fulfill scholars' paradigms. Old Greek Comedy, as a term used in classical scholarship, refers to the style of comic drama staged in Athens from c. 476 B.C. until the early fourth century B.C., in contrast to New Comedy, which begins in the late fourth century B.C. and has much more in common with situation comedy and comedy of manners. The sparse fragments surviving from Middle Comedy indicate a period of transition, with no distinctive or distinguishing traits other than a possible tendency to prefer plots that burlesque myth and the disappearance of choral odes written especially for each play.

2. Directed by Colin Higgins, screenplay by Higgins and Patricia Resnick, story by Resnick. The title sometimes appears alphabetically as *Nine to Five*. To those with no previous reading in the area of film genres I suggest as a starting point *Film Genre: Theory and Criticism*, ed. Barry Keith Grant (Metuchen, N.J.: Scarecrow Press, 1977). Gerald Mast, *The Comic Mind: Comedy and the Movies*, 2nd ed. (Chicago: University of Chicago Press, 1979), is a more specialized examination of film comedy.

3. Mast, *The Comic Mind*, 331–337.

share with *9 to 5* certain other features of form and content.[4] My purpose is to demonstrate how closely *9 to 5* corresponds to an eclectic view of the form and style of Aristophanes' plays, the sort of general picture we might get by reading the most readily available translations and commentaries.

174

CLASSICAL

MYTH &

CULTURE

IN THE

CINEMA

One of the most distinctive features of Aristophanes' comedies is the outrageous, fantastic "happy idea" or "grand scheme," which provides what little there is of a plot.[5] The happy idea may be presented to the audience in several different ways. In some plays, such as *Lysistrata* and *Frogs*, the comic heroine or hero has already conceived the scheme before the play begins and merely spells it out in the prologue and first episode; in others, such as *Wasps*, *Birds*, and *Clouds*, the hero begins the play with a plan, which, however, is dropped in favor of a new option or undergoes as many metamorphoses as do the characters themselves in response to opposition and opportunities. Like *Acharnians*, *9 to 5* is in a third category. The prologue only serves to present the main character or characters, who initially have no clue about a solution to their distress but then invent a fantastic scheme before our very eyes as an extemporaneous response to the forces oppressing them. In *9 to 5*, what might pass for the equivalents of an Aristophanic prologue and *parodos*, the processional ode sung by the chorus as they enter, are interwoven as the main characters are awakened at the beginning of a workday, each by a style of alarm clock appropriate to her personality; they then join the throng of clerical workers whose pendulum-like, synchronized legs are emphasized by several sidewalk-level shots interspersed among other rush-hour scenes during the opening credits. There is also a bit of foreshadowing of the critical role that coffee, especially spilled coffee, will play in the plot, but there is not the slightest hint of any grand scheme until the film has run through nearly half of its length. Likewise, as Kenneth McLeish has pointed out, performance of the parodos, the *agôn* (mock debate or trial), and the *parabasis* (choral address to the audience) could easily fill the first half of

4. Kenneth McLeish, *The Theatre of Aristophanes* (New York: Taplinger, 1980), 15–22 and 64–66, examines how farce, comedy, and other forms blend in Aristophanes. Much of what McLeish says of Aristophanes' plays also applies to *9 to 5*, but the film is not unique in this regard: Dover, *Aristophanic Comedy*, 237–240, discusses Aristophanic aspects of Peter Ustinov's play *The Love of Four Colonels* (1951) and Jacques Feyder's film *La Kermesse héroïque* (1935). Louis E. Lord, *Aristophanes: His Plays and His Influence* (1925; rpt. New York: Cooper Square, 1963), 75–175, and Alexes Solomos, *The Living Aristophanes*, tr. Solomos and Marvin Felheim (Ann Arbor: University of Michigan Press, 1974; rpt. 1982), 244–276, provide useful surveys of the high points of Aristophanes' influence since the Renaissance.

5. For a discussion of the progression from reality to fantasy in Aristophanes' structural design and of the question of why the happy idea is acceptable to the audience see McLeish, *The Theatre of Aristophanes*, 64–78.

the performance time of some of Aristophanes' plays before the action becomes frenetic.[6] Only when the trio of heroines of *9 to 5* is enjoying its first *kômos* (revel), which begins with alcohol at Charlie's Bar and progresses to "Maui Wowie" (according to the film, a premium grade of marijuana) at Doralee Rhodes's apartment, does each of them muster the courage to describe to the others her individual fantasy about overthrowing the old order of the office in a truly Aristophanic combination of binding, castration, and death symbols.[7] The *kômos* in a play of Aristophanes frequently comes near the end. It is a scene in which the hero or heroine abandons inhibitions and often sobriety to celebrate the restoration of the pleasures of peacetime, wine, food, and sometimes sex, as a result of the victory of the happy idea. *Acharnians*, however, is an exception that provides a close parallel to *9 to 5*. Dikaiopolis starts a celebration of the Rural Dionysia early in the play, but he is interrupted by the reality of the threats of violence from the Acharnian chorus and does not complete his celebration until the very end. In *9 to 5*, the joyous intoxication, good food, and fantasizing of the first revel give way quickly to the reality of another day's drudgery at the office. Like Dikaiopolis, these women do not drink the toast of ultimate victory until a second revel at the end of the film.

Although their fantasies are revealed in the first revel scene, no unified plan of action begins to emerge until after the end of the next workday when, along with forceful reminders of the injustices and irritations they have been enduring, the accidental—at least on the conscious level—substitution of rat poison for sweetener in the boss's coffee forces the three to extemporize responses that resemble the fantasies expressed in the revel. This is true to the Aristophanic model. As McLeish points out, the Aristophanic hero moves through a gradual progression from alienation to action in the implementation of his or her idea.[8] The three then begin a series of maneuvers which overthrow the authoritarian, patriarchal, and patronizing establishment, represented by their boss, Franklin Hart, and create a new order in the office, using the tools they each understand best as well as whatever else falls to hand, as Aristophanic heroes and hero-

6. McLeish, *The Theatre of Aristophanes*, 50–53.

7. On the festival aspects of old comedy see Kenneth J. Reckford, *Aristophanes' Old-and-New Comedy*, vol. 1: *Six Essays in Perspective* (Chapel Hill: University of North Carolina Press, 1987), 3–52 and 443–498. For the importance of the overthrow of the old order and the binding, emasculation, or death of the old king in the ritual theory of the origins of Greek drama see Cornford, *The Origin of Attic Comedy*, 3–55, but see also the more modern and moderate views of Reckford, 39–42, 447–448, and 496–497.

8. McLeish, *The Theatre of Aristophanes*, 64–71.

176

CLASSICAL

MYTH &

CULTURE

IN THE

CINEMA

ines generally do.[9] The scheme develops in three stages. First, they drive Mr. Hart, bound and gagged, to his house to try to persuade him that the poisoned coffee was an accident. When that fails, they hold him prisoner (still in his own house) while trying to get the necessary evidence to prove that he is guilty of embezzlement so that they can blackmail him into accepting their story about the poison. Finally, having usurped his place at the office to conceal his absence, they begin to enact the reforms that lead to their final triumph.

Once set on their course of revolt, they exult in *ponêria* (the behavior of scoundrels and mythic tricksters, discussed later) and in the breaking of taboos and legal and social barriers. The prime examples of such amoral conduct in Aristophanes' plays are Dikaiopolis in *Acharnians*, who proceeds, once his own victory is secure, to take unfair advantage of others suffering the same distress from which he has just escaped, and Pisthetairos of *Birds*, who uses his new-found strategic advantages to establish himself as a virtual tyrant of the universe, the very essence of the trickster myth in many of its versions (see *Acharnians* 729–958, *Birds* 851–1765). The success of the ponêria of the three heroines of *9 to 5* also leads to a final revel and the proclamation of the beginning of a new regime, grown directly out of their fantastic schemes in perfectly Aristophanic fashion.

Some scholars think that the parabasis, the choral address to the audience, is the chief distinguishing feature of Aristophanes' style. The function of the chorus common to all Greek drama is to sing songs from the point of view of an ideal spectator and thus to deepen the stage audience's understanding of what has been enacted and to prepare the mood for what is to follow. In addition to this, the choruses of most of Aristophanes' plays at some point break the flow of the action to address the audience directly, both as a group and through their leader. Their words are usually something of an editorial, either praising the merits of the comic poet or offering advice of a popular sort on practical social and political problems.[10] Some may think it difficult to find a parabasis in a film in which the chorus, if we dare use that term for the roomful of clerical office workers, does little but process paperwork and the choral leader, Margaret Foster, is an alcoholic typist, but we should not underestimate her importance in carry-

9. On the women of *Lysistrata* and their use of women's expertise to end the war see Jeffrey Henderson, "*Lysistrata*: The Play and Its Themes," *Yale Classical Studies*, 26 (1980), 153–218, especially 167–169.

10. See Reckford, *Aristophanes' Old-and-New Comedy*, 187–191 and 483–491, and G. M. Sifakis, *Parabasis and Animal Choruses: A Contribution to the History of Attic Comedy* (London: Athlone Press, 1971), 7–70; also Cornford, *The Origin of Attic Comedy*, 91–100, and Dover, *Aristophanic Comedy*, 49–53.

ing on the ancient chorus's dramatic function as both a representative and shaper of audience opinion. Although her comment: "Sure, let's all revolt," is a sarcastic sigh of resignation and a clever bit of foreshadowing rather than a call to arms, she interjects "Atta girl!" with increasing enthusiasm each time one of the three main characters storms out of the office toward Charlie's Bar after a series of individual confrontations with the boss. She thus provides a necessary nudge of encouragement just before the beginning of the first revel, which starts the process of metamorphosis of the three from resentful workers to revolutionary reformers. It is true, nevertheless, that a proper formal parabasis is impossible in any dramatic tradition concerned with dramatic illusion, something that bothered the Greeks very little.[11]

If, however, we change our focus from form to content, we find at least one genuine Aristophanic precedent for exactly what happens in *9 to 5* in one of Aristophanes' own frequent deviations from the hypothetical structural schemata that scholars impose on his surviving works. In *Lysistrata*, the formal parabasis (lines 614–705) seems, to judge from the text, to have been a reversion to the kind of stripping, flashing, and "grossing out" by insults that may have been typical of the parabases of Aristophanes' predecessors or even competitors, or of an earlier ritual-and-revel procession of a Mardi Gras or Mummers' Day sort that evolved into or at least contributed its spirit to Old Comedy. The presentation of topical and often partisan advice to the citizens, however, which forms the usual content of Aristophanes' own parabases, is given by Lysistrata herself in the striking "wool carding" speech (567–586), a part of her debate (agôn) with the Athenian *proboulos* (commissioner or magistrate).[12] Similarly, in *9 to 5* Violet Newstead leads the chairman of the board, as awesome a figure as a real Athenian proboulos, on a tour of the office, now rejuvenated by the women's reforms as successfully as the city of Athens is in Aristophanes' most optimistic finales. Violet's description of these reforms takes on a certain note of political oratory in her sudden change of tone to patriotic realism, a move typical of Aristophanes' parabases and of Lysistrata's speech to the proboulos, and eloquently presents the women's specific political agenda. But in formal terms, because of its position in the film and its triumphant tone, the tour of the office might better be

11. See Sifakis, *Parabasis and Animal Choruses*, 7–22, and William E. Gruber, *Comic Theaters: Studies in Performance and Audience Response* (Athens: University of Georgia Press, 1986), 11–41.

12. For an analysis of the advice to the city in this speech and of the formal parabasis of the play see Douglas M. MacDowell, *Aristophanes and Athens: An Introduction to the Plays* (Oxford: Oxford University Press, 1995), 235–243.

compared to the victory procession leading up to the final revel of an Aristophanic comedy.[13]

178

CLASSICAL

MYTH &

CULTURE

IN THE

CINEMA

This same appeal to consider content more critical than form might also help us find the agôn of *9 to 5*. Whether or not the agôn originated in some sort of ritual combat, in Aristophanes' plays it has been transformed into a formalized verbal contest or battle of wits between two characters or between the hero and all or part of the chorus.[14] The veneer of realism of all the parts of the film preceding the first revel, mentioned earlier, rules out the kind of parodies of courtroom rhetoric that distinguish an Aristophanic agôn. But in a more general sense of the Greek word, whose literal meaning is "contest" or "struggle," the entire first half of the film is a struggle of wills between Mr. Hart and the three individual women, each with a separate cause for complaint. There are brief moments of verbal confrontation between Ms. Newstead and Mr. Hart and Mrs. Rhodes and Mr. Hart, and these intensify into two separate major confrontations of an agonistic character after the revelation that Ms. Newstead's expected promotion has been given to a less qualified man. Ms. Bernly meanwhile is drawn into the struggle by her sympathy for a typist fired for revealing her salary. Although isolated by false impressions of one another in the first part of the film, the three women now discover a common bond in their shared feeling of oppression at the beginning of the first revel, the centerpiece and turning point of the film, which follows immediately after these confrontations. Not only the modern expectation that the dramatic illusion be preserved but also the tripling of heroines has altered and expanded the manner in which the typical material of an agôn, the essential conflict of the drama, is presented throughout the film's first half.

The Aristophanic hero or heroine has to deal with several specific kinds of antagonists. Three of the most important types are the Old King, the Impostor, and the Informer.[15] The Old King is the leading representative of the oppressive old order, who must be driven out, defeated, emasculated, or slain to make room for the new springtime of happiness. The Impostors impede the progress of the happy idea in various ways. Some resist its advance in the name of the old order, but others try to turn the success of the hero to their own selfish advantage. Informers spy on the hero for the sake of the scheme's antagonists. The Old King of *9 to 5* is Mr. Hart, who also fulfills the Impostor role by stealing credit for the "color coding of accounts" idea developed by Ms. Newstead. Rosalind

13. I owe this point to my colleague Lewis W. Leadbeater.

14. On the typical Aristophanic *agôn* see Dover, *Aristophanic Comedy*, 66–68, and Cornford, *The Origin of Attic Comedy*, 27–46.

15. See Cornford, *The Origin of Attic Comedy*, 13–15 and 115–133.

Keith, Mr. Hart's administrative assistant, is a genuine Informer who nearly nips the plot in the bud and is suppressed by being sent to Aspen for French lessons, just as the Athenian informer is crated and shipped like a precious vase to Boeotia by Dikaiopolis in Aristophanes (*Acharnians* 910–958). The slapstick scenes between the hero and his or her adversaries that are typical of the second half of Aristophanes' comedies are exactly where they should be in *9 to 5*. The hilarious theft and return of an anonymous corpse mistaken for Mr. Hart's, his subsequent abduction and escape attempts, not to mention the later snags such as the constant delays in acquiring the Ajax Warehouse inventory, the return of Mrs. Hart and Judy Bernly's ex-husband, and Mr. Hart's refilling of the warehouse—all these are Aristophanic threats to the happy idea and are met with an increasingly confident application of ponêria by the trio.

In spite of the problems presented by Mr. Hart's attempt to restore himself to power, the three women win their victory and celebrate the festive achievement of "fantasy triumphant," as McLeish calls it, in a second revel worthy of Aristophanes' final scenes. They enjoy a bottle of champagne expropriated from their ex-boss in the office that was formerly his but is soon to be officially occupied by Ms. Newstead upon her promotion. The final credits begin to roll with a series of texts that present an account of the aftermath, a set of transformations as mythic and Aristophanic as the play-long metamorphoses of the main characters of Aristophanes' *Birds*. Mr. Hart is transferred to Brazil, where he is then kidnapped by a tribe of Amazons. (Aristophanes would have loved such mythical-geographical confusion.) Doralee Rhodes achieves fame to the point of heroic immortality as a country-and-western singer; since the part is played by Dolly Parton, this now does amount to a humorous violation of dramatic illusion not unlike some of Aristophanes' references to the real people of Athens in the original audience or cast. Finally, in accordance with the great efforts which F. M. Cornford exerted to find some slim evidence of a *hieros gamos* (a sacred marriage of the new king and queen) at the end of every Aristophanic comedy, the text reveals that Judy Bernly eventually joins in holy matrimony with the Xerox representative.[16]

It is impossible to make any comparison to the plays of Aristophanes without dealing with Old Comedy's abundance of sexual and scatological humor and slang.[17] *9 to 5* has no shortage of the sort of material that many

---

16. On the sacred marriage in the ritual theory see Cornford, *The Origin of Attic Comedy*, 56–66.

17. Jeffrey Henderson, *The Maculate Muse: Obscene Language in Attic Comedy*, 2nd ed. (New York: Oxford University Press, 1991), provides an exhaustive study of the sexual

180

CLASSICAL

MYTH &

CULTURE

IN THE

CINEMA

people take as the first meaning of the adjective "Aristophanic," if in somewhat subtler forms of expression. Near the beginning of the film, Ms. Newstead expresses her opinion of her boss by holding a manila folder over the nameplate on Franklin Hart's door so that only the letters F and ART are visible and responds to Rosalind Keith's orders to post an oppressive, authoritarian memo with the exclamation: "I know just where to stick it." She also suddenly and unexpectedly tells the innocent, friendly candy striper at the hospital: "Piss off!" Mr. Hart's favorite expression of surprise is "Holy shit!" (He encounters numerous surprises in the course of the film.) Upon her return from six weeks of intensive French lessons, Rosalind Keith discovers the three heroines celebrating the overthrow of her beloved boss and mutters: "Holy *merde!*"

The most prominent sexual theme is castration.[18] Mr. Hart welcomes Ms. Bernly to the company with a speech about the teamwork needed to "cut the balls off the competition," which is what the team of three women do to him, metaphorically and symbolically. Doralee Rhodes responds to her discovery that Mr. Hart has been making false claims about his success in seducing her with a threat to get her pistol from her purse and to metamorphosize him "from a rooster to a hen with one shot." Her rapid, slashing gestures while saying this graphically emphasize the nature of the threat. When she has usurped his identity by forging his signature to enact the reforms in the office, she conceals his absence from Rosalind Keith by leaving a burning cigar, a traditional symbol of male potency, on his desk and then stubs it out when the ruse succeeds. Furthermore, anyone familiar with the oversized leather phalluses worn during the original performances of Aristophanes' plays should not be startled by the position and angle in front of his fly at which Mr. Hart holds the bottle of champagne presented to him by the chairman of the board, a prize he soon surrenders to Mrs. Rhodes as his emasculating defeat is completed.[19]

---

and scatological vocabulary of Aristophanes and its function in the plays. For different views on the nature of the breaking of taboos and the religious and social reasons for this see Dover, *Aristophanic Comedy*, 38–41; McLeish, *The Theatre of Aristophanes*, 93–108; Reckford, *Aristophanes' Old-and-New Comedy*, 14–15; and Cedric H. Whitman, *Aristophanes and the Comic Hero* (Cambridge: Harvard University Press, 1964), 209–210.

18. On the subtleties of castration and impotence versus erection humor in *Lysistrata* see Dover, *Aristophanic Comedy*, 150–161.

19. Popping corks and champagne bottles foaming over have been symbols for sexual climax almost from the beginnings of filmmaking. Hollywood has never been at a loss to find ways of symbolizing or suggesting a phallus while avoiding censorship troubles or outcries from respectable citizens or organizations—As an obvious *alazôn* (braggart, charlatan) type of Impostor, Franklin Hart invites comparison with Pyrgopolynices of Plautus' *Miles gloriosus (The Braggart Soldier)* and all his derivatives in the later European comic tradition. Pyrgopolynices is threatened with castration at the end of the play, a traditional

Mrs. Rhodes, upon learning that her coworkers think that she is having an affair with Mr. Hart, exclaims: "They think I'm screwin' the boss!"—an echo of Ms. Newstead's earlier "She is bangin' the boss," with its Aristophanic alliteration.[20]

Other elements of Aristophanes' complex techniques for eliciting laughter are present in the film. The three fantasies of the first kômos each parody a major film genre—jungle adventure films, westerns, and animated cartoons—but there are also several points of parody of stage tragedy, one of Aristophanes' own favorite targets.[21] During an argument regarding marijuana, her son says to Ms. Newstead about his grandmother: "She doesn't understand moderation" and: "Harm springs from excess," both Apollonian maxims from the moralizing world of Greek tragedy; the three women exult in breaking these precepts during their first revel. In a similar manner, Dikaiopolis in *Acharnians* and Pisthetairos in *Birds* violate social restraints in exhilaration at the success of their schemes. Another genuinely Aristophanic moment is the mock-tragic crescendo of fears for the future spoken at the hospital by the panicky Ms. Newstead, which culminates in bathos: "I'm no fool—I've killed the boss—you think they're not going to fire me for a thing like that?" The effect closely matches the sudden change of tone at the end of the mock-tragic dialogue at *Lysistrata* 706–715. After lamenting in the most tragic of terms and poetic styles the dangerous loss of resolve to continue the sex strike among her corps of Athenian women, Lysistrata suddenly sums up the problem with the shocking expression *"binêtiômen!"*[22]

There is also some typically Aristophanic burlesque of myth in *9 to 5*. Besides the reference to Amazons in the epilogue, Ms. Bernly's fantasy of revenge clearly derives from the tale of Artemis and Actaeon: Hart (note the deer name), a sport hunter whose office wall is decorated with

---

Roman punishment for adultery with a citizen's wife. For Aristophanes' Lamachos of *Acharnians* as a comparable braggart soldier see Solomos, *The Living Aristophanes*, 78–85. I will treat the none-too-subtle castration aspects of Ms. Bernly's fantasy later.

20. The paperback novel derived from the filmscript—Thom Racina, *Nine to Five* (New York: Bantam Books, 1980)—contains many more examples of castration, phallic, and ejaculation humor as well as explicit sexist remarks by both male and female characters, but it seems impossible to determine whether these items are the scriptwriters' ideas, perhaps cut to maintain a PG rating, or are additions by the novelist, as I suspect.

21. On Aristophanic parodies of tragedy see Dover, *Aristophanic Comedy*, 72–77, 162–164, and 183–189. I examine the parody aspects of the fantasies later.

22. With apologies to those whose sensibilities may be offended: Given the grammatical voice, the desiderative form, and the crudity of the verb, as amply demonstrated by Henderson, *The Maculate Muse*, 151–153, the only linguistically accurate and contextually appropriate translation of this word is: "We wanna fuck!"

182

CLASSICAL

MYTH &

CULTURE

IN THE

CINEMA

a mounted deer head, becomes the hunted as she pursues him around the office with a double-barreled shotgun after he takes refuge there to escape pursuit by the other office workers and their bloodhounds, as it were.[23] He runs helplessly back and forth, changing directions after each blast like a mechanical animal in a shooting gallery.

It is not only possible but, indeed, easy to point to equivalents in *9 to 5* for many of the important typical features of an Aristophanic play. There is a fantastic plot based on a wild scheme and dependent on plenty of ponêria, a kômos or two, a series of agônes, something resembling one of Aristophanes' own alternatives to the parabasis, and a thoroughly Aristophanic festive close. In addition to these structural features we can find bawdy humor, bathos, parody of ancient myth and modern film, and just the right kinds of antagonists. Indeed, *9 to 5* fits the formal paradigm better than many of Aristophanes' plays do themselves.

2. *9 to 5* and *Lysistrata*

The character types of Aristophanes' plays have been studied by scholars from ancient times down to the present.[24] Underlying substantial variations, there remains one common thread: that the Aristophanic hero is, in varying degrees, a "tolerable scoundrel"—tolerable partly because he or she fulfills the escapist fantasies widely attested in fairy tales and especially in the comic forms of the trickster myth (Reynard the Fox, Till Eulenspiegel, Robin Hood, Nanabozho, and the Roadrunner, for example) and partly because the hero usually begins the play as the innocent victim of an oppressive social situation and progresses from credible idealism to fantastic ponêria in response to highly unfair treatment or the opposition of genuinely outrageous scoundrels or impostors.[25]

23. Compare the myth of Actaeon and Diana in Ovid, *Metamorphoses* 3.131–255.

24. McLeish, *The Theatre of Aristophanes*, 53–56 and 127–143, provides a compact treatment and a convenient chart of the stock types as they appear in Aristophanes' plays. The comic hero has been the special focus of several monographs; see Whitman, *Aristophanes and the Comic Hero*, and Dana Ferrin Sutton, *Self and Society in Aristophanes* (Washington, D.C.: University Press of America, 1980). The phrase "tolerable scoundrel" (below) is Sutton's.

25. See Sutton, *Self and Society in Aristophanes*, 17–33, 47–54, and 83–92; Reckford, *Aristophanes' Old-and-New Comedy*, 76–112, and, on the trickster myth in general, Joseph Campbell, *The Masks of God*, vol. 1: *Primitive Mythology* (1959; rpt. New York: Penguin, 1991), 267–281. For the progression from victim to trickster in the character of Dikaiopolis see Gwendolyn Compton-Engle, "From Country to City: The Persona of Dicaeopolis in Aristophanes' *Acharnians*," *The Classical Journal*, 94 (1999), 359–373.

The same is true of all three women in *9 to 5*. Almost realistic in the first half of the film, they become caricatures in the second half as much as their opponents do. Contrary to Aristophanes' concentration on a single hero or heroine, however, the writers of the screenplay have taken great care to draw their major female characters in some depth and in the context of three different problems of modern working women. Doralee Rhodes is a target of sexual harassment. Violet Newstead is a victim of discrimination regarding promotion and the assignment of office tasks and has the credit for her managerial accomplishments stolen by her immediate supervisor, Mr. Hart. Judy Bernly has been the victim of an immature, totally egocentric husband, whose divorce has now deposited her into the working world without any preparation.

Rather than compare them to Aristophanic heroes in general, I will argue that Mss. Newstead, Bernly, and Rhodes match quite accurately the specific characters Lysistrata, Myrrhine, and Lampito of Aristophanes' *Lysistrata*. Each of the three is a different personality type, closely comparable to the personalities of the Aristophanic heroines, and in both the ancient play and the film the women's individual situations bring them together in a common feeling of frustration and abuse. As a fourth parallel we might compare Margaret Foster, the alcoholic typist, to Kalonike, the bibulous old woman of *Lysistrata*, a stereotype of ancient comedy.[26]

Violet Newstead is Lysistrata. The protagonist of Aristophanes' play is a woman of strong will balanced by careful restraint of her aggressive urges, as befits the leader of an antiwar conspiracy. She has excellent insight into the social, political, and economic realities of wartime Athens, yet states her proposals for a solution in terms of woolworking and weaving, the basic ancient symbol of civilized femininity (*Lysistrata* 567–586). Although her husband is not mentioned in the play, every aspect of her characterization indicates that she is a married woman approaching early middle age. In the typology of Aristophanic heroes, she is a *spoudaia*: competent, visionary yet energetic, and earnest.[27]

Ms. Newstead is a widow with four children. She has repeatedly lost promotions to less qualified men in spite of her spirit of "Anything men

26. See *Lysistrata* 194–208. Because of textual problems, some editors and commentators attribute to Myrrhine or even Lysistrata some or all of the lines suggesting addiction to wine that I feel certain belong to Kalonike. Other examples of women and wine in ancient comedy appear in Aristophanes, *Thesmophoriazusae* 630–761, and Terence, *Andria* 228–233. On bibulous women in Greek art, especially vase painting, and other forms of literature see Marjorie Susan Venit, "Women in their Cups," *The Classical World*, 92 (1998), 117–130.

27. See McLeish, *The Theatre of Aristophanes*, 53–56. Whitman, *Aristophanes and the Comic Hero*, 201–202, gives a useful summary of Lysistrata's personality.

184

CLASSICAL

MYTH &

CULTURE

IN THE

CINEMA

can do, I can do better," demonstrated by her competence at everything from installing garage door openers to reforming office procedures and working conditions. She does not dominate the action as completely as Lysistrata does, since the film spreads out its social concern and liberal propagandizing over several different problems plaguing the women of the office, but she is clearly the leader of the group, even when they are carrying out Doralee Rhodes's or Judy Bernly's ideas. It is true that her panic, thinking that she has accidently poisoned the boss, goes far beyond the doubt of herself and her women that Lysistrata expresses in her mock-tragic speech, but it exemplifies the same moment of human weakness that many of Aristophanes' heroes exhibit when their survival or that of the grand scheme seems to be in danger. The film's concluding shots emphasize the irony of her brief panic by running a flashback of her flight through the hospital with the corpse on the gurney while juxtaposing a text which states that she was promoted to Hart's job "because of her ability to remain calm under pressure." Her usual character is better demonstrated by the poise and confidence with which she escorts the chairman of the board in a victory procession around the reformed office while the defeated Hart trembles in fear even as he is receiving credit for the rejuvenation and revitalization of the office that have resulted from the women's efforts. Athena, a goddess who was honored as patroness of many traditionally masculine crafts and skills and who was usually portrayed with a personality like Lysistrata's, would have been proud to call Ms. Newstead "sister."

Ms. Newstead's fantasy appears third at the first revel. It is a Disneyesque fairy tale—"gruesome and horrible and real gory, but kinda cute," as she herself describes it—that grows straight out of the most demeaning aspects of her job. Hart treats her, the senior supervisor of his staff, like an errand girl by making her fetch him his coffee and blames her and Mrs. Rhodes, rather than the maintenance men, for a constant problem with his office chair, yet she must do her motherly best to protect the rest of the office staff from other injustices. All three of the women's fantasies involve inflicting on Hart a violent death involving emasculation, binding, or ritual expulsion like a scapegoat's; this last is reminiscent of the overthrow of the Old King in myth. Ms. Newstead therefore imagines herself adding some unspecified crystalline substance from a secret compartment in her ring to Hart's coffee, enough to dissolve the spoon instantly. As the coffee begins to take effect on him, she uses his chair as an ejector seat to hurl him out of the twelfth-floor window to the cheers of Bambi, Thumper, et al.[28] The rest of the workers, seen in a medieval

28. For the Disneyesque dimensions of certain of Aristophanes' plays see Sifakis, *Parabasis and Animal Choruses*, 73–103 (on the choruses in animal costume in *Wasps*,

dungeon, find their chains dropping off as their fairy godmother (Violet) announces their liberation, just the effect that the real reforms later produce.

The next day, distracted by her rage at yet another incident of degrading treatment from Hart, Ms. Newstead carelessly picks up a box of rat poison when she is intending to add "Sweet and Skinny" to Hart's coffee, but, ironically, Hart's defective chair saves him as he tips over backward and spills his coffee without drinking a drop. When she discovers her mistake, her uncharacteristic panic sets in motion the events that force the women to conspire for their common defense; this in turn leads to the birth of the grand scheme.

Judy Bernly resembles Myrrhine, the centerpiece of the most outrageously hilarious scene of Aristophanes' play (*Lysistrata* 845–1013).[29] Under the direction of Lysistrata, this young woman alternates between flirting with and stalling her amorous husband, Kinesias, running off on errand after errand to fetch a bed, a mattress, a pillow, a blanket, and perfumes in preparation for the nuptials with which she teases him. Her strength of will, however, prevails; once she has Kinesias' oath to work for peace, she runs off again, keeping her oath to abstain from sex until peace is accomplished and leaving her thoroughly aroused husband unrelieved. Ms. Bernly is attractive, if a bit atmosphero-cephalic at first, but otherwise an "ordinary housewife."[30] Very seriously disoriented by the change in lifestyle which her husband's misconduct and the resulting divorce have forced on her, Ms. Bernly, like Myrrhine, nevertheless finds hidden resources of strength when the chips are really down. While the others are panicking over the discovery that they have the wrong body in the trunk, she shouts them back into order; when her husband attempts to seduce her into a reconciliation, she at first wavers but then sees through his egocentric emptiness and casts him out. The effect on the male is, at least psychologically, like the effect of Myrrhine's stalling and ultimate rejection on the painfully ithyphallic Kinesias. When Hart nearly escapes from his imprisonment, she beats him back into submission with a pil-

---

Birds, and *Frogs*). In the film, also note the brief animalization of the Xerox machine, which belches at Ms. Bernly during her first morning on the job.

29. On the meaning of the name "Myrrhine," roughly equivalent in its ambiguities to the American "Pussy," see McLeish, *The Theatre of Aristophanes*, 99; for possible connections to a contemporary Athenian priestess by the same name and other aspects of the name that might have resonated with meaning for Aristophanes' original audience see A. M. Bowie, *Aristophanes* (Cambridge: Cambridge University Press, 1993), 194–195.

30. Exactly the term Henderson, "*Lysistrata*," 161, uses to describe Myrrhine.

low, one of the several bedroom items used by Myrrhine in the discomfiting of Kinesias.

186

CLASSICAL

MYTH &

CULTURE

IN THE

CINEMA

Ms. Bernly's fantasy, which begins with the parody on the myth of Artemis and Actaeon mentioned earlier, shows a side of her personality very different from anything depicted earlier, but it is in accord with an Artemis-like blend of innocence and reserve combined with unrelenting viciousness once angered, and her drill-team twirling of the shotgun recalls the hunter-goddess's archetypal skill with the bow.[31] At the end of her fantasy, Hart is cornered in a restroom stall, crouching on a toilet seat like the bewildered men on chamber pots early in Aristophanes' *Ecclesiazusae*, and she accomplishes his final "dethroning" with a single point-blank shot. The squatting, hunched-over posture that Hart assumes to try to protect himself and, next, his undamaged head mounted in place of the deer's on his office wall indicate that her aim was not "right between the eyes" but rather "right between the thighs." Given the phallic implications of her weapon, this shows not only obvious aspects of castration but also an Aristophanic role-reversal aspect of her fantasy. Back in reality, late in the afternoon on the day after Hart's emergency trip to the hospital, when chaos breaks out in the office, she does indeed stop his escape by emptying Doralee Rhodes's revolver at him, although only the office windows and furnishings suffer ill effects.

Doralee Rhodes is a perfect Lampito, the Spartan representative to Lysistrata's conspiratorial council. Her Doric dialect, robust physique, and rural aphorisms were meant to draw laughter from the ethnic prejudices of the Athenians against the Spartans. Likewise, at the beginning of the film Doralee Rhodes is the least credible and most stereotypical of the three women. As a Texan, she is exposed to the same kinds of bigotry the Athenians held against the women of Sparta and other Doric Greek regions, most notably the stereotype of excessively bold, "unladylike" behavior and outlandish speech patterns. Prejudices of ignorance and rusticity about speakers of the southern dialects of American English are so prevalent in other parts of our society that it is only appropriate that Douglass Parker gives Lampito something of a hillbilly style of speech, while Jack Lindsay has her speak Scots dialect, reflecting parallel biases in the British Isles.[32]

31. For evidence of these characteristics of Artemis see Ovid, *Metamorphoses* 2.401–507 (the transformation of Callisto), 3.138–255 (the death of Actaeon), and 6.148–315 (the slaughter of Niobe's children).

32. Parker's version: *Aristophanes: Lysistrata* (Ann Arbor: University of Michigan Press/New York: New American Library, 1964; several reprints); Lindsay's: *The Complete Plays of Aristophanes*, ed. Moses Hadas (New York: Bantam, 1962; rpt. 1981), 287–328. A number of years ago, within one month CBS aired two made-for-TV specials in which fictional people who were rural, poor, and uneducated were depicted as such by a

As far as behavior is concerned, Doralee shows Doric traits. In line with the "hick" stereotype the Athenians had of the Spartans, she drives a pickup truck and drinks beer while the others have more urbane drinks like margueritas or daiquiris. She is an accomplished rodeo athlete— Spartan women had a reputation for athletic competition in public—and dresses a good bit more boldly than the other office workers, just as the Doric *peplos* was somewhat more revealing than the Attic *chitôn*. Finally, Doralee and her husband seem to have a relatively open and equal—albeit unpolished and even uninhibited—relationship, of a sort found frequently in rural societies, including ancient Sparta.

Aristophanes' plays contain several scenes describing the physical attributes of a supposedly attractive female character in some detail while she, the character present for the audience's admiration, is played by a male.[33] At such moments the ancient audience would have been expected to get quite a laugh out of the basic incongruities required by their stage convention, and the same is true for Elizabethan performances of Shakespeare's comedies. This is a special form of drag humor, as it were, akin to the humor of "self-referential" film or metadrama. A few scholars have argued that such graphic descriptions of women in the texts must have required the presence of a real, and in some cases quite naked, woman as an "extra" for these scenes to be convincing. Most critics, however, consider this quite unlikely, not least because the festival of the Lenaia, at which comedies were performed, took place in January–February—unless Attic men had a goosebump fetish to be added to all their other well-documented crimes against womankind. Some have argued for the more discreet technique of representing the beautiful woman by a statue or mannequin; this makes some sense in one, and only one, of the scenes in question, involving the goddess Peace in the play named after her, but the other scenes suggested require the women characters to participate in too much movement and activity for a statue, even one with well-lubricated rollers.[34]

---

random mixture of Georgia, Carolina, and Tennessee phonetics, although the one film was set near Sacramento, California, and the other in Oregon.

33. J. Michael Walton, *Living Greek Theatre: A Handbook of Classical Performance and Modern Production* (New York: Greenwood, 1987), 206, maintains that "*Lysistrata* is at heart a 'drag' play," but his treatment is primarily directed toward performability in a modern theater, not to its ancient Greek cultural setting. A more thorough approach to the same subject, based on feminist and film theory, is in Lauren K. Taaffe, *Aristophanes and Women* (London: Routledge, 1993), especially 48–73.

34. Many commentators, however, have assumed that the tradition of men playing female roles was so well established that, given a delivery with all the impact that ancient rhetoric could muster, the words themselves would be sufficient to overcome any visual

188

CLASSICAL

MYTH &

CULTURE

IN THE

CINEMA

Dolly Parton's not entirely natural hypertrophic figure has obvious relevance to *Lysistrata*. (Although she often appears to be engaging in self-parody, Ms. Parton takes her professional persona very seriously, not least in regard to those traits for which she is most famous.) At the entrance of Lampito and the other foreign delegates, Lysistrata first points out Lampito's thoroughly masculine, even Heraclean, musculature: "How healthy you are, how strong your body is! You could strangle a bull!" (79–80). In comparison, the film explicitly stresses Doralee's calf-roping abilities, and her binding of Mr. Hart with a telephone cord is a funny variation on her rodeo abilities.

Kalonike, who plays the clown (*bômolochos*) in contrast to Lysistrata's more dignified spoudaia role, then points out Lampito's (artificial) feminine traits: "What a bodacious bunch of boobs you've got!" (83). Lampito's response—"Y'all are pawing me over like a sacrificial victim!" (84)—suggests that this last comment was accompanied by some fondling of the parts mentioned, possibly in such a way as to emphasize the artificiality of the padding. The Boeotian and Corinthian representatives receive similar attention in just those parts of the bodies that were presumably artificial and made the compliments most incongruous. Lysistrata's remark to Lampito some lines later provides an ironic capstone to the metadramatic drag humor of the scene: "Oh, you are a real *dear*, the only *woman* of these!" (145). In scenes such as this, Aristophanes does not have his characters wax eloquent about women's bodies to arouse his audience's lust but rather, by drawing attention to the incongruity between words, appearances, and reality, to heighten their hilarity. The theme of words–versus–appearances–versus–reality is present elsewhere in Aristophanes' plays

---

evidence to the contrary and that the audience accepted the idea that the male actor arrayed and described as a beautiful woman was a beautiful female character with only a minimum of adolescent giggles or tittering. Dover, *Aristophanic Comedy*, 28, mentions the possibility of drag humor but then dismisses it in a short sentence without due consideration; McLeish, *The Theatre of Aristophanes*, 151–156, discusses the "travesty" aspects of certain other plays that have scenes involving characters who change clothes while remaining "in character," which is not what is happening in this passage. Jeffrey Henderson, *Three Plays by Aristophanes: Staging Women* (New York: Routledge, 1996), 17, continues to deny that drag humor and metatheater are possible in Aristophanes' plays, but his own vivid description of this scene in "*Lysistrata*," 162–166, convinces me of the opposite, in spite of his contention that the male actors are costumed as naked women. My argument depends on our awareness of how different from our modern theatrical experiences the relationships between actor, character, and audience must have been in the Old Comic theater, especially in regard to an apparent lack of inhibition about dramatic illusion and a willingness to slip in and out of character whenever there was a joke to be found in the transition.

as well. From that point, it is an easy step to self-referential metadrama aimed at the conventions of the Greek theater itself.

9 to 5 also engages in self-referential comments. We have already seen that the other women's fantasies during the revel are self-referential or metafilmic in their parody of some of Hollywood's most appealing genres and some of their most unrealistic conventions, especially with Judy Bernly's ability to fire many more than two shots in rapid succession from a double-barreled shotgun without loading, a parody of Hollywood's heroic western tradition. But the casting of Dolly Parton as a modern Lampito is a far more clever stroke.

Lampito's entrance in *Lysistrata* could serve as a perfect preface to Mrs. Rhodes's fantasy, which is an all-out role reversal. At a rodeo and barbecue Hart is first sexually harassed to the point of emasculation, then calf-roped, hog-tied, and finally roasted, bound to the shaft of a Texas barbecue spit.[35] As in the other women's fantasies, there is enough castration, binding, and "ritual slaughter of the old god" material in these few shots to fulfill the hypotheses of not only F. M. Cornford and the other members of the Cambridge School but also of Freudians and neo-Freudians regarding ritual and psychological origins of drama. When the actual overthrow of Hart begins (after her previous threat of castration by pistol shot), Mrs. Rhodes indeed binds him up twice. First, he is briefly tied like a rodeo calf in his own office, then he spends six weeks in a strait-jacket, which combines features of harness making, part of Mrs. Rhodes's expertise with horses, and Ms. Newstead's mastery of garage door openers into a perfect parody of the stage machinery of the theater of Dionysus in Athens, on whose perilous operation Trygaios comments during his flight on the dung beetle in Aristophanes' *Peace* (lines 82–176).[36] Similar bindings of males by women occur in *Lysistrata*—the commissioner, an ineffectual authority figure parallel to Hart, is bound with feminine veils, wrapped in the garb of a corpse, and crowned with symbols of death—and in *Thesmophoriazusae*, where Euripides' relative Mnesilochos is tied to a plank, the ancient Attic equivalent of handcuffing. Mrs. Rhodes, meanwhile, follows the archetype of the early generations of Earth Mothers even further by usurping the fallen male's power, perhaps even his identity, by buying the equipment for his binding with his own Mas-

---

35. A student of mine commented, during class discussion, that this shot reminded her of the myth of Ixion, bound to a wheel rotating between extreme heat and cold in punishment for attempting to seduce Hera, queen of the gods and patroness of marriage.

36. In the novel version Ms. Newstead refers to Hart as "Peter Pan" (Racina, *Nine to Five*, 106), an obvious reference to the resemblance of her contrivance to the elaborate apparatus used to make Mary Martin fly in the play and film by that name.

190

CLASSICAL

MYTH &

CULTURE

IN THE

CINEMA

ter Card (!) and forging his signature on the memos that announce the first reforms in the office. It is, in fact, this first small step to improve conditions that moves the trio from purely defensive plotting into active usurpation of Hart's place and makes possible the positive side of their scheme, the total rejuvenation of their working environment.

The men of the film are caricatures throughout, as was typical of Aristophanic villains as well: Lamachos (*Acharnians*), Kleon (the Paphlagonian in *Knights*), Socrates (*Clouds*), and Kleisthenes (*Thesmophoriazusae*). The film's women undergo a metamorphosis from almost credible, albeit stock characters to caricatures as they pass from helpless suffering through panic and despair to defensive plotting and finally to enthusiastically reveling in the success of their scoundrelry. Meanwhile they release the repressed urges and talents first expressed in their fantasies and become more and more enthusiastic in their Dionysiac smashing of barriers. Aristophanes' Lysistrata does not undergo so radical a transformation, since she begins the play with her plot already developing and, unlike a trickster figure, retains a certain nobility and dignity in triumph.[37] Her modern descendants progress from voicing individual grievances to applying the kind of teamwork that Hart had claimed only real men—those who had played football—could learn, a statement that comes back to haunt him through the chairman of the board's nonrefusable offer to him of a place on his company's Brazilian management team. A parallel to Aristophanes' *Peace* is the theme of the importance of pan-Hellenic teamwork to rescue the goddess Peace from the pit in which War has buried her; this theme receives special emphasis in the play when the farmers from various parts of Greece have to learn to pull together to hoist her out of this pit (lines 416–542).

But how is it that the team of heroines of *9 to 5* retain our sympathy and even excite our enthusiasm as they resort more and more to skullduggery? After all, not too many people outside the Teamsters Union would argue that the achievement of fair working conditions justifies assault with a deadly weapon, kidnapping, illegal imprisonment, forgery, and blackmail. (Ms. Newstead mentions Jimmy Hoffa's missing body as a precedent when she steals what she thinks is Hart's corpse.) What *9 to 5* offers is, in essence, the thrill of a modern Aristophanic comedy. The Aristophanic hero abandons all principles and breaks down almost all

---

37. This is an important part of the evidence that convinces me that Aristophanes modeled her character more on that of the goddess Athena than upon any real woman in Athens at his time. Henderson, "*Lysistrata*," 187–188, considers the same possibility but also emphasizes possible connections with Lysimache, priestess of Athena Polias in 411 B.C., when the play was first produced.

barriers or inhibitions, whether from social taboos or law, even though the revolt usually arises from and for a good cause. The opposition is usually left vanquished and often in unrelieved distress or pain, although the *Lysistrata* revels in reconciliation and reunion at its finale. F. M. Cornford saw this kind of scoundrel-like behavior as the comic equivalent of tragic hubris: an arrogant self-assertion that leads not to a tragic fall but to the comic reversal of fortunes in which the oppressed victim becomes triumphant.[38] Cedric Whitman has argued that the Aristophanic heroes are individualists, out for their own gain regardless of the social benefits for Athens that may sometimes be a side effect of their victories, and pointed out how this fits the contemporary attitudes on the part of the sophists and of Euripides, whom Aristophanes often seems to be attacking. Whitman has also expounded on the parallels between Aristophanic characterization and surrealist art, in which distortion serves to emphasize the true reality behind outward appearances.[39] But these approaches may be oversophisticated. It is quite likely that the fundamental appeal of Aristophanes' protagonists, and that of the three women of *9 to 5*, is hidden in everybody's less-than-noble fantasies of the sort represented by such contemporary colloquial aphorisms as "Don't get mad, get even!" and "Nothing's illegal if you don't get caught"—precisely the kind of fantasies that Dana Sutton and Kenneth Reckford discuss for Aristophanes. Reckford also revives the hypothesis of a comic catharsis, which turns the release of these fantasies into a cleansing and purifying experience for the soul.[40]

I mention one final bit of empirical evidence to support my analysis of *9 to 5* as Aristophanic comedy. Whenever I have taught ancient comedy, nothing, not even a taped performance of *Acharnians, Birds,* or even *Lysistrata,* has been as successful at bringing the students close to the essence of Aristophanes' works as a carefully prepared screening and guided discussion of this film. Matters such as the structural elements of the ancient plays, the character types, and the possible revelry, festival, and ritual aspects of Old Greek Comedy cease to be mere abstractions to be learned from secondary sources. Instead, they come alive when students confront them in modern costume. The most important insights gained from viewing *9 to 5*, however, have to do with those questions of

38. Cornford, *The Origin of Attic Comedy*, 180–191.

39. Whitman, *Aristophanes and the Comic Hero*, 21–58 and 259–280.

40. Reckford, *Aristophanes' Old-and-New Comedy*, 12–13, 213–214, 231–232, and 272–275. See also the criticism and applications of the catharsis theory on the basis of the literary theories of Northrop Frye and the psychological theories of Alfred Adler in Sutton, *Self and Society in Aristophanes*, 89–90. See also Sutton, *The Catharsis of Comedy* (Lanham, Md.: Rowman and Littlefield, 1994).

192

CLASSICAL

MYTH &

CULTURE

IN THE

CINEMA

artistic unity and audience response surrounding the metamorphosis of the Aristophanic hero from frustrated victim to triumphant, uninhibited fulfiller of fantasies, which are often surprisingly difficult to communicate in a discussion based on a printed translation of Aristophanes' plays. After viewing *9 to 5*, students—and others—better comprehend the nature of the appeal of the lovable scoundrel, not just to ancient peoples or simpler societies but even to space-age sophisticates.

IX

Ancient Poetics and Eisenstein's Films

J. K. Newman

The application of filmic principles to criticism of classical literature is now well established and includes interpretation drawn from the Soviet director Sergei M. Eisenstein.[1] My essay has a different purpose: to link certain procedures of ancient narrative and the critical maxims they generate, notably in Aristotle, with specific aspects of Eisenstein's writings. This approach is encouraged by Eisenstein's habit of quoting widely from the most disparate sources, although his incidental acknowledgments of classical predecessors are never supported by sustained examination of ancient texts. In that respect, an essay such as this fills a gap in the great filmmaker's own explication and defense of his artistic positions.

My methodology is simple. After first discussing certain classical narrative passages and critical points, I link the principles illustrated in them with precepts and examples set forth by Aristotle in his *Poetics* and by Eisenstein himself in what his Soviet editors call his "theoretical researches."

1. Greek Poetics from Homer to the Hellenistic Age

At the beginning of the *Iliad,* the priest Chryses asks for his daughter back from Agamemnon. The other Greeks agree enthusiastically. But Agamemnon refuses, "enjoining on him a violent word":

> "Let me not find you, old man, by the hollow ships, either lingering now or coming again later, lest the staff and garland of the god avail you nothing. Her I will not release: before that old age will come upon her in my

---

1. See in particular the pioneering article by Fred Mench, "Film Sense in the *Aeneid*," first published in 1969 and reprinted in slightly revised form in this volume.

palace at Argos, far from her native land, as she toils at the loom and tends
my bed. Off with you, don't provoke me, so that your return may be safer."

At this, the old man felt a stab of fear, and heeded [the king's] word.
And he went in silence along the shore of the gurgling sea.[2]

194

CLASSICAL

MYTH &

CULTURE

IN THE

CINEMA

It is hardly an exaggeration to say that the whole future of European
narrative technique is contained in these lines. Several points may be
noted:

1. The *Iliad* is an epic, but this is a *dramatic confrontation*. In a fashion typical of later Attic drama, two violently opposed characters face each
other before what may be considered a chorus, in this case the Achaean
soldiers.

2. The scene is filled with *irony*. As Homer's audience knew from the
myth, Agamemnon was not in fact destined to enjoy Chryseis' sexual
favors. Although he appeared fearful and powerless in the presence of the
mighty king, Chryses was going to win this conflict, and on terms so crushing that they form the whole tragedy of the *Iliad*. Agamemnon's bluster
leads to Achilles' withdrawal from the fighting, to the deaths of Patroclus
and Hector, and to the eventual confrontation between Priam and Achilles and the realization of the mortal condition affecting us all.

3. There is great use of *antithesis*. While the other Greeks, for example,
had only one verb to indicate their approval at line 22, Agamemnon speaks
his disapproval at length. Chryseis is young, but she will be old. She was
free and a virgin here; she will be a slave and the king's mistress there.
The old priest is silent, but nature, the "gurgling sea," takes up and mag-
nifies his indignation for him.

4. The dramatic scene convinces by its use of *concrete, telling detail*.
Agamemnon does not say: "your sacred rank" but "the staff and garland
of the god." He does not say: "Your daughter will be my slave and mistress" but singles out tasks vividly denoting the role of such a slave and
mistress. The silence of the priest, contrasting with the noisy sea, particularizes what "the old man felt a stab of fear" means.

5. *Characterization* is not spelled out in authorial generalizations but
emerges from linguistic structure. Agamemnon is violent, crude, and
egotistical. In a more literal translation than the one given above he says:
"Off with you—don't go on provoking me—so that you may return
safer." The word order shows his agitation. With the interjection he is
projecting his own wrongdoing onto the priest. He is really the one provoking; if he is provoked, it is by his own lust. "Safer" (*saôteros*) is an

---

2. *Iliad* 1.26–34. Throughout, translations from Greek, Latin, and Russian are my own
unless stated otherwise.

idiom of the type found, for instance, in the Homeric phrase "more feminine women" (*Iliad* 8.520), where women are not being contrasted with other women but with men. The suffix -*ter*- implies a contrast (more antithesis), here not between two types of safety but between safety and what could happen to Chryses—what the king desires to do to him.

6. *Pathos* is developed by a peculiar technique in which the listener is required to collaborate with the verbal construct. Homer is aware of what it means for the old man to lose his daughter in defiance of all morality, because afterward (36) he makes Apollo, "son of fair-tressed Leto" and therefore himself aware of family ties, quick to answer his priest's call. The priest will say in his later prayer: "May the Greeks pay for my tears with your arrows" (42). But what we are not told is that the priest weeps here and now, only that he is afraid and silent. We have to read his distress beyond this fear and silence retroactively into the scene, unless we learn how to get the most out of poetry on first reading.

7. The phrase "the gurgling sea" offers a hint of the priest's inner storms. But on the other side this *powerful image* symbolizes the world as it is given by the gods, greater than our concerns, not to be disturbed by human willfulness: "There is the sea, and who shall quench it?"[3]

8. *Repetition.* Homer says that Agamemnon "enjoined on him a violent word" at the start (25), and this is the "word" the old man obeys at the end (33). This is the ring composition which may have been essential in an oral technique, later developed to extraordinary lengths. It is a device prevalent in all Greek literature, including the prose of Herodotus and Thucydides. From the Greeks it passed to the Romans.

9. *Musicality.* This cannot be divorced from repetition, one of the most characteristic procedures in music. Implied here is more than euphony and assonance. If we examine the lengths of the individual segments making up the narrative in lines 17–52, we find the following:

I.	Chryses asks for his daughter back:	5 lines
II.	The other Greeks agree:	2 lines
III.	Agamemnon disagrees:	2 lines
IV.	He speaks threateningly:	3 + 4 = 7 lines
V.	Chryses goes off in fear:	4 lines
VI.	He prays:	6 lines
VII.	Apollo responds by assailing the Greeks:	10 lines

3. Aeschylus, *Agamemnon* 958. To anticipate my argument, we may compare Eisenstein's remarks about the function of the vast, cathedral spaces in his film *Ivan the Terrible* (two parts, 1943 and 1946). See Eisenstein, *Izbrannye Proizvedeniya v shesti tomakh* (Moscow: Izdatel'stvo Isskustvo, 1964), vol. 3, 353. (Later references to Eisenstein's writings in these volumes will be abbreviated as *I.P.*)—Eisenstein's theories as they are rele-

196

CLASSICAL

MYTH &

CULTURE

IN THE

CINEMA

Chryses' departure and prayer (V, VI) and the response (VII) are in perfect balance: ten and ten lines; compare his first prayer (I) of five lines. Agamemnon's jarring isolation from the other Greeks during his speech (IV) is suggested by his anomalous seven lines. But even they echo, antithetically or antiphonally, I and II. We may be skeptical about this kind of analysis because we divorce music from poetry and both from mathematics; the ancients did not. "I remember the numbers; if only I could think of the words!" exclaims Lycidas in Virgil's *Ninth Eclogue* (9.45).

Normative as it was for later Greek poets, the Homeric technique could still admit refinement. Homer's epics had presumed the existence of other types of poetry, for example the wedding song on the shield of Achilles (*Iliad* 18.493–495). In particular, the choral lyric as developed by Stesichorus seems to have had an epic dimension and to have acted as a bridge between the two styles. The fragmentary state of much choral poetry prevents us from tracing post-Homeric development in any detail, but Simonides, Pindar's older contemporary, is credited with the saying that painting is silent poetry and poetry painting that speaks.[4] He is also cited in a passage of the anonymous treatise *On the Sublime*, whose author, discussing special effects of imagination (*phantasiai*), declares:

> In general, imagination may be defined as any thought which in its occurrence produces speech. In this context the term is most common nowadays when, under the influence of enthusiasm and emotion [*pathos*], you seem to see what you are saying, and then communicate that vision to your hearers. (15.1)

---

vant to this essay are available to the English-speaking reader in Eisenstein, *Nonindifferent Nature*, tr. Herbert Marshall (Cambridge: Cambridge University Press, 1987; rpt. 1994). They are summarized here, however, directly from the Russian of Eisenstein, *I.P.*, vol. 2, 329–483, and vol. 3, 33–432. See also Eisenstein, *Izbrannye Stat'i* (Moscow: Izdatel'stvo Iskusstvo, 1956). The best-known selections of Eisenstein's writings in English translation are in *The Film Sense*, ed. and tr. Jay Leyda (1942; rpt. New York: Harcourt Brace Jovanovich, 1975), and *Film Form: Essays in Film Theory*, ed. and tr. Leyda (1949; rpt. San Diego: Harcourt Brace Jovanovich, 1977). *S. M. Eisenstein: Selected Works*, vol. 1: *Writings 1922–1934*, ed. and tr. Richard Taylor (Bloomington: Indiana University Press, 1988; rpt. 1996), contains a useful introduction; Taylor calls Eisenstein "by general consent the single most important figure in the history of cinema" (ix). Recent interpretive works in English include David Bordwell, *The Cinema of Eisenstein* (Cambridge: Harvard University Press, 1993); James Goodwin, *Eisenstein, Cinema, and History* (Urbana: University of Illinois Press, 1993); and Håkan Lövgren, *Eisenstein's Labyrinth: Aspects of a Cinematic Synthesis of the Arts* (Stockholm: Almquist and Wiksell International, 1996). For descriptions and illustrations of Eisenstein's working methods see Leyda and Zina Voynow, *Eisenstein at Work* (New York: Pantheon/Museum of Modern Art, 1982).

4. Plutarch, *On the Glory of the Athenians* 3 (*Moralia* 346f–347c).

Euripides, we go on to learn, is a good example of this. But there are also cases in Homer, Aeschylus, Sophocles—and Simonides. In the two authors mentioned last, the shade of Achilles appeared above his tomb to the army leaving Troy for the last time, "a scene which nobody perhaps has depicted as vividly as Simonides" (15.7).[5]

In Pindar we find both a polemic against Homer and a modification—in essence a concentration and intensification—of his narrative techniques. Scholars single out, for example, the myth of the *First Nemean Ode*.[6] The miraculous deed by which the infant Heracles signaled his more-than-human birth is related in a series of dramatic, painterly scenes. In the following translation I have attempted to preserve some of the affective word order of the original. In normal English, Heracles, for instance, would be "seizing the twin serpents by their necks with his two ineluctable hands," but the poet presents his picture in the abnormal order given here, telling

how, when from his mother's womb immediately into the marvelous light the son of Zeus fleeing the birth pang with his twin brother came—how not escaping golden-throned Hera the saffron swaddling clothes he entered. But the queen of the gods, angry at heart, sent serpents forthwith. They, as the doors flew open, into the broad recess of the chamber entered, around the children their swift jaws to wrap eager. But he raised his head and made his first trial of combat with both his the-two-serpents-by-the-necks-seizing, ineluctable hands. And as they were strangled, time breathed out the lives from their unspeakable limbs. Unbearable fear struck the women who were in attendance at Alcmena's bed. She herself got to her feet unrobed as she was and rushed from the couch in spite of all, and tried to ward off the insolence of those monsters. And swiftly the Theban chiefs with bronze weapons ran up all together, and in his hand Amphitryon brandishing a sword naked from its scabbard arrived, by sharp distresses stricken.

At this point, the poet breaks off to remark: "For what is close to home oppresses every man alike, but straightway the heart feels no pain for another's care." The story now resumes:

There he stood, by astonishment, both unbearable and yet happy, confused. For he witnessed the unwonted spirit and power of a son. Backward-tongued the immortals made for him the news of the messengers, and he summoned his neighbor, the eminent spokesman of most high Zeus, right-prophesying Tiresias.

5. Cf. Apollonius, *Argonautica* 2.911–929 (Sthenelus' tomb).

6. Cf. Leonhard Illig, *Zur Form der pindarischen Erzählung: Interpretationen und Untersuchungen* (Berlin: Junker und Dünnhaupt, 1932), 20–25. The lines translated hereafter are *Nemean* 1.35–61.

198

CLASSICAL

MYTH &

CULTURE

IN THE

CINEMA

Tiresias then delivers a prophecy, muffled in the circumlocutions of reported speech, about the victorious career of Heracles, culminating in his
fight on the side of the gods against the snake-limbed Giants. Heracles'
own life comes full circle in an existential ring composition. Following
Athenian tradition, Pindar passes straight from Heracles' battle against
the Giants to his apotheosis. He ignores within the economy of his poem
the details we find, for example, in Sophocles' *Women of Trachis*.

This story proceeds in a series of pictures: the birth, the sending of the
serpents, the mysteriously opening doors, and the response of the baby
son of Zeus. The interlocking word order in the strangulation of the two
serpents cuts from the baby's grasp to what he is grasping, until we finally realize with relief that around their necks he has his hands. But this
high point is anticipation. The story cuts back to the serving women, and
then particularizes the reaction of the mother, struggling in her weak-
ened state to get out of bed and not even bothering to seize a robe. Negative adjectives ("ineluctable," "unspeakable," "unbearable," "unrobed")
force us to supply their positive counterparts since negatives in themselves
make no appeal to the imagination. Now the Theban chiefs arrive, armed
in bronze, and again someone is singled out among them: father Amphitryon, his bare sword flashing.

Verbs of movement have so far predominated: "fleeing," "came," "entered," "sent," "entered," "eager," "rushing," "ran, " "arrived," but here
the narrative halts (cf. 55: *esta*) as the poet reflects on his version of the
old adage that blood is thicker than water. This has been thought of as
merely a holding remark, unimportant in itself, and intended to allow the
listener to savor the vivid picture so far presented. But it is more, as the
sequel shows.

Amphitryon reacts ambiguously. Wonderment is the appropriate reaction to a divine epiphany, and the unity of opposites illustrated by pain
and pleasure together (55–56) is also part of this extraordinary mystical
etiquette. His intervention, as it turns out, is not needed. The boy is quite
able to look after himself, and the alarming news brought by the messengers is reversed. What did these messengers say? Perhaps: "Your sons are
in mortal danger." The situation now proclaims: "Not only are your sons
not in mortal danger, but this miracle also shows that the bolder of them
is not your son." No wonder Amphitryon's feelings were mixed as he
struggled to assimilate this conclusion, simultaneously flattering and
devastating. Perhaps some inkling of it caused him to send for the spokesman of Zeus, because, as we were told at the beginning of the myth (35),
the father of the child is none other than Zeus most high.

This sheds another light on the poet's reflections on the miracle. In cold
logic, Amphitryon has been bothered about "another's care," since Heracles

is now shown to be no child of his. Amphitryon's trouble was wasted, his assumption of responsibility premature, his weapons were unneeded, and, like all cuckolds, he is left looking rather a fool. Like Homer's Agamemnon in his middle-aged lusts, the hero is caught in a less than heroic moment. All he can really do is stand there.

Pindar's *Fourth Pythian Ode*, his most elaborate, contains a long narrative of the seizure of the Golden Fleece.[7] It strikingly illustrates a technique by which Pindar, following Homer, seeks his listener's cooperation in the fashioning of the work of art. Jason has just completed his plowing with the brazen bulls commanded by Aeëtes:

> And at once the wondrous child of the Sun [Aeëtes] told of the shining fleece and where the sword blows of Phrixus had stretched it out. He was hoping that this toil at least Jason would not fulfill. For it lay in a thicket and clung to the savage jaws of a serpent that in bulk and length outdid a fifty-oared ship finished by the blows of the iron. It is long for me to travel the cart road. Time presses, and I know a certain shortcut. To many others I am a leader in the poet's craft. He slew the fierce-eyed, spangle-backed serpent with arts, Arcesilaus, and stole Medea with herself, the murderess of Pelias. And they plunged into the expanses of Ocean and the Red Sea, into the tribe of Lemnian women who slew their husbands.

At the height of the action the poet simply abandons his story. He breaks off to congratulate himself on his poetic prowess. But this desertion of the story is part of his very prowess, for in our impatience, and drawing on our familiarity with longer narrative poetry, we reconstruct the combat in our imagination. Presumably we are perfectly satisfied with our own creative work. The poet's thesis and claim of mastery have been triumphantly vindicated.

In fact, Pindar has offered hints at what he wants us to do: "blows of iron" in his narrative, although, at first sound, blows of shipwrights' hammer and mallet, could just as well in another application be sword blows (cf. line 242). As it were, the Argo has metamorphosed into, and itself subsumed, this final confrontation, just as the serpents almost blended into the Giants in the *First Nemean Ode*. This is why, in that ode, Time (the word is repeated a little later at line 69) "breathed out the life from their unspeakable limbs." So in this, although we do not hear a great deal about what will happen to Medea and Jason, we are told that she will be

---

7. On this see my *The Classical Epic Tradition* (Madison: University of Wisconsin Press, 1986), 96–99. Individual studies of the ode are Charles Segal, *Pindar's Mythmaking: The Fourth Pythian Ode* (Princeton: Princeton University Press, 1986), and Bruce K. Braswell, *A Commentary on the Fourth Pythian Ode of Pindar* (Berlin: de Gruyter, 1988). The lines below are *Pythian* 4.241–252.

the death of Pelias and the first stop on the voyage home is to be the island of women who murdered their menfolk. The root *phon-* ("murder") is repeated twice in three lines.

200

CLASSICAL

MYTH &

CULTURE

IN THE

CINEMA

Pindar, congratulating himself on his virtuosity as narrator, both implies and develops a whole narratology.[8] He opens the *Second Dithyramb*, for example, by remarking: "Earlier there crawled the *schoinos*-length song of the dithyrambs and the false *san* from men's lips." The schoinos is an ancient unit of measurement, and so this is an objection to irrelevant length in poetry. There may be an allusion in *san*, an old name for sigma, to some experiment perhaps by the poet's teacher Lasus of Hermione in avoiding the use of the consonant *s*.[9] The Alexandrian Callimachus picks up the language of the schoinos in the preface to his *Aitia* (18: *schoinoi*).

At *Paean* VII.B.11 Pindar refers to Homer's "cart track," a term already familiar from the *Fourth Pythian Ode* (line 247) and later to be adapted by Callimachus (preface to the *Aitia*, 25). In a now fragmentary passage, the chorus were perhaps advised not to travel along it and not to ride on other people's horses.

Pindar's polemic must not be exaggerated. Every poet stakes out his own terrain by distinguishing himself from his immediate predecessors. For the Greeks, long-dead Homer was an immediate predecessor, partly because of his lasting prestige, particularly in education, and partly because he was the nominal patron of a great mass of poetry loosely associated with his tradition. Pindar has reinforced certain Homeric features noted in our extract from the *Iliad*. He has carried selectivity and compression even further. In the *First Nemean Ode* he heightens the emotional element; the interplay between human and divine veers toward the tragicomic. There are careful lighting effects: "light," "golden-throned," "saffron," "bronze," "brandishing a naked sword." Everything moves from divine to human and back to a new apprehension of the divine, toward a stillness of the kind familiar from Japanese Kabuki theater. At the climactic moment the armed father, his chiefs behind him, stands in the doorway and, staring with a mixture of awe-struck emotions at his (or not his?) triumphant baby son, ponders what it all might mean.

8. This does not mean that Pindar was anti-Homeric any more than Callimachus, but he was far more reflective about his art than Homer. It is to Pindar, for example, that the controversial Callimachus looks back; see my *Augustus and the New Poetry* (Brussels: Collection Latomus, 1967), 45–48, and "Pindar and Callimachus," *Illinois Classical Studies*, 10 (1985), 169–189.

9. Dionysius of Halicarnassus, *On the Arrangement of Words* 14. Perhaps Pindar was objecting to sigmatism of the kind for which the comic playwright Plato later criticized Euripides (Fr. 30 Kock).

Simonides' famous saying about poetry and painting may perhaps be paraphrased that poetry is painting with a soundtrack. We do not know how soon Greek painting caught up with poetry or what poetry had previously borrowed from painting. But the sophisticated technique of narration by omission, already familiar in the poets, became famous in the visual arts of the classical period with the painter Timanthes of Sicyon. Cicero relates that Timanthes, in a painting of the sacrifice of Iphigenia, indicated varying degrees of sorrow among the spectators waiting at the altar. We may interpret Cicero's remarks. The priest Calchas stood there, sorry, of course, although for him this sacrifice may have been no more than the almost routine fulfillment of a religious duty. Next was Odysseus, hardened, shrewd, but perhaps less impervious to human feeling than his clerical colleague. Then Menelaus. With what eyes could he watch his virginal niece, in the flower of her youthful beauty, being cut down for the sake of his honor and desire to recover his adulterous wife? Finally the girl's father, Agamemnon. What were his feelings? His daughter was to die to preserve his position and prestige as commander-in-chief. Did he weep? Did he try to seem resolute? How would he look? The painter showed him turned away, his head muffled in his robe. It was for the spectator to supply the father's feelings from his own heart and to his own satisfaction.[10]

This leap into another dimension, from showing to not-showing, made Timanthes' picture famous throughout antiquity. This technique of antithesis was familiar to the Athenian playwrights. The ancient *hypothesis* (introductory summary) to Euripides' *Medea* notes that some critics had condemned him for inconsistencies in his heroine's character: "He is blamed for not sustaining Medea's role and for her resort to tears when plotting against Jason and his wife."[11] Horace later seems to echo this critical blame when he urges that characters should remain true to one

---

10. Cicero, *Orator* 22.74: "The painter saw, when at the sacrifice of Iphigenia Calchas was sad, Ulysses more sad, Menelaus in mourning, that Agamemnon's head had to be muffled, since he could not depict with the brush that supreme degree of grief." Cf. Pliny, *Natural History* 35.73: "He veiled the face of her actual father, unable to depict it satisfactorily." A version of Timanthes' painting from the House of the Tragic Poet at Pompeii is preserved in the Museo Nazionale, Naples. See also the relief on the circular marble altar signed by Cleomenes (latter half of first century A.D.), now in the Uffizi Gallery, Florence.

11. In a similar vein Eisenstein remarks: "In ancient tragedy one is frequently struck not so much by a double, divided nature but at times and above all by the unmotivated breakdown of a character into another extreme incommensurate and irreconcilable with the first, into another contradiction" (*I.P.*, vol. 3, 137). The difference is that he approves of this method of composition.

guiding emotion, "in agreement with themselves" (*Art of Poetry* 119). But the Greek writers knew differently. So did the painter Parrhasius when he depicted the Athenian people as a mass of contradictory emotions:

202

CLASSICAL

MYTH &

CULTURE

IN THE

CINEMA

> His painting of the Athenian *dêmos* [people] also shows great talent. He portrayed it as fickle, passionate, unjust, changeable, yet flexible, compassionate and lenient, boastful, proud and humble, bold and cowardly, in a word, everything alike.[12]

The route by which this complex legacy was transmitted to the later world has not always been accurately traced. Greek civilization did not pass directly from Athens to Rome. The importance of Alexandria in Hellenistic Egypt for the mediation of Greek antiquity even to Byzantium, the New Rome, and from there to Russia, is too easily forgotten. The duty of the Alexandrian poets in the third century B.C., led by Callimachus, was to assess the legacy of the past at a time when they were beset on two fronts, by the achievements of fourth-century prose and by the monopolization of the epic manner on the part of writers like Choerilus of Iasos, who, following a pattern set by his earlier namesake Choerilus of Samos, supposed that unthinking imitation of Homer's mannerisms could serve the propaganda needs of modern conquerors. Alexander the Great had remarked that he would sooner be Homer's Thersites than Choerilus' Achilles.[13] But the bitter polemic that eventually developed between the Callimacheans and the anti-Callimacheans over the question of epic shows that not all Hellenistic grandees were as fastidious as Alexander.

Callimachus, in rethinking the task of narrative poetry, was much influenced by the example of Pindar. In particular, he takes over some of Pindar's terms. In one place, tellingly an imitation of Pindar, he appears from our perspective to think ahead to a filmmaker's verb: "Let [the reader] add his own thought and so cut length off the song."[14]

Although often considered a great innovator, Callimachus here simply repeats an idea already attributed to Pindar's contemporary Aeschylus, reputed to have said that his plays were "cuts," that is, slices, from Homer's banquets.[15] Closer inspection of Callimachus's implied poetic reveals a num-

---

12. Pliny, *Natural History* 35.69; quoted from Pliny, *Chapters on the History of Art*, tr. Katherine Jex-Blake (1896; rpt. Chicago: Ares, 1982), 112. See my later mention of Homer's Andromache "laughing through her tears"; see also Callimachus, Fr. 298 Pfeiffer; Apollonius, *Argonautica* 4.1165–1167; Quintus Smyrnaeus, *Posthomerica* 7.635.

13. The ancient commentator Porphyrio (on Horace, *Art of Poetry* 357) has preserved Alexander's comment.

14. Callimachus, Fr. 57.1 Pfeiffer. See Peter J. Parsons, "Callimachus: *Victoria Berenices*," *Zeitschrift für Papyrologie und Epigraphik*, 25 (1977), 1–50.

15. Athenaeus, *The Deipnosophists* 347e.

ber of principles: analogy with music; selection of detail; vivid presentation that concentrates especially on emotion; balance and recurrence in language and overall setup; seriocomedy (irony) of tone. It is a measure of the importance of his poetic that it illumines not only him but also Virgil.

Between Callimachus and Virgil came Apollonius of Rhodes.[16] The subtle unifying of his new epic, *The Argonautica*, by repetition of key images has only recently become clear. In particular, the red-gold of the Fleece recurs throughout the poem in many guises: in the blushing cheek of love, in the hero's red cloak assumed for his visit to Hypsipyle, and eventually in the red stain spreading over a sister's silvery dress while her unarmed and unsuspecting brother is foully done to death in the shrine of Artemis by Jason.[17]

Greek eulogists such as Choerilus of Iasos may have invented for their poems strict parallels between modern patrons and the great heroes of old. An important aspect of the Hellenistic theory of allusion, which is a prominent feature of Apollonius' epic and reveals the erudition these Greek poets and their Roman emulators prized highly, is the abandonment of any search for exact or logical correspondences between the characters in a scene evoked from an earlier original and the later poets' adaptations. It is enough that the motifs should be recalled, even if they are now found differently distributed. This again is something Apollonius was to hand down to Virgil. (In Eisenstein's epic *Ivan the Terrible*, a dense pattern of reminiscences from earlier Russian literature lends resonance to the filmic narrative without any insistence on precise linkage. This is the inevitable outcome of a preoccupation with musical technique in all these artists.) Form elevates sense into something manipulable, suggested, transrational. Even where a scene is recalled from within the same work, its elements may be rearranged.

2. Aristotle's Poetics and Eisenstein's Theories of Film

Behind all the surface differences of meaning or form in ancient and modern works there lies a common human nature—more significantly, a

16. Hermann Fränkel, *Noten zu den Argonautika des Apollonios* (Munich: Beck, 1968), 324–325, uses film as an analogy to the art of the *Argonautica*: "wie wenn in einem laufenden Film," etc.

17. Eisenstein is critical, however, of the use of a symbolic red cloak in Rouben Mamoulian's 1935 film *Becky Sharp*, based on William Makepeace Thackeray's *Vanity Fair* (I.P., vol. 2, 372). In general, this metamorphosing image is an example of the concept of the "basic thought" mentioned later. For more on the use of connected images in the *Argonautica* see my *Classical Epic Tradition*, 74–88.

204

CLASSICAL

MYTH &

CULTURE

IN THE

CINEMA

common tradition, without understanding which we are bound to miss what individual works of art mean. Such a tradition is of vital importance for anyone dealing with antiquity and its continuing influence, and it is the supreme justification for the kind of investigation undertaken here.

Because of this shared tradition, I have already employed a terminology dependent on both Aristotelian and filmic principles to illuminate ancient poetic techniques. I spoke, for example, of drama, selectivity and characterization in Homer (all Aristotelian insights), and of the unity of opposites and a Kabuki-like quiet (both filmic principles) in Pindar's *First Nemean Ode*. Aristotle, the greatest of the ancient critics, was himself a creative artist, a poet. Let us compare his reflections with those of the greatest of the modern theoreticians of the film, Sergei Eisenstein, one of the cinema's foremost visual poets. If the theories of the two can be drawn together, my examination of them will be striking proof that a cinematic analysis of Greek poetry and its Roman heirs is neither intrusive nor anachronistic. Indeed, Eisenstein's thoughts correspond to the deepest insights of an ancient critic whose mind played over the whole range of classical Greek literature.

On the modern side, however, things begin ominously enough. Lenin had emphasized that in the class struggle the cinema was the most important of all arts. Eisenstein was a propagandist of revolution, his task to expose the corruption of the old system and the compelling common sense of the new order, one not in need of hypocritical pretenses or disguises. One might have thought at the time that it would have been enough for him merely to picture some sort of "scientific," objective truth. What is therefore extraordinary is his frank admission that the artist, even the Communist artist, is engaged in systematic distortion. Eisenstein points out, for example, how extensively in his agricultural film *The Old and the New* (1926–1929) he used "lens 28," rejected by other filmmakers because of its wide-angle distortion of the image. With this 28mm lens Eisenstein aimed at making objects go out of themselves, beyond the dimensions of the scope and forms nature prescribed for them. This deformation, as he goes on to explain, was also marked by irony or even satire. The hulk of the sleeping *kulak* (wealthy peasant), for example, from whom the activist member of the village cooperative, Martha Lapkina, hoped in vain to borrow horses for her plowing, was shot to look like the body of the dead Christ in a painting of Andrea Mantegna. The horses themselves were overlarge, and poor Martha ends up using her old cow. The kulak's bull became monumental until it looked like the mythical bull that had abducted Europa. During the shooting of *Battleship Potemkin* (1925), Eisenstein's cameraman Eduard Tissé hung netting or tulle over the lens in order to muffle the contours of objects in some of his shots. But this distortion is not at the service of narrow personal feelings, although Eisenstein declares that an artist is needed who writes with the blood of his own heart. The artist is only interested in the personal as far as it can be universalized. El Greco, to use Eisenstein's examples, may (or may not) have subsumed personal feelings in his "Storm over Toledo" or Leonardo da Vinci in his drawings of machines. This recalls the Aristotelian interest in what is *katholou* ("universal"; *Poetics* 1449b8).

The artist, continues Eisenstein, may have a twofold relationship to his material. He may wish to reflect it simply: sadness, jollity, and so on. But he may also have a comment to make. At this point irony enters, the deliberate transgression of the bounds of normality and expectation. As this transgression becomes more marked, there may occur a unity of opposites to secure a single artistic effect. Here is where Pindar's description of Amphitryon as "unbearable and yet happy" (*Nemean* 1.55–56) and, before him, Homer's famous phrase about Andromache ("laughing through her tears"; *Iliad* 6.484) secure their rationale. With the Presocratic philosopher Heraclitus, Eisenstein believes in the essential flux of phenomena, not in order to argue with Plato that they are unknowable or contemptible but to urge that they are growing and that they are doing so according to mathematically determinable laws. This is why he so strongly defends, for example, the use of the Golden Section and is pleased to note its occurrence in his films.

Although the cinema was a new art in the 1920s, Eisenstein uses a great many terms of classical rhetoric to describe it. Amplification, for example, is one of his basic concepts. By this he means the reshaping of reality to larger-than-life dimensions in order to serve an artistic purpose. He analyzes the novels of Emile Zola to point out how that master of realism distorted reality. He notes that, in a letter of October 24, 1894, Zola compared his use of repetition, for example, with Richard Wagner's use of the leitmotif and argued that in this way he secured greater unity for his works. Similarly, adds Eisenstein, in his preface to *Pierre et Jean*, Guy de Maupassant claimed that critics usually fail to discover the most subtle threads, hidden and often invisible, that certain modern writers use in place of the previous single thread, the intrigue. Eisenstein claims that he is the heir of the past.[18]

Eisenstein advances criteria of appreciation for the classics which go well beyond mere commonplaces. The following principles of his poetic are the most important. Before I discuss them in greater detail, I list each point with a reference to a passage of Aristotle's *Poetics* that advances a similar argument.

18. *I.P.*, vol. 3, 238.

206

CLASSICAL

MYTH &

CULTURE

IN THE

CINEMA

1. *The primacy of the theatrical among artistic genres.* The real heir to ancient epic is modern drama. Eisenstein thought that his acted art was the culmination and encapsulation of the art of the past. With some adjustments, this is the thesis of chapter 26 of the *Poetics.* In the same vein, Aristotle had characterized Homer's artistry as "dramatic" (*Poetics* 1448b35).

2. *The actor's art is paradigmatic for the creative artist,* but this does not mean that the actor matters more than the story. The Russian cinema rejected the Hollywood star system. To Aristotle, the plot (*mythos*) is the soul of tragedy, and the actor helps complete the script with his gestures as indicated or designed by the poet (*Poetics* 1450a38 and 1455a29).

3. *Metaphor is the chief and unteachable poetic gift.* To Aristotle, "much the most important thing is to be metaphorical" (*Poetics* 1459a6).

4. *Factual or historical truth is irrelevant to the artist's need for figurative truth.* According to Aristotle, "poetry is something more philosophical and serious than history" (*Poetics* 1451b5–6).

5. *Clarity in unwavering attention to artistic goals is essential, aided by careful selection of detail.* The film director's achievement lies chiefly in his ability to cut effectively, a point also crucial to Eisenstein's contemporary, director and film theorist Vsevolod Pudovkin. Aristotle's praise of Homer is especially relevant here (*Poetics* 1451a22).

6. *The work of art must have a controlling rhythm,* to be derived from the director's overall concept of what his work is meant to express. This parallels *Poetics* 1451a30–35.

7. *The artist must make use of pathetic structure.* In this way the recipient of his work is continually torn between opposite poles of emotion until this movement becomes so violent that there is a breakthrough or leap into another dimension. This may occur on a small or on a large scale; if the latter, then with climactic and shattering emotional effect. With this we may compare the Aristotelian concept of catharsis (*Poetics* 1449b28).

As the parallels in Aristotle show, Eisenstein's points apply to Greek poetry. My discussion now amplifies the observations with which this essay began.

1. The theatrical has priority because all great art tends toward drama. Plato had disparaged Homer as "the leader of the modern tragedians" (*Republic* 595b–c). Aristotle developed Plato's point for the Attic tragedians but reversed his judgment, especially at the end of the *Poetics.* Shakespeare would have been a supreme illustration of Aristotle's thesis, but because we take Shakespeare for granted we cannot see what an amazing argument in defense of "modern" poetry Aristotle, a conservative Greek, advanced. He dismissed all flaccid epic writing, which passed itself off as Homeric by aping the external mannerisms of the grand style, and

seized upon the real merit of the *Iliad*, in particular that it was "dramatic" and "tragic." The dramatic scenes in the *Iliad* and their speeches prove the correctness of Aristotle's insight.

Stesichorus early turned the choral lyric toward dramatic themes, and the tenth-century Byzantine Suda lexicon attributes dramas even to Pindar. Whatever these may have been, the dramatic confrontations and character painting of, for example, the *Fourth Pythian Ode* are clear. Pelias is a crude, cunning and bombastic liar; Jason, the soul of honor. Euripides, who raised tragedy to new heights while—in Eisenstein's words—"visibly preserving the features of its line of inheritance from earlier (lower) stages of intensity," was to be acutely conscious of lyric drama. (I return to this quotation from Eisenstein at greater length later.) Such drama reached its climax on so traditional a theme as that of Euripides' *Bacchae*, whatever the novelty of certain details.

2. Eisenstein admired the Russian stage directors Konstantin Stanislavsky and Vsevolod Meyerhold and, although he does not mention him, was in his way also a disciple of Duns Scotus with his theory of *haecceitas* (literally, "thisness"). You cannot depict grief, Eisenstein says in a famous passage, you can only depict this grief in this person in this context, because only by visualizing and feeling your way into the specifics of the pathetic situation can you recreate them convincingly for the spectator.[19] Horace, depending on Aristotelian tradition, says exactly the same thing: "If you want me to weep, you have to weep yourself first of all. Then your misfortunes, Telephus or Peleus, will bruise me" (*Art of Poetry* 102–103). Aristotle had said something broader. The playwright, if he hopes to persuade, should act out each part to himself. Commentators have found this odd, although there are parallels with Charles Dickens or Henrik Ibsen. But if this is indeed odd, why does the comic poet Aristophanes depict the tragedians Euripides and Agathon as wearing their characters' clothes while writing their plays?[20] Agathon explains his behavior in quite intelligible terms. He says he changes his attitude according to what he has on:

> I wear clothing to suit my frame of mind. For a poet must suit his character to the plays he has to write. For example, when he writes about women, he must physically share in their character.[21]

19. *I.P.*, vol. 3, 37.

20. Aristophanes, *Acharnians* 412 and *Thesmophoriazusae* 148–152 (quoted later).

21. This is an insight effectively exploited by Bertolt Brecht in *Galileo*, when the liberal Cardinal Maffeo Barberini, dressing on stage in his papal robes after his election as Urban VIII, becomes more and more illiberal as he assumes the garb appropriate to his new office.

Writer and stage or film director must be imaginatively inside their characters' minds if they wish to present them persuasively. Only then will they be able to call forth the desired emotions in the spectator.

208

CLASSICAL

MYTH &

CULTURE

IN THE

CINEMA

3. After noting certain individual features in *The Old and the New*, Eisenstein remarks that the film also needed an overall metaphor. In this piece of propaganda for the collective farm, the metaphor was that of a fountain of milk, recalling peasant proverbs about "rivers of milk." Eisenstein also argues for the importance of metaphor in general, of the feel by the author for an image that controls all individual representations of the action. The content of Homer's and Vladimir Mayakovsky's metaphors is different, he remarks, but the principle of metaphor is the same in both.[22] Just so, music may change, but rhythm is essential to all of it. Without such a metaphor, the details of a composition will tend to fall to pieces. This already implies the principle of selectivity, since what is irrelevant to the reinforcement of the metaphor must be cut out. If modern critics of classical literature had grasped this point, their appreciation of Apollonius' *Argonautica*, and the significance in it of the Golden Fleece, would have been immeasurably deeper. In many odes of Pindar, a governing image is metamorphosed time and again to lend a musical unity to the whole. Eisenstein and Stanislavsky agree that without some overarching aim (*sverkhzadacha*, "basic thought") as organizational principle the artistic production simply disintegrates.

4. Eisenstein handled the events of the Potemkin mutiny with great freedom. In general he was opposed to the literalness that cripples poetic imagination. But the conflict between historical poetry and imaginative larger-scale writing is ancient. The preface to Callimachus' *Aitia*, for example, gives us some inkling of the bitter intensity with which this creative war was pursued in Alexandria. Why this clash of opinion matters so much beyond Hellenistic culture can only be fully understood outside the Greek world, since the principal protagonists when the battle continued were, at least probably, the Roman epic poets Ennius and Virgil. An inability to understand this irreconcilable division is the likely reason for the failure of Petrarch's epic *Africa*.[23] The imaginative writer is asking for freedom to develop a larger truth, and that truth may not always be flattering to heroes.

5. Selectivity is obvious in Pindar and the Alexandrian poets. But long before them, Homer chose one particular episode from the ten-year siege

22. *I.P.* vol. 3, 200.

23. Petrarch wanted to be a second Ennius, that is, a writer of historical epic, but his genius was too Ovidian, and the poem died in the fight between ambition and inclination. I develop this thesis in more detail in *The Classical Epic Tradition*, 282–292.

of Troy to encapsulate the entire experience of men at war.[24] The scene is set in the passage from the *Iliad* I cited at the beginning. Brutal, irreligious self-gratification has taken over in Agamemnon's mind from any larger purpose. As he defends his action in his dramatic confrontation with Achilles later in Book 1, it becomes evident that no sacrifice of his will end the war, since he has no imagination, no new method, but only the persistence with the old and failed. Achilles will break out of the stereotype and in so doing become the first tragic hero of European literature. In Books 20–22 we will not hear the name of Agamemnon at all. The commander-in-chief becomes irrelevant. This is also why Homer, who knew about the Trojan Horse (*Odyssey* 4.272), says nothing about it in the *Iliad*, where it might have made a difference. Not clever tactics but the sacrifice of flesh and blood in mortal combat changes history; the profound meditation on what that means changes poetry. Homer closely illustrates the following remarks by Eisenstein:

> Composition takes the structural elements of the phenomenon represented and from them creates the law of the thing's structure. Moreover, in the first instance, it takes these elements from the structure of the emotional behavior of the human being connected with the experience of the content of this or another represented phenomenon. . . . Precisely for this reason genuine composition is necessarily deeply human.[25]

6. Eisenstein, like the Roman elegist Gallus, was also an engineer, and so he was not afraid of the slide rule. He believed that pathos can only be present when there is an almost biological relation between the work of art and the laws of life and growth. Eisenstein sees this relation in the spiral graph of the Golden Section. He considered *Battleship Potemkin* a five-act tragedy. Tragedy, he says, has five acts because of the Golden Section. This allows for a transition into a sharp opposition, in which the organic growth of the work of art breaks through into new levels of development without losing its coherence and structure.

To suggest that ancient epics or dramas must have a controlling rhythm opens the door to speculations about numerical composition, in whose labyrinthine complexities the too-often innumerate critic can become quickly lost. But Aristotle claims that there must be some degree of measure when he argues that a work of art must be "easily viewable as one" (*eusunopton*) and when he rejects the notion of a hypothetical creature

---

24. On the timelessness of this see in particular Jonathan Shay, *Achilles in Vietnam: Combat Trauma and the Undoing of Character* (1993; rpt. New York: Simon and Schuster, 1995).

25. *I.P.*, vol. 3, 38.

of ten thousand stades. Not to measure is to lose control. This is the point of the later polemic against the turgid Antimachus, whom Plato had admired. "The *Lyde* [of Antimachus] is a crass piece of writing and not clear," was Callimachus' judgment (Fr. 398 Pfeiffer). "But let the common herd take pleasure in swollen Antimachus," said Catullus (95.10). As Attic tragedy recapitulates its development in Euripides, we see symmetry reclaiming its prominence in, for example, *The Trojan Women*.[26]

7. Like Aristotelian catharsis, "pathetic structure" is a difficult concept. It is best to let Eisenstein speak for himself:

> Pathetic composition in essence is a measure of the formation of expressive methods, matching the measure of the pathetic apprehension by the author of his theme. At that point, the composition acquires the tokens of a new quality but at the same time visibly preserves the features of its line of inheritance from earlier (lower) stages of intensity, which it is possible to feel and detect through the lines of this new quality. . . . Pathos is what causes someone to go out of himself. It is the same as ecstasy. And ecstasy is the transition into another quality. . . . Pathos is the unity of opposites within the actual principle of composition. The unity of the later and the simultaneous.[27]

Part of this restates, although in somewhat different terms, the argument of the treatise *On the Sublime*, which praised phantasia as the power of imagination so vivid that it communicated the artist's emotion (pathos) to his audience. The vision of dead Achilles recreated for the departing Greeks and their Trojan captives all the tragic memories of what ten years of war had cost them. In this passage, the ancient author is moving in traditional areas, as his kinship with Greek Stoic thinkers and, on the Latin side, with Horace and Quintilian shows. The technique was familiar to the Renaissance. Erasmus remarks:

> We use this [*evidentia*] whenever, for the sake of *amplifying*, adorning or pleasing, we do not state a thing simply, but set it forth to be viewed as if portrayed in color on a panel, so that it may seem that we have painted, not narrated, and that the reader has seen, not read. We will be able to do this well if we first conceive a mental picture of the subject with all its attendant circumstances. Then we should so portray it in words and fitting figures that it is as clear and graphic as possible to the reader.[28]

26. On this see Werner Biehl, "Quantitative Formgestaltung bei Euripides: Die Trimeterszenen der *Troades*," *Philologus*, 126 (1982), 19–43. See also his *Textkritik und Formanalyse zur euripideischen Hekabe: Ein Beitrag zum Verständnis der Komposition* (Heidelberg: Winter, 1997).

27. I.P., vol. 3, 39, 60–61, and 381.

28. Modified from Erasmus, *On Copia of Words and Ideas*, tr. Donald B. King and Herbert David Rix (Milwaukee: Marquette University Press, 1963; rpt. 1999), 47. Horace's

We already saw that "amplification" was one of Eisenstein's favorite terms. To him, the artist in essence recreates the original process in himself, and the spectators recreate it again under his artistic guidance. Imaginative feeling, in which the artist and his actors project themselves into the characters they are portraying, determines the visualization of the work. This leads the artist to select those details for portrayal that will most effectively convey a character's feelings. But these details will also be juxtaposed in such a way as to throw the observer off balance. When this happens often enough, a breakthrough occurs to a new dimension of feeling, what the author of *On the Sublime* called *ekplêxis*, knockout astonishment. This term is Aristotelian (*Poetics* 1455a17), although Aristotle does not use it with quite as narrow or drastic a scope as it was to acquire later.

Greek poet and Russian filmmaker alike select the telling detail for more than its vividness. The artist who narrates everything not only will bore his audience to death, as Antimachus seems to have done with his *Thebaid*, but he will leave nothing for it to do. If, on the other hand, he offers a few significant details after the principle that a part may stand for the whole, viewers or listeners will be drawn into working these details into a total picture. Engaged in the artistic process, they will be the more susceptible to its effect. This is why the old priest's tears in Homer were not mentioned at the time of the original insult. We deduced his grief by the contrast between his silence and the noise of the surging ocean. We must think into the text. This became so marked a feature of the Greco-Roman theater in its later pantomimic period that "eloquent silence" was then, as now, a cliché.[29]

Even the ancient Greek commentators understood the power of a repeated image.[30] Great artists possess a plasticity of imagination by which they see the similarity in difference. This is why Aristotle thought that metaphor was the chief and unteachable poetic gift. Eisenstein transforms his images again and again.[31] In *Battleship Potemkin* mutinous sailors are

---

famous phrase *ut pictura poesis* ("poetry like painting"; *Art of Poetry* 361) is already an Aristotelian insight; see *Aristotle: The Poetics*, ed. D. W. Lucas (Oxford: Clarendon Press, 1968; rpt. 1990), 56, on *Poetics* 1447a18.

29. Cf. Otto Weinreich, *Epigrammstudien*, vol. 1: *Epigramm und Pantomimus* (Heidelberg: Winter, 1948), 144–145.

30. Cf. Robin R. Schlunk, *The Homeric Scholia and the Aeneid: A Study of the Influence of Ancient Homeric Literary Criticism on Vergil* (Ann Arbor: University of Michigan Press, 1974), 41.

31. The following remarks on *Battleship Potemkin* are paraphrased from *I.P.*, vol. 3, 264, and show what Eisenstein wished to emphasize rather than what may be valid in a total description of his film. See also his essay on organization and pathos in the composition of the film in *Izbrannye Stat'i*, 243–251.

212

CLASSICAL

MYTH &

CULTURE

IN THE

CINEMA

to be executed on the quarter-deck by a firing squad drawn from their own comrades. A rolled-up canvas is brought in, carried so that it already looks like a shrouded corpse. In real life, this canvas would have been spread on the deck to catch the blood of the victims. Eisenstein had the idea of draping it instead over their heads, so that they are both dehumanized and buried while still alive. Later, Eisenstein wryly reports, the survivors of the mutiny recast their memories of the event in accordance with his artistic reconstruction.[32] A command is barked out, and the firing squad raises its rifles. There is an agonizing wait, ended by the muffled cry of "Brothers!" The entire crew heeds the cry and joins the mutiny, but one sailor, Vakulinchuk, is killed. The ship now sails for the harbor of Odessa, which is wrapped in a gray mist symbolic of mourning. Slowly the gray polarizes into black and white, culminating in the laying of the white-shrouded body on the black stones of the quay. A tiny candle is placed between the corpse's fingers. The element of fire grows into the towns-people's fiery anger and on into the raising over the ship of the fiery red flag of socialist revolution. It reverses into the fire of the black-and-white uniformed militia of the czar, who ruthlessly charge and massacre the unarmed protesting civilians on the steps leading down to the harbor. The battleship fires back its defiance, shaking the theater building in which the czar's generals are discussing their plans. (This detail is meant symbolically, because they are only irrelevant extras on the stage of events.) The linkage of all these scenes by recurring images is the rediscovery of an ancient technique. Eisenstein himself remarked: "Let us begin, as always, from our ancestors." These ancestors for him included the Greeks.[33]

If the principle of pathetic style should appear to explain too much— Greek, Russian, whatever—the explanation lies in the shared humanity of the artist's psychology, which may be engaged "either consciously or in some inspirational way." This is Eisenstein's phrase, and again there is agreement with Aristotle.[34] Eisenstein closely shares with Aristotle the belief that the actor's art is that of the author, that the true test of poetic genius is the use of metaphor, that music is the "sweetest" of the embellishments on which tragedy can call, that epic finds its natural culmination in drama, and that in drama not the hero but the action is of primary importance.[35] He also shares with him something else, the belief that the ultimate aim of pathetic structure is the leap into another dimen-

32. *I.P.*, vol. 2, 370.
33. *I.P.*, vol. 2, 393. On the Greeks see, for example, *I.P.*, vol. 3, 136.
34. *I.P.*, vol. 3, 200; cf. *Poetics* 1451a24: "either through art or natural gift."
35. The traditional translation "sweetest" (*Poetics* 1450b16) is, however, too mawkish. The connection of the adjective *hedys* ("sweet") with *hêdonê* ("pleasure") must not be forgotten.

sion of consciousness that raises the spectator beyond himself, projects him perhaps into that *katharsis tôn pathêmatôn*, that "purging of the passions," that for centuries has been found puzzling and fascinating in Aristotle's *Poetics*. Eisenstein does not think that this leap into another dimension occurs once or that it is the mechanical discharge of ugly and unwanted humors. The multiplying of pathetic details leads to a sharp transition into another level of apprehension. Pathetic structure, moving between antithetical polarities all the time, eventually pushes its patient into an ecstasy of pathos.

So it was that in *Battleship Potemkin* a revolutionary flag filmed in black and white suddenly looked red under pressure of the fire imagery that pervades the entire film. So in Homer the cheers of the applauding Greeks who were quite willing for Chryses to get his daughter back passed into Agamemnon's angry words, into silence, into the noise of the elemental sea, and into prayer and the supernatural sound of Apollo's bow: "And terrible was the clang of his silver bow" (*Iliad* 1.49). Apollo would later guide the arrow that kills Achilles (Virgil, *Aeneid* 6.56–58).

3. Performance: Roman Literature and Film

In their recent appreciations of classical literature, scholars have increasingly come to understand the central importance of performance. For this there are clues in the ancient sources, not only Plato's description, in the *Ion*, of Ion's presentations from Homer but also stories of Herodotus or Apollonius reading from their works. Virgil is said to have displayed "voice and utterance and acting skill," while Horace and Ovid note the public recitals of their Augustan contemporaries.[36]

As the impulse of Greek drama became assimilated in Rome, the Roman theater moved back from tragedy and comedy toward mime and pantomime. (We may think of pantomime as the ancient precursor of silent cinema.) The pantomime was known in classical Athens, but Roman poets pressed the ideal of performance even further.[37] By Virgil's day, there were amazing performers. Bathyllus, the comic actor from Alexandria, was a particular favorite of Maecenas. The tragedian Pylades of Cilicia lectured the emperor on the value of the theater to despots and composed a book on his art. He introduced some reforms, including the enlargement of the

---

36. Donatus, *Life of Virgil* 28; Horace, *Epistles* 2.2.90–105; Ovid, *Tristia* 4.10.43–50 and *Ex Ponto* 4.2.33–34.

37. On the Greek pantomime see Weinreich, *Epigramm und Pantomimus*, 125 and plate 1 (facing page 176).

214

CLASSICAL

MYTH &

CULTURE

IN THE

CINEMA

orchestra that accompanied his performances. When asked to define his innovations, he replied with a Homeric line: "The call of flutes and pipes and the hubbub of humankind" (*Iliad* 10.13). Pylades felt the excitement of Homer's martial and heroic verses. His choice of "Pylades" for a stage name—Pylades was the companion of mad Orestes, "harried over the stage," in the words of Virgil (*Aeneid* 4.471)—hints that he claimed a place, however subordinate, in the heroic world.

This tragic pantomime, which at Rome came to prevail over its comic counterpart, singled out particular highly charged episodes instead of telling a connected story. A sung narrative accompanied the actor's studied dance. From these episodes the performer extracted the greatest possible pathos. To judge from surviving titles, there was a preference for characters caught at moments of crisis and collapse or fluttering on the borderlines of sanity and madness, of one world and another.[38] Such art, biased toward the unnatural, violent and frenzied, inevitably influenced more formal literature. The *Aeneid*, for instance, is the product of an age that both relished such tastes and asserted that they had borrowed something from Homer. Nero himself wanted to dance the role of Virgil's Turnus; later, Dido became a special favorite of pantomimes.[39] The Roman aesthetic in general is essentially carnivalesque, theatrical, pantomimic, musical, lyrical. Eisenstein believed that all performance art, including cinema, grew out of vaudeville and the circus.[40] Mikhail Bakhtin speaks of the carnival as theater without footlights, a description applicable to Roman life.[41] The following are some basic interrelated principles of the Roman "cinematic" aesthetic, which was indebted to the Greeks and transmitted by Byzantium to Russia:

1. The *appetite for outdoing all that went before*. This means borrowing from the past as a way of making it contribute to a new and more complex present.

2. *Nonlinear (vertical) time*. Everything is here now; yet what is present has value only as a symbol, one half of a whole to which the au-

---

38. Ludwig Friedlaender, *Darstellungen aus der Sittengeschichte Roms in der Zeit von August bis zum Ausgang der Antonine*, vol. 2 (10th ed.; Leipzig: Hirzel, 1922), 127, lists, among others, *Atreus and Thyestes, Ajax Mad, Hercules Mad, Niobe, Hector, Aphrodite and Adonis, Aphrodite and Ares, Apollo and Daphne, Phaedra and Hippolytus, Meleager and Atalante, Jason and Medea.*

39. Suetonius, *Nero* 54; Macrobius, *Saturnalia* 5.17.5.

40. He speaks fondly of his early stage production in 1922–1923 of an experimental farce with the proverbial title *Every Wise Man Is a Bit of a Fool*, after Alexander Ostrovsky's nineteenth-century comedy (*I.P.*, vol. 2, 453). Miming occurs in the first part of *Ivan the Terrible*.

41. Mikhail Bakhtin, *Rabelais and His World*, tr. Hélène Iswolsky (Bloomington: Indiana University Press, 1984), 6–7.

dience must fit a second half from their own experience, memory, and understanding—for example in the *Aeneid* the prophetic anticipations of Augustus' Rome and of limitless empire in Books 1 and 6 and Latinus' quite unrealistic palace in Book 7 (7.170–191). The tarpaulin scene in Eisenstein's *Battleship Potemkin* is a related example, as we saw. Nothing directly presented is exclusively concrete or specific.

3. *Mixing or dissolving* serial sequence by the combination of different stages and models of the past. This is particularly clear in Virgil's reverse-sequence imitation of Homer's two epics in both halves of his *Aeneid*, but it also occurs in his treatment of character.

4. *The use of form to transcend form* (in Eisenstein's phrase, the "leap into another dimension"). Since the Roman imagination was profoundly theatrical—to us, cinematic—what looks like, but rarely is, plain narrative in Roman poetry tends to dissolve into the scenic, involving both sight and sound. The phrase "a scene [*scaena*, i.e., theatrical backdrop] among shimmering woods" (*Aeneid* 1.164) occurs as the fugitive Trojans land in Africa, where they will find Dido building a theater at Carthage (1.427–429; cf. 4.471, mentioned earlier). The funeral games for Anchises take place in a *theatrum* ("theater"; 5.664), even a round stage evocative of classical Greek drama (*theatri circus*; 5.288–289). Hence also the prominence of rhetorically presented speeches and the entrusting of what actors call "business," that is, the added details intended to flesh out a performance, to the professional interpreter ("hypocrite") and to readers trained like him.[42] Here key words of Virgil's aesthetic such as "shadow" (*umbra*) and "reflection" (*imago*) find their proper context. Virgil's fascination with fires in the night, supremely illustrated in Book 2, is a particularly telling example. "Shadow-painting"—*skiagraphia* is Plato's term (*Critias* 107d)—is allied to the use of chiaroscuro ("darkness visible"), which is part of the control of interior space or emotionalism. Dido and Turnus, both deranged, haunted, became favorite pantomime parts.

While a libretto, sometimes composed by poets as gifted as Lucan or Statius, was sung, a virtuoso dancer interpreted the words by his gestures and movements in a process Eisenstein would have instantly recognized as an example of his "leap into another dimension." Tacitus tells us that some authors of his day were delighted to find their compositions sung and danced and that orators and actors received and enjoyed interchangeable compliments (*Dialogue on Orators* 26.3). It is hard to believe that

42. Cf. again Callimachus' statement quoted earlier: "Let [the reader] add his own thought, and so cut length off the song." Silent reading was not the rule in antiquity.

such skillful performances did not influence some of the surviving literary masterpieces.[43]

Eisenstein speaks of drunkenness and dreams as the closest approximation by normal consciousness to primitive emotion and thought.[44] Apollonius makes effective use of dreams, a token of the restless atmosphere of the Hellenistic world. They illustrate the thematic harmony in the structure of his epic.[45] Dreams play a notable part in Book 3 of the *Argonautica*, when the poet portrays lovelorn Medea's tormented mind. Yet psychological and even fantastic dreams were old. In the *Odyssey*, Homer had given a waking vision like a nightmarish trance, in which the seer Theoclymenus, one of Penelope's suitors, sees the palace walls running with blood.[46] The suitors' heads are wrapped in darkness, and this is in effect their "death-dream."[47] After Homer and before Apollonius, the Greek tragedians incorporated such psychological dreams into their plays, with a marked interest in women as dreamers. Atossa in Aeschylus' *Persians* and Euripides' Iphigenia are well-known instances.

These explorations of the dissolving bounds of perception are a further anticipation of film technique. Early Russian cinema knew the "Kuleshov effect," the ability of the cinema to juxtapose dimensions of perception in order to generate new apprehensions of time and space. This might be at the level of simple social criticism, as when a shot of soldiers dying in war was immediately followed by a scene of feverish activity on the St. Petersburg Stock Exchange in Pudovkin's *The End of St. Petersburg* (1927). It might be the method of entering a mind teetering on the brink of madness, as in the first part of Eisenstein's *Ivan the Terrible*. Such extremes had always attracted tragedy. Euripides' *Orestes* and *Bacchae* presented examinations of a crumbling mind, and in the latter play Pentheus' double vision was the "cinematic" symptom of his altered state. Hellenistic theater, known to us only in fragments, inherited and further developed these techniques. Roman adaptations give us some inkling of

216

CLASSICAL

MYTH &

CULTURE

IN THE

CINEMA

43. I have argued this case for Catullus and Propertius in *Roman Catullus and the Modification of the Alexandrian Sensibility* (Hildesheim: Weidmann, 1990), 343–366, and *Augustan Propertius: The Recapitulation of a Genre* (Hildesheim: Olms, 1997), 176–177.

44. *I.P.*, vol. 3, 424.

45. See my *Classical Epic Tradition*, 86.

46. *Odyssey* 20.345–358. Cf. Circe's dream in Apollonius, *Argonautica* 4.664. In general see A. Leo Oppenheim, *The Interpretation of Dreams in the Ancient Near East with a Translation of an Assyrian Dream Book* (Philadelphia: American Philosophical Society, 1956; rpt. 1974), 179–374.

47. The term is from Oppenheim, *The Interpretation of Dreams*, 213.

the powerful effects of its aesthetic, aided by the swiftly changing rhythms of voice and flute.

In Ennius' *Alexander*, for example, adapted from a play of Euripides, mad Cassandra indulges in extraordinary outbursts. Paris unexpectedly returns to the royal court, and his sister foresees that he will prove the ruin of Troy. Her song switches rapidly between rhythms—different meters—and visions:

> Here, here is the torch, wrapped in blood and fire, hidden for many years. Citizens, help, quench it! . . . And now on the mighty sea a swift fleet is being built, speeding a cargo of dooms. A savage band will come and fill our shores with its ships. . . .
>
> O light of Troy, my own brother Hector, why is your body so torn, and you so pitiful? What dragging is this before our very eyes?
>
> With a great leap a horse pregnant with men-at-arms has jumped over [our walls], and when it gives birth it is to bring low lofty Pergamum.[48]

The audience knew well the story of Troy's downfall. Yet to Cassandra's hearers on stage, these were events still to come. For the moment, they could dismiss her as mad. The tension generated by conflicting times and truths produces a kind of theater that foreshadows the cinema. For a full realization of its visual qualities and its quick movements from mental image to mental image, this theater needs the resources of the cinema, especially camera and editing.

In Ennius' *Alcmaeon*, probably taken from another Euripidean model, the hero, slayer of his own mother, has a vision of divine punishment. The Furies, aided by the gods, are assailing him:

> Bring me help, drive from me this plague, the fiery force which tortures me! Here they come, girt with black snakes, surrounding me with their blazing torches. Long-haired Apollo bends his golden bow, leaning on the moon. On the left, Diana hurls a brand.[49]

An Apollo leaning on the moon is virtually a Symbolist image, passed quite beyond the scope of any sort of realism. Again, only the cinema, or a stage borrowing from the cinema, could do full justice to such effects.[50]

---

48. The text is most easily accessible in *Remains of Old Latin*, ed. E. H. Warmington, vol. 1: *Ennius and Caecilius*, rev. ed. (Cambridge: Harvard University Press; London: Heinemann, 1967), 234–245; the passages translated (*Alexander* 67–72 and 76–81) are at 242 and 244.

49. Ennius, *Alcmaeon* 32–36; text at Warmington, *Ennius and Caecilius*, 232. Warmington's text and translation accept a modern emendation, which I do not adopt.

50. Mench, "Film Sense in the *Aeneid*," is especially good on this aspect of the film-maker's art.

218

CLASSICAL

MYTH &

CULTURE

IN THE

CINEMA

Much work still remains to be done before we can appreciate the full impact of the vivid, dramatic, painterly, musical, metamorphosing art of ancient narrative on its audiences. For scholars, it will not be enough to develop parallels between the ancient and the modern by random discovery. But when they look to filmmakers for a systematic theory, elaborated into what the Greeks would have called a poetic, to provide them with guidance, they would do well first to consult the pages of Sergei Eisenstein.

X

Film Sense in the *Aeneid*

Fred Mench

EDITOR'S NOTE: This essay originally appeared in *Arion*, 8 (1969), 380–397. An earlier detailed study of Book 1 of the *Aeneid* as filmic text is Paul Leglise, *Une oeuvre de pré-cinéma: L'Enéide: Essai d'analyse filmique du premier chant* (Paris: Debresse, 1958). See also A. Malissard, "Homère, Virgile et le langue cinématographique," *Caesarodunum*, 5 (1970), 155–169.

. . . workers in the art of film should not only study playwriting and the actor's craft, but must give equal attention to mastering all the subtleties of montage creation in all cultures.
— Sergei M. Eisenstein

The literary critic should study not only philology or comparative literature but also the techniques employed by the filmmaker if he wishes to appreciate those literary works that utilize a kinetic visual approach: montage, variation of viewing angle, alternation of close-up and distance shot, and the like.

In "Word and Image," the chief essay in *The Film Sense*, Eisenstein analyzes a number of authors, especially Alexander Pushkin and John Milton, to show that they used essentially cinematic techniques to give dynamic emphasis to scenes.[1] One short quotation will illustrate the nature of his analysis:

---

1. Sergei M. Eisenstein, "Word and Image," in *The Film Sense*, ed. and tr. Jay Leyda (1942; rpt. New York: Harcourt Brace Jovanovich, 1975), 1–65. The epigraph appears at 65, the following two quotations at 58–60.

220

CLASSICAL

MYTH &

CULTURE

IN THE

CINEMA

Paradise Lost itself is a first-rate school in which to study montage and audio-visual relationships. . . . Studying the pages of his [Milton's] poem, and in each individual case analyzing the determining qualities and expressive effects of each example, we become extraordinarily enriched in experience of the audio-visual distribution of images in his sound montage.

But here are the images themselves:

(*The Approach of the "Host of Satan"*)

> . . . at last
> Farr in th' Horizon to the North appeer'd
> From skirt to skirt a fierie Region, stretcht
> In battailous aspect, and neerer view
> Bristl'd with upright beams innumerable
> Of rigid Spears, and Helmets throng'd, and Shields
> Various, with boastful Argument portraid,
> The banded Powers of *Satan* hasting on
> With furious expedition. . . .

Note the cinematographic instruction in the third full line to *change the camera set-up*: "neerer view"!

Eisenstein then goes on to a line-by-line analysis of a passage from one of the battle scenes, transcribing fifteen lines of the poem "arranged in accordance with the various compositional set-ups, as a shooting script." I cite Eisenstein not because he formed the springboard for my analysis (in fact, I was directed to Eisenstein only after I had written the core of this essay) but because of his clear articulation of the *effect* the montage technique has on the reader and because of his skill and perception in applying the critical methods of one discipline to another to show that each is creating basically the same effect with the same technique.

Most people who think of Virgil's artistry in visual terms tend to describe him as a painter, citing, for example, the backdrop painting of the harbor scene in Book 1 of the *Aeneid* (1.159–169). But actually more striking is the extent to which he employs the techniques of a film director, of which montage is but one. This can most readily be seen, I think, if we look at a few passages in the *Aeneid* as if they were the scenario for a film. I attempt in my translations to retain where possible the line-by-line structure of the Latin, with some consequent sacrifice of English fluency and Latin syntax, in order to facilitate references and to indicate run-on or end-stopped lines and to approximate the succession of words and images as Virgil gives them.

1. *Aeneid* 4.68–93

A good passage to start with is the sequence in which Virgil presents a montage on the theme of Dido's preoccupation with Aeneas to the exclusion of her duties as queen and caps it with a striking shot of the effects of this preoccupation:

> Luckless Dido burns with love and wanders over the whole
> city in frenzy, just like a deer when an arrow is loosed,
> the doe is caught off-guard amid Cretan forests
> by a hunter's chance shot; his swift shaft hits the mark
> unknown to him; the doe flees through grove and glade
> on Mount Dicte, the fatal shaft stuck in her side.
> Now Dido leads Aeneas around the walls
> and shows him the Tyrian riches in the city she has built.
> She starts to speak but checks herself in mid-word.
> Now she proposes banquets in the waning light
> and is mad to hear again of Troy's tribulations;
> she demands it and hangs from his every word.
> Afterward, when all have left, a fitful light from a hazy
> moon struggles in, and the setting stars suggest sleep;
> alone in the deserted hall Dido weeps and, on the couch he has just left,
> stretches out. Him she hears and sees even when apart,
> and holds Ascanius in her lap, taken by his likeness to his father—
> holds him to see if she can outwit love.
> Though started, the towers no longer rise; military training
> ceases, and harbors and protective battlements
> lie neglected; standing unfinished are the threatening
> huge walls, atop which a heaven-reaching crane stands against the sky.
> As soon as Dido was seen succumbing to this disease
> by Jove's dear mate (wagging tongues in no way inhibited her madness, as
>   Juno saw),
> with such words did Saturn's daughter approach
> Venus. . . .

Although nearly every line takes the reader-viewer on to a new scene or image, the basic absence of end-stopped lines ties groups of images or scenes together. From lines 68 to 73 there is no real end-stopping: Love-struck Dido wanders in frenzy through the city and the deer wanders the forest as the camera follows them in a dizzying whirl until the sequence ends with the close-up of the arrow sticking in the doe's side:

> uritur infelix Dido totaque vagatur
> urbe furens, qualis coniecta cerva sagitta,
> quam procul incautam nemora inter Cresia fixit
> pastor agens telis liquitque volatile ferrum
> nescius: illa fuga silvas saltusque peragrat
> Dictaeos; haeret lateri letalis harundo.

The wanderings of Dido and the deer are contrasted with, and separated by, the picture in line 70 of the unsuspecting deer standing quietly unaware of her danger (*incautam*). But *we* are aware of the danger; at the end of the preceding line we have watched the flight of the arrow; the very arrangement of the words (*coniecta cerva sagitta*) already shows the deer encompassed.

If we were going to write this particular segment as a shooting script, it would probably go something like this:

222

CLASSICAL

MYTH &

CULTURE

IN THE

CINEMA

1.
Dido, sighing with passion (close-up).
She wanders through deserted city (long shot)
. . . in frenzy (camera zooms in to her face; hair unkempt, streaming).

2.
A deer is standing (dream-sequence haze or soft-focus throughout deer
   scene). Dissolve to an arrow speeding through the air (flight of arrow
   tracked briefly in close-up). Dissolve back to:
The deer still grazing peacefully (medium shot) in the surrounding
   forest (pan over verdant woods).
The arrow hits (sound only—arrow thunking, doe snorting—while
   camera is still on woods?).
Dissolve to hunter-shepherd (with Aeneas' features), holding bow, back to:
Deer, leaping forward; arrow can be seen in its side.
Hunter peers in direction of arrow's flight, unable to tell whether he has
   hit or not.
Deer in flight through deserted forests and clearings (long shot).
Camera moves in to gradual close-up of arrow protruding from flank.

3.
Immediate cut (haze drops abruptly) to Dido and Aeneas walking calmly
   together through city, Aeneas peering about as Dido gestures to
   points of interest.

We shift then to the more staccato series of images in lines 74–79, in which there is stopping at the end of 75 and 76. Dido shows Aeneas the sights of Carthage; we see them standing together looking out at the city. We zoom to Dido to see her start to speak of the main subject on her mind, then break off in embarrassment. Instead, she asks Aeneas to renew at another banquet the stories he told in Books 2 and 3, the stories that caught her admiration and love. She is mad to do this or mad doing it (*demens*) or both. She hangs motionless on his words (*pendet*), just as the walls are going to stand (*pendent*), no longer rising, in line 88 (to be quoted later):

nunc media Aenean secum per moenia ducit
Sidoniasque ostentat opes urbemque paratam,
incipit effari mediaque in voce resistit;
nunc eadem labente die convivia quaerit,
Iliacosque iterum demens audire labores
exposcit pendetque iterum narrantis ab ore.

In line 81 we see the banquet hall empty; at least it appears to be empty. The moon—Dido's theme (see 1.498–503 and 742; 4.522–530 and perhaps 609; and 6.450–455, the last especially related to this passage)—is giving a sporadic light (cut to the sky seen through a window, clouds fitfully scudding over the face of the moon) to a distant shot of Dido standing alone in the hall, her weeping amplified by the stillness of the night and the resonance of the hall, the banqueting debris scattered all about her. Then, suggestively, Dido moves over to the couch where Aeneas had been reclining and lies down on it (80–83):

> post ubi digressi, lumenque obscura vicissim
> luna premit suadentque cadentia sidera somnos,
> sola domo maeret vacua stratisque relictis
> incubat.

For the culmination of this Freudian imagery compare 4.650 (*incubuit toro*), where Dido, lying on her bed atop the funeral pyre, just before stabbing herself with Aeneas' sword, kisses the bed they had shared (*os impressa toro*, 4.659).

What follows in lines 83–85 could be interpreted in either of two ways:

> illum absens absentem auditque videtque,
> aut gremio Ascanium genitoris imagine capta
> detinet, infandum si fallere possit amorem.

One could assume that the scene shifts to successive days when Dido thinks of Aeneas even when he is not present and, as it were in transference, holds Ascanius in her lap. (Remember Cupid taken for Ascanius at 1.715–722.) I think, however, that it would be better to visualize Dido still in the deserted banquet hall, with Aeneas' words still ringing in her ears (coming to her out of the corners of the room) and Aeneas' face in spectral form materializing in the semidarkness while she thinks back to a day or so before when she was holding Ascanius in her lap (a scene that would be done in a dream-sequence technique, fading in and dissolving out again).

Then the camera would slowly recede from Dido and move out the window to pan over the unfinished building projects in the city. Whether the time sequence is contemporary with Dido in the hall or subsequent to it by many days is not made precise nor should it be in the film; in one fluid succession of images (86–88) there is a telescoping of time for a pair who have all too little of it:

> non coeptae adsurgunt turres, non arma iuventus
> exercet portusve aut propugnacula bello
> tuta parant . . .

Dido's love for Aeneas has brought her to a standstill, reflected in its effects on the city, a cessation of the industrious activity described in 1.421–436. The succession of images is then (88–89) capped by

224

CLASSICAL

MYTH &

CULTURE

IN THE

CINEMA

> pendent opera interrupta minaeque
> murorum ingentes aequataque machina caelo.

The camera moves along the walls (close-up from below, as indicated by *minaeque/murorum ingentes*) and comes to rest on a single symbol, a solitary but enormous—and rather phallic—crane atop the wall, a crane that seems from the camera angle to fill the whole sky (*aequata . . . caelo*). There is a strong pause after *caelo*, indicated by the meter, as the camera backs off and slowly recedes to a silent long-shot fade-out. Compare, for effect, the dance-of-death close of Ingmar Bergman's *The Seventh Seal* (1957) or the gate and castle closing Akira Kurosawa's *Rashomon* (1950) and *Throne of Blood* (1957), respectively.

Abruptly now mood and scene are shattered by a cut to Juno's cynical celestial dialogue with Venus, which is introduced at lines 90–92:

> quam simul ac tali persensit peste teneri
> cara Iovis coniunx nec famam obstare furori,
> talibus adgreditur Venerem Saturnia dictis.

The angle shot from beneath the walls past the crane has pointed the way to this scene in heaven. In line 89 the sky (*caelo*) is the background against which something earthly was measured; in line 90 it is the setting for a dialogue between the two goddesses. The camera angle has been reversed; instead of looking up to heaven past the crane, the camera now looks down from above heaven, with the actions on earth seen dimly and indistinctly in the far distance beyond Juno and Venus.

In the montage of lines 68–89 Virgil not only has told what was going on in Carthage but has also revealed Dido's inner state, even though from 74–89 the only word explicitly describing her state is *maeret* (82). Instead of merely stating the character's mood, Virgil *represents* it with a series of images dynamically spliced; he is less interested in conveying information than in creating an emotional effect. As Eisenstein points out, this use of montage causes the spectator himself to create the fusion of separate images and thus derive an inner excitement that would not have been generated by seeing or reading a mere expository account of the mood or emotion.[2] Consequently, dynamic rather than static images and emotions arise. We are explicitly told that Dido is alone and sad, but this is framed by images that help us feel her emotion, not merely register the fact of its existence. The culmination of the whole sequence is the magnificent

2. Eisenstein, "Word and Image," 35.

image of the abandoned crane, not unlike the clock tower of Robert Frost's poem "Acquainted with the Night":

> And further still at an unearthly height
> One luminary clock against the sky
> Proclaimed the time was neither wrong nor right.

The crane is both a symbol of Dido's abandon and a foreshadowing of her own abandonment.

2. *Aeneid* 10.246–290

Equally cinematographic are lines 228–311 in Book 10, of which I give only lines 246–290 here. Most striking, perhaps—other than the pictorial vividness of the scenes—is the alternation of distant and close shots with constantly shifting camera angles and points of focus:

> Cymodocea finished talking and, as she was leaving, gave with her right
>   hand a push—
> as she well knew how—to the lofty ship. It flew through the waves
> swifter than a javelin or an arrow that races the winds.
> Then the others are sped on their course. In puzzled amazement he—
> the Trojan son of Anchises—stood, but the omen raises his spirits.
> Then briefly, looking at the overarching vault of heaven, he prays:
> "Kind Idean mother of the gods, to whom are dear Didyma
> and turreted cities and the chariot yoked to a lion pair,
> be now the leader in my fight; confirm in due course
> this omen and aid the Trojans, goddess, by standing by us."
> Thus he spoke. Meanwhile, rushing in its turn,
> day with its first beams had routed night.
> He gives the initial orders to his comrades. "Follow the signals!
> Ready your spirits and weapons! Prepare for battle!"
> And now Aeneas has in view the Trojans and his camp
> as he stands aloft on the stern. When he raised
> in his left hand his burning shield the Trojans on the walls
> raised a shout to heaven. Renewed hope buoyed their courage,
> they hurled javelins as thick as when cranes under black clouds
> signal their approach as they noisily swim the air,
> outracing the south wind in their trailing clamor.
> But Turnus and the other Italian commanders thought strange the
>   renewal of Trojan spirit
> until they spotted behind them the ships' stems turned for landing
> and the whole sea gliding Aeneas' fleet toward them.
> Aeneas' helmet burns, and flames pour from his crests;
> the golden boss of his shield spews out great fires—

226

CLASSICAL

MYTH &

CULTURE

IN THE

CINEMA

just as when bloody comets on a clear night
mournfully glow red, or when blazing Sirius
(the one that brings thirst and plague to suffering mortals)
is born and saddens the sky with its baleful light.
By no means, however, is Turnus deserted by his daring or his confidence
that they can seize the shore and push the newcomers from the land.
In fact, he fires his men's spirits with his own will and challenges them:
"What you've been praying for has come, a chance to break the enemy
   to bits hand to hand.
In your hands is Mars himself, men! Now let wife
and home be remembered by each of you! Now relive those great
feats which won your ancestors their renown. Don't wait, run to the
   breakers
while the enemy is off balance disembarking
and can't get a firm footing for those first steps.
It's the bold that Fortune favors."
He says this and tries to figure whom he can lead against the shore assault
and to whom he can entrust the continuance of the siege of the camp.
Meanwhile Aeneas dispatches his men from the lofty ships
by gangways; many others watch for the retreat
of the ebbing waves and leap into the shallows.
The oars helped others. Tarchon, looking at the shore . . .

When Cymodocea, the ship that has been transformed into a sea nymph,
finishes her admonition to Aeneas, she reaches out her hand to his ship
(focus on hand and ship) and gives it a shove (246). Virgil presents the
ship cleaving the waves; with a dissolve the ship is replaced for a few in-
stants by the image of a javelin or an arrow (248); dissolve back to the
ship. Then the rest of the ships dart forward (249). Immediately (249–
250) we cut to Aeneas' face, on which momentary puzzlement gives way
to joy as he accepts the omen and the help. He turns his eyes (and the
camera follows his gaze) to heaven (251) and prays. With "Thus he spoke"
the camera returns from heaven to Aeneas momentarily (256) to show in
the background day breaking behind the hero. The temporary beauty and
tranquility of the scene is broken by a flurry of activity as Aeneas issues
commands (258–259).

Suddenly and dramatically the camera shifts from Aeneas—through
his eyes—to the Trojan camp, which has just come into view (260). Almost immediately the camera angle is reversed, and we see Aeneas with
upraised shield on the stern of the ship just as the besieged Trojans see
him (261–262). The Trojans raise a shout (263) that causes the camera to
reverse again to show them invigorated by his return, showering javelins
on the enemy (264)—zoom to the javelins themselves, which dissolve to
cranes, thick and noisy.

Now a third camera angle enters, one that has been artfully delayed. Cut to Turnus and the Italian commanders with their backs to the shore, as *respiciunt* (269) makes clear, hence unable to tell what is going on. We see puzzlement on the face of Turnus and then on the faces of a number of others (267). The camera backs off from individual faces to show the Italian forces in the middle distance and Aeneas' fleet coming up behind them in the slightly out-of-focus background. The Italians turn (269: *respiciunt*) and spot the ships, which, suddenly sharply focused, seem to cover the entire sea. If one were actually filming this sequence, Virgil's text would need very little change to provide a shooting script; all the basic camera directions that I use are implicit in or readily deduced from the text.

Now lines 269–276: the mass of ships in the distance; a flame gleams in the midst (*ardet apex*, 270). The camera moves in toward the gleam, which is only gradually found to be a helmet. Virgil does not specify whose, but everyone knows, Turnus, Trojans, and reader-viewer:

> respiciunt totumque adlabi classibus aequor.
> ardet apex capiti cristisque a vertice flamma
> funditur et vastos umbo vomit aureus ignis:
> non secus ac liquida si quando nocte cometae
> sanguinei lugubre rubent, aut Sirius ardor
> ille sitim morbosque ferens mortalibus aegris
> nascitur et laevo contristat lumine caelum.
> haud tamen audaci Turno fiducia cessit . . .

A tongue of fire resolves itself into a crest. The camera moves closer, like a moth drawn to a light. The even greater brilliance of the reflection of the morning sun on the golden shield overwhelms the eye as the camera moves into the very midst of the dazzling light (271). A blinding red-gold light fills the screen. Gradually the light retreats, framed by black (272), until it contracts into a comet streaking through the sky. The red of the comet (273) progressively fills the screen with its glow. The red contracts again (a nearly complete iris-out) to a point now seen to be a fixed star, Sirius, whose baleful effects are shown by a turn of the camera angle to view (through red filter?) the earth with men and animals parched and sick, staggering or lying about (274). A last turn back to the red foreboding sky, before an instant cut to Turnus in the breaking dawn urging his men on (276, 279–284).

The camera picks out, one after another, various of his men (*quisque*, 281) to whom occur images of wife and home, a portrait hall of ancestral busts. Turnus points (and the camera follows his arm) to the Trojans slipping in the breakers. Then, as Turnus ponders whom to send to repel the invaders and whom to keep at the siege of the camp, we shift to his opponent Aeneas disembarking his men.

228

CLASSICAL

MYTH &

CULTURE

IN THE

CINEMA

From the single figure of Aeneas (287) we shift to masses of Trojans leaping into the shallows (*multi . . . alii*, 288–290). A sudden shift fixes on the Etruscan king Tarchon (290), a single figure, who harangues his men, panned over by the camera. Line 308 turns back to Turnus at the head of his men, and 311, after the script direction *signa canunt* ("the trumpets blow"), to Aeneas again.

A director could film this scene just as written; all the instructions are there. The shifts of focus are particularly remarkable from a thematic standpoint. One could maintain from the fact that Turnus and his men bracket the simile (*respiciunt*, 269; *audaci Turno*, 276) that the destructive effects of the dazzling comet/Sirius simile are restricted to Turnus and the Rutulians alone. But part of the irony of the passage beyond that of light and beauty bringing night and destruction is that the impending ruin, although formally seeming to apply only to Turnus and the Rutulians, actually applies to Aeneas' forces also. Such destructive force cannot be channeled into strictly discrete streams but inevitably spills over to harm friend as well as foe. It is Turnus and his men who see Aeneas in this baleful aspect (although Turnus, characteristically and wrongly, rejects the omen), but the interweaving of Trojan and Rutulian points of view (camera angle) is emblematic of the interaction of their destinies. What affects one will affect the other, too. Bodies will litter the ground on both sides. Montage and camera shifts give rapidity of motion to the external action, which mirrors the agitated emotions of the participants. Also effective is the alternation between mass and individual, letting the champions stand out against the background of their forces. The fight is essentially between Aeneas and Turnus, but the principal victims will be the masses on both sides.

3. Other Instances

I have discussed these two passages in some detail in order to illustrate one way of visualizing Virgil's flow of images. If we analyze any lengthy segment of the *Aeneid*, we cannot fail to see that Virgil marshals not only words but images, meter, and scene in much the same way a director marshals film and score—cutting, juxtaposing, shifting focus, emphasizing breaks, or tying sequences together. In the remainder of this essay I sketch more briefly a few other passages in the *Aeneid* that embody cinematic techniques of various types.

1. An extreme example of cutting occurs at 1.192–193. Aeneas, out hunting with Achates, shoots seven deer:

nec prius absistit quam septem ingentia victor
corpora fundat humi et numerum cum navibus aequet

Aeneas did not stop until seven huge bodies had been triumphantly
poured out on the ground, equaling the number of ships

Then immediately this line (194):

hinc portum petit et socios partitur in omnis.
then he heads for the harbor, and divides [the deer] among his comrades.

No mention is made of how Achates and Aeneas got seven deer back to
the ships. Virgil really does not care; the detail would advance neither plot
nor theme. So he merely juxtaposes the shooting and the sharing, with
hinc portum petit serving the function of a fade between them. The abrupt-
ness is more pronounced if we compare the lengthy detail given at *Odyssey* 10.156–173, where Odysseus shoots one deer and with great difficulty
staggers back to the shore to share it with his comrades.

2. The ant simile of 4.401–407 is an excellent dissolve. Aeneas and his
men are carrying provisions from Carthage to their ships at the shore (401):

migrantis cernas totaque ex urbe ruentis

You could see them leaving, rushing from the city.

The men are then compared to ants carrying grain from a larder to their
nest in a steady double line. The camera is obviously looking at the men
from a distance (and from above: *arce ex summa*, 410) as they scurry
about, barely distinguishable as humans. Then we get a dissolve to ants
swarming over a sandy stretch. Line 408 tells us what we had not known
before, that we are looking through Dido's eyes; and line 410 reveals that
she is looking down from her lofty citadel. (Compare Alain Resnais's technique in *Hiroshima Mon Amour* [1959], as the sleeping Japanese dissolves
before the actress's eyes into the form of her dying German lover.) The
ant simile has been perfectly appropriate. It suggests not only the indus-
try of the ants and the visual effect of looking at the scene from a height
but also the dehumanized nature of the departing Trojans and their leader.

3. Lines 4.450–473 are a splendid succession of images that whirl about
Dido, some actual events, some dream sequences or the product of a dis-
ordered mind:

452–456   Dido pours wine onto the altars and sees it turn to blood before
          her eyes (visual).
457–461   She hears the voice of her dead husband calling to her out of his
          mausoleum in the shadows of the night (*nox . . . obscura*, 460)—
          with imagined sound (?).

230

CLASSICAL

MYTH &

CULTURE

IN THE

CINEMA

462–463   The screech of a solitary owl succeeds the voice of her husband—with real sound.

464–465   Within her head ring the terrifying words of earlier prophecies—with remembrance of past sounds.

465–466   Visions of Aeneas torment her in her dreams (back to visual stimuli).

466–468   Then, one of the finest images. She imagines herself wandering alone through the desert looking for her countrymen:

> semperque relinqui
> sola sibi, semper longam incomitata videtur
> ire viam et Tyrios deserta quaerere terra.

> always she sees herself left
> alone, always companionless on a long journey
> and seeking her Tyrians through desert wastes.

This image embodies Dido's loneliness without Aeneas (*sola*) and the estrangement that her affair with him has caused between her and her people (*incomitata . . . Tyrios quaerere*). Then this scene, already dreamlike, is further removed from reality by a dissolve from Dido wandering the desert to the maddened mythical character Pentheus, confronted by the Furies (469–470). The picture of the Furies, and perhaps the pursuing, vengeful mother implicit in the reference to Pentheus, leads to an alternative comparison (*aut*, 471) with Orestes pursued by Clytemnestra and the Furies (471–473)—not a real Orestes even in the mythical sense, however, but specifically one who is being played on a stage (*scaenis*, 471). By this final image reality is taken even further away, to a stage presentation of a mythical character as seen in a dream. The whole sequence is a dizzying, whirling montage of real and unreal, sight and sound, waking and sleeping, of the same order as Bergman's opening to *Wild Strawberries* (1957). One thing turns into another; the links are thematic, imagistic, and surrealistic but not logical.

    4. Consider next the cinematic possibilities of the ending of the *Aeneid* (12.938–952), with a stop-action zoom at lines 941–946. Aeneas has stayed his sword on listening to Turnus' plea. But just as he is about to be persuaded—we can imagine the camera recording the emotion on Aeneas' face, softening, then suddenly hardening as his eye falls on Pallas' sword belt, which Turnus is wearing:

> stetit acer in armis
> Aeneas volvens oculos dextramque repressit;
> et iam iamque magis cunctantem flectere sermo
> coeperat, infelix umero cum apparuit alto
> balteus et notis fulserunt cingula bullis
> Pallantis pueri, victum quem vulnere Turnus

straverat atque umeris inimicum insigne gerebat.
ille, oculis postquam saevi monumenta doloris
exuviasque hausit, furiis accensus et ira
terribilis: "tune hinc spoliis indute meorum
eripiare mihi? Pallas te hoc vulnere, Pallas
immolat et poenam scelerato ex sanguine sumit."
Hoc dicens ferrum adverso sub pectore condit
fervidus; ast illi solvuntur frigore membra
vitaque cum gemitu fugit indignata sub umbras.
      Aeneas stood fierce in his armor
glancing about, and checked his right hand.
More and more, as Aeneas delayed, Turnus' pleas
were beginning to take effect—when on his shoulder the unlucky
baldric gleamed, the belt with its well-known decorations—
those of young Pallas, whom Turnus had run through
and killed; Turnus was now wearing on his shoulder that hostile badge.
Aeneas spotted this memento of his cruel grief—
the spoils—and inflamed by fury and terrible in his
wrath shouted, "You, wearing my comrade's spoils,
shall you get away from me? Pallas deals this blow, Pallas
kills you and revenges himself with your accursed blood."
With this cry he buries the blade in Turnus' chest,
burning with rage. Turnus' limbs go slack and cold;
his life with a groan flees—indignantly—to the shades below.

Virgil takes six lines to tell of Aeneas spotting that baldric; nothing moves in the plot line. The action freezes as Aeneas thinks of Pallas; as Aeneas looks at the baldric, Pallas' face gradually appears and dissolves again on it. The spell breaks; Aeneas shouts that Pallas is exacting his revenge and buries his sword in Turnus' chest. The pause or freeze before violent action employed here corresponds to Virgil's similar use of scenes of quiet and rest before a sudden outbreak or resumption of frenzy, as in 4.522–529 (*nox erat* to *at non infelix animi Phoenissa*) or at 2.268–271. It is the lull before the storm or the eye of the tornado, comparable perhaps to the scene in Richard Brooks's *Something of Value* (1957), in which the former African houseboy (now a Mau-Mau) is sitting beside the sleeping children of the family who had employed him, reluctant to kill them. This quiet, almost tranquil scene, during which the viewer wonders if he will spare them, is torn apart by the noise of a terrible screeching and the immediate cut to the living room downstairs, where the other Mau-Mau are hacking to bits a piano. The hellish noise is that of their machetes on the piano strings.

    5. An understanding of Virgil's cinematic approach to writing may elucidate one passage that seems logically inappropriate. At 2.557–558 Aeneas, who has just witnessed the death of Priam, says:

232

CLASSICAL

MYTH &

CULTURE

IN THE

CINEMA

iacet ingens litore truncus
avulsumque umeris caput et sine nomine corpus.

Lying huge on the shore a body,
its head torn from its shoulders, a nameless corpse.

Commentators have noted the similarity to the death of Pompey, which Virgil may have had in mind.[3] But, applied to Priam's body, the description does not accord with Aeneas' tale. Aeneas saw Priam stabbed in the palace; he never saw his body decapitated and flung on the beach, because he left immediately after the stabbing. Possibly he envisioned the scene in his mind's eye from a consideration of what might have happened or from some account given by a Trojan refugee encountered later, perhaps by Andromache. Or Aeneas may have been speaking metaphorically, comparing Troy to a body with its head (i.e., Priam) severed. Actually, I do not think Virgil cared how or whether Aeneas knew or whether it was a metaphor. The image occurred to Virgil, and once he had seen it I believe he could not dismiss it from his mind. It was a perfect fade-out, visually as unimpeachable as the crane in Book 4. And the phrase *at me tum* of the next line ("but then I [was surrounded]") brings us joltingly back to Aeneas, just as the image brought Aeneas joltingly back to himself.

Virgil is much closer to being a film director than a painter or a dramatist. The canvas or the stage set must be presented essentially all at once. Except perhaps by diligent and complicated lighting, the artist or dramatist can only single out in a limited way what he wants us to concentrate on at any given moment. The painting is there, the stage set and cast are present. Actors, by their lines or actions, can attempt to fix our attention on one character or object. But the film director, like the poet and the novelist, can move in on a single object, stay on it as long as he wants to, and cut away at will—and force us to go along. He can cut in an instant from heaven to hell, remove or present a scene or character as slowly or quickly as he wishes, disregard any temporal or spatial limitations. A painter or playwright can accomplish some of this in a limited way, but it would be difficult to sustain. The flexibility that we associate with the cinema is a hallmark of Virgil's epic.

3. See, for example, the notes on lines 506–558 and 557–558 in the commentary by R. G. Austin, *P. Vergili Maronis Aeneidos liber secundus* (Oxford: Clarendon Press, 1964; rpt. 1980), 196–198 and 214.

XI

Peter Greenaway's *The Cook, The Thief, His Wife and Her Lover*: A Cockney Procne

Janice F. Siegel

Although Peter Greenaway did not consciously model *The Cook, The Thief, His Wife and Her Lover* (1989; abbreviated hereafter as *CTWL*) on the mythological tale of Procne and Philomela, there is evidence to suggest unbidden influence. A film like *A Zed and Two Noughts* (1985) shows Greenaway's knowledge of and interest in mythological conflicts and themes, and he admits to being particularly partial to Ovid.[1] His vision of Prospero in *Prospero's Books* (1991), a reworking of Shakespeare's *The Tempest*, developed from his certainty that any successful humanist scholar must owe a great debt to Ovid.[2] Greenaway traces the tradition of the classic revenge tragedy, from which he claims *CTWL* springs, to its ancient roots. This tradition, he has said,

---

1. Greenaway: "Many of *Zed and Two Noughts*'s characters are actually Olympian gods: Castor and Pollux, the twins who arose from an act of bestiality, are the film's two main characters. Venus or the prostitute is one of the two principal women; always two: Juno, fecund, is the other. Mercury guards the gates of the zoo and carries flying wings on his hat. The villain, Pluto, who of course bears a Walt Disney badge in order to identify himself, collects zebras, black and white emblems of the judgmental society. Meanwhile Neptune looks after those in the fish house and Jupiter governs the whole zoo." Quoted from Kathy Acker, "The Color of Myth: The World According to Peter Greenaway," *The Village Voice* (April 17, 1990), 61, 65, and 67; quotation at 67. Holly Haynes, "Escape and Constraint: Female Desire and Narrative Bondage in Aeschylus' *Oresteia* and Peter Greenaway's *The Cook, The Thief, His Wife and Her Lover*," *Intertexts*, 4 (2000), 58–73, provides an examination of Greenaway's film from another classical perspective. I am grateful to Martha Davis, Ulrich Schmitzer, Mary-Kay Gamel, and Timothy Peters for helpful suggestions.

2. As Greenaway said in an interview: "A scholar who had accumulated a large amount of knowledge—as Prospero surely must and as Shakespeare surely must—would, in a visual sense, have taken much of it from the classical pictorial imagination, through Ovid

234

CLASSICAL

MYTH &

CULTURE

IN THE

CINEMA

starts with Seneca and goes on through Jacobean drama to be picked up later by people like de Sade, and then much later by people like Genet, Bataille, and it even continues with Ionesco's Theatre of Cruelty and Peter Brook's Theatre of Blood, and perhaps it is also picked up by film-makers like Buñuel and Pasolini.[3]

As a specific model for *CTWL* Greenaway suggests John Ford's *'Tis Pity She's a Whore*, a play "that looks seriously, compassionately and with-out flinching, at a taboo subject on the far reaches of experience."[4] The taboo subject in *CTWL* is cannibalism, and the obvious candidate for its Senecan model is *Thyestes*, which scholars understand to have been pro-foundly influenced by the tale of Procne and Philomela in Book 6 of Ovid's *Metamorphoses*.[5]

There is further reason to connect Ovid and Greenaway in terms of theme and structure. Greenaway explains that *CTWL* was originally in-tended to be the second of a trilogy of films, the other two also having mythological models. The first was to be based on the Medea myth, about an archeologist who kills her own child, to be called *The Love of Ruins*. Greenaway's goal was to "make an audience sympathetic to a woman who kills her own child."[6] The third was to be based on the story of Marsyas, the satyr who is flayed alive by Apollo after losing a musical contest with him. The stories of Marsyas and Medea both appear in Ovid's *Metamor-phoses*, Marsyas at 6.382–400 and Medea at 7.1–424. They are separated from each other only by the tale of Procne (6.424–674), with the addition of two short but thematically significant transitional scenes (6.401–423, about Pelops, and 6.675–721, about Boreas). Greenaway was interested in linking the two murdering mothers thematically, and so was Ovid. In addition to juxtaposing their tales in the *Metamorphoses*, Ovid regu-larly pairs Medea and Procne, either chastising them for their crime (*Ars Amatoria* 2.381–384), showing them as paradigms of the unjust avenger

---

and the Renaissance scholars (*The Tempest* was written in 1611), and I wanted, as it were, to repopulate the island on which Prospero had arrived through the characters of his mental universe. It would have been a classical Humanist universe." Quoted from *An Auto-biography of British Cinema: As Told by the Filmmakers and Actors Who Made It*, ed. Brian MacFarlane (London: Methuen, 1997), 236–243; quotation at 242.

3. Marlene Rodgers, "*Prospero's Books*—Word and Spectacle: An Interview with Peter Greenaway," *Film Quarterly*, 45 no. 2 (1991), 11–19; quotation at 12.

4. The quotation is from the introduction to the screenplay: Peter Greenaway, *The Cook, The Thief, His Wife and Her Lover* (Paris: Dis-Voir, 1989), 7.

5. For example, R. J. Tarrant, "Senecan Drama and its Antecedents," *Harvard Stud-ies in Classical Philology*, 82 (1978), 213–263, points to the similarity between the can-nibalistic recognition scenes in Ovid and in Seneca's *Thyestes* in terms of "characteriza-tion and rhetoric" (263).

6. Quoted from Rodgers, "*Prospero's Books*," 19.

(*Amores* 2.14.29–32), or blaming them for committing crimes against their families (*Fasti* 2.627–630). Given his obsession with structure and organization, Greenaway surely would not pass up such a classical triad as model for his mythologically inspired film trilogy.[7]

As Ovid's rendition of the myth goes, the Thracian king Tereus marries the Athenian princess Procne and takes her back to his country, where they live for several years and have a son, Itys. When Procne asks her husband to fetch her sister Philomela for a visit, Tereus dutifully returns to Athens but falls madly in lust-at-first-sight with his virginal sister-in-law and returns with her to Thrace. Instead of bringing her to the palace and to Procne, he rapes her in the woods and, in response to her threats to expose his crime, cuts out her tongue and imprisons her. Then he deceives Procne into thinking that her sister died en route to Thrace. During the next year Philomela, victim of Tereus' repeated rapes, weaves a tapestry in which she reveals his crime. After this tapestry is delivered to her, Procne frees Philomela, and the two sisters conceive of a plan for revenge. They kill Tereus' son and serve the child to his father at a banquet. After being shown whom he has just eaten, Tereus pursues the sisters, and all three are turned into birds in midflight.

Greenaway's *CTWL*, set in contemporary Britain, concerns the plight of an abused woman, Georgina, married to a pathologically possessive and culturally challenged low-level mobster named Albert Spica. Most of the film's action occurs inside a gourmet French restaurant, which Albert has recently taken over. The resident chef, Richard, and his kitchen staff abet the affair that Albert's wife Georgina begins with a patron, the modest middle-aged bookkeeper Michael, an affair that unfolds right under Albert's nose. Once the affair is discovered, Albert tracks down the lovers' hiding place and has Michael tortured and killed. At this time Georgina is visiting a child in the hospital, whom Albert had tortured for information about the lovers' sanctuary. Upon discovering her husband's crime, Georgina enlists Richard's help to prepare Michael's body for Albert's last meal. The film ends with the climactic cannibal scene in which Georgina gets her revenge on her husband.

Both Greenaway and Ovid use preexisting names for their characters. Ovid is bound by the mythographic tradition. Greenaway, in his original work, adopts a kind of predestined naming system, too. He names his characters after the actors he had originally chosen for the four principal parts: Richard the Cook (Richard Bohringer), Albert the Thief (Albert Finney), Georgina the Wife (Georgina Hale), and Michael the Lover

---

7. See Jonathan Hacker and David Price, *Take Ten: Contemporary British Film Directors* (Oxford: Oxford University Press, 1992), 210 and 216.

(Michael Gambon). Eventually, Helen Mirren and Alan Howard played Georgina and Michael, and Michael Gambon was granted his request to play Albert.[8]

236

CLASSICAL

MYTH &

CULTURE

IN THE

CINEMA

My comparison of the two works begins with the similar plots and tangled interrelationships among the principal characters of each: the husband (Tereus, Albert), his wife (Procne, Georgina), the one beloved by the wife (Philomela, Michael), and the cooked or cook (Itys, Richard). The husbands perpetrate violence against someone who is beloved by their wives (rape and mutilation, torture and murder), and the wives' discoveries bring about a crucial shift in the balance of terror. At this point, the newly empowered wives deliberate, determine on, and deliver an appropriate response to their husbands' savagery. Their retribution is a cannibal feast for the husband, a punishment facilitated by the one cooked or by the cook himself, who provides either the goods (Itys) or services (Richard) necessary for the wife to effect her revenge.

More than the plot itself, it is Greenaway's sub-surface thematic play, the expression of human weaknesses and drives, his specific techniques used to bring these tortured psyches to life, that reminds us of Ovid. Comparison of the two artists' techniques reveals the distinctive difference between both husbands, which determines the direction of the tale. Each husband is a watcher, for example, but Tereus' watching is predatory; Albert's is passively voyeuristic. Each has a voracious appetite, but Tereus craves sex and food; Albert only eats. Each husband in his way attempts to control social, sexual, and verbal intercourse, but unlike Tereus, whose violence is sexually motivated, Albert's barbarity replaces his sexual drive.

Each wife also eventually dethrones her husband. (Tereus is a king, Albert aspires to a comparable state in his societal circles.) Each husband's crime precipitates a shift in the balance of power, and each shift is heralded by a flight and a liberation, a revelation of the husband's past crimes, and a final scene of discovery and revenge. Although the specific aspects of rape and mutilation and of torture and murder are very different, the artists' renditions of these savage acts are remarkably similar. Symbolically, they are even identical. Each is an act of disempowerment with a strong sexual overtone. Each husband resorts to violence, although Albert's inability to effect punishment himself reveals his true impotence.

In either case, the wife's cannibal feast is an apt retribution for the husband's crime. The nature of the crime dictates the nature of the punishment and also determines the degree of the avenger's guilt. Georgina

8. See Alan Woods, *Being Naked Playing Dead: The Art of Peter Greenaway* (Manchester: Manchester University Press, 1996), 262.

becomes the hero when she forces Albert to eat the flesh of her dead lover. Throughout the film, Albert's tiresomely repeated threats, tantrums, and assaults have seduced the audience into rooting for his appropriately vulgar demise. Georgina and Richard harm nobody except Albert. At the end we are relieved that Albert has gotten his just deserts. Procne seizes on the idea of feeding Tereus his own child, whom she rejects along with her marriage. Our reaction to Procne's child-feast, however, is ambivalent. We are glad to see Tereus punished, but we are horrified at the toll her act has taken. In their hunger for vengeance, the sisters perpetrate a crime worse than the original. Even in Ovid's sympathetic portrait, Procne and Philomela are eternally marked as killers, not avengers.

1. The Husband: Speech as Weapon

Despite the complaints of some critics, the one-dimensionality of Albert's character is not an error on Greenaway's part.[9] Rather, it is intentional: "I wanted to create deliberately, almost in a technical way, a character of great evil, who had no redeeming features. Not like a Machiavelli or a Richard III, who have charisma, which is attractive. I wanted to create a man who *had* to be mediocre."[10] Greenaway constructs a clear-cut division between Right and Wrong and firmly plants his characters on one side or the other. Albert fancies himself the leader of an elite force, attempting a real-life imitation of the painting in the dining room of his restaurant, Frans Hals's *Banquet of the Officers of the St. George Civic Guard* of 1616.[11] In reality, Albert is a mean-spirited mobster, and his associates are "small-time crooks, pimps, gigolos, busted boxers, cheap whores, bullies, hairdressers, faggots and hoods," in the words of a guest invited by Albert but unimpressed by his show.[12] His wealth is stolen, his taste plebeian; his friends are bought. Albert's braggadocio clashes with the posh interior of the restaurant and its upscale clientele. The crooks

9. Terrence Rafferty, "Conspicuous Consumer," *The New Yorker* (May 8, 1990), 88–91, at 88: "Albert is loathsome through and through, an evil lout who just does one evil, loutish thing after another for two solid hours"; Sean French, "Spit Roast," *Sight and Sound*, 58 (1989), 277–278, at 277: "I wish Greenaway had found a co-writer to lend more interest to Michael Gambon's rants."

10. Greenaway in an interview with Gavin Smith, "Food for Thought," *Film Comment*, 26 no. 3 (1990), 54–60; quotation at 58.

11. David Pascoe, *Peter Greenaway: Museums and Moving Images* (London: Reaktion Books, 1997), 171–188, discusses Greenaway's use of paintings as models for scenes in *CTWL*.

12. Amy Lawrence, *The Films of Peter Greenaway* (New York: Cambridge University Press, 1997), 165, calls *CTWL* a "prime exponent of the 1980s British gangster film."

238

CLASSICAL

MYTH &

CULTURE

IN THE

CINEMA

look ridiculous in their billowing blouses (after Hals) and matching scarves, a detail Albert mistakes for a sign of class. And he is not good enough for his long-suffering wife, who has no choice but to endure the crass attentions of this physically repulsive, morally reprehensible man.

Albert considers speech a formidable weapon. He wields it unilaterally and irresponsibly, and he severely limits others' access to it. For the first half of the film he never stops talking and makes himself the center of attention. With his loud prattle he lives up to his name, a low-class mauling of the word "speaker."[13] When his associates fail to meet his expectations, Albert's self-possession invariably deteriorates, and he attacks them verbally. His lectures are monotonous, uninformed, and scatological, more often than not revealing some ugly truth about himself. He is "sadistic, bullying, nagging, crude, loud, callous, self-important, sanctimonious, anti-Semitic, racist, misogynist, homophobic, drunken, unlettered, and possessed of a poor French accent."[14] Most of Albert's attention is directed at Georgina, who stoically endures his never-ending strings of invective. But Albert's voice is most conspicuous in its absence; whenever Michael and Georgina are alone, they escape to a world of silence. Particularly jarring is each of their reentries into the boisterous dining room of the restaurant. Greenaway visually emphasizes this contrast. He intercuts every scene of Michael and Georgina making love in other rooms of the restaurant with scenes of Albert loudly lording it over the table.

Whereas Greenaway allows Albert to reveal his ugly character through speech and action, Ovid presents a Tereus whose words and actions are designed to deceive; they do not reflect his thoughts. Procne misses her family after living for several years in faraway Thrace and asks her husband the favor of fetching her sister for a visit. Only hindsight allows us to see that Tereus' initial agreement to this request reveals a controlling hand: Procne was powerless to leave her adopted home and had to ask her husband to act on her behalf. Still, Tereus lacks any sinister attributes at this early stage; he is introduced as a famous leader with a shining reputation (6.425 and 436). Even his barbarian nationality, revealed in the first line of the story (424), is not problematic until he falls victim to the lust innate in himself and his people (458–460). Tereus' lust makes him eloquent (469), and he abuses language in order to dupe his father-in-law

13. Michael Walsh, "Allegories of Thatcherism: The Films of Peter Greenaway," in *British Cinema and Thatcherism*, ed. Lester Friedman (Minneapolis: University of Minnesota Press, 1993), 255–277, at 274: "Homophonically, and especially given the film's play with the Cockney tendency to add an 'r' to a final vowel, we may even be reminded of 'Mr. Speaker,' the bewigged parliamentarian of the British House of Commons, who is comparable with Spica in both the atavism of his dress and his authority over speech."

14. Walsh, "Allegories of Thatcherism," 272.

Pandion: "with a lust-inspired speech he returns to Procne's requests and carries out his own wishes as if they were hers" (467–468).

Albert's is an evil we know immediately. Tereus is much more terrifying because his is a hidden threat, revealed to his victim only when it is too late. Ovid achieves suspense by interweaving Tereus' outward politeness and the pleasing effect of his deceitful words on his listeners with the inner turmoil he suffers for his illicit lust. Ovid misses no opportunity to point out the contrast. An authorial intrusion bemoaning the blindness of human beings accompanies Tereus' initial decision to pursue his own goal as if it were still Procne's (472–473). Dramatic irony is at its highest when ignorant Pandion finally gives Tereus permission to take Philomela away, basing his decision on the misconception that this is all Procne's idea: "The father is conquered by the entreaty of both [daughters]: unlucky [Philomela] rejoices and gives thanks to her father and believes that thing succeeded for the two of them which will be disastrous for the two of them" (483–485).

Tereus does not allow an opponent, who threatens to use speech, to thwart him. After being raped by the brother-in-law she had trusted, Philomela embarks on a long speech of recrimination, in which she promises to reveal Tereus' crimes by telling about them (544–548). Tereus' response is to negate her power over him, to remove her weapon of speech.[15] He further abuses speech by lying to cover up his crimes and to ensure future illicit sessions with his captive. It will be part of Procne's quid pro quo retribution to appropriate Tereus' power over language by using similar methods of deception when she executes her vengeance.

2. The Husband's Insatiability

Ovid emphasizes Tereus' innate greed to reveal his salaciousness, for Tereus' double insatiability for food and sex is a key element necessary for the appropriateness of his punishment.[16] Ovid lays the foundation for this in his description of lust-struck Tereus suffering through a banquet on the night before he is to leave with Philomela. Ovid combines imagery of food and sex to reflect the state of Tereus' mind and body. Although

15. The symbolic interpretation of a tongue as a weapon was as familiar to the Greeks and Romans as it is to us. Cf. Shakespeare's Hamlet: "I will speak daggers to her, but use none" (Hamlet, act 3, scene 2).

16. The comment by Walter Burkert, Homo Necans: The Anthropology of Ancient Greek Sacrificial Ritual and Myth, tr. Peter Bing (Berkeley: University of California Press, 1983), 104, concerning the punishment of Thyestes, another man forced to eat his own sons, is applicable to Tereus: "the 'eater' could not restrain himself sexually either."

sleep should come easily to someone who had just feasted on food and wine, Tereus cannot sleep because of his burning lust (488–493):

240

CLASSICAL

MYTH &

CULTURE

IN THE

CINEMA

> A regal feast is set out on the tables, and wine in golden cups; hence they give their swollen bodies over to gentle sleep. But the Odrysian king, although he departed, burns with her and, recalling her figure and mannerisms and hands of the sort he desired, he imagines that which he has not yet seen and he sustains his fires, his preoccupations keeping him from sleep.

Greenaway also makes greed the chief flaw in Albert's character. But while Albert has a huge appetite for food—when asked by Richard if he is ready to eat, he replies: "Always!"—his hunger lacks a sexual dimension. The film is crammed with images of Albert presiding over his table and eating his food, and Greenaway cuts away time and again to scenes of Michael making love to his wife. Although there is a lot of sex, Albert is party to none of it. Ovid and Greenaway show the husband controlling his wife and others, but it is only Tereus whose sexual appetite drives him to his crimes. By contrast, Albert is hungry for power and sees sex and food only as human drives that can be controlled, two more ways to maintain his grip on those around him:

> I'm an artist in a way and combine my business and my pleasure: money's my business, eating's my pleasure, and Georgie is my pleasure too. Though in a more private kind of way than stuffing the mouth and feeding the sewers, though the pleasures are related because the naughty bits and the dirty bits are so close together. It just goes to show how eating and sex are related.

Albert is, in fact, terrified by the close relation between sex and excretion. In an attempt to control both, and thereby to conquer their hold on him, we see him wield excrement like a weapon. As the film opens, Albert is terrorizing Roy, a local businessman reluctant to pay protection money. Careful not to soil his evening wear, Albert strips Roy naked, smears him with dog excrement, forces some of it into his mouth, warning that it will be his own next time, and then urinates on him: "Now I've given you a nice dinner. Here's a little drink." When Albert does not control or use filth, he crusades to annihilate it. Throughout the first half of the film, he publicly harangues Georgina each time she returns from the lavatory. Suspicious about why she is taking so long in the bathroom one evening, Albert barges in and berates Georgina through the stall door, crudely exerting his proprietary control over her. He does not realize that he has unwittingly intruded on Georgina and Michael's first sexual encounter, through which Georgina secretly asserts her independence from her husband. Georgina erodes Albert's power over the sexual and the personal by using a visit to the toilet as an excuse to meet her lover, even after they have stopped making love in bathrooms. Although he eventually senses that something is wrong, Albert does not understand the truth until the affair is revealed to him in a fitting juxtaposition of slang terms: "Why do you think Georgie's been spending so much time in the john? You blind bat! She doesn't have the fucking shits every five minutes!" Albert's fears have come true. The naughty bits and the dirty bits are indeed related, and he has lost control over both.

To Albert, filth conceived in the mind or expressed in language is no different from filth excreted. Throughout the film, he gets his strength from rooting out sexual depravity and destroying it. Yet Albert is just as likely to knead Georgina's breasts at the table or to lift her skirts in the parking lot. These actions have nothing to do with sex but are crude expressions of ownership. Albert's pathological need to possess Georgina extends into every realm of behavior. In one grand display, he drags Michael over to his table and introduces Georgina as his wife, but he fails to make an impression because Michael and Georgina are already lovers. Michael's transgression is to have appropriated command of Georgina's body from Albert. Albert will be motivated to murder Michael more by the prospect of losing a prize possession than by any sense of personal betrayal.

3. The Husband as Watcher

Albert established control over Georgina with physical violence and forced her to perform degrading personal tasks for him. We learn that she even had to endure sexual penetration with various objects: "If I didn't do it whilst he watched, then he'd insist on doing it himself. At least when I did it, it hurt less." Georgina's report of this sexual perversion reveals that all of Albert's attacks lack a sexual component: "He wasn't really interested in sex—not with me—not with women." The attacks on Georgina and that on Michael are proof of Albert's impotence. Greenaway includes a wooden spoon, later the instrument of Michael's torture, in Albert's chest of sex toys to make the parallel unmistakable.

As Georgina reveals, Albert had been happy to play the voyeur. Ovid, too, characterizes Tereus as a watcher, but his conclusions are much more dire. The view of Tereus as watcher is linked to a play on words that dates back at least as far as Sophocles' lost play *Tereus,* in which Tereus is described as *epoptês* ("overseer"), a foreshadowing of his eventual metamorphosis into an *epops* ("hoopoe"). "Tereus," a name which first appears in Sophocles' play, may derive from *têrein*, "to watch, guard."[17] Ovid accordingly highlights this characteristic in Tereus and plays with words referring to sight. In his farewell speech, Pandion seals Philomela's fate by saying that he wishes Tereus to "look after her with fatherly love" (499). Tereus' earlier fantasy has already shown what kind of father he would be to Philomela: an incestuous one (482). Ovid shows us how Tereus perverts this fatherly request by watching not as a guardian but as a predator (514–518):

> Barbarous, he exults and he scarcely delays his joys in his mind and never turns his eye away from her, not unlike when some predator with hooked talons, a bird of Jove, deposits a hare in his high nest. There is no escape for the one captured; the robber watches his prize.

242

CLASSICAL

MYTH &

CULTURE

IN THE

CINEMA

4. The Husband's Subversion of Standards

Both Greenaway and Ovid see disrespect for moral and social behavior as central to the husband's character. Albert neither respects nor is restrained by social rules. He interrupts the conversations of others at will, showing no regard for etiquette, and intrudes on physical space just as easily, as his breaking through doors, bursting into rooms, and kicking open toilet stalls dramatically illustrate, in a manner that is highly effective in a visual medium. Albert goes wherever he wishes, and Greenaway's camera captures his proprietary air. The film is full of panoramic shots of Albert swooping into rooms without warning, descending on innocent people going about their business, and wreaking havoc that fills the scene with noise, frenetic activity, or flying objects. There is nothing terribly profound about Albert's actions; he simply needs to own and control. His most highly prized possession is Georgina.

Ovid focuses more on the moral side of Tereus' transgressions and on the consequences of his breaches of trust. After she recovers from the initial shock of rape, Philomela lashes out at him, enumerating his immoral acts: breaking his promise to his father-in-law and destroying the bond of sisterhood, her innocence, and the sanctity of his marriage (534–536). The dissolution of family bonds is a theme Ovid stresses throughout, choosing specific vocabulary to define the characters' shifting familial alliances. In lines 440–450, they are described in terms of their bond of kinship with one another. In this way, family devotion becomes para-

17. A. C. Pearson, *The Fragments of Sophocles*, vol. 2 (Amsterdam: Hakkert, 1963), 226 (note on fr. 581.1).

mount. But when Tereus meets Procne's sister, she is simply called Philomela (451). Just as Tereus and Procne were earlier united by verbal juxtaposition (*viro Procne*, 440), so now Tereus and Philomela are similarly bonded (*virgine Tereus*, 455). During the course of Tereus' wooing of Philomela, Ovid fortifies our impression that Tereus has shed his role as Procne's husband by referring to Procne only by name, thus refusing to acknowledge her as his wife (468, 470). But only Tereus' perception has shifted. Everyone else remains focused on the familial bond that holds them all together, and Ovid reveals this by an overuse of terms signifying familial relations. Philomela begs permission to visit her sister (476), Pandion gives permission as their father (483, 484), and, in a speech designed to emphasize the dramatic nature of the horror brewing, he hands over his daughter to his "dear son-in-law" (496), still thinking that family loyalty links them together (507). Upon landing in Thrace, Philomela asks where her sister is (523), but Tereus rapes the virgin (524) to whom he no longer feels a bond of kinship while she calls out to father, sister, and finally the gods (525–526). Philomela's cry: "You have mixed up everything" (*omnia turbasti*, 537) blames Tereus for the utter disruption of the family, including her relationship with her sister, who she thinks now has the right to seek vengeance on her (538). In response to her threats of exposure, Tereus hacks out her tongue even as she cries the name of her father (555).

Procne unwittingly highlights the familial disintegration Tereus has perpetrated by asking her husband where her sister is (564) and, in response to his lie, mourns her death (570). Once Procne learns the truth, Ovid emphatically has her liberate her sister (582, 598, 604, 610, 613), not from her husband but from the "savage tyrant" (*saevi ... tyranni*, 581) he revealed himself to be when he cut out her tongue (*feri ... tyranni*, 549). From this point on, Procne calls him only by name (615), acknowledging that he has forever broken the bonds of marriage. It is poetically justified that Itys becomes Procne's victim in linguistically the same way that Philomela became Tereus': He becomes the object of her revenge as an unrelated victim (620). When a surge of maternal feeling causes Procne to hesitate in her murderous intent, mother and son are momentarily reunited (*natus matrique*, 624). But deeper blood ties win out over broken marital ones: "He calls me mother, why can't she call me sister?" (633). Tereus, responsible for both circumstances, is Procne's target, and in her desire to destroy him she rejects her son—even as he cries out for his mother (640)—along with her marriage. We come to understand that Itys can no longer claim a link to either woman when they are identified by name only as they are killing and dismembering him (641, 643). At the cannibal feast Ovid shows a wife (647) wreaking vengeance on a husband

244

CLASSICAL

MYTH &

CULTURE

IN THE

CINEMA

she has utterly rejected (647, 650) by making him eat his own flesh and blood (651). Philomela points to the dire familial consequences of Tereus' atrocity by shoving the head of the child into his father's face (658–659). Procne's vengeance proves effective; Tereus bemoans the loss of his son (665). The only familial bond to survive intact is the one Tereus had underestimated, the blood bond of sisterhood (666).

5. The Husband's Crime

The turning point in each story arrives when the husband commits a crime so dastardly and reckless that he seals his own doom. Tereus and Albert, barbaric husbands, disdain their helpless victims. Despite obvious differences, their deeds are symbolically identical and even similar in some details. Tereus holds Philomela by her hair (552); Albert orders his henchman Mitchel to do the same to Michael. Tereus ties Philomela's hands behind her back (552–553); Michael's hands, too, are bound. Tereus attacks Philomela's mouth, holding her tongue with a kind of forceps and slicing it off with his sword (556–557); Mitchel stuffs pages down Michael's throat with the handle of a wooden spoon.

Ovid has been charged with having "revelled in bloodthirsty and repulsive descriptions of human agony simply because he liked cruelty."[18] A comparison with Michael's torture, however, reveals that Ovid's scene is a stylized poetic exercise rather than any attempt to capture the full reality of violence. When Greenaway's camera focuses on Michael, his chest and face covered in blood, his eyes wide with horror and pain, his gaping mouth emitting a series of increasingly desperate gagging sounds, we have all the gore missing from Ovid's account and all the victim's suffering. Although Ovid had earlier compared Philomela, just raped, to a dove cowering in a corner, her feathers soaked with her own blood and too frightened to believe herself safe (529), there is no mention of the torrent of blood that must have gushed from Philomela's mouth or flowed down her throat, causing her to choke, as her tongue was sheared at its root (557). Ovid does not mention a single drop of blood; he leaves the

---

18. G. Karl Galinsky, *Ovid's Metamorphoses: An Introduction to the Basic Aspects* (Berkeley: University of California Press, 1975), 129; he continues: "This is evident, for instance, in his detailed description of Philomela's mutilation by Tereus and in its counterpart, the death of Itys. Both scenes are characterized by extreme cruelty and a loving depiction even of the smallest sadistic detail. It is almost as if the poet were giving stage directions—one might think of Artaud's theater of the cruel—to make sure that every horrid effect is exploited to the fullest. This is especially true of Tereus' attack on Philomela. . . . The passage needs little *explication de texte*" (129–130).

horror to our imagination. Of course, verisimilitude is not his goal, or Tereus would not use a pair of magically appearing forceps to clamp onto Philomela's tongue. (By contrast, the origin of Mitchel's wooden spoon is all too painfully clear.)

Ovid is interested in the symbolism of the act, as his choice of words to describe Tereus' attack effectively reveals: *vagina liberat ensem*—"he frees his sword from its sheath" (551). In Ovid, this phrase is sexually charged; here and elsewhere it describes a male's violent reaction after illicit sex.[19] Tereus is about to engage in an activity symbolically equivalent to his rape. Tereus' attack on Philomela is a horrifying parody of a sexual encounter as yet another orifice of her body is violated. Her mutilated and helpless state makes Philomela an even more alluring prize to him (561–562): "And after this villainous deed was done (I could scarcely believe it), it is said that he repeatedly sought with lust her mangled body." As Leo Curran comments:

> In what is probably the most repellent passage in all of Ovid, Tereus is represented as repeatedly deriving sexual pleasure from Philomela's mutilated body and the language implies that the mutilation was itself a further sexual stimulant (6.549 ff.). Ovid understands male sexuality at its most savage.[20]

Michael's torture is an equally horrifying parody of a violent sexual encounter. He lies face up on the floor, stretched out with his hands bound, as Mitchel slowly and with great relish plunges his spoon down Michael's throat again and again as he clenches Michael's head between his leather-clad thighs. But Albert himself takes no part in the torture; his henchman penetrates Michael's body. Albert only directs his attack, and in this detail lies his crucial distinction from Tereus. After focusing on Michael's face only long enough to reveal the exact procedure involved in his torture, the camera shifts to focus on Albert, who deliberately turns his back on the others and walks toward the camera while he delivers a progressively lunatic diatribe complaining about the wrongs he has suffered. Albert's figure blocks our view, his girth a reminder of his true appetites. Greenaway conveys the savaging going on in the background through the sounds of Michael's choking.

Ovid also uses a single detail to convey the horror of the crime, a kind of close-up of Philomela's severed tongue flopping on the ground, a mute

19. Cf. *vagina deripit ensem* (*Metamorphoses* 10.475; the episode of Cinyras and Myrrha) and *vagina liberat ensem* (*Fasti* 2.793; Tarquin and Lucretia).

20. Leo C. Curran, "Rape and Rape Victims in the *Metamorphoses*," *Arethusa*, 11 (1978), 213–241; quotation at 219.

246

CLASSICAL

MYTH &

CULTURE

IN THE

CINEMA

witness to her earlier threat, now eradicated (557–560): "the tongue it-self lies trembling on the dark earth and murmurs, just as the tail of a mutilated snake is wont to twitch, and the severed tongue writhes and, dying, seeks the feet of its mistress." We see the effects of Tereus' tor-ture of Philomela, we hear Michael's agony. Since the victim no longer offers a threat to the attacker or its orchestrator, neither Philomela nor Michael appears in the final moment of the scene. The objectification of both victims is complete. Just as Philomela was transformed from a vir-ginal princess into a "lacerated body" (562), so Michael is reduced to being a piece of meat, but one that will revisit Albert.[21] But in Ovid's tale Philomela survives. Tereus leaves no body behind, so the source of the later cannibal feast must lie elsewhere.

Albert chastises Mitchel for almost ruining the effect he wishes to create:

> I didn't mean you literally have to chew his bollocks off. . . . I meant it metaphorically. . . . I don't want this to look like a sex murder. It's what it is—a revenge killing, an affair of the heart. A *crime passionelle*. I want no evil gossip spread around about me. They are going to say it was a digni-fied revenge killing. They will admire the style. He was stuffed and Albert liked good food—he was stuffed with the tools of his trade. He was stuffed with books. The crummy little bookkeeper . . .

But Albert's concern that someone would misunderstand the attack on Michael as being sexually motivated ("savaged by young sex maniac") is curiously misplaced; having to hire someone to do this for him only re-veals his inability to do it himself. At the climactic moment, almost sob-bing with rage and despair, Albert admits his impotence before scream-ing the death order. Particularly significant is how Albert commands Mitchel to murder Michael: "Close his mouth! Hold his nose! Ram the bloody books down his throat! Suffocate the bastard!"

Typically, when Albert finds that he cannot control his victim's speech, he overpowers its mechanism. Earlier in the film Michael and Georgina appropriated control of a conversation that Albert had intended for his own self-aggrandizement. Albert now manages to find a way to shut Michael's mouth permanently and on his own terms, a grand display of his constant attempts to "rule dictatorially over orifices."[22] Those who fail to see that the film's scenes of violence reveal Albert's underlying

---

21. See Amy Richlin, "Reading Ovid's Rapes," in *Pornography and Representation in Greece and Rome*, ed. Richlin (New York: Oxford University Press, 1992), 163–164, for a detailed study of Ovid's grammatical objectification of Philomela.

22. Walsh, "Allegories of Thatcherism," 275.

pathology also fail to find anything more than shock value in it.[23] All of the violent attacks in the film show an Albert desperate to prove his authority by violent control of social, verbal, and personal expression. His attacks reveal his underlying impotence: punching Georgina, kneeing an old man in the groin, slapping the child Pup. His victims are weak and defenseless; his weapons, when he wields them, are smooth, soft, feminine. The one time he wields a weapon in anger and successfully penetrates a victim occurs when he instinctively reacts to the sting of being labeled a cuckold. But even then he does not quite get it right, stabbing the woman who revealed Georgina's affair in the face with a fork. The attack on the child Pup is particularly instructive. Albert wants to force him to reveal Michael and Georgina's hiding place. When his threats fail to make the boy cooperative, Albert proves his authority by deciding what will go into Pup's mouth. First, he gives his standard order: "Open your mouth"; then he force-feeds the child the buttons—smooth objects without sharp, damaging edges—from his clothing. Next, Albert horrifies even his own gang: "Take down his pants!" The men refuse, begging Albert not to launch a sexual attack ("He's just a kid"), but Albert has something entirely different in mind. He borrows Mitchel's knife—significantly, he does not have one of his own—to carve out the child's navel and stuff it down his throat. There is something sinisterly feminine about this act involving the last vestige of a snipped umbilical cord, a false opening marking the broken connection between mother and infant.

6. The Wife's Transformation from Victim to Avenger

In either tale, the wife is her husband's victim along with his principal target, the one she loves. Georgina has suffered endless acts of humiliation, pain, and torment at Albert's hands. As primary victims, Michael

23. For example, Rafferty, "Conspicuous Consumer," 89–90, delivers a scathing denouncement of the film based on this very misconception: "The Motion Picture Association of America did the movie the enormous favor of giving it an X rating (the distributors released it without a rating), and thus made Greenaway seem a kind of martyr, like Robert Mapplethorpe—a victim of repressive philistinism. (It must be a role he relishes.) Some prominent critics, flashing their anti-censorship credentials, proclaimed the movie a masterpiece, and a lot of filmgoers must feel compelled to buy a ticket as a protest against attempts to muzzle artistic expression. Also, because everyone knows by now that the movie features several gross-out scenes, including a climactic act of cannibalism, it is, in a sense, a perfect date movie for a certain audience—the intellectual's equivalent of a 'Friday the 13th' picture. To sit through it with a worldly, unshockable air and then deliver a lengthy opinion about it is to display, irrefutably, one's liberal *cojones*. The movie is doing big business at the art houses. . . . The film's success is a ghastly joke."

248

CLASSICAL

MYTH &

CULTURE

IN THE

CINEMA

and Philomela provide texts—his body stuffed with books, her inscribed robe—that silently reveal to each wife the painful truth about her husband. As secondary victims, Georgina and Procne have suffered a long series of indecencies from a tyrannical husband; Procne's horror is the more acute because she was unaware of the truth for so long. Both Georgina and Procne become empowered when they discover the true nature of their husbands and give it voice. Georgina addresses the dead Michael; in the presence of her mutilated sister, Procne rages against Tereus' crimes and lists numerous avenues of vengeance. Each wife then conceives of her cannibal plot and is thus transformed from victim into avenger.

Georgina and Philomela also have much in common. Both are attacked by husband figures. Although he is officially married only to Procne, Philomela calls Tereus a bigamist immediately after the rape (538).[24] Georgina feels trapped in a marriage from which she has tried to escape; Philomela is kept in a prison. Both regard their treatment at the hands of their victimizer as unspeakable. Ovid describes Philomela's rape as a *nefas* (524), a crime contrary to divine law. The term derives from the Latin verb *fari*, "to speak." A *nefas* is literally a crime so dire that it is unspeakable. Tereus' next crime is designed to be left unspoken. But Philomela is able to thwart his plot. Her tapestry speaks for her—Sophocles had referred to "the voice of the shuttle" in his *Tereus* (fr. 595). Later, in Procne's presence, Philomela uses her hands to communicate (609). Although Philomela eventually loses her speech for good when she becomes a bird, her ability now to rise above her handicap separates her from the vast multitude of other characters in the *Metamorphoses* who lose their speech in their transformation without having a chance to complain about or draw attention to their suffering.

For both Georgina and Philomela, voicing their experience of suffering offers liberation from that suffering. Georgina tells Michael the truth about her husband's barbaric treatment of her only after she finds him dead. Before, her shame had always kept her silent. Only by reappropriating her own speech can she break Albert's hold on her. Philomela, too, is shamed by Tereus' treatment (604). She feels such shame not only because of her rape but also because she has become a rival to her sister, whom she believes she has made her enemy (537–538). But Procne embraces her and enlists her aid in avenging their common injustice. She completes the empowerment process begun by Philomela's weav-

---

24. Tereus' bigamy is part of the mythographic tradition. In Apollodorus, *Library* 3.14.8, Tereus lies to Philomela, claiming that Procne was dead, and takes her as a second wife. In Hyginus, *Fabulae* 45, Tereus tells the same lie, but to Pandion, and again gains Philomela as a second wife.

ing. Philomela, too, is now fully transformed from victim to avenger. From now on, Procne and Philomela act in concert as a kind of wife doubled. They and Georgina will adopt much the same strategy toward their husbands.

Without realizing it, each wife provides her husband with the opportunity to savage her beloved. Her very kindness allows the tragedy to occur. Georgina visits Pup in the hospital and leaves Michael vulnerable to Albert's attack. Procne's acceptance of the false news of her sister's death gives Tereus the freedom to continue raping her. In the film there is never a suggestion that Georgina should bear blame or guilt for having started an affair with Michael; Albert is responsible for every terrible act, and Georgina remains unsullied. Things are different in the tradition of the ancient story. Procne is vilified even before she actually perpetrates her unspeakable deeds. The ancient commentator Servius places total responsibility for all the events in the myth squarely on her head because her request to see her sister put everything into motion.[25]

Ovid and Greenaway dramatize the wife's ignorance of her husband's crime by alternating scenes focusing on the husband with scenes focusing on her. Ovid establishes simultaneous events by presenting the impact of Tereus' actions on both women in a rapid alternation of scenes spanning only fourteen lines (561–574). Greenaway employs changes in sound and light to sharpen his contrasts: the hospital is gleaming, white, spacious, neat; the book depository is dark, crowded, cluttered.[26] Haunting strains of the *Miserere*, the song, based on Psalm 51, previously sung by Pup, emanate from loudspeakers in the walls of the ward, while the attack on Michael is accompanied by booming, ominous percussion.

7. Scene of Liberation

In order to proceed, both plots must provide a dramatic escape for their victimized characters. The stories both contain a harrowing scene in which the wife and her beloved flee from the husband's tyranny; its function is

25. Servius on Virgil, *Georgics* 4.15, identifies Procne as "the cause of that crime; for she herself had sent Tereus to bring back her sister." This interpretation is not unknown in modern criticism, either. Cf. P. M. C. Forbes Irving, *Metamorphosis in Greek Myths* (Oxford: Clarendon Press, 1990), 103: "By then bringing her sister into her house she inevitably wrecks it, since the one home cannot have two brides." Irving too easily dismisses Tereus' responsibility for his rape of Philomela: "Tereus . . . merely reveals his true character as a savage barbarian, someone who never did belong in the house" (102).

26. Bridget Elliott and Anthony Purdy, *Peter Greenaway: Architecture and Allegory* (Chichester: Academy Editions, 1997), 72, call the book depository "a sanctuary of learning and history that proves all too vulnerable in times of barbarism."

250

CLASSICAL

MYTH &

CULTURE

IN THE

CINEMA

to move the couple from a place of danger to one of relative or temporary safety. Procne liberates Philomela on the night the Thracian women celebrate their festival of Bacchus, and their mad nocturnal dash through the woods is steeped in religious frenzy. A Fury-like Procne joins the native revelers to hide evidence of her secret purpose from Tereus. Michael and Georgina have to run for their lives; they escape in an abandoned meat wagon. The slimy heads of animals hanging from ceiling hooks bash into them; worms and maggots crawl in rotting meat, flies buzz all around. Greenaway intends the scene to be a journey through hell. Both escapes have an otherworldly quality. They are outside the normal range of human experience and are tinged with spirituality and horror. While all the escapees seek liberation from an unbearable reality, only Procne and Philomela are successful. But they have been transformed—contaminated—by the deeds of the barbarian Tereus. Georgina and Michael seek to escape violence; Procne and Philomela willingly and unnecessarily embrace it.

From this point on, the tales somewhat diverge. Procne and Philomela's choice of punishment for Tereus does not serve justice. They cannot see beyond the moment of vengeance and have no regard for the consequences of their actions. By contrast, Georgina's goal is to end the cycle of Albert's brutality with an appropriate response to his act of murder. Her plan helps him fulfill the very threat he had screamed out when he first discovered her affair with Michael: "I'll bloody eat him! I'll kill him and then I'll eat him!" Georgina now takes her cue from these words. Her plan comes as a kind of comic relief, Richard confessing that he had feared even worse horrors:

GEORGINA: "Cook Michael for me."

RICHARD: "No!"

GEORGINA: "This was his favourite restaurant." (*There's a little pause.*) "It's also mine. Cook Michael for me."

RICHARD (*quietly*): "If I did—who would ever eat here again?"

GEORGINA (*with a smile*): "What would make you change your mind? Do you want to sleep with me? You can do what he did." (*Richard sadly shakes his head.*) "How can I persuade you?"

RICHARD: "You can't. You may have loved him . . ."

GEORGINA: "You know I did—you saw me."

RICHARD: ". . . but you don't have to eat him, Georgina. Do you have some idea that by eating him he can become part of you?" (*She smiles and shakes her head.*) "You can't believe that by eating him" (*he pauses*) "you can always be together."

GEORGINA (*with a broad grin*): "*I'm* not eating him." (*Richard looks perplexed.*) "*Albert is.*"

The questioning look on Richard's face slowly relaxes. There is a long pause. Georgina opens her bag and begins to take out a large sum of money in large notes.

RICHARD: "Albert?"

There is a long pause.

GEORGINA: "There's eleven thousand pounds. It's Michael's."

RICHARD: "Put your money away. Where is he?"[27]

Greenaway has been taken to task for his scenes of violence as being intended for pure shock effect.[28] But if he wanted utterly to disgust his audience, he surely missed a great opportunity. There is never a hint at how Michael's body is transformed from murder victim to main course. In a film so cluttered with cooking scenes, this one is conspicuously missing. But such an omission suits Greenaway's real purpose: Richard and Georgina can remain positive figures even as they conspire to force-feed one human to another. Such cannibalism brings purification. Only after making the arrangements for the feast does Georgina give her grief for her loss of Michael free rein. We associate neither her nor Richard with the horror of preparing Michael's body for food. Instead, we pity Georgina and even applaud Richard for his courage in going along with her plan.

Greenaway finds it ironic that Georgina, in order to triumph, "has to use the violence of her husband to turn it on him and win."[29] But even so she appears largely guiltless to us because Michael was already dead. Procne and Philomela, however, must change from victims to victimizers. In her quest to achieve justifiable vengeance, Procne crosses a moral line: "But about to confound right and wrong, Procne rushes forth and she is wholly absorbed in imagining the punishment" (585–586). Procne is determined to commit a crime in order to avenge one. Because of their misguided sense of justice, Procne and Philomela perpetrate unspeakable violence against an innocent child to effect their vengeance. Procne's response to the news of her husband's crimes is burning anger, but she never cries, nor does she allow Philomela to cry once she has rescued her. When

27. Greenaway, *The Cook, The Thief, His Wife and Her Lover*, 88.

28. Rafferty, "Conspicuous Consumer," 89: the film's "imagery is more violent than usual and thus evokes fear and disgust—not the most enlightening emotions a movie can produce, but two more than Greenaway generally allows us to feel."

29. Marcia Pally, "Cinema as the Total Art Form: An Interview with Peter Greenaway," *Cinéaste*, 18 no. 3 (1991), 6–11 and 45; quotation at 8.

252

CLASSICAL

MYTH &

CULTURE

IN THE

CINEMA

Procne wavers in her resolve to kill her child, her eyes fill with tears against her will (628). But this return to near-humanity lasts for only a moment. Her icy resolve returns and emotionally separates her from her victim. She does not even look away as she murders Itys (642).

Ovid paints Procne and Philomela in the worst possible light. He describes the sisters' act in detail and even shows them enjoying the butchery. Herein lies the tragedy of the myth. Their great success at empowering themselves causes them to fall victim to the same savagery they had despised before and to lose the reader's sympathy (641–646):

> Procne wielded her sword and stuck him through the side into his breast, nor did she turn away. That one wound was enough for the deed: Philomela then cut his throat with the sword, and they tore into pieces the limbs still alive and retaining something of his spirit: part leaps up from the bronze cauldrons, part shrieks on the spits; the interior of the house drips with gore.

8. The Wife's Reappropriation of Power

In their respective final scenes, the two wives have appropriated the power previously wielded by their husbands. They ensure the husband's presence at the meal by exploiting his egomania. Procne tells Tereus that he is invited to be the guest of honor at a ritual feast based on a tradition from her homeland (648–649).[30] Since we already know that Procne has mixed right with wrong (*fasque nefasque/confusura*, 585–586), it is particularly chilling that she evokes the concept of *fas* ("that which is divinely right"), in her deception to get Tereus to eat his own child.

Georgina sends Albert a special invitation, and we are informed of the celebratory nature of the evening: "FRIDAY: The Restaurant is closed for a private function." Although he really is powerless from the moment he enters the restaurant, Albert comes to realize this only very slowly. And this time Georgina does not submit to his bullying. While Albert rages loudly and ridiculously, Georgina is soft-spoken as she ominously hints at the reason for this special occasion: "It's an anniversary I shall always celebrate, even if you won't. And you won't." Albert is desperate to get Georgina back on his side, begging her to admit that Michael meant nothing to her. But his pathetic behavior strikes only contempt in her—and in

---

30. The child-feast is a Greek mythological tradition. Pausanias, *Description of Greece* 10.4.6, however, claims that Tereus' banquet is the first such pollution of the table, omitting the myth of Pelops. By introducing his tale of Procne with a summary of the Pelops story (6.403–411), Ovid places the Itys feast in an established tradition.

the viewers. Georgina resolutely mocks him, listing the faults her troglo-dyte husband sees only as sterling attributes, and specifically refers to that all-important appetite of his. In both stories the husband is the only eater of the meal: Tereus sits at table alone (648–649); Georgina prevents any-one else from sitting down: "No, this is Albert's special treat." Canni-balism is not taken lightly and is not meant to be indulged in by just anyone.

The climactic scene that follows dramatizes the shift in power from husband to wife, or to wife and accomplice. Now Georgina is in charge, commanding Albert: "Go on, Albert. Eat!" Procne appears submissive to ensure that ignorant Tereus eats his food (647). Ovid emphasizes Tereus' blindness to his fate when he calls for Itys to be brought to him after he has eaten him (652). Each wife takes satisfaction from orchestrating events in such a way that her ignorant husband must request information. The husbands, we might say, "ask for it," and the wives oblige. Both of them employ black humor as they revel in their new superiority. Procne even responds with a riddle to her husband's request to see his son. As Tereus had reveled in "his joy" (514) when he was anticipating his rape of Philo-mela, so Procne and Philomela now revel in theirs (653–660):

> Procne is unable to disguise her cruel joy and, desiring to be the messen-ger of his destruction, now says: "You have him, whom you seek, inside." He looks around and asks where he is; and as he asks and calls, Philomela, just as she was with hair bespattered by the furious slaughter, springs forth and shoves the bloody head of Itys into his father's face. Never was there a time when she wished she could speak more, so that she could show tes-tament to her joy with deserved words.

Greenaway delights in comparable outrageousness. Georgina mocks everything in which Albert takes pride. As he stares in helpless horror at Michael's body, she pleasantly wishes him "Bon Appetit!" and adds: "That's French," reminding him and us of all the times she had tried to correct his bad French pronunciation but earned a thrashing for her trouble. She also derives pleasure from a kind of inside joke: "Try the cock, Albert. It's a delicacy and you know where it's been." Greenaway's Georgina shows no less flair for the dramatic than Ovid's Philomela as she reveals the exact nature of her vengeance by whisking the cover off the serving table. Both Tereus and Albert immediately recognize the fea-tures of the human being served to them as food. Philomela thrusts the gory head of his decapitated son smack in his father's face, the moment dramatically rendered by Peter Paul Rubens in his *Feast of Tereus* of 1636. Since she cannot speak, Philomela must rely on Tereus' close view of Itys' head for effect. To achieve this, Ovid diverges from the usual way classical authors reveal to a cannibal the identity of his food.[31] In contrast to Ovid, Michael is laid out in toto, and Greenaway's camera lingers on Michael's face, catching a puff of steam wafting upward from behind his ear.

254

CLASSICAL

MYTH &

CULTURE

IN THE

CINEMA

Central to each story is the idea that a cannibal feast is a particularly justified recompense for the behavior of the husband toward the wife (and her doublet). But Ovid takes the symbolism of this child-feast to a much deeper level. In order for Procne's vengeance to fit his crime, Tereus' punishment must have a sexual dimension. As Tereus gorges himself, Ovid's word order underscores that he is eating his own flesh and blood: "He feeds, and he fills his stomach with his own flesh" (*vescitur inque suam sua viscera congerit alvum*; 651). But Tereus is filling more than his stomach, for *alvus* means both "stomach" and "womb." And he is eating more than meat, for *viscera* means both "flesh" and "children." The pun makes Ovid's story go beyond the regular reasons why child-feasts are prevalent in Greek mythology. Page DuBois has commented:

> If children are baked in the oven, which is the mother's womb, then, like loaves of bread, they are meant to be eaten. . . . In the most important myths of cannibalism of the Greeks, the consumed are children. And they are usually cooked and served to their fathers. . . . If children are cooked in the oven of the mother's uterus, then they are cooked again in these myths of cannibalism. Sons are cooked, and then, most often, devoured by their unwitting fathers.[32]

By forcing Tereus to take his own son into his *alvus*, Procne metaphorically impregnates her husband, knowing that he lacks the power to give birth to any child, particularly to *this* child. Tereus sobs that he has become "the wretched tomb of his son" (665).[33] To put it differently: Tereus'

31. The traditional method of identification is to display a basket containing some combination of the victim's head, hands, and feet, by which the feaster is able to identify the nature of his meal. (So Herodotus, *Histories* 1.120). In Seneca's *Thyestes*, Atreus uncovers the platter filled with his sons' "severed heads, torn-off hands, and feet broken off from shattered shins" (*Thyestes* 1039–1040), so that Thyestes can see the source of his meal. But Hyginus, *Fabulae* 88, claims that only the head and hands of the boys identified them as Thyestes' sons. Achilles Tatius, *Leucippe and Clitophon* 5.3, reports that the head and hands of Itys were brought to Tereus in a basket; he may be modeling his version on Servius' commentary on Virgil, *Eclogues* 6.79.

32. Page DuBois, *Sowing the Body: Psychoanalysis and Ancient Representations of Women* (Chicago: University of Chicago Press, 1988; rpt. 1991), 117.

33. Galinsky, *Ovid's Metamorphoses*, 155 note 22, lists additional instances of this image. Cf. Shakespeare's Romeo upon finding Juliet dead, as he thinks: "womb of death / Gorg'd with the dearest morsel of the earth" (*Romeo and Juliet*, act 5, scene 3). Ovid's emphasis elevates this point above the level of a tedious literary conceit (so Galinsky, 131–132).

womb has becomes Itys' tomb. One would expect a man who has just eaten his own flesh and blood to vomit forth his meal, but Tereus, metaphorically impregnated by his wife, can only bemoan the lack of an opening through which he could bear this necessarily still-born child (663–664).

Ovid's cannibal feast reaches a symbolic height that Greenaway's cannot because Albert's meal is not his own flesh and blood. Albert can and does vomit all over himself. But the theme of death *in alvo* is also at the heart of Georgina's suffering and vengeance, as Greenaway himself has made clear: "*Cook, Thief,* for me, functioned as a metaphor about the conflict between creativity and consumption, and the way they are destabilized by desire and excess."[34] Several times during the film Albert claims to want children and blames their childlessness on Georgina: "She doesn't eat properly, that's her problem." But Georgina believes that she is infertile because of the internal damage sustained from three miscarriages, all due to Albert's beatings. (The screenplay reveals that Georgina had had previous lovers, a circumstance that would account for these pregnancies, but the film leaves this out.) Given Greenaway's care in developing the elaborate metaphor of Albert's impotence, it seems reasonable to assume that Albert is not responsible for the conceptions. He is, however, responsible for the fetuses' terminations. While Procne causes Tereus to enwomb-entomb a child because he is the parent, Albert kills children in his wife's womb because he is not.

Once she has succeeded in getting her husband to sit down at the table, each wife proceeds to knock him off his pedestal. Tereus is specifically described as "sitting high on his ancestral throne" (650). He will not comprehend the depths of his disempowerment, sexual or otherwise, until he impotently tries to pursue the sisters with "a mere sword" (666). Albert, too, pulls a weapon, but Georgina's associates disarm him and give his gun, an obvious phallus substitute, to Georgina in an all-too-obvious redistribution of power. In the final manifestation of her power Georgina unseats the tyrant when the force of her bullet sends Albert and his chair crashing to the floor.

9. Metamorphosis

The metamorphoses which the characters in the Procne myth undergo are all for the worse. As birds they symbolize the horrific aspects of their earlier existence. Tereus becomes a hoopoe, disgusting, predatory, mired

34. Smith, "Food for Thought," 56. In another Greenaway film, *The Belly of an Architect* (1987), the protagonist's stomach is being eaten away by cancer as his wife's pregnancy advances; the film culminates in his suicide and her delivery of a child.

256

CLASSICAL

MYTH &

CULTURE

IN THE

CINEMA

in filth. The bird's feathered crest inspired Indian and Egyptian mythologies to revere it as a regal solar emblem, but this characterization is absent from the Greco-Roman tradition, which focuses on the bird's dirty habits.[35] Pliny the Elder reports that the hoopoe is a foul-feeding bird and suggests that it eats dung, and both Aristotle and Aelian observe that it smears human feces on its nest to warn people away.[36] (We are reminded of the opening scene of *CTWL*, in which Albert smears dog shit all over Roy.) The fact that both Tereus and Albert become cannibals reveals that their wives have only fleshed out, as it were, their innate depravity. The hoopoe's beak, crest, and tail are reminders of Tereus as sexual predator. But the warlike disposition of Tereus transformed is more important to Ovid. The bird's crest stands stiffly on his head like a helmet, and his beak is like a sword. He is poised for attack.[37] In this characterization of the hoopoe as an angry warrior, Ovid follows Sophocles, who had described the metamorphosed Tereus as "a bird in full armor" (*Tereus*, fr. 581).

While Tereus' bird form suggests that he is at least partially justified in his pursuit of his son's killers, the nightingale and the swallow are forever marked with the bloody evidence of slaughter (669–670). Ovid does not mention that because of Philomela's muteness the swallow has no birdsong and can only twitter unintelligibly. Nor does he tell us that the nightingale is known for her mournful song, doomed to bemoan the loss of a once beloved child. His description of the birds indicates that they have been punished not only for their crime but also for their gloating. They are remembered as murderers, not avengers, and Tereus as a warrior, not a rapist. Their savagery has overshadowed his.

In the film all the characters who do not change die; those who adapt survive. Albert Spica is despicable from beginning to end and meets with a well-deserved death. Michael, whose habits and dress had been the most regular, also dies. He had worn the same suit every evening, and this consistency distinguishes him from other characters who undergo a series of costume changes even within the same scene. In the long and complicated opening sequence, Georgina's dress appears black to Albert although she calls it dark blue; it is green in the kitchen, red in the dining room, and white in the bathroom. Michael always wore brown. Even when he is naked his skin has a light-brown hue, in the raw and in the cooked state.

Georgina adapts and survives. Most of Albert's entourage survive by defecting. (They are forever changed by their experiences.) Richard the

35. Cf. Aelian, *On Animals* 10.16 and 16.5.

36. Pliny, *Natural History* 10.86; Aristotle, *History of Animals* 616b1; Aelian, *On Animals* 3.26.

37. Pliny, *Natural History* 10.86.

cook undergoes a kind of transformation, too, from passive observer to active participant. His black tuxedo not only marks the final scene as ceremonial but also identifies the theme of change as momentous for the entire film. This is the first time that he wears anything other than a chef's white.

While Procne and Philomela are and remain stained with the bloody evidence of their crime, Georgina is washed clean, innocent of crime, free of Albert, free to pursue life. In Ovid, the avian metamorphoses are the end of a human tragedy and the beginning of an eternity of pursuit, doomed to be replayed over and over in the natural world of predators and prey. Georgina has put an end to such a cycle in her own life. Tereus and Albert suffer the foul treatment their foul dispositions demand, but in the end Albert is not transformed into anything. He is simply dead, powerless to hurt Georgina or even to haunt her. After she shoots him, Georgina has the last word, her voice dripping with contempt: "Cannibal!" Justice is served.

XII

The Social Ambience of Petronius' *Satyricon* and *Fellini Satyricon*

J. P. Sullivan

EDITOR'S NOTE: J. P. Sullivan died in 1993. Except for some minor changes and emendations and a few additions in the notes, his essay appears here essentially as it did in 1991. Among the numerous publications on Fellini, the following may be of particular interest to readers (most of them have appeared since Sullivan's essay was written; page numbers refer to *Fellini Satyricon*): Bernard F. Dick, "Adaptation as Archaeology: *Fellini Satyricon* (1969) from the 'Novel' by Petronius," in *Modern European Filmmakers and the Art of Adaptation*, ed. Andrew Horton and Joan Magretta (New York: Crossroads, 1981), 145–167; rpt. in *Perspectives on Federico Fellini*, ed. Peter Bondanella and Cristina Degli-Esposti (New York: Hall, 1993), 130–138; Bondanella, *The Eternal City: Roman Images in the Modern World* (Chapel Hill: University of North Carolina Press, 1987), 238–245, and *The Cinema of Federico Fellini* (Princeton: Princeton University Press, 1992), 237–261, with additional references; John Baxter, *Fellini* (1993; rpt. New York: St. Martin's, 1994), 237–253; Fabrizio Borin and Carla Mele, *Federico Fellini*, tr. Charles Nopar and Sue Jones (Rome: Gremese, 1999), 100–106; Maria Wyke, *Projecting the Past: Ancient Rome, Cinema and History* (New York: Routledge, 1997), 188–192. *Federico Fellini*, ed. Lietta Tornabuoni, tr. Andrew Ellis, Carol Rathman, and David Stanton (New York: Rizzoli, 1995), is lavishly illustrated. Axel Sütterlin, *Petronius Arbiter und Federico Fellini: Ein strukturanalytischer Vergleich* (Frankfurt a. M.: Lang, 1996), is a detailed comparison of novel and film, but see my review in *Petronian Society Newsletter*, 27.1–2 (1997), 8–9. *Fellini: A Director's Notebook* (1970), directed by Fellini and written by him and Bernardino Zapponi, is a poetic "documentary" on Fellini just before *Fellini*

Satyricon, which combines the Roman past with the present. *Ciao Federico* (1972) is a film essay directed by Gideon Bachmann on the making of *Fellini Satyricon*. Both are available on video.

Fellini Satyricon (1970) has proved something of a puzzle to some critics, whose reaction to the film can hardly be construed as favorable. Classical scholars have been particularly troubled by its syncopation of events, its drastic redistribution of incidents among the characters, and, above all, its non-Petronian sources.[1] Perhaps a reevaluation of these sources will throw more light on the film. I shall argue that Fellini, faced with the battered torso of this ancient novel, with only a tenth or twentieth of it still extant, felt justified as a director and creative translator to supplement the fragmentary narrative with incidents and details from more or less contemporary literary and historical works.[2]

1. The following reviews of and articles on Fellini's film by classicists are particularly noteworthy: Gilbert Highet, "Whose *Satyricon*—Petronius's or Fellini's?" *Horizon*, 12 no. 4 (1970), 42–47, rpt. in *The Classical Papers of Gilbert Highet*, ed. Robert J. Ball (New York: Columbia University Press, 1983), 339–348; Barry Baldwin and Gerald Sandy, reviews in *Petronian Society Newsletter*, 1 no. 2 (1970), 2–3 and 3; William R. Nethercut, "Fellini and the Colosseum: Philosophy, Morality and the *Satyricon* (1970)," *The Classical Bulletin*, 47 (1971), 53–59. In addition see Alberto Moravia, "Dreaming Up Petronius," tr. Raymond Rosenthal, *The New York Review of Books* (March 26, 1970), 40–42, rpt. in *Federico Fellini: Essays in Criticism*, ed. Peter Bondanella (New York: Oxford University Press, 1978), 161–168; Charles Samuels, "Puppets: From *Z* to *Zabriskie Point*," *The American Scholar*, 39 (1970), 678–691; John Simon, "*Fellini Satyricon*," in *Movies into Film* (New York: Dial Press, 1971), 211–219. Those interested in the making of the film may consult Eileen Lanouette Hughes, *On the Set of FELLINI SATYRICON: A Behind-the-Scenes Diary* (New York: Morrow, 1971). The published text of the film is in *Fellini Satyricon*, ed. Dario Zanelli (Bologna: Cappelli, 1969); English translation, as *Fellini's Satyricon*, by Eugene Walter and John Matthews (New York: Ballantine, 1970).
2. It should be remembered that Fellini had philological advisers for the film: Luca Canali of the University of Pisa, a Marxist, and the scriptwriter Bernardino Zapponi, who together called on the expertise of Ettore Paratore, the author of a long and inconclusive commentary on Petronius (*Il Satyricon di Petronio*, 2 vols. [Florence: Le Monnier, 1933]). Not that these would prove any block for Fellini's imagination in his film *Roma* (1972), when he exercised it on the subject of Nero's Rome, which he seems to have seen as the substrate underlying the Eternal City in the twentieth century. [EDITOR'S NOTE: See *Conversations with Fellini*, ed. Costanzo Costantini, tr. Sohrab Sorooshian (San Diego: Harcourt Brace, 1995), 74–75: "That my film might be thought to have little in common with Petronius, I consider more a compliment than an indictment. . . . My intention was to make a film outside of time, an atemporal film, but it was impossible for me not to see that the world described by Petronius bore a remarkable similarity to the one in which

260

CLASSICAL

MYTH &

CULTURE

IN THE

CINEMA

This is not to say that Fellini wished, even creatively, to "adapt" the *Satyricon* as though it were a defective film script based on a historical novel. As he himself insisted: "I've tried first of all to eliminate what is generally called history. . . . Thus the atmosphere [of the film] is not historical but that of a dream world."[3] But even dreams have a certain logic and usually a consistent tone, often of fear, passivity, pleasure, or some other emotional state. And so the supplementary material is naturally drawn from congenial sources. The atmosphere may be sometimes exotic, but it is never, in any pictorial way, modern. The *Satyricon*, in any case, was an "open" work to begin with, that is to say a work consisting of scarcely related episodes, and it has been further opened by the massive textual losses in the manuscript tradition. This provided even more of a stimulus to Fellini's inventive ingenuity, which turned for inspiration to the scanty remains of Roman painting and sculpture, as was noticed by Alberto Moravia. It is highly appropriate that the last glimpse the audience has of the film's antiheroes, Encolpius and Giton, is in a freeze-framed faded fresco of Pompeian colors.[4]

What were these external, non-Petronian materials that Fellini used to flesh out the fragmentary narrative?[5] The basic plot of Petronius consists of the picaresque adventures of the antihero Encolpius and his young and fickle boyfriend Giton. An early offense against the sexual divinity

---

we live, me included. Petronius's characters are prey to the same devouring existential anxieties as people today. Trimalchio made me think of Onassis: a gloomy, immobile Onassis with the stony glare of a mummy. The other characters reminded me of hippies. It may be that I have also projected my personal fantasies into the film, but why not? Am I not the film's creator?"]

3. Quoted from Edward Murray, *Fellini the Artist*, 2nd ed. (New York: Ungar, 1985), 179. Murray's overall evaluation of the film is negative: "Both artistically and humanistically . . . Fellini's single out-and-out failure" (189). [EDITOR'S NOTE: See Fellini as quoted in *Federico Fellini: Comments on Film*, ed. Giovanni Grazzini; tr. Joseph Henry (Fresno: California State University, Fresno, 1988), 172–173: "a great dream galaxy sunken in the darkness and now rising up to us amid glowing bursts of light. . . . The ancient world, I told myself, never existed, but no doubt we dreamed it. My job [making the film] will be to eliminate the borderline between dream and imagination; to invent everything and then to objectify the fantasy; to get some distance from it in order to explore it as something all of a piece and unknowable."]

4. [EDITOR'S NOTE: See Fellini as quoted in Charlotte Chandler, *I, Fellini* (New York: Random House, 1995), 171–172: "It [Petronius' novel] has come down to us in fragments. . . . I was even more fascinated by what wasn't there than by what was there. Stimulated by the fragments, my imagination could roam. . . . I was like an archaeologist piecing together fragments of ancient vases, trying to guess what the missing parts looked like. Rome itself is an ancient broken vase, constantly being mended to hold it together, but retaining hints of its original secrets."]

5. Most of these, but not all, were spotted by Highet, "Whose *Satyricon*?"

Priapus, reinforced by subsequent unwitting offenses, causes the god to hound him in various ways, just as Poseidon hounded Odysseus in the *Odyssey* and Juno persecuted Aeneas in the *Aeneid*. The *Satyricon* is in this sense a parody of the *Odyssey* and the *Aeneid*, but it is also a parody of contemporary Greek love-romances. Encolpius' misadventures—temple violation, condemnation to the amphitheater, burglary and murder, and the flight from various avengers—are compounded by his troubles with temporary companions, who try to take Giton away from him. These are Tryphaena the courtesan, Ascyltus, his burly and untrustworthy companion for a while, and the devious and deviant poet Eumolpus. In Croton, living out a dangerous confidence trick, he adds to his troubles by taking up, as a pretended slave, with the arrogant Circe, a Roman Lady Chatterley, who expects the inferior men she prefers to perform well.[6] She is highly indignant when Priapus' anger induces in Encolpius a chronic impotence with her. Onto the fantastic narrative thread, already replete with suicide attempts, elaborate banquets, cannibalism, violence, and trickery, Petronius could hang literary digressions relating to contemporary writers, which Fellini had naturally to forgo, substituting instead the extraneous literary and historical material which he in turn felt was *ben trovato*. So he draws upon Juvenal's third satire for the decrepit state of his Roman tenements (*Satires* 3.193–196). He borrows medieval material about Virgil the magician for the obscene and fiery fate of the witch Oenothea, possibly adding here an indecent motif from Martial.[7] Encolpius in the novel had at some time been a gladiator; this is elaborated by Fellini into the gladiatorial mime in which Encolpius playing the part of Theseus has to fight a gladiator made up as the Minotaur in a labyrinth and then, after winning Princess Ariadne, has to take her in full sight of a large audience. His predictable failure and her impatient anger hark back to Encolpius' failure with Circe in the *Satyricon*, but the scene as a whole depends on similar episodes in the second extant Roman novel, written about a century later than the *Satyricon*, Apuleius' *Golden Ass*. Here the antihero, Lucius, has a number of tricks played on him during a festival in honor of the god of mirth. For instance, he is tricked into puncturing three wineskins filled with blood under the impression that he is killing some robbers. He is hauled off to a mock court, held in a theater, to stand

6. For an analysis of the character type in Latin literature see my "Lady Chatterley in Rome," *Pacific Coast Philology*, 15 (1980), 53–62.

7. Cf. *Epigrams* 3.93. On the medieval background of this episode in the film see Domenico Comparetti, *Vergil in the Middle Ages*, tr. E. F. M. Benecke, 2nd ed. (1908; rpt. Princeton: Princeton University Press, 1997), 325–336, and, for a more detailed account, John Webster Spargo, *Virgil the Necromancer: Studies in Virgilian Legends* (Cambridge: Harvard University Press, 1934; rpt. 1979), 136–206.

262

CLASSICAL

MYTH &

CULTURE

IN THE

CINEMA

trial for his life and is threatened with ghastly tortures before the farce is finally exposed to the great amusement of the assembled townsfolk (2.31–3.11). This and Lucius' forced copulation later (10.34), while he is in ass's shape, with a condemned female criminal in the arena, presumably inspired the grotesque "public performances" that Fellini took delight in presenting in his film, most notably in the sexual encounters of Encolpius with Ariadne and then with Oenothea. This aspect of ancient entertainment Fellini could easily have found documented in Jérôme Carcopino's *Daily Life in Ancient Rome*, one of the works he read in preparation for making the film.[8] Martial reports the executions and mutilation on stage in mythological and historical playlets, and nude spectacles by prostitutes were part of the spring rituals of the Floralia in Rome. This would have appealed to Fellini's almost obsessive preoccupation with circuses (*La Strada* [1954]), stage performances of an unorthodox kind (*Ginger and Fred* [1986]), indeed with exhibitionism in general (*8½* [1963]), and is not incompatible with his delight in masks. All of this surfaces in the tragic-comic mime scenes and the appearances of Vernacchio, the buffoonish actor who turns up early in *Fellini Satyricon*.

The haunting sequences of the suicides of the handsome upper-class couple in their ornate villa are based on the deaths of Thrasea Paetus, the Stoic opponent of Nero, and his wife.[9] Their significance in the film is not only to provide a link with the imperial world of the novel, but again to provide a play within a play—this time a tragedy, which will be quickly converted to comedy when the trio of antiheroes arrives. At first impressed and awed by the mournful spectacle, they are soon engaged in a sexual romp with the young Oriental slave girl they find there. The mood is finally broken by the burning of the body of the master of the villa. Short though the whole sequence is, it provides a good example of how swiftly Fellini, with his eye for detail and coloring, generates a convincing atmosphere or, more generally, ambience in quite brief scenes.[10]

8. According to Murray, *Fellini the Artist*, 178. Jérôme Carcopino, *La vie quotidienne à Rome à l'apogée de l'empire* (Paris: Hachette, 1939); in English: *Daily Life in Ancient Rome: The People and the City at the Height of the Empire*, tr. Emily Overend Lorimer (New Haven: Yale University Press, 1940; rpt. 1992). An Italian translation appeared in 1941.

9. See, for example, Martial, *Epigrams* 1.13; Tacitus, *Annals* 16.33–35; and Pliny the Younger, *Letters* 3.16.6.

10. [EDITOR'S NOTE: Fellini on this episode: "Petronius himself appears in *Satyricon*. He is the wealthy freedman who commits suicide with his wife after he has freed his slaves"; quoted from Chandler, *I, Fellini*, 173. There is, then, a direct parallel between Petronius and Fellini: "What wasn't there [in the text] appealed to me most because it created the opportunity for me to fill it in using my imagination, and I could actually become a part of the story" (Chandler, 172).]

One episode, which has particularly puzzled critics, is the kidnapping by the trio of a frail albino bisexual, who is worshiped as the living god Hermaphroditus but who dies of thirst and exhaustion in the desert during his abduction. I suggest that this is based on a pseudo-Petronian poem sometimes printed along with the *Satyricon*.[11] This late piece describes the strange debate in heaven over the birth and death of Hermaphroditus: Should he die by drowning, stabbing, or crucifixion? In the poem he climbs a tree by a river, transfixes himself with his own sword, and his head falls into the river, with his body hanging from the tree.

There is also a possible allusion in the scene depicting the marriage of Lichas and Encolpius to the transvestite emperor Elagabalus, who reigned from A.D. 218 to 222. Born Varius Avitus, the young ruler took his name from the sun god of Emesa, Elah-Gabal, whose hereditary priest he was and whose religion he spent his short life promoting. Reaching Rome in 219, he built two enormous temples for the Oriental deity and celebrated his midsummer festival with outlandish and obscene ceremonies.[12] He and his powerful mother, Julia Soaemias, were eventually murdered by the Praetorians.

For some of the scenes involving Lichas and his "marriage" to the humiliated Encolpius, Fellini has apparently drawn not just on the *Satyricon* but also on certain anecdotes about Nero's mock marriages to his freedmen Doryphorus and Pythagoras, pruriently detailed by the imperial biographer Suetonius and also by the historian Tacitus. Again, these additions are appropriate to the Neronian setting in which the *Satyricon* itself was written.[13]

One could say more about the possible sources, but the fundamental question to be asked is: Why does Fellini allow himself these liberties? Fellini, I suggest, is using the creative translator's method of "equivalences." What cannot come across to the modern audience—for example, the literary and very topical digressions on Neronian literature with their parodies of Seneca and Lucan[14]—Fellini jettisons and substitutes often silent episodes, such as an emperor surrounded and assassinated by sol-

11. For example, in the edition of Maurice Rat (Paris: Classiques Garnier, 1938); numbered as fragment LVII in my translation: *Petronius: The Satyricon and Seneca: The Apocolocyntosis*, rev. ed. (Harmondsworth: Penguin, 1986), 179.

12. Herodian, *History of the Empire* 5.8; Dio Cassius, *Roman History* 79.33 and 80.3–17.

13. Suetonius, *Nero* 29, and Tacitus, *Annals* 15.37, describe Nero's marriages. On the background of Petronius' *Satyricon* and the audience for which it was intended see my *Literature and Politics in the Age of Nero* (Ithaca, N.Y.: Cornell University Press, 1985), 19–73 and 153–179.

14. See the chapter on criticism and parody in my *The Satyricon of Petronius: A Literary Study* (London: Faber, 1968), 158–213.

264

CLASSICAL

MYTH &

CULTURE

IN THE

CINEMA

diers, a monstrous effigy of an emperor's head dragged through the streets (based on the death of Vitellius in A.D. 69), or a new Caesar, dignified and soldierly, marching on Rome. For the literary dimension, impossible to convey on the screen, Fellini has substituted a political dimension. This may be interpreted as the representation of the martial, highly masculine Rome which the director is undercutting or marginalizing through the sexual mysticism of other, more amplified and indeed grosser, scenes in the film. Fellini has always believed that pagan Rome has certain analogies with our modern world, not least that represented by his own films *La Dolce Vita* (1960) and *Roma*. But for him Rome as an ideal, admittedly pagan ideal, was distorted by Mussolini's fascism, which emphasized its military and organizational virtues. It was also distorted by the moralistic views of Christianity, which rejected as vice what the pagans regarded as happiness and contentment. Fellini's view of ancient and modern Rome is simultaneously pagan and pessimistic, but he is not above parodying the more optimistic alternatives. So the hermaphroditic divinity, who works miracles and is worshiped by peasants, may even be considered a parody of the infant Jesus in his manger, and Fellini has heightened the cannibalistic scene around the dead Eumolpus toward the end of the *Satyricon* by "elevating" the solemn reading of Eumolpus' will and the instructions for this cannibalism into a grotesque Last Supper. The Fellini aficionado may be reminded of the enormous flying statue of Christ that opens *La Dolce Vita*.

Where Fellini is astonishingly true to his model is, however, in the atmosphere he engenders in his film. Although more graphic and, of course, visual, than his original, he succeeds in expressing its spirit in a number of ways. A few things may be said about Petronius and his audience of which Fellini must have been aware. Here is part of Tacitus' description of Petronius' way of living (*Annals* 16.18):

> Gaius Petronius spent his days sleeping and his nights working and enjoying himself. Industry is the usual foundation of success, but with him it was idleness. Unlike most people who throw away their money in dissipation, he was not regarded as an extravagant sensualist but as one who made luxury a fine art. Yet as proconsul in Bithynia, and later as consul, he showed himself a vigorous and capable administrator. His subsequent return to his old habits, whether this was real or apparent, led to his admission to the small circle of Nero's intimates as his Arbiter of Elegance. In the end Nero's jaded appetite regarded nothing as enjoyable or refined unless Petronius had given his sanction to it.

Seneca, Petronius' philosophical opposite and his political rival at court, was familiar with this type of personality and in the *Epistles* severely attacked such an unnatural lifestyle. Such people were "night-owls"; he says of them:

they pervert the activities of day and night, and they don't open their eyes, heavy from yesterday's hangover, before night begins to fall. How can they know how to live who don't know when to live? Do they fear death when they've buried themselves alive? (122.3)

Seneca argues that this depravity of avoiding the day and living at night is part of the viciousness that delights in being completely at odds with nature. It is the aim of luxuriousness to delight in perversity and in departing as far as possible from the correct way of behaving, in fact to do its opposite. Seneca points to the perverse taste for roses and lilies in winter, to transvestite affectations, and to the cultivation of gardens on rooftops (122.8).

He might also have mentioned other perversities of some of his contemporaries, not least Nero's habit of slumming—wandering from his palace in disguise late at night through disreputable parts of Rome, breaking into shops, and playing malicious jokes on whomever he encountered. This is recorded with appropriate distaste by Suetonius; other emperors and at least one Ptolemy shared this taste, and it is presumably a symptom of *nostalgie de la boue*, that longing for degradation not uncommon in ages when material luxury and artistic sophistication seem to breed a certain decadence and a keen desire for thrills to tickle jaded palates. One thinks of the 1890s in England and France, the period of Joris-Karl Huysmans' *À Rebours* (1884)—*Against Nature* is the title of the English translation—and Oscar Wilde's *The Picture of Dorian Gray* (1891), but one could equally well think of the society portrayed by Fellini himself in *La Dolce Vita*.

The *Satyricon* has to be put in the same class as such works—indeed, Huysmans specifically mentions it as one of the works his hero dotes on. Here is the Duc Des Esseintes in his library:

> The author he really loved ... was Petronius. Petronius was a shrewd observer, a delicate analyst, a marvellous painter; dispassionately, with an entire lack of prejudice or animosity, he described the everyday life of Rome, recording the manners and morals of his time in the lively little chapters of the *Satyricon*.
>
> Noting what he saw as he saw it, he set forth the day-to-day existence of the common people, with all its minor events, its bestial incidents, its obscene antics.
>
> Here we have the Inspector of Lodgings coming to ask for the names of any travellers who have recently arrived; there, a brothel where men circle round naked women standing beside placards giving their price, while through half-open doors couples can be seen disporting themselves in the bedrooms.
>
> Elsewhere, in villas full of insolent luxury where wealth and ostentation run riot, as also in the mean inns described throughout the book, with

266

CLASSICAL

MYTH &

CULTURE

IN THE

CINEMA

their unmade trestle beds swarming with fleas, the society of the day has its fling—depraved ruffians, like Ascyltus and Eumolpus, out for what they can get; unnatural old men with their gowns tucked up and their cheeks plastered with white lead and acacia rouge; catamites of sixteen, plump and curly-headed; women having hysterics; legacy-hunters offering their boys and girls to gratify the lusts of rich testators, all these and more scurry across the pages of the *Satyricon*, squabbling in the streets, fingering one another in the baths, beating one another up like characters in a pantomime.

There are lightning sketches of all these people, sprawled round a table, exchanging the vapid pleasantries of drunken revellers, trotting out mawkish maxims and stupid saws, their heads turned towards Trimalchio, who sits picking his teeth, offers the company chamberpots, discourses on the state of his bowels, farts to prove his point, and begs his guests to make themselves at home.

This realistic novel, this slice cut from Roman life in the raw, with no thought, whatever people may say, of reforming or satirizing society—this story fascinated Des Esseintes; and in its subtle style, acute observation, and solid construction he could see a curious similarity, a strange analogy with the few modern French novels he could stomach.[15]

This quotation, with only few changes, could very well stand as a description of Fellini's film. *Nostalgie de la boue*, the fascination that rags hold for riches, the urge to wallow in the gutter or stoop to conquer, whether in the male desire for prostitutes or ladies' predilections for slaves, is patently mirrored in both versions of the *Satyricon*.

In Petronius, many of the scenes take place at night. The rites of Priapus are nocturnal; Encolpius' crime must be expiated by an all-night vigil in Priapus' honor; banquets go on through the night; Trimalchio's friend Habinnas in particular wants to turn night into day, and so the all-night feasting is prolonged by a second bath; only cock-crow breaks up the party, sending Encolpius, Ascyltus, and Giton wandering through the last shades of night without a torch. The ghost stories of Trimalchio and his guests about witches and werewolves all take place in the night. It is in darkest night on board ship that Encolpius, Giton, and Eumolpus plan their escape from their pursuers and so shave their heads by the light of the moon. This atmosphere of darkness, torches, and obscure, dingy dwellings and bathhouses Fellini successfully evokes in the opening scenes of the film.

This psychological complex accounts for much more than the physical atmosphere of both novel and film. It extends also to the social planes on which they operate. Again we are presented only with characters and scenes drawn from the seamier side of Roman society. One particularly interesting character is Circe, the rich and beautiful lady who falls in love at the sight of the pretended slave Encolpius. She above all expresses *nostalgie de la boue* in her desire for sexual degradation. Here is her maid's description of her to Encolpius:

> "You say you're just a poor slave, but you're only exciting her desire to boiling point. Some women get heated up over the absolute dregs and can't feel any passion unless they see slaves or bare-legged messengers. The arena sets some of them on heat, or a mule-driver covered with dust, or actors displayed on the stage. My mistress is one of this type. She jumps across the first fourteen seats from the orchestra and looks for something to love among the lowest of the low."
>
> I said in a voice full of sweetness: "Tell me, are you the one who is in love with me?"
>
> The maid laughed heartily at such an unlikely notion.
>
> "I wouldn't make you so pleased with yourself. I have never yet gone to bed with a slave, and heaven forbid I should ever see a lover of mine crucified. That's for ladies who kiss the whip-marks. Even though I'm a servant, I've never sat anywhere except in the lap of knights."
>
> I couldn't help some surprise at such contrasting sexual desires. I thought it very strange that the maid should cultivate the superior outlook of a lady and the lady the low taste of a maid.[16]

But the theme of sexual degradation has been struck earlier in the tale of the virtuous widow of Ephesus, who had vowed to remain faithful to her deceased husband till her own death but falls for a common soldier and saves him by putting her husband's body up on the cross which the soldier had been guarding (*Satyricon* 111–112).

The incidental references in the Feast of Trimalchio to mistresses who have affairs with their slaves are not to be omitted from this general picture. This perversion of the natural order of things among the upper-class ladies is paralleled by the pathetic attempts to rise on the social scale by Trimalchio and many of his friends, who hope that through the ostentatious use of their newly acquired money they can ape their betters in taste, luxury, and extravagance. The inspection of the vulgarity of the circle, on Petronius' part, is *de haut en bas*, and Fellini's fascination with his Trimalchio is quite unlike the amused and objective coolness which the Roman author brings to his satire, just as Fellini's fondness for grotesques and cripples goes beyond the cooler observation of Petronius. Examples of Fellini's eye for the bizarre and the eccentric are especially frequent in his

16. *Satyricon* 126.5–11; quoted from my translation, 142.

268

CLASSICAL

MYTH &

CULTURE

IN THE

CINEMA

Satyricon, but viewers will remember also how pervasive that element is in *La Dolce Vita*, most notably in the monstrous goggle-eyed fish dragged up from the depths near the end of the film, and the troupe of midgets in *Ginger and Fred*.[17] Nevertheless there are wizened and oversexed old ladies, gross male prostitutes, and a lecherous old bisexual poet in Petronius' *Satyricon* as well, and the hero himself, after all, is for much of the narrative a hopeless sexual cripple, a facet of the story that Fellini finally confronts directly in the brief scene depicting Encolpius' fiasco with Princess Ariadne.

The social ambience, then, of Petronius' *Satyricon* is not too unlike that presented, at least in the first half of the film, in *Fellini Satyricon*, if we allow for the greater vividness and shocking detail that the modern visual medium permits and encourages. We go on an intellectual slumming tour in Petronius' company as well as in Fellini's. To observe the lower classes and the criminal elements of Roman society and to have portrayed even upper-class ladies who sink to that level excited a frisson in the highly class-conscious Roman society or, among the respectable members of the senatorial caste, a strong repugnance. Fellini's audience is wider; the differing reactions to his film are worth recalling.[18]

Granted the resemblances and differences between the Roman novel and its cinematic version by Fellini, is there a critical view expressed in Fellini's recreation of that world?

There is a school of thought represented in different nuances which tries to discern in Petronius, a man at home if not enthroned in Nero's court, an elevated and subtle satirist.[19] This critical theory is partly based on T. S. Eliot's use, as an epigraph for *The Waste Land* (1922), of the pathetic story of the Sibyl in the Bottle as told by Trimalchio. When asked by little boys what she wanted, she cried out in Greek: "I want to die" (*Satyricon* 48.8).

Helen Bacon elaborated this into a theory about the *Satyricon* as a prototype of *The Waste Land*.[20] She stressed Trimalchio's obsession with death, the use of food for everything except its proper purpose, money and materialism as the only shared values of the Roman society Petronius

17. For further instances see Murray, *Fellini the Artist*, 130 and passim. He also documents the many grotesque minor characters whom Fellini parades in most of his work.

18. For example, that by Simon, "*Fellini Satyricon*."

19. Thus Highet, "Petronius the Moralist," *Transactions of the American Philological Association*, 72 (1941), 176–194; rpt. in *Classical Papers*, 191–209; William A. Arrowsmith, "Luxury and Death in the *Satyricon*," *Arion*, 5 (1966), 304–331; Froma I. Zeitlin, "*Romanus Petronius*: A Study of the *Troiae Halosis* and the *Bellum Civile*," *Latomus*, 30 (1971), 56–82. Contrast these views with that argued in my "Petronius: Artist or Moralist?" *Arion*, 6 (1967), 71–88.

20. Helen H. Bacon, "The Sibyl in the Bottle," *The Virginia Quarterly Review*, 34 (1958), 262–276.

depicts, the lack of love, and the world of famine in which luxury tries to tease the satiated senses into the appearance of life. For her, the Sibyl symbolizes Petronius' own Waste Land, except that to Petronius the Sibyl does not seem to suggest the possibility of rebirth when longed-for death is achieved. Against this William Arrowsmith has argued:

> Miss Bacon sees . . . that the *Satyricon* is not a symptom of a corrupt society, but a penetrating *description* of it, remarkably like Fellini's *La Dolce Vita*. . . . But when she forces the whole book to yield that Christian, almost Manichaean, desolation of Eliot's *Waste Land*, she goes . . . deeply wrong. And when, in order to support this view, she denies that the *Satyricon* is basically comedy, and that the characters are not alive, I think she is violating her text, its plain comic ambitions and its extraordinary liveliness. . . . Miss Bacon tends to assume either that comedy and moral seriousness are incompatible, or that deep gaiety and the description of cultural decay are incompatible. . . . Petronius sets his charming rascals and rogues in sharp contrast to society's greater immoralism, hypocrisy and vulgarity.

Arrowsmith points instead to a hope of which Petronius, even in the midst of so much degradation and death, never loses sight:

> If society has organized itself around the satiety that brings death, man's hope is to rediscover the old pagan landscape, the radiance here and now, in which everything had *numen* [divine presence], and nobody needed eternal life because life itself was good and had god in it. . . . Petronius is . . . the last great witness to the pagan sense of life, and the last classical author in whom we can feel the firmness of moral control that underlies the Greek tragedians. . . . Petronius is squarely in the Latin moralist and satirical tradition—and the greatest moralist of them all.[21]

Arrowsmith's interpretation still presents Petronius as ultimately a great moralist, although now he is a pagan moralist, satirizing the excesses he sees in Roman society with its emphasis on luxury as a way of escaping death.

How would such an analysis apply to Fellini, particularly when we take into account not only *Fellini Satyricon* but also *La Dolce Vita* and *Roma*, all of which have much in common? Certainly Fellini has a satirical eye and an eye for the grotesque, particularly in his casting for minor roles, and a willingness to exaggerate by emphasis as well. This, incidentally, he can do very effectively with his selection of vivid, sometimes scaring,

---

21. The quotations are from Arrowsmith, "Luxury and Death in the *Satyricon*," 325–327 and 329–330.

images; for instance, the handless arm spouting blood that is shown early in *Fellini Satyricon*. But what are his positives?

I suggest that he has, in common with Petronius, an amused tolerance and acceptance of life as it is lived, a willingness to face his perceived reality and an impatience with false solutions, such as Mussolini's fascism. So, like Petronius, he has more of an artist's than a moralist's eye, although some social comment is often implicit in his choice of themes.

We have here, then, two contrasting views of Petronius, and the analogies for Fellini are obvious. There is Petronius the complex moralist as described by Arrowsmith and others, and there is Petronius as seen by, for example, the Duc Des Esseintes in Huysmans' novel. In the latter the comedy of life is seen as irresistible: After a while there is nothing you can do but laugh. To illustrate this point, there are several scenes which Fellini found worth adapting to illustrate this ancient theater of the absurd. References in Petronius to mimic laughter, to the world as a stage, to role-playing and disguises are frequent enough. Fellini plays up this farcical element by introducing his "underground" theater in the film's opening scene and by inventing a new character, the absurd actor Vernacchio, who farts musically, quaffs a beaker of urine, and then cuts off the arm of the pretended Muzio Scevola with a great axe.[22]

Is there a solution to this critical conflict in which Huysmans, Arrowsmith, and Fellini all seem involved? T. S. Eliot, in "Tradition and the Individual Talent" (1919), alluded to the phenomenon whereby each new classic rearranged the order of all its predecessors in the great *musée imaginaire* that is Western literature. This in a way was an early and striking statement of the principle nowadays called intertextuality: Every literary work has roots and connections that cannot be ignored, however hard we try to treat it as a self-subsistent work of art. Its history is part of its essence—for us, part of its *lisibilité*. And, to go even further, the reinterpretations become part of the reading we give it, either through reaction to or sympathy with earlier readings. This is particularly the case with the Latin and Greek classics; our heads are already full of interpretation, conscious or not, because of what we have had to do just to read them. So no text is sacred.

Interpretations then become preliminary, not unnecessary, of course, to what we nowadays call deconstruction of the work and of the author.

22. The motif of Mucius Scaevola, the Roman hero who defied the besieging Etruscan king Porsenna by burning his right hand in a blazing fire, is actually taken from Martial, *Epigrams* 1.21. The story appears in Livy, *From the Foundation of the City* 2.12. If the connection seems somewhat recherché, consider that in *Ginger and Fred* the hero claims that his high-school Latin teacher compared his rhyming aphorisms to Martial's epigrams.

270

CLASSICAL

MYTH &

CULTURE

IN THE

CINEMA

Fellini, in a manner of speaking, "deconstructs" Petronius' *Satyricon* and, particularly in the very last shot of his film, lays out the characters in a frozen immobility which transcends the age in which it was written and renders null and void the motives that other critics have attributed to the author. This ending is a clue to one plausible interpretation of *Fellini Satyricon*. The restless cinematographic images of the sometimes inferior actors that have led us such a bewildering dance through the film—and the dance, not the dancers, is at issue here—are pinned to a fragmentary mural and so are taken out of time. The random confusion of life, reflected in one way in the fragmentary state of Petronius' own text, is now given a timeless quality. The characters' story becomes history, as it were, not in a conventional sense, which Fellini has rejected anyway, but as a slice of the past held up for aesthetic rather than inquiring contemplation.

To end with a truism: The Greek and Latin classics discussed here all have to be reinvented in every age and for every new audience. Fellini's version of the fragmentary *Satyricon* is a worthy part of that continuing endeavor, and critics' complaints about the lack of fidelity to the often uncertain text are beside the point. The text itself has many meanings; to suggest that only one view is the right one is itself to distort that text. Fellini's interpretation, or rather presentation, of Petronius now becomes part of the *Satyricon*'s "literary history" and of its meaning for the modern reader.

XIII

Star Wars and the Roman Empire

Martin M. Winkler

A wide variety of sources influenced George Lucas in his *Star Wars* trilogy, which was released from 1977 to 1983, rereleased in a "Special Edition" in 1997, and followed in 1999 by *Star Wars: Episode I— The Phantom Menace*. Among Lucas's literary sources are archetypal hero myths as described by C. G. Jung, popularized by Joseph Campbell, and exemplified in the stories and novels of J. R. R. Tolkien, American pulp fiction, and comic strips; among his cinematic sources are science-fiction and war films, medieval epics, westerns, and film noir. Also markedly evident is the influence of individual films, such as Fritz Lang's *Metropolis* (1926), Leni Riefenstahl's *Triumph of the Will* (1935), Victor Fleming's *The Wizard of Oz* (1939), John Ford's *The Searchers* (1956), and Akira Kurosawa's *The Hidden Fortress* (1958). There is, however, one other aspect of popular culture, generally overlooked, that plays a major part in Lucas's imagination of the future.

The films' theme is the struggle of the forces of Good against absolute Evil. Their eternal opposition is a fundamental feature linking traditional hero myth, romance, and epic to modern fiction and films. In such tales the hero's actions are invariably deeds of valor and violence, committed for the purpose of restoring justice to the community and helping to bring about a better society. Literary and cinematic narratives of this kind tell thrilling stories full of exciting action. The fight of Good versus Evil frequently evolves on a large scale in clashes of battles and wars. Lucas has described the purpose he pursued with *Star Wars* in the following words:

> I wanted it to be a traditional moral study, to have some sort of palpable precepts in it that children could understand. There is always a lesson to be learned. Where do these lessons come from? Traditionally, we get them

from church, the family, art, and in the modern world we get them from
media—from movies.[1]

Bible

273

Star Wars

& the

Roman

Empire

In Lucas's film world, Evil is represented by a galactic empire. While
twentieth-century history and its transformations into filmic narratives,
especially those involving World War II, provide the most obvious factual parallels to the films' plot, there is another, more distant, era of the
past which is equally important. Lucas's evil empire parallels the Roman
Empire and conforms to the negative view of imperial Rome generally
present in popular culture. Moreover, the first three *Star Wars* films bear
close resemblances to one specific historical film: *The Fall of the Roman
Empire* (1964), directed by Anthony Mann. I will describe, first, Lucas's
galactic empire as an *imperium Romanum redivivum,* so to speak, and,
second, the similarities between *Star Wars* and Mann's film.

1. Parallel Societies and Histories

In *The Eternal City*, Peter Bondanella has traced the modern survival of
ancient Rome in the high and low culture of western Europe and the
United States. He has shown conclusively the connections between Edward
Gibbon's *History of the Decline and Fall of the Roman Empire* and *Star
Wars*, with Isaac Asimov's *Foundation* trilogy providing the direct link
between the two.[2] Asimov himself acknowledged as much: "I modeled

1. Quoted from John Seabrook, *Nobrow: The Culture of Marketing—The Marketing
of Culture* (New York: Knopf. 2000), 146, in a chapter entitled "The Empire Wins" (131–
160), first published as "Why Is the Force Still with Us?" *The New Yorker* (January 6,
1997), 40–53.
2. Isaac Asimov, *Foundation* (1951), *Foundation and Empire* (1952), *Second Foundation* (1953), published mostly in magazines from 1942 to 1949. For a plot outline see
Peter Bondanella, *The Eternal City: Roman Images in the Modern World* (Chapel Hill,
N.C.: University of North Carolina Press, 1987), 227–237 and 270 (notes). On Asimov
and on the tradition of galactic empires in science fiction see Oliver Morton, "In Pursuit
of Infinity," *The New Yorker* (May 17, 1999), 84–89. Asimov also published two books
on Roman history for juvenile or popular audiences: *The Roman Republic* (1966) and *The
Roman Empire* (1967). In the wake of the *Star Wars* trilogy he took up writing further
installments of the Foundation saga in the 1980s, with other science-fiction authors taking over from him after his death in 1992. The latest addition to date is David Brin,
Foundation's Triumph (1999). Further examples of Asimov's influence on modern science fiction appear among the stories collected in *Far Horizons: All New Tales from the
Greatest Worlds of Science Fiction*, ed. Robert Silverberg (New York: Avon Eos, 1999).
Silverberg is himself the author of stories about an alternative Roman empire that never
fell. For a Greek parallel to ancient Rome in galactic-empire fiction see Brian Herbert and
Kevin J. Anderson, *Dune: House Atreides* (1999), a sequel—or rather, "prequel"—to the

my 'Galactic Empire' . . . quite consciously on the Roman Empire," and: "When I first wrote the Foundation trilogy, I did indeed have Gibbon in mind." On *Star Wars* Asimov noted:

274

CLASSICAL

MYTH &

CULTURE

IN THE

CINEMA

> Galactic empires reached the cinema with this group of films, which here and there offered more than a whiff of the Foundation. (No, I don't mind. Imitation is the sincerest form of flattery, and I certainly imitated Edward Gibbon, so I can scarcely object if someone imitates me).[3]

Asimov's trilogy seems to have provided Lucas with the chief source of his transposition of the historical past into the mythical future of science fiction. From this perspective, the well-known motto of *Star Wars*—"A long time ago in a galaxy far, far away"—receives a specific connotation which goes beyond its general nature as a variation of the traditional opening phrase of fairy tales: "Once upon a time . . ." The "long time ago" in the *Star Wars* films is, from the statement's point of view, a past that to the spectators is still in the future, but we may also regard it as a reference to an era in our own long-ago past, that of Rome's empire.[4]

The imperial tyranny in *Star Wars* parallels imperial Rome beyond the general theme of an evil power and its decline as described factually by Gibbon and imaginatively by Asimov. Lucas's galactic empire has overthrown an earlier republic and, as in Roman history, the new monarchy has preserved the original republican governing body, the senate. Early in the trilogy's first film the usurping emperor dissolves the senate. Except for this, the film's senate parallels the history of the imperial Roman

---

Dune novels by Frank Herbert. The noble house of Atreides are descendants of Homer's Agamemnon.

3. The quotations are from Bondanella, *The Eternal City*, 229, 270 note 11, and 233. Mary Henderson, *Star Wars: The Magic of Myth* (New York: Bantam, 1997), 146, traces several mythical and historical parallels in the *Star Wars* trilogy but gives only the briefest reference to ancient Rome—and this one is to Julius Caesar rather than to the time of the empire. She does not mention Gibbon or Asimov. Morton, "In Pursuit of Infinity," 87, quotes Asimov's jingle: "you'll find that plotting is a breeze, / With a tiny bit of cribbin' from the works of Edward Gibbon and that Greek, Thucydides." Morton's observation that "Asimov had an Enlightenment love of reason above all things" (88) explains Asimov's affinity for Gibbon.

4. The ambitious scope of Lucas's mythmaking in the *Star Wars* saga with its multiple settings in time and space also parallels Tolkien's multigenerational myths of Middle Earth. In narrative terms the first three *Star Wars* films comprise the second of two trilogies (episodes IV–VI). *The Phantom Menace* is the initial installment of the first trilogy, whose other parts are scheduled to appear in 2002 and 2005. Lucas seems to have abandoned his original intention to continue the story with a third trilogy. On Lucas and myth see in general John Baxter, *Mythmaker: The Life and Work of George Lucas* (New York: Avon/Spike, 1999).

senate. Tacitus, the chief historian of early imperial Rome, emphasizes that after Augustus the Roman senate progressively lost its influence and prestige and most of its administrative functions to the increasing usurpation of power by successive emperors and that it rapidly declined into a claque of imperial flatterers. In particular, his stark statement about the beginning of Tiberius' rule provides a concise summary of this phenomenon: *At Romae ruere in servitium consules patres eques*—"Meanwhile at Rome consuls, senate, knights, precipitately became servile."[5] While the historical Roman senate continued to exist as an administrative figurehead, the imperial senate's dismissal in the film is the logical next step to be taken by any tyrant who need not preserve even a façade of legitimate government. So Governor Tarkin announces: "The imperial senate will no longer be of any concern to us. I have just received word that the emperor has dissolved the council permanently. The last remnants of the old republic have been swept away." The speaker's name echoes that of the Tarquins, the last dynasty of Roman kings, which had become synonymous with tyrannical monarchy and, according to the Romans' own perspective on their early history, had directly led to the abolishment of monarchy in the late sixth century B.C. From this perspective the situation in *Star Wars* is a reversal of Roman history.

The popular American view of the Roman Empire, especially in its reincarnation in the cinema, has almost invariably been that of a degenerate totalitarian society characterized by militarism, slavery, religious persecution, bloody games, sexual debauchery, and spiritual emptiness.[6] It is doomed to be overthrown, and Christianity provides the only path still open to Romans toward moral regeneration. (Much of this stereotypical view is historically inaccurate.) The American founding fathers had therefore modeled their own government on the Roman republic, not on the empire.[7]

The dichotomy of good republic and evil empire fits Lucas's futuristic society seamlessly. Obi-Wan Kenobi, the wise teacher and spiritual leader of the resistance to the empire, tells Luke Skywalker, the young hero-to-be: "The Jedi Knights were the guardians of peace and justice in the old republic, before the dark times, before the empire." Even the visual and

5. Tacitus, *Annals* 1.7.1; quoted from *Tacitus: The Annals of Imperial Rome*, tr. Michael Grant (rev. ed.; Harmondsworth: Penguin, 1977; rpt. 1996), 35.

6. Cf. my "The Roman Empire in American Cinema After 1945," *The Classical Journal*, 93 (1998), 167–196, with further references. For a general overview of Rome in cinema see Maria Wyke, *Projecting the Past: Ancient Rome, Cinema and History* (New York: Routledge, 1997), 1–33.

7. See, for instance, the recent detailed examination by Carl J. Richard, *The Founders and the Classics: Greece, Rome, and the American Enlightenment* (Cambridge: Harvard University Press, 1994).

276

CLASSICAL

MYTH &

CULTURE

IN THE

CINEMA

verbal references in *Star Wars* to the most evil of all modern empires, Nazi Germany, are consistent with the standard portrayal in American films made after World War II, in which Rome appeared as a totalitarian system modeled on Hitler's Germany.[8] From this point of view the historical continuity from the Roman Empire to the Holy Roman Empire of German Nation, the empire of 1871–1918, and on to the third empire in German history, Hitler's Third Reich, may be extended to the galactic empire in *Star Wars*. The films' references to imperial army units as both legions and storm troopers are anything but surprising.

In ancient Rome, an absolute monarchy replaced the free republic, what Romans called the *libera res publica*. The same occurs in Lucas's galactic world. His emperor, as did his historical precursors, uses a particularly powerful henchman to carry out his will. In Rome, this was the prefect of the Praetorians, the emperor's elite guard. Such men walked in the innermost circles of power and often were the most influential advisers to the emperor. Little was possible without their consent. Men like Sejanus under Tiberius and Tigellinus under Nero are generally depicted as two of the most villainous creatures in Roman history, not only because of their own ruthlessness but also because of their close association with rulers considered to have been quintessential tyrants. The archvillain of the *Star Wars* trilogy fulfills a similar function in the new imperial power structure. The figure of Darth Vader presents a striking parallel to imperial Roman henchmen. He is swift and energetic in carrying out his master's plans, and consequently the emperor has no need himself to become active. (Except for a brief appearance in a holographic image in the second film, he remains off-screen until the trilogy's climax.) Tacitus' description of Sejanus and his character traits, the best-known historical source for this prefect's rise to power and for his eventual fall, applies to Darth Vader as well: "Of audacious character and untiring physique, secretive about himself and ever ready to incriminate others, a blend of arrogance and servility."[9] These last two aspects of Sejanus' character are clearly present in Darth Vader. We may compare his supercilious and cruel treatment of those below himself in rank and his obsequiousness toward the emperor, which is expressed in faux-archaic English: "What is thy bidding, my master?" Tacitus also refers to Sejanus' *industria ac vigilantia*, his energy and vigilance (*Annals* 4.1.3).

8. Details and additional references in my "Roman Empire in American Cinema After 1945." For Nazi overtones in *Star Wars* see, for example, the final scene in the first film, which is modeled on *Triumph of the Will.* Cf. in general Dan Rubey, "*Star Wars*: Not So Far Away," *Jump Cut*, 18 (1978), 9–14, and Henderson, *Star Wars*, 144–147.

9. Tacitus, *Annals* 4.1.3; quoted from Grant, *Tacitus*, 157. For Tigellinus see Tacitus, *Histories* 1.72.

Nero.
Julius Caesar
Praetorian guards
-Storm troopers

Vader
– Antony
–Octavian
– Nero's henchmen

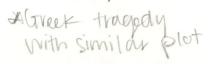
*Greek tragedy with similar plot

Even more than Sejanus, Nero's Tigellinus has been a regular example of a "bad guy" in Hollywood's Roman films. Cecil B. DeMille's *The Sign of the Cross* (1932), which was reissued in a "modernized production" in 1944, presented an explicit analogy between Nero and Hitler; DeMille's Tigellinus was an ice-cold sadist.[10] In Mervyn LeRoy's *Quo Vadis* (1951), the first of Hollywood's post–World War II Roman films, the same analogy recurs, and Tigellinus is more than willing to obey his master blindly. While it is unlikely that Lucas intentionally modeled Darth Vader on Sejanus or Tigellinus, the similarities between these historical and cinematic villains indicate that all of them are equally diabolical and have become stereotypes. Even Darth Vader's turning against his emperor at the trilogy's end, when he overthrows his master both literally and figuratively, has historical parallels in the Praetorians' palace coups in which one emperor is replaced by another. The examples best known to Americans are those of the emperors Tiberius and Caligula, popularized as characters in Robert Graves's novels *I, Claudius* (1934) and *Claudius the God* (1935) and, even more so, in the 1976 BBC television series based on them.[11] But there were several other cases in Roman history. In the first to third centuries A.D., Praetorians were involved in the overthrow of Domitian, Commodus, Caracalla, Gordian III, Gallienus, and Numerianus. Tacitus reports that the Praetorian prefect Macro, Sejanus' successor, caused the murder of Tiberius, the man who had raised him to power (*Annals* 6.50.5). While Darth Vader kills his emperor for the sake of a last-minute plot reversal in which he finally acknowledges and saves his son Luke and also redeems himself in the audience's eyes, men like Sejanus and Tigellinus appear to have had no positive qualities.

The parallels between Darth Vader and the Praetorian prefects, especially in connection with Tiberius, point to the reason why the "shuttle," which Luke Skywalker and Han Solo seize from the enemy in order to infiltrate the new Death Star in *Return of the Jedi*, is called Tiberium. Not surprisingly, Ian McDiarmid, the actor who plays the galactic emperor, resembles George Relph, the Tiberius of William Wyler's *Ben-Hur* (1959), the most popular and best-known of all Roman Empire films. Both actors appear somewhat emaciated and possess rather hawklike facial features.[12] As with Caligula in Henry Koster's *The Robe* (1953) and Delmer Daves's

---

10. On Nero in American and Italian films see Wyke, *Projecting the Past*, 110–146. See my "Roman Empire in American Cinema After 1945," 178–182, on Nero as Hitler in American cinema.

11. Bondanella, *The Eternal City*, 234, points to Praetorian parallels to Darth Vader but does not examine them in detail.

12. Bondanella, *The Eternal City*, 234, also adduces the modern incarnations of Tiberius in the BBC's *I, Claudius* and in Tinto Brass's film *Caligula* (1980).

278

CLASSICAL

MYTH &

CULTURE

IN THE

CINEMA

Demetrius and the Gladiators (1954) and with Tiberius in *Ben-Hur*, the galactic emperor must be approached via a flight of steps, if a considerably less grandiose one. Both Tiberius and Lucas's emperor sit on a throne or thronelike seat from which they can overlook their domain, in one case Rome, in the other the galaxy.

The galactic emperor's body guard, which appears on-screen in the third film, is dressed in garb of blood-red cloaks and tight-fitting helmets.[13] While it looks medieval, it has, however, a close Roman or quasi-Roman parallel. The guards' outfit resembles that worn by Fredric March as prefect of the city of Rome in *The Sign of the Cross*. The Jedi Knights themselves are a case in point for Lucas's mixture of ancient and medieval cultures. While popular imagination primarily associates knights and swords with the Middle Ages, Roman society also had a class of knights throughout its history. Despite obvious differences between Roman and medieval social and class structures, the Roman *equites* ("horsemen") are the historical precursors of the medieval knights; they ranked immediately below the aristocratic senatorial class and well above the rest of the population.[14] The feudal hierarchy of the Middle Ages is a direct result of the rigid vertical organization of ancient Roman society. (Medieval Florence, for example, believed, or at least claimed, that the city and its nobility were a Roman foundation later refounded by Charlemagne.) Such a hierarchy reappears virtually unchanged in Lucas's trilogy.[15] The name of the usurping emperor, the former senator Palpatine, is a case in point: it carries echoes of both medieval and imperial Roman history and culture.[16]

The dialogue of Hollywood's historical films also links Roman, medieval, and futuristic societies. In such films, those of low social status generally use a simple modern idiom. Lucas's Han Solo is the best example of a thinly disguised all-American of the mid–twentieth century, as his standard exclamation makes evident: "I have a bad feeling about this!" On the other hand, the aristocrats in historical epics are assigned elevated

13. A convenient illustration in Henderson, *Star Wars*, 146.

14. See, for example, Frances Gies, *The Knight in History* (New York: Harper and Row, 1984; rpt. 1987), 8 and 209 note 2 (references) on the origin and rise of medieval knighthood. Maurice Keen, *Chivalry* (New Haven: Yale University Press, 1984), discusses the chivalry of the Romans in medieval context.

15. Cf. Rubey, "*Star Wars*," 10–11.

16. Medieval: "paladin"; Roman: *Palatinus* ("imperial"; as noun: "chamberlain"). Cf. also the name of presidential candidate Charles Palantine, who becomes the target of a political assassination attempt in Martin Scorsese's *Taxi Driver*, a film released the year before the first *Star Wars* film. Palpatine's guard in *The Phantom Menace* wears ancient-looking helmets with two crests, which seem to be patterned after similar double- or triple-crested helmets on view in some European films set in Greek or Roman antiquity. An example from a later film is Achilles' helmet in Michael Cacoyannis's *Iphigenia* (1977).

diction, which is often rather flowery and sometimes bathetic. The most telling verbal connection between *Star Wars* and the past is a linguistic standby of historical American films set in antiquity or the Middle Ages. Deferential addresses to Darth Vader such as "My Lord" or "Lord Vader" directly echo the apostrophes both to medieval kings or heroes and the standard way in which Roman emperors are addressed in these films. We may compare the tautologous phrase "My Lord Cid" in Anthony Mann's *El Cid* (1961) and "My Lord Caesar" in *The Fall of the Roman Empire*. All this is another bridge from the past to the future.

These parallels between the Roman Empire and its usual portrayal in American cinema on the one hand and the science-fiction empire in *Star Wars* on the other can hardly be overlooked. The fundamental historical similarity between Rome and America is as quintessentially American as it is Roman, that of expansionism and the concept of the frontier. Both Rome and the United States rose from humble beginnings to world power, and both periods of history, ancient and modern, are characterized by military campaigns and territorial annexation as far as geography would permit. The limits of the Roman Empire were set by the Atlantic Ocean in the northwest and west, by the impenetrable forests and swamps of central Europe in the north and northeast, and by the deserts of Arabia and Africa in the east and south. The American empire came to stretch from sea to shining sea, its military presence extending from the halls of Montezuma to the shores of Tripoli and eventually throughout most parts of the globe. And it is on the borders of both empires that the battles for the continuing presence of Romans and Americans in territories originally belonging to other peoples were regularly carried out. The maintenance of imperial power is, almost by definition, a border problem. Just as Indians raided American border settlements or wagon trains, both in history and in the cinema, so Germanic and other barbaric tribes invaded the Roman frontiers, again both historically and on film. In modern American culture, space is the final frontier, and this concept applies to the *Star Wars* films in equal measure. The connections between the science-fiction film and the western are obvious.[17]

17. American science fiction films are, by and large, westerns transplanted to outer space, or to *Outland*, as Peter Hyams's 1981 sci-fi remake of Fred Zinnemann's *High Noon* (1952) calls it. Lucas himself has acknowledged as much: "I became very fascinated with how we could replace this mythology that drifted out of fashion—the Western. One of the prime issues of mythology was that it was always on the frontier, over the hill. It was always in this mysterious place where anything could happen"; quoted from Henderson, *Star Wars*, 136. And: "That sort of stuff . . . is always big adventure out there somewhere. It came all the way down through the western"; quoted from Rubey, "*Star Wars*," 10. See further the quotation from Lucas at Henderson, 126. For an overview of archetypal

280

CLASSICAL

MYTH &

CULTURE

IN THE

CINEMA

The American western has regularly carried overtones of medieval culture.[18] Arthurian romance has influenced American popular fiction since the nineteenth century, in particular through Tennyson's *Idylls of the King* and the historical novels of Sir Walter Scott, the spiritual father of James Fenimore Cooper, Owen Wister, Zane Grey, Max Brand, and Louis L'Amour, to name only the most prominent.[19] Just like westerns, the *Star Wars* films are modern morality plays, although less sophisticated than their cinematic precursors. Important models for both are medieval mystery plays and chivalric epics. These in turn go back to Greek and Roman epic and drama based on myth.

2. *Star Wars* and *The Fall of the Roman Empire*

The Fall of the Roman Empire is a film with specific parallels to Lucas's futuristic cinema. Although Lucas has never acknowledged any direct or conscious influence, he was probably familiar with Anthony Mann's film.[20]

Generally, and since the earliest epic stories (*Gilgamesh, Iliad*), the fate of society hinges on the heroism of one man. Often he has learnt from a teacher or father figure that physical prowess must be based on an awareness of justice and responsibility. The hero's fatherly teacher in *Star Wars* is Obi-Wan Kenobi. He is first the living and then the spiritual embodiment of the Force, a quasi-religious philosophy of the distinction between

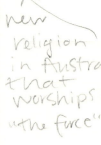

new religion
in Australia
that
worships
"the force"

connections between ancient myth and the western, with additional reference to science-fiction cinema, see my "Classical Mythology and the Western Film," *Comparative Literature Studies*, 22 (1985), 514–540, especially 535.

18. Details are in my "Mythologische Motive im amerikanischen Western-Film," in *Mittelalter-Rezeption*, vol. 3: *Mittelalter, Massenmedien, Neue Mythen*, ed. Jürgen Kühnel et al. (Göppingen: Kümmerle, 1988), 563–578. See also the examples in Frank McConnell, *Storytelling and Mythmaking: Images from Film and Literature* (New York: Oxford University Press, 1979; rpt. 1980), especially 83–137. For the reverse—western overtones in a medieval film—see my "Mythical and Cinematic Traditions in Anthony Mann's *El Cid*," *Mosaic*, 26 no. 3 (1993), 89–111, at 105–107.

19. See John Fraser, *America and the Patterns of Chivalry* (Cambridge: Cambridge University Press, 1982), especially 3–14, and Alan Lupack and Barbara Tepa Lupack, *King Arthur in America* (Rochester, N.Y.: Brewer, 1999).

20. Lucas's first feature-length film, THX 1138 (1971), an expansion of an earlier short film made while he was a student in film school, deals with rebellion against an oppressive system and so reflects the theme of Mann's film and foreshadows his own *Star Wars* trilogy. I give detailed information about the plot of *The Fall of the Roman Empire*, its use of historical sources, and Mann's approach to history in "Cinema and the Fall of Rome," *Transactions of the American Philological Association*, 125 (1995), 135–154.

right and wrong and of the meaning of life in the universe. That the Force is a secular substitute for traditional religion becomes evident, none too subtly, in the fact that it can move physical objects by sheer exercise of will resulting from faith, just as belief in Christianity is said to be able to move mountains.[21] As master teacher of the Force, Obi-Wan naturally functions as repository of wisdom, experience, and traditional values, those qualities that had made the galaxy great before renegade Jedi Knights were corrupted by Evil and went over to "the dark side of the Force." Obi-Wan personifies man's highest aspirations and represents everything good and noble in mankind.

Parallel to this kind of figure in Roman history is the philosopher-emperor Marcus Aurelius, a major character in *The Fall of the Roman Empire*. The filmmakers' conception of Marcus Aurelius is closely based on his reputation as an ideal or perfect man, whom Matthew Arnold, for instance, called "perhaps the most beautiful figure in history" and "one of the best of men."[22] Several of Marcus Aurelius' words and speeches are, in their philosophical thrust, similar to Obi-Wan's teachings about the Force, while others fit Obi's character so well that no viewer would be surprised if they came from his mouth. Marcus' words in the film's opening scene, addressed to his friend and counselor, the fictitious Greek philosopher Timonides, point to his premonition both of the impending fall of the Roman world, no longer ruled by someone good like him, and of his own death, expressed in the image of darkness: "When I was a child, Timonides, I had a secret fear that night would come and would never end, that we would live out our lives in total darkness. It was a small fear then." Later he adds: "I have tried to convince myself that my fears for the empire are unreasonable. But my fears *are* reasonable." One of his main principles of government in the multinational and, to use a current term, multicultural Roman Empire—a world paralleled in the *Star Wars* films by the various races of humans and other creatures—is to promote mutual acceptance: "We must try to understand other people more." What he says to his daughter Lucilla presents, in a nutshell, what Obi-Wan teaches Luke Skywalker: "Learn to pity, learn to have compassion. The future will make great demands on you."

21. Matthew 17:20 and 21:21, Mark 11:23, 1 Corinthians 13:2.

22. Matthew Arnold, "Marcus Aurelius," *The Victoria Magazine*, 2 (1863), 1–19; quoted from *The Complete Prose Works of Matthew Arnold*, vol. 3: *Lectures and Essays in Criticism*, ed. R. H. Super (Ann Arbor: University of Michigan Press, 1962), 133–157; quotations at 140. On ancient and modern views of Marcus Aurelius and his age see my "Cinema and the Fall of Rome," 139–140 note 17. The most recent tribute to Marcus is by Nobel Prize-winning author and poet Joseph Brodsky, "Homage to Marcus Aurelius," in *On Grief and Reason: Essays* (1995; rpt. New York: Noonday, 1997), 267–298.

282

CLASSICAL

MYTH &

CULTURE

IN THE

CINEMA

Shortly before his death Marcus holds a memorable interior dialogue with himself, in which he wrestles with his painful sickness and imminent death. He summarizes his life's philosophy, his responsibility for the empire, and the sacrifice of his comfort for the sake of the world he governs in simple but effective terms: "I do not seek pleasures, or friendship, or love; I speak only of Rome, and when I say Rome, I mean the world, the future. For my part, I am prepared to live in pain." The same could be said about Obi-Wan. In view of the latter's self-sacrifice at the hands of Darth Vader, Marcus' belief—"Death is in the order of things" although it remains a "mystery of mysteries"—equally applies to Obi. When Marcus resigns himself to death ("come for me when you will"), we may remember that Obi-Wan voluntarily accepts death by putting down his light saber during his duel with Vader. And some of Marcus' last words could summarize Obi's lessons to Luke about the Force: "there is a great truth we have not yet divined." When he sacrifices himself to the cause of the Good in the first film, Obi wears a hooded cloak, a garment in which he is seen for much of the film. In Mann's opening scene, Marcus Aurelius wears a similar-looking cloak and also appears with his head veiled—in Roman terms, *capite velato*—at a sacrifice. Both Marcus' and Obi's garments look medieval, like the habit of a monk, but, more important, these cloaks as well as the beards the men wear in both films are meant to signify that they are simple but upstanding figures of moral authority. Each embodies the epitome of his civilization. Tellingly, both characters are played by the same actor. The casting of Alec Guinness as Obi-Wan creates a strong link to his portrayal of Marcus Aurelius, especially for anyone who in 1977 remembered seeing the earlier film.

The enduring philosophical legacy of the historical Marcus Aurelius resides in his famous *Meditations*, as they are usually called—rather loosely, for their original Greek title simply means "To Himself" and indicates that Marcus' observations, instructions, and aphorisms were originally intended only for his own eyes and mind. Marcus' interior dialogue, mentioned earlier, is a moving adaptation of the *Meditations* to a visual medium.[23] The parallels between Mann's Marcus Aurelius and Lucas's Obi-Wan make the *Meditations* the dramatic equivalent of the Force in that both are philosophical teachings rooted in practical applicability; they direct us toward spiritual enlightenment and the responsible exercise of power. As we have seen, the Force is a kind of secular religion; in antiquity, philosophy also provided a substitute for traditional religious

23. For examples of dialogue in individual meditations by the historical Marcus see *Meditations* 5.6, 8.40, and 12.36, the latter on death and pain. Death is a regular topic throughout, often in connection with pain; see especially *Meditations* 6.28 and 49, 7.21 and 32–33, 8.47, 9.3, 10.36, and 11.3.

beliefs. The connections from Marcus Aurelius to Obi-Wan become even more obvious if we remember that Stoicism was a strong influence on early Christianity, which in turn has provided most of the population of the United States with spiritual guidance since 1776.[24] With the rising popularity of Eastern philosophies and their impact on both popular culture and the counterculture of the 1960s and later, Christianity as redemptive force could be replaced by a new system of morals such as Lucas's Force, which is nondenominational and undogmatic in nature, fitting everybody.

This comparison of Marcus' Stoicism with Lucas's Force is not meant to imply that all the naive talk about the Force in the *Star Wars* films is as profound or moving as are the *Meditations*. But the thematic importance of the *Meditations* in Mann's film points the way to Lucas's use of an analogous, if simpler, presentation of the spiritual. Marcus' soliloquy before his death, when we hear both himself and his disembodied voice in dialogue, is comparable to the voice of Obi-Wan as Luke hears it on several occasions after Obi-Wan's death. But the parallel becomes clearest in the following words spoken by Lucilla when she deposits her father's writings in a Roman temple: "I ask that you guard these, the *Meditations* of my father Marcus Aurelius. Whatever else happens in the days to come, let not these be destroyed, for this is Rome." If we make a few changes, we could imagine Luke Skywalker describing the lasting validity of the Force: "I ask that you guard these, the teachings of my spiritual father Obi-Wan Kenobi. Whatever else happens in the days to come, let not these be destroyed, for this is the future."

The characters who learn most from their teachers are the principal heroes of their respective films, Livius and Luke. Livius is the chief commander of the Roman legions stationed on the Danube frontier, whom Marcus Aurelius has chosen for his successor. As is Luke to Obi-Wan, Livius is a surrogate son to Marcus. Both Livius and Luke have been adopted into positions of increasing responsibility and power; both are being groomed for leadership, and their journey toward heroism and victory over their enemies is necessary for the survival of their worlds. In the *Star Wars* films, this survival is eventually accomplished with the fall of the evil empire. In Mann's film historical fact prevents such a victory

---

24. The historical Marcus' disquisition on the gods at *Meditations* 6.44 are a case in point for the spiritual affinity between Stoicism and Christianity: "the gods" could easily be replaced with "God," and so on. The widely read translation of the *Meditations* by clergyman Maxwell Staniforth has an introduction that closes with a section entitled "Stoicism and Christianity": *Marcus Aurelius: Meditations* (Harmondsworth: Penguin, 1964; rpt. 1985), 23–27. This translation was published in the same year *The Fall of the Roman Empire* was released.

284

CLASSICAL

MYTH &

CULTURE

IN THE

CINEMA

More modern comparison: gladiator

look 70s

even in a partly fictitious plot and requires Livius, himself an invented character, to reject offers of the throne. But Livius is, as Timonides says, "the real heir of Marcus Aurelius," just as Luke is Obi-Wan Kenobi's. And both Livius and Luke undergo the processes of learning and the rites of passage which in traditional tales are obligatory for apprentice heroes before they can become full-fledged hero figures themselves.

The side of evil is represented in *The Fall of the Roman Empire* by Commodus, Marcus' successor and believed to be his son (as he was, historically), and in the *Star Wars* films by Darth Vader. The protagonists and antagonists in both film worlds are either related by blood or at least close friends; the family is the social unit through which the fate of the world is determined in either case.[25] The parallels between the heroines, Princess Lucilla, Marcus' daughter, and Princess Leia, Luke's sister, further reinforce this aspect of the films' plots. Both of them play prominent parts in the rebellions against an evil empire. (During most of her on-screen appearances Leia wears a white dress, which almost gives her the appearance of a Vestal Virgin.) The close family ties between the good and the bad reinforce the similarities in the films' portrayals of evil. The theme of true parentage is also crucial to both plots. In *Star Wars*, the hero learns that the villain is his father, a former Jedi knight corrupted by the dark side; in *The Fall of the Roman Empire*, the revelation that the true father of Commodus is not Marcus Aurelius but only a gladiator explains Commodus' innate instability and evil.

A parallel to the dark side of the Force are Lucilla's words to the power-mad and irresponsible Commodus, now emperor: "You've had only one idea, to smash and destroy everything Father did." These words could equally well describe the evil emperor's and Darth Vader's intentions in regard to what Obi-Wan and the Jedi Knights had built. Commodus represents the dark side of Marcus and Livius; appropriately, Livius kills him in the film's climactic duel.[26] Anthony Mann points to the extent of tyranny in the empire as ruled by Commodus most clearly in a scene set in the Roman senate. One of Commodus' henchmen is as unscrupulous about the extermination of rebels against Commodus' tyranny as Darth Vader is about the Rebel Alliance against *his* emperor: "crucify their leaders, sell

25. While dramatic stories have presented and worked through large and complex issues in family units since the beginning of Western civilization, this has been the standard strategy in historical fiction and film to make a distant past more easily accessible. See the discussion by Robert Rosenstone, *Visions of the Past: The Challenge of Film to Our Idea of History* (Cambridge: Harvard University Press, 1995), 54–61.

26. In a stylistic parallel between this combat and the final duel in *The Phantom Menace*, the evil Darth Maul wields his light saber the way Livius and Commodus handle their spears at certain moments in their fight to the death.

the rest as slaves. Teach them once and for all what it is to make war on Rome." Dramatic pause; then: "*That* is the Roman way."

In the same scene Timonides describes the traditional scorched-earth tactics in the Romans' treatment of other nations, which he and Livius want to overcome. His speech is not only a concise summary of the standard American view of Rome as an evil empire, with which cinema audiences have by this time become thoroughly familiar, but also a close parallel to the galactic empire of *Star Wars*:

> We have burned their villages, we have crucified their leaders, we have enslaved their young; the fires go out, the dead are buried, the slaves die, slowly, but the hatred that we leave behind us never dies. Hatred means wars. Wars mean tribute torn from our provinces, taxes, hunger, disease. How costly that is, how wasteful! And yet the answer is simple. We must have no war.

Timonides then calls for what would bring about the kind of society that Lucas shows us at the end of his trilogy:

> Let us share the greatest gift of all, let us give these men the right of Roman freedom, and they will spread the word that Rome has accepted them as equals. Then we will have our human frontiers: the Roman peace that Marcus Aurelius promised.

It is, however, too late for this to come about, and Timonides' thoroughly American vision of democratic equality and liberty must wait for a different future, one unconstrained by historical fact and one that can become real only in a modern filmmaker's wishful thinking. Clearly, as the *pax Romana* came to be lost in the second century A.D. and no lasting *pax Americana* was to be achieved in the twentieth century, universal peace—a *pax galactica*, as it might be called—can come about only in the imagination, by a creative artist's say-so. The people's misguided celebration at the end of *The Fall of the Roman Empire* takes on added poignancy if we compare it to that at the end of *Return of the Jedi*. The latter is a genuine expression of joy over freedom regained, while the former is an instance of the proverbial dance on the volcano, the people oblivious to their impending ruin.

In *The Fall of the Roman Empire* we see the change of a good empire into a bad and doomed one; the *Star Wars* trilogy presents the overthrow of an evil empire and the restoration of liberty. Thus the films contrast in the ultimate resolution of their plots. But in both cases we are shown what benevolent and civilized forms of society and centralized government can be like. Since antiquity, the time of Marcus Aurelius has been considered a golden age in the history of mankind, a return, as far as such was at all possible, to the principles of the free republic that had made Rome great.

The years 96–180 A.D., the period of a series of good emperors culminating in the rule of Marcus Aurelius, received their highest praise during the Enlightenment in the famous verdict of Edward Gibbon:

286

CLASSICAL

MYTH &

CULTURE

IN THE

CINEMA

> In the second century of the Christian era, the Empire of Rome comprehended the fairest part of the earth, and the most civilised portion of mankind. . . . If a man were called to fix the period in the history of the world, during which the condition of the human race was most happy and prosperous, he would, without hesitation, name that which elapsed from the death of Domitian to the accession of Commodus.[27]

Anthony Mann in his film laments the passing of such a society, as Gibbon had done before him; George Lucas resurrects a comparable one before our eyes. The old republic and the new society in *Star Wars* here come to correspond to the Roman Empire under Marcus, and the galactic empire to that under Commodus.

That both the Roman and the galactic empires are indeed comparable appears with particular clarity in the prologue of the novel version of *Star Wars*, which accompanied the first film's release and became a national bestseller, read by many who had seen the film. It provides a description of what the galactic world used to be like. With a few simple changes in the wording, we could hear a summary of Roman history:

> The Old Republic was the Republic of legend, greater than distance or time. . . . Once under the wise rule of the Senate and the protection of the Jedi Knights, the Republic throve and grew. But as often happens when wealth and power pass beyond the admirable and attain the awesome, then appear those evil ones who have greed to match.

The prologue further describes the fall of the galactic republic and the rise of tyranny in Roman terms: there were "restless, power-hungry individuals within the government," and: "Imperial governors and bureaucrats instituted a reign of terror. . . . Many used the imperial forces and the name of the increasingly isolated Emperor to further their own personal ambitions."[28] The novel version of the third film recapitulates this theme:

27. Edward Gibbon, *The History of the Decline and Fall of the Roman Empire*, 6 vols. (New York: Knopf, 1993); quotations from vol. 1, 3 and 90. Gibbon's work was first published 1776–1788.

28. George Lucas, *Star Wars: From the Adventures of Luke Skywalker* (1976), quoted from *The Star Wars Trilogy* (1987; rpt. New York: Del Rey, 1993), 3. This is a collection of the novel versions that accompanied the films upon their first release. The other novels are Donald F. Glut, *The Empire Strikes Back* (1980), and James Kahn, *Return of the Jedi* (1983). Lucas's novel was ghostwritten by Alan Dean Foster; see Baxter, *Mythmaker*, 225–226.

Back in the days when he [the emperor] was merely senator Palpatine, the galaxy had been a Republic of stars, cared for and protected by the Jedi Knighthood that had watched over it for centuries. But inevitably it had grown too large—too massive a bureaucracy had been required, over too many years, in order to maintain the Republic. Corruption had set in.[29]

But we also find two specific parallels to Mann's film in the prologue to the first *Star Wars* novel, when we read on its opening page: "Like the greatest of trees, able to withstand any external attack, the Republic rotted from within, though the danger was not visible from outside." This echoes the narrator's last words in *The Fall of the Roman Empire*, provided by historian Will Durant, which summarize Gibbon's perspective on Roman history: "A great civilization is not conquered from without until it has destroyed itself from within."[30] The metaphor of the tree for the empire also appears in Mann's film. In its first grand set piece, Marcus Aurelius says to the assembled leaders of the empire: "like a mighty tree with green leaves and black roots, you are the unity which is Rome."

Another parallel between *The Fall of the Roman Empire* and the *Star Wars* films is not of a thematic or narrative nature, as are those discussed so far, but rather concerns the most popular aspect of historical epics and science-fiction films: their action sequences. In Mann's film a quarrel between Livius and Commodus turns into an unexpected chariot race—unexpected because viewers are surprised to see a race where none has ever taken place before, along a narrow mountain road and on into a forest. The placement of this race comparatively early in the film and the fact that it is a duel in natural surroundings rather than a large-scale race in the Circus Maximus or similar arena are conscious signals to the audience that with his film Mann intends something different from the standard Roman epic on the order of the famous *Ben-Hur*.[31] Both the loca-

---

29. *Star Wars Trilogy*, 382. A little later the description of the emperor's usurpation of power "through subterfuge, bribery and terror" parallels the perspective of Tacitus on the rise of the first Roman emperors, and the galactic emperor's megalomania—"he *was* the Empire; he *was* the Universe" (383)—reminds us of the madness of Caligula, Nero, or Commodus. The same novel contains a detail which is not in the film but which reinforces the analogy between Darth Vader and Roman Praetorians, when an ambitious Vader intends to overthrow the emperor and rule in his place (372–373).

30. Will Durant, *Caesar and Christ: A History of Roman Civilization and of Christianity from Their Beginnings to A.D. 325* (1944; rpt. New York: MFJ Books, 1992), 665, minimally altered in the film.

31. On this see my "Cinema and the Fall of Rome," 142–143. The two races and their stunts were staged by the same second-unit director. On the creation and filming of the race in *The Fall of the Roman Empire* see Yakima Canutt and Oliver Drake, *Stunt Man: The Autobiography of Yakima Canutt* (1979; rpt. Norman: University of Oklahoma Press, 1997), 202–205.

288

CLASSICAL

MYTH &

CULTURE

IN THE

CINEMA

tion and the hair-raising stunts of the race are likely to have left audiences gasping.

To anyone remembering *The Fall of the Roman Empire*, the speeder chase in *Return of the Jedi* will look very familiar indeed. The flight of some storm troopers and their pursuit by Luke and Princess Leia on "speeder bikes," a kind of futuristic motor scooter, also takes place in a forest. Advanced computer technology makes it possible for the speed of this chase to be several times faster than that attainable by horse-drawn chariots in the 1960s and to present some spectacular crashes exciting to audiences who have come to depend on ever more advanced special effects for their thrills. But the fundamental idea behind the newer sequence—that is, to present a thrilling chase in an impossible-looking locale—is identical to that in Mann's film. Even so, there is a telling difference. With the help of his second-unit director and two first-rate stuntmen, Mann shows us a real race. Lucas and his director, on the other hand, have to rely entirely on technical gadgetry and can only show us something that was put together in the lab or, rather, on the computer. We know it to be fake as we are watching it. Old-fashioned as it will appear to audiences accustomed to computerized special effects, Mann's chariot race, with its carefully prepared tricks and stunts, and the traditional expertise of an action director and his team contrast with the soulless machinery of modern filmmaking. Not least for this reason, Mann's is the more exciting action sequence of the two.

Lucas's most recent installment of his saga also contains a high-speed race in a desert "arena," as it were. Numerous critics and reviewers noted that the pod race in this film "has a gutsy, Roman-circus buzz to it" and specifically refer to the race in the 1959 *Ben-Hur*.[32] But the widespread disappointment that greeted *The Phantom Menace* upon its release is revealing. Effective storytelling depends on how much the teller cares for the characters in his tale. Lucas, however, concentrates almost exclusively on his technological expertise, and the result is that the spectacular digital effects dwarf his protagonists: "Lucas is so fatally gulled by the latest tricks of his trade that he abandons the actors to their fate."[33] As is not

32. The quotation is from Anthony Lane, "Star Bores," *The New Yorker* (May 24, 1999), 80–84, at 82. The "bad guy" in the pod race fights unfairly and bumps other pods, just as the evil Roman Messala does to other chariots in *Ben-Hur*. As happens to chariots in *Ben-Hur*, two pods get entangled, and one of them crashes. Before the race starts, Jabba the Hutt enters with a pomp similar to that of Pontius Pilate in *Ben-Hur* (or Nero's in the arena sequence of *Quo Vadis*).

33. Lane, "Star Bores," 82. In his capsule review of the film, which appeared in subsequent issues of *The New Yorker*, Lane is even more blunt: "With this film, Lucas demonstrates two facts: one, that he has kept abreast of the recent leaps in special effects, and

the case in the earlier films, the numerous overtones of Roman history and of Hollywood's Roman cinema in *The Phantom Menace* do not enhance its narrative quality or cohesion.[34] We may contrast Anthony Mann's approach to his film, which for its time was a comparably large-scale undertaking, with immense logistical problems regarding its set constructions and its huge battle sequences:

> one must be careful not to let the concept of the spectacular run away with you. . . . the spectacle [in my film] is done entirely differently to what you would expect. . . . the characters bring you into the spectacle rather than it being imposed on you without dramatic reason.[35]

In spite of its often strange appearance, Lucas's galactic world is not all that different from an actual and specific era of history—or, more accurately, from the presentation of that history in the cinema. In the popular media of today, both the recreations of the past and the imaginative creations of the future necessarily reveal the moment of their making. But as practically all science-fiction films show, visions of the future quickly look dated. This is true even for Lucas's trilogy, which less than fourteen years after the release of its last installment was technically enhanced for a special edition. By contrast, and despite the liberties it takes with historical fact for the sake of a coherent plot, Mann's Roman world looks as good and convincing today as it did over thirty-five years ago.

---

two, that he hasn't a clue what to do with all the nondigital figures, otherwise known as 'people'." The logical next step is that the two remaining films will be made completely on the computer; Lucas has already said that he intends to do so. As one critic has pointed out about the earliest film in the series: "*Star Wars* helped make the dawning digital age seem fun. But it also helped make fun merely digital." The quotation is from Louis Menand, "Billion-Dollar Baby," *The New York Review of Books* (June 24, 1999), 8–11, at 11.

34. The most obvious Roman aspects in *The Phantom Menace*, besides those noted already, are the following: Baroque architecture and statuary and immense barrel-vaulted halls with columns and polychrome marble, reminiscent of the palace architecture in *The Fall of the Roman Empire*; a huge statue of a man in a toga (the *togatus* was a popular type of Roman statuary); the triumphal scene, recalling the triumph sequences in *Quo Vadis* and *Ben-Hur*; trumpeters blowing fanfares as they do in *Quo Vadis* and other Roman films; the square formations in the land battle at the end, patterned after those of the Roman army in Stanley Kubrick's *Spartacus* (1960); the rolling balls that explode on impact, a parallel to the rolling fire logs with which the slave army in *Spartacus* beats back the Roman advance; enslavement versus freedom, the same theme as in *Spartacus*. The peace scene at the conclusion imitates the final scene of *Demetrius and the Gladiators*. Chancellor Valorum bears a fake Latin name, and much of the music score echoes Carl Orff's popular *Carmina Burana* (1937).

35. Anthony Mann, "Empire Demolition," in *Hollywood Directors 1941–1976*, ed. Richard Koszarski (New York: Oxford University Press, 1977), 332–338; quotations at 332 and 335. Mann's article was originally published in *Films and Filming* (March 1964).

290

CLASSICAL

MYTH &

CULTURE

IN THE

CINEMA

This is because a highly accomplished vision of the past such as his better preserves its fascination. It becomes even more appealing when we realize that it also provided a thematic parallel to, perhaps even a model for, a popular imperial saga set in the future. The historical Marcus Aurelius as much as predicted all this, even if he was referring only to historical fact and not to works of the imagination, when he observed: "Look back over the past, with its changing empires that rose and fell, and you can foresee the future too. Its pattern will be the same."[36]

36. *Meditations* 7.49, quoted from Staniforth, *Marcus Aurelius: Meditations*, 113. Cf. Mann, "Empire Demolition," 332, on past and future.

XIV

Teaching Classical Myth and Confronting Contemporary Myths

Peter W. Rose

The most striking development since the first appearance of this essay has been the dramatic escalation and general success of the right-wing assault on education and culture. Stanley Aronowitz and Henry Giroux, assessing the Reagan-Bush era, note the following developments:

> During these years, the meaning and purpose of schooling at all levels of education were refashioned around the principles of the marketplace and the logic of rampant individualism. Ideologically, this meant abstracting schools from the language of democracy and equity while simultaneously organizing educational reform around the discourse of choice, reprivatization, and individual competition.[1]

The Republican control of Congress, combined with President Clinton's apparent determination to steal Republican issues, has meant that the Clinton era has seen a vast escalation of rhetoric about improving education, but only token gestures have actually been enacted. Meanwhile the rhetoric of "choice in education" by means of school vouchers has already turned into reality.[2] William Bennett is still preaching a simplistic "moral literacy."[3] A host of right-wing culture warriors, usually

---

1. Stanley Aronowitz and Henry A. Giroux, *Education Still under Siege*, 2nd ed. (Westport, Conn.: Bergin and Garvey, 1993), 1. My thanks to Steven A. Nimis for comments and suggestions on the first version of this essay; also thanks to many perceptive students who have helped enlighten me over the years.

2. "Few Clear Lessons From Nation's First School-Choice Program," *The New York Times* (March 27, 1999), A10.

3. See *The Book of Virtues: A Treasury of Great Moral Stories*, ed. William J. Bennett (New York: Simon and Schuster, 1993).

292

CLASSICAL

MYTH &

CULTURE

IN THE

CINEMA

funded by right-wing think tanks, are hard at work discrediting any intellectuals in the public sphere who have dared to proclaim themselves progressive or who have even been admired by progressives. Nobel Prize–winner Rigoberta Menchú, earlier targeted by Dinesh D'Souza, is now the subject of a book-length assault.[4] The antifeminist backlash, well analyzed by Susan Faludi in 1991, has succeeded in muting, if not totally silencing, public objections to the most blatantly sexist advertising.[5] Verbal and physical violence against gays, including murder, has escalated grimly.

In the field of classics we have Mary Lefkowitz triumphantly "refuting" Afrocentrism to rescue Socrates and Cleopatra from any taint of Africa.[6] Victor Davis Hanson and John Heath have scolded classicists, myself included, for indulging in theory by hurling bizarre rhetorical questions that seem to imply the utter absurdity of classicists presuming to bite the hand of capitalism that feeds them.[7]

In the context of this alleged demise of classical education, making a case for the use of popular film in teaching classical culture or literature runs the inevitable risk of handing ammunition to the enemy. Without positioning myself like some Solon in the middle, I should also note that there is a less strident but perhaps more distressing attack from the left: Walter Benjamin, we are told, was against film; and the name of one of the founding fathers of cultural studies, Stuart Hall, in my view widely and justly re-

---

4. David Stoll, *Rigoberta Menchú and the Story of All Poor Guatemalans* (Boulder, Colo.: Westview, 1999). Cf. Dinesh D'Souza, *Illiberal Education: The Politics of Race and Sex on Campus* (1991; rpt. New York: Vintage, 1992), chapter 3 ("Travels with Rigoberta: Multiculturalism at Stanford"). Stoll's preface makes clear his real agenda: "dissecting the legacy of guerrilla warfare. . . . It continues to be romanticized, as illustrated by the aura surrounding Che Guevara, and it has hardly disappeared, as demonstrated by news reports from Colombia, Peru, and Mexico" (x). There are many "truths" to be revealed. Stoll is clearly not interested in the truth of the United States' heavy complicity in the chain of horrors inflicted on the "poor people of Guatemala," beginning with the CIA's coup d'état in 1954. For a thoughtful assessment of Stoll's book and issues of truth in Guatemala see Peter Canby, "The Truth About Rigoberta Menchú," *The New York Review of Books* (April 8, 1999), 28–33, and the exchange between Stoll and Canby, *The New York Review of Books* (October 21, 1999), 72–73.

5. Susan Faludi, *Backlash: The Undeclared War against American Women* (New York: Crown Books, 1991).

6. Mary Lefkowitz, *Not Out of Africa: How Afrocentrism Became an Excuse to Teach Myth as History* (New York: Basic Books, 1996). Contrast the review by Martin Bernal, *Bryn Mawr Classical Review*, 96.4.5 (1996), published electronically.

7. Victor Davis Hanson and John Heath, *Who Killed Homer? The Demise of Classical Education and the Recovery of Greek Wisdom* (New York: Free Press, 1998). See Peter Green, "Homer Lives!" *The New York Review of Books* (March 18, 1999), 45–48, and the "Forum" on *Who Killed Homer?* in *Arion*, 3rd ser., 6 no. 3 (1999), 84–195, and 7 no. 2 (1999), 172–184.

vered on the left, is likewise invoked against the subtle elitism involved in using popular culture only to demonstrate its inferiority.[8]

In classics, apart from heated discussions of the various options available for teaching beginning and intermediate language courses, pedagogy is rarely discussed.[9] The explicit use of popular culture, while not unheard of, is equally rare. Indeed, educational theorist Henry Giroux points to this parallel between pedagogy and popular culture:

> Pedagogy is often theorized as what is left after curriculum content is determined. It is what follows the selection of ideologically correct content. . . . Popular culture is still largely defined in the dominant discourse as the

8. So Maria Wyke, "Classics and Contempt: Redeeming Cinema for the Classical Tradition," *Arion*, 3rd ser., 6 no. 1 (1998), 124–136 (review essay, *Classics and Cinema*), at 124 and 127. Wyke seriously misreads Benjamin, who argues that "theses about the developmental tendencies of art under present conditions of production . . . brush aside a number of outmoded concepts, such as creativity and genius, eternal value and mystery— concepts whose uncontrolled (and at present almost uncontrollable) application would lead to a processing of data in the Fascist sense. The concepts which are introduced into the theory of art in what follows . . . are completely useless for the purposes of Fascism. They are, on the other hand, useful for the formulation of revolutionary demands in the politics of art." The quotation is from "The Work of Art in the Age of Mechanical Reproduction," in *Illuminations*, ed. Hannah Arendt, tr. Harry Zohn (1968; new ed. New York: Schocken, 1969; rpt. 1986), 217–251; quotation at 218. Far from wallowing in nostalgia for a lost aura, as Wyke suggests, Benjamin dialectically points to its revolutionary potential in film: "in permitting the reproduction to meet the beholder or listener in his own particular situation, it reactivates the object reproduced. These two processes lead to a tremendous shattering of tradition which is the obverse of the contemporary crisis and renewal of mankind. Both processes are intimately connected with the contemporary mass movements. Their most powerful agent is the film" (221). Regarding Hall see my note 22.

9. It is one of the merits of Hanson and Heath's book *Who Killed Homer?* that they engage directly with some of the problems. But their ideal teaching situation seems limited to large lectures in which they envision a charismatic lecturer mesmerizing passive students with a heavy dose of "Greek wisdom." I find quite disturbing the relentlessly repeated assumption that the goal of truly effective teaching on this subject is to make students be "like the Greeks" and that this is best achieved by those who are themselves most "like the Greeks." It is clear from Hanson's *The Other Greeks: The Family Farm and the Agrarian Roots of Western Civilization* (New York: Free Press, 1995), why he considers himself like a Greek. After assuring us that he has "lived on the same ranch for all of my forty years" (xiii), he proclaims his central thesis: "agrarian pragmatism, not intellectual contemplation, farmers, not philosophers, 'other' Greeks, not the small cadre of refined minds who have always comprised the stuff of Classics, were responsible for the creation of Western civilization" (xvi). But even if we grant that this is entirely true as stated, there seems a curious contradiction between his view and the indictment of those of us who are not full-time farmers but full-time teachers of that "stuff of Classics" which was, for better or worse, actually composed by a "small cadre of refined minds." It must be a sign of the times that both *The Other Greeks* and *Who Killed Homer?* were republished by the same academic press in the same year (Berkeley: University of California Press, 1999).

cultural residue which remains when high culture is subtracted from the overall totality of cultural practices; it is the trivial and the insignificant of everyday life, a form of popular taste often deemed unworthy of both academic legitimation and high social affirmation.[10]

294

CLASSICAL

MYTH &

CULTURE

IN THE

CINEMA

Not without some misgivings, but with no apologies, I will here examine my use of contemporary film in teaching mythology. I will both outline and interrogate my rationale for doing so. I describe how I have presented Greek myth and offer a detailed account of the uses to which I put some specific films: *Clash of the Titans, Jason and the Argonauts, Return of the Jedi,* and *Superman.* Two of these are based on Greek myths, two evoke contemporary American myths. Finally, I will attempt to sum up the implications of this sort of pedagogy. Since pedagogical practice is an eminently personal as well as a political act embedded in a concrete time and place, I make wider use of the first person pronoun than I would do in the critical analysis of a text. Readers should assess the relevance of what I have done or now do in the light of their own specific pedagogical circumstances and goals.

1. Rationale

The first question I pose to myself in this connection is: "What am I doing when I teach a course in ancient Greek mythology?" Mythology was not something most classicists were taught in graduate school, nor did it occur to most classics departments to offer it as an undergraduate option until the late 1960s and early 1970s, when more standard offerings had been decimated by the call for relevance. Today, although I have seen no hard statistical data, I suspect from my direct experience in a variety of institutions that at a great many colleges and universities mythology courses draw the largest number of students taught by classicists.[11] They not only constitute a deeply invested bread-and-butter issue for classicists' material well-being but for many students they also represent their *only* exposure to the civilization of ancient Greece. The first factor has tended to foster a certain meretricious mindlessness in some presentations

10. *Popular Culture, Schooling, and Everyday Life,* ed. Henry A. Giroux and Roger I. Simon (Granby, Conn.: Bergin and Garvey, 1989), 221.

11. A January 1999 e-mail posting on the teaching of classical mythology at the University of Maryland confirms my impression: the myth course "is . . . crucial to our department's financial well-being. . . . approximately two thirds of our students each year are enrolled in only one of our courses"—the myth course.

of the subject.[12] The second is a consideration that should recall us to our moral responsibilities as educators of future citizens.[13]

Beginning in the 1980s, the political significance of teaching the classics in general came under considerable scrutiny. On the one hand, classical texts are a key component in the educational agenda of the New Right, most clearly identifiable in the positions taken by President Reagan's secretary of education, William Bennett, and in the highly popular bestseller by Allan Bloom, *The Closing of the American Mind*.[14] For both Bennett

12. See John J. Peradotto, "Myth and Other Languages: A Pedagogic Exercise, with a Preface on Interpretive Theory in the Undergraduate Classroom," *The Classical World*, 77 (1984), 209–228. He begins his meditation on the problem of teaching theory in the classroom with an ironic allusion to the passing of a "Golden Age . . . in which classical mythology could be taught in innocent disregard of interpretive theory, by the simple dissemination of the data" (209). That "Golden Age" is still alive and well in classics departments where theory is rigorously absent from the classroom, not to mention from the studies of professors.

13. On the issue of educating for citizenship see especially Giroux, *Schooling and the Struggle for Public Life: Critical Pedagogy in the Modern Age* (Minneapolis: University of Minnesota Press, 1988), especially chapter 1 ("Schooling, Citizenship, and the Struggle for Democracy"). As noted earlier, the obliteration of effective, critical, and engaged citizenship from the goals of American public education is a high priority of the New Right's educational agenda.

14. Bennett's general views may most clearly be seen in William Bennett, *A Nation at Risk: The Imperative for Educational Reform*, report of the National Commission on Excellence in Education (Washington, D.C.: United States Department of Education, 1983). Follow-up: Bennett, *American Education, Making It Work: A Report to the President and the American People* (Washington, D.C.: United States Department of Education, 1988). See also Allan Bloom, *The Closing of the American Mind: How Higher Education has Failed Democracy and Impoverished the Souls of Today's Students* (New York: Simon and Schuster, 1987). The most explicit contemporary case for a fixed and ultimately despairing view of human nature of which I am aware is laid out by classicist Thomas Fleming, *The Politics of Human Nature* (New Brunswick, N.J.: Transaction, 1988; rpt. 1993). He concludes solemnly: "The laws and decrees enacted by human government are mutable and sometimes tyrannical, but the laws of human nature, curled in the spirals of the genetic code, are unchanging and just. More than just, they are justice itself in this sublunar sphere" (231). The final phrase suggests the fundamentally religious inspiration of his doctrine, despite all the invocation of the pseudoscience of sociobiology. See also his citation, in refutation of Christian civil disobedience, of Saint Paul's injunction: "let every person render obedience to the governing authorities, for there is no authority except from God, and those in authority are divinely constituted, etc." (224). For some assessments of the pedagogical implications of such agenda see Aronowitz and Giroux, "Schooling, Culture, and Literacy in the Age of Broken Dreams: A Review of Bloom and Hirsch," *Harvard Educational Review*, 58 (1988), 172–194, and in the same issue Peter L. McClaren, "Culture or Canon? Critical Pedagogy and the Politics of Literacy," 213–234. For a well-documented overview see Ellen Messer-Davidow, "Manufacturing the Attack on Liberalized Higher Education," *Social Text*, 36 (1993), 40–80. See now also Aronowitz, *The Knowledge Factory: Dismantling the Corporate University and Creating True Higher Learning* (Boston: Beacon Press, 2000).

296

CLASSICAL

MYTH &

CULTURE

IN THE

CINEMA

and Bloom, the classics constitute immutable reservoirs of fixed truth about a fixed human nature, a fixed human condition. So taught, the classics can convey to students precisely the message of the severe limits of possibility that it has been the goal of the New Right to impart to the dominated majorities of the world.[15] On the other hand, subordinated groups such as women, African Americans, and other ethnic minorities whose historical relation to Western civilization is by no means unequivocally positive have raised serious and legitimate questions about the misogynistic, patriarchal, and ethnocentric strains embedded in the classical texts. All of these developments have made it, I hope, somewhat more difficult for classicists to see their pedagogical activities as devoid of political implications. What the late J. P. Sullivan said about the teaching of history is equally true of the teaching of the classics: there can be no unideological teaching. The question is whether teachers are consciously aware of their approach and perspective.[16] Although Greek literature has been more directly implicated in this debate, Greek mythology, which we know primarily from Greek literary texts, can, depending on how we present it, also be enlisted in support of a certain politics of a critically unexamined, allegedly monolithic Western tradition. We all know of mythology courses in which the students learn a few hundred names in the interest of cultural literacy, see some fleshy Renaissance nudes to bring home the continuity of the tradition, and perhaps even listen to an opera or two—all without the slightest hint that there is anything distinctly *odd*, distinctly *different* about Greek myth seen from the perspective of the twentieth-century United States. Indeed the prime goal of many mythology teachers is to demonstrate with a vast panorama of

15. Giroux gives a succinct summary of the constituent elements, implications, and positions of this phenomenon in *Schooling and the Struggle for Public Life*, 220–221.

16. J. P. Sullivan, "Editorial," *Arethusa*, 8 (1975), 6. What I find most galling, if all too predictable, in the pronouncements of New Right ideologues is their pretense to be apolitical: They attack the left for injecting politics into the previously pure garden of classical studies. Mary Lefkowitz, for example, explains with a coyly impersonal construction that "there is a need . . . to indicate that the motives behind it [Afrocentrism] are political, and that this politicizing is dangerous because it requires the end to justify the means" (*Not Out of Africa*, xiii). Hanson and Heath protest that they are "more interested in the behavior and the culture of the Classicist than in his politics" (*Who Killed Homer?* xvi) after offering the tendentious claim that "our present Western notions of constitutional government, free speech, individual rights, civilian control over the military, separation between religious and political authority, middle-class egalitarianism, private property, and free scientific inquiry . . . derive from the ancient Greeks" (xvi). This list is soon recycled as "a free market, democracy, military dynamism, technology, free speech, and individualism" (xviii).

repeated motifs that "there is something deeply human" in these motifs' very persistence.[17]

While there is a serious, perhaps necessary, case to be made for the basic unity of the human species, I agree with anthropologist Clifford Geertz that "it may be in the cultural peculiarities of people—in their oddities— that some of the most instructive revelations of what it is to be generically human are to be found."[18] Thus for me the liberating potential for students of an encounter with Greek civilization in general and with Greek myth in particular is first and foremost the possibility for engaging with the culturally Other. Not that there are no continuities or similarities available or worthy of study. But I see my first responsibility as challenging the belief of most of my students that anything different from what they know is either undesirable or unattainable. The profoundly ahistorical or antihistorical cast of most of what constitutes students' cultural experience—something that therefore deeply determines their own subjectivities, their own perceptions of their individual and collective life options—seems to me a major obstacle to the transformation of our society into one that is truly democratic and humanely decent.[19] To put it differently, if I ask myself why so many students seem easily to consent to a view of the future characterized by an escalating threat of human extinction through war and environmental pollution, by ever more bitter divisions between the self-centered rich and the desperate poor, between the First World and the Third, between the white minority and the colored majority, between the empowered male half and the exploited female half of humanity, their acquiescence seems to me due to the success of their cultural environment in conveying to them the message that they are powerless to change a world whose parameters are dictated by

17. Cf. Erling B. Holtsmark, "The *Katabasis* Theme in Modern Cinema" in this volume. It is not surprising that Holtsmark invokes Jung and his archetypes.

18. Clifford Geertz, *The Interpretation of Cultures: Selected Essays* (New York: Basic Books, 1973), 43. He acknowledges that "'the basic unity of mankind'" is "the governing principle of the field [of anthropology]" (36) but then argues: "Culture, the accumulated totality of such patterns [organized systems of significant symbols], is not just an ornament of human existence—but the principal basis of its specificity—an essential condition for it" (46).

19. Giroux, *Schooling and the Struggle for Public Life*, 15, cites a recent survey: "The majority of young people in grades seven through twelve believed that some form of global catastrophe would take place in their lifetimes. [In] discussions with high school students across the country, very few of them believed that adults can effect any changes in democracy working as collective citizens. . . . None of them had studied an interpretation of *history* in which trade union struggles, civil rights struggles, or feminist struggles had any impact on *changing* the course of human history" (my emphases).

298

CLASSICAL

MYTH &

CULTURE

IN THE

CINEMA

an immutable human nature. Of course, to call this posture ahistorical or antihistorical is to invoke a conception of history as the realm of possibility, where a whole set of choices from the most individual to the most broadly societal have directly led to the conditions of possibility in any particular social and historical context.[20] A serious encounter with a different civilization can be liberating if we present that other civilization not simply as a repository of *better* choices but rather as a model of a social totality in which the *consequences* of choices in various spheres— economic, political, social, educational, cultural—introduce students to the very fact of choice and thus break the hold of the belief in "natural" necessity.[21]

Students cannot, I believe, readily deal with such an encounter if it is completely divorced from the mechanisms by which they deal with the rest of their daily experience. This seems to me the most relevant context for understanding broadly the role of popular culture in the experience of students. It is not a matter of seeking a level of relevance that merely confirms their current individual perceptions of what is important. In differing degrees and different contexts depending on a whole array of socioeconomic factors, rock music, advertisements of all sorts, games, toys, street practices (e.g., males casting remarks at passing females), television, computers, and film all play a decisive role in students' attempt to forge a sense of themselves and their moral values and life options.[22] By incorporating elements of that culture in a course on ancient mythology, I hope to engage the students in a double, if not exactly simultaneous, interrogation of their own cultural practices as well as those of a radically different society.

There is, I believe, a particular similarity between popular culture and mythology that constitutes an additional pedagogical attraction in such a combination and, at the same time, a special problem. Both myth and popular culture appeal to students, when they do appeal, on a visceral level, which students are extremely reluctant to subject to an intellectual scru-

---

20. To quote Geertz, *The Interpretation of Cultures*, 45 (perhaps in a sense quite unintended by him): "we all begin with the natural equipment to live a thousand kinds of lives but end up having lived only one."

21. I owe my conception of the "social totality" primarily to György Lukács, *History and Class Consciousness: Studies in Marxist Dialectics*, tr. Rodney Livingston (Cambridge: MIT Press, 1971; rpt. 1999).

22. Giroux, *Popular Culture, Schooling, and Everyday Life*, 18: "The popular cannot be ignored because it points to a category of meanings and affective investments that shape the very identities, politics, and cultures of the students we deal with." This seems to me the best answer to Wyke's attempt in "Classics and Contempt" to enlist Stuart Hall's very early (1964) comment on using film.

tiny they tend to reject as "cold." With both sorts of cultural experience students are especially likely to complain: "Why can't we just enjoy the stories? Why do we have to ruin them by analyzing them?" Not just concepts or systems of beliefs are at stake; pleasure is at stake.[23] Of course, the degree of particular students' emotional investments in any given cultural object will depend on a host of very specific factors—their economic level, class background, and gender most obviously, but also their age. Here I mean only that the age at which students have first encountered some of the more mythic films I use plays a great role in the depth of their emotional investment in *not* subjecting them to analysis. There are some students who are particularly resistant to the appeals of Greek mythology and some who may be particularly resistant to the sorts of films I have tried to use. I can only say that the students I teach seem, by and large, to feel rather strongly the visceral attraction of both myth and film. My institution, Miami University, is part of the Ohio State system, but its rural location and exclusive entrance mechanisms have brought an extremely homogenized, well-to-do, white middle-class student body. The proportion of minority students, despite some strenuous recruitment efforts inspired by federal legislation, remains strikingly low (7.44 percent) for a tax-supported school.

2. Course Overview

Since everyone who teaches Greek myth seems to do it very differently and since any assessment of the usefulness of my approach to film implies, at least in part, an assessment of the context in which I use it, I will try briefly to describe the overall structure of my course and the assumptions underlying this structure.

The most basic problem I perceive in presenting Greek myth may be summed up in the tension between—to use Claude Lévi-Strauss's terms—the synchronic approach and the diachronic approach: between, on the one hand, treating Greek myth in its entirety as a meaningful, internally self-reinforcing system of narratives and, on the other, presenting mythic narrative as itself a historical problem, a problem to which Greek culture

---

23. This point is made especially well by Lawrence Grossberg, "Teaching the Popular," in *Theory in the Classroom*, ed. Cary Nelson (Urbana: University of Illinois Press, 1986), 177–200. For a more radically skeptical view of the pleasure of spectacle in cinema see Dana B. Polan, "'Above All Else to Make You See': Cinema and the Ideology of Spectacle," in *Postmodernism and Politics*, ed. Jonathan Arac (Minneapolis: University of Minnesota Press, 1986), 55–69.

300

CLASSICAL

MYTH &

CULTURE

IN THE

CINEMA

offered a variety of solutions over time.[24] Many contemporary critical approaches that I find engaging in various degrees are radically ahistorical and treat myth as a mode of discourse preceding historical consciousness. Accepting, so to speak, myth's own philosophy of time, they proceed to analyze particular myths with little or no interest in the impact of historical changes on the meanings of myths. Among these are Freudian and Jungian psychoanalytic approaches, Lévi-Straussian structuralist analyses and, with a few equivocations, the work of such figures as Bronislaw Malinowski, George Dumézil, and Mircea Eliade.[25] For them history is at best an intrusion; the interpretive enterprise consists in finding the atemporal cores of meaning. On the other hand, one of the traditional fascinations of a history of the written remnants of Greek culture involves tracing the emergence of an ever-growing self-consciousness in the poets about narrative as itself a problem and the parallel forging of an increasingly abstract language.[26] Side by side we find either the attempt to force narrative to bear an ever heavier burden of abstractly conceived meaning or the movement toward a nonnarrative alternative, signaled by the development of strident critiques of Homer and Hesiod in the Presocratics and culminating in Plato's head-on assault on narrative and poetry.

My course attempts to introduce students to both ahistorical and historical dimensions of the study of myth by, in a sense, covering the ground

24. Claude Lévi-Strauss, "The Structural Study of Myth," in *Structural Anthropology* [vol. 1], tr. Claire Jacobson and Brooke Grundfest Schoepf (New York: Basic Books, 1963; rpt. 1978), 202–228. The familiar theme of the movement from *mythos* to *logos* has been set on a footing different from the simple progression its original German propounders envisioned—for example, Wilhelm Nestle, *Vom Mythos zum Logos*, 2nd ed. (Stuttgart: Kröner, 1942; rpt. New York: Arno, 1978)—by the research of Milman Parry, *The Making of Homeric Verse: The Collected Papers of Milman Perry*, ed. Adam Parry (Oxford: Clarendon Press, 1971), and Albert B. Lord, *The Singer of Tales* (1960; rpt. Cambridge: Harvard University Press, 1981), on the oral nature of Homeric verse. See Carlo Brillante, "History and the Historical Interpretation of Myth," in *Approaches to Greek Myth*, ed. Lowell Edmunds (Baltimore: Johns Hopkins University Press, 1990), 91–138, especially 96, where his primary source on the impact of orality is the work of anthropologist Jack Goody.

25. Jungians include the prolific Joseph Campbell and Erich Neumann. For bibliography and a brief assessment of these and others named in the text see John Peradotto, *Classical Mythology: An Annotated Bibliography* (Urbana, Ill.: American Philological Association, 1973; rpt. 1981). I should point out, however, that Lévi-Strauss in one essay directly explores the impact of history on myth, yet his title suggests the ultimate incompatibility of history and myth as he conceives it: "How Myths Die," in *Structural Anthropology*, vol. 2, tr. Monique Layton (New York: Basic Books, 1976), 256–268.

26. See especially Eric A. Havelock's numerous works, in particular *A Preface to Plato* (Cambridge: Harvard University Press, 1963; rpt. 1987) and *The Literate Revolution in Greece and Its Cultural Consequences* (Princeton: Princeton University Press, 1982).

twice. (Miami University has a fifteen-week semester. I would have a hard time indeed compressing my approach into a ten-week quarter, but I hope at least some of my assumptions about how to teach myth are adaptable to such a time-frame.) In the first half of the course I use Tripp's *Handbook* to present the major stories in as detailed and interpretively neutral a manner as possible.[27] At the same time I introduce students to three critical approaches. The psychoanalytic approach (Bruno Bettelheim, Sigmund Freud, Philip Slater) stresses the parallels between myth and dreams as a radically narrative means of dealing with what society defines as unacceptable desires and fears.[28] The structuralist approach (Lévi-Strauss) offers both a methodology for grasping the grammar, so to speak, of these peculiar narratives and an account of their function, that is, to overcome unresolved intellectual contradictions in a spurious repetitive spiral of narrative mediations. Finally, the overtly political, historical approach (Malinowski, Karl Marx) stresses the role of myth as a self-interested source of validation for actual social and political institutions— in short, as ideology.[29] Students are invariably shocked at the heavy theo-

27. Edward Tripp, *Crowell's Handbook of Classical Mythology* (New York: Crowell, 1970). There are several reprints under slightly different titles.

28. From the voluminous output of Sigmund Freud I usually assign selections from chapter 6 ("The Dream-Work") of *The Interpretation of Dreams*, vols. 4 and 5 of *The Standard Edition of the Complete Psychological Works of Sigmund Freud*, ed. James Strachey (London: Hogarth Press, 1953), and selections from *The Ego and the Id* (Standard Edition, vol. 19). Bruno Bettelheim, *The Uses of Enchantment: The Meaning and Importance of Fairy Tales* (1976; rpt. Harmondsworth: Penguin, 1991), is rather eclectically Freudian. I find his analysis of "Jack and the Beanstalk" (183–193) not only a relatively painless introduction to Freud but, because of his insightful use of the repetitions in the story, a nice anticipation of the approach of Lévi-Strauss. Philip E. Slater, *The Glory of Hera: Greek Mythology and the Greek Family* (Boston: Beacon Press, 1968; rpt. 1992), has an implicit historicizing dimension despite the primary emphasis on Freudian categories: Slater's whole analysis depends on the peculiar dynamics of the family in fifth- and fourth-century Athens, a period for which we have abundant if indirect evidence. This approach excludes the question of the nature of the Greek family during the period when the broad outlines of Greek myth were drawn, presumably in the Mycenaean period, as Martin P. Nilsson argued in *The Mycenaean Origin of Greek Mythology* (Berkeley: University of California Press, 1932; rpt. 1983).

29. I usually assign the well-known essay by Malinowski, "Myth in Primitive Psychology" (1926), rpt. in *Magic, Science, and Religion and Other Essays* (1948; rpt. Westport, Conn.: Greenwood, 1984) and as *Myth in Primitive Psychology* (Westport, Conn.: Negro Universities Press, 1971). I realize that I am grouping Malinowski with ahistoricists. Nonetheless his concept of myth as a "charter" for specific historical claims offers a decisive basis for grasping one key aspect of a historicizing approach to myth as ideology. For Marx I usually assign the selections and comments in *The Rise of Modern Mythology 1680–1860*, ed. Burton Feldman and Robert Richardson (Bloomington: Indiana University Press, 1972; rpt. 1975), 488–504.

302

CLASSICAL

MYTH &

CULTURE

IN THE

CINEMA

retical component in a course many of them take because they associate myth with stories of a painlessly self-evident meaning. The variety of theoretical perspectives that I offer not only reflects what I find most relevant to the study of myth but also aims at introducing students to the very fact of theoretical variety. Conversations with students have led me to conclude that they are rarely confronted with more than one theoretical set of assumptions in any given course, and even that one view is rarely placed within the theoretical background that has formed their teacher's pedagogical practice. Moreover, my bias toward primary theoretical texts—Freud, Lévi-Strauss, Marx in their own words rather than in a potted summary—derives from my conviction that students are more empowered if they come to realize that with a little effort and adequate help from their instructor they can understand major thinkers as those thinkers actually expressed themselves. If we are serious about developing genuine critical thinking in our students, these future citizens must develop the capacity to grasp the significant presuppositions of the intellectual, moral, and political options offered them. To assume that only graduate students are fit to engage with serious thinkers is to doom the majority of college graduates to permanent intellectual puberty. I find it ironic that so many New Right ideologues lament the inadequate study of great books of the past while expressing their horror or scorn of professors who dare bring into the classroom the work of the finest minds of the nineteenth and twentieth centuries.

3. The Perseus Myth

In the second half of the course I include a necessarily abbreviated historical survey from Homer to Plato. Film plays a key role in my attempt to effect a transition between the halves of the course—to suggest the explanatory power of some ahistorical approaches (psychoanalytic and structuralist) and at the same time to confront the students with the reality of historical change. The primary vehicle for this encounter is a film based on the Perseus myth, *Clash of the Titans* (1981).

The students have already read a considerable number of myths in Tripp's *Handbook* and are familiar with the critical approaches mentioned earlier, including Slater's analysis of the ambiguity of snake symbolism as part of an "oral narcissistic dilemma." I now ask them to read Slater's analysis of the Perseus myth and view *Clash of the Titans*. I then ask them to analyze the film's and Slater's contemporary approaches in the light of the ancient data on the myth available in the *Handbook*. The vehicle for their response has sometimes been an in-class hour test, sometimes an outside essay. The size of my classes, usually fifty to sixty students, precludes the dialogic explorations of popular culture advocated by progressive theorists. At the same time, I see distinct advantages in asking the students to write about the film before I have said anything about it. Not only do I write abundant comments and questions on their texts, but I also devote at least a full class after the hour test to summarizing the range of their comments, offering my own understanding of the film, and inviting their comments. Because they have already engaged with the film on their own, they are often readier to speak up on these occasions than they might be otherwise, despite the inhibiting size of the class.

I am well aware that a majority of classicists who know of Slater's work do not like it; in general, Freudian approaches to classical mythology have met with indifference at best, active scorn at worst. I doubt anything I could say in this context would convert the committed anti-Freudian, so I address my comments to those willing to entertain the possibility that there is something of value in this approach. Personally I can only endorse John Peradotto's assessment of Slater:

> Classical specialists will find here and there points of misplaced emphasis over which to argue, but to merit the right to criticize Slater as he deserves they must be prepared to venture into his bailiwick at least as deeply as he has come into theirs.[30]

Slater's general thesis is based on Freud's view that the emotional life of adults is significantly determined by their earliest relationships to those who bring them up. He argues that the circumstances of Greek society that dictated the relative seclusion of legally married women and encouraged the relative nonparticipation of fathers in the rearing of young children led to a deeply ambivalent mother–son relationship. This pattern is reflected in the misogyny and male narcissism prevalent in Greek myth. In the absence of a strong husband and father, the mother simultaneously pushes the male child to be an overachiever and makes emotional demands on him that fill him with a sense of terror and doom. He wants complete possession of the mother to nurture him literally and, metaphorically, to

---

30. Peradotto, *Classical Mythology*, 29. See also Richard S. Caldwell, "The Psychoanalytic Interpretation of Greek Myth," in *Approaches to Greek Myth*, 344–389. Caldwell calls Slater's book "the most important contribution to the subject since Freud" (386). Caldwell's own introductory book is very useful: *The Origin of the Gods: A Psychoanalytic Study of Greek Theogonic Myth* (New York: Oxford University Press, 1989; rpt. 1993). I have long been impressed by Frederick Crews's lapidary formulation of the Freudian problematic; he defines human beings as "the animal destined to be overimpressed by his parents" in "Anaesthetic Criticism," in *Psychoanalysis and Literary Process*, ed. Crews (Cambridge, Mass.: Winthrop, 1970), 1–24; quotation at 12.

304

CLASSICAL

MYTH &

CULTURE

IN THE

CINEMA

foster his ideal self-image. But the very intensity of her emotional concentration on him fills him with fear of being "engulfed" by the mother.
Slater calls this ambivalence the "oral-narcissicistic dilemma" and seeks
to organize the major hero figures of Greek myth as, in effect, a system
of different attempts to overcome this dilemma. Thus Zeus' exaggerated
displays of sexual prowess are one way of attempting to deny the threat
by overcompensation. Orestes' or Alcmaeon's mother-murder is another
extreme solution, echoed in various slayings of female monsters. Dionysus
illustrates "identification with the aggressor," becoming like the threatening mother in hopes of dispelling her threat. Lame Hephaestus, variously
rejected by both parents, represents symbolic self-emasculation in the
hopes of ingratiating himself with his ferocious mother. Apollo is presented as primarily dealing with the threatening female by "antisepsis"—
by a posture, not always successfully maintained, of hostile distance from
all hints of female fertility. Heracles, whose name furnishes Slater with
his title, *The Glory of Hera*, illustrates the richest variety of responses:
vast displays of male potency, repeated triumphs over female monsters,
transvestism with Omphale, homosexuality with Hyllus, symbolic mother-
murder of Megara, and finally tragic defeat at the hands of Deianeira, whose
name means "man/husband-destroyer."

Within this configuration Slater presents Perseus under the rubric of
"maternal de-sexualization." Perseus, completely deprived of any positive adult male role models, perceives males solely as sexual competitors
for his mother Danae's attentions. Acrisius, Danae's father, who imprisons her in a tower or under ground to keep away suitors, especially
his brother Proetus, out of fear that the child will kill him as predicted by
a prophecy, only mirrors Perseus' own obsessive concern with his mother's
chastity—the motive force behind his heroic quest for the Medusa head
and his subsequent murder of Polydectes and company. Perseus' fascination with his mother's sexuality is further evidenced by the strong emphasis on looking at the forbidden place—"scopophilia" in Freudian terms—at
the same time that he is terrified by the prospect of the ferocious return
gaze should he be caught looking. Here the parallels of Actaeon, torn to
shreds for seeing forbidden female nakedness, or Tiresias, blinded in some
accounts for the same crime, come to mind.[31] Perseus' radical solution to
the dilemma of a mother he wants desperately to keep but whose sexuality is frightening for him is to cut off the offending part.

31. Slater does not cite these directly, but see *The Glory of Hera*, 327. See also Caldwell,
"The Blindness of Oedipus," *The International Review of Psychoanalysis*, 1 (1974), 207–
218. The "equivalence of Oedipus and Teiresias" (208) is a key element in his analysis,
substantially recapitulated in his contribution to *Approaches to Greek Myth* cited earlier.

Slater's identification of the Medusa head with the mother's genitalia is the centerpiece of his analysis. Those who find in Medusa's paralyzing look quaint folklore of the evil eye or the Sartrean horror of the reifying stare of the Other will not be moved by Slater's citation of a sexual psychopath's dream in which the pubic hair of an adult woman is perceived as menacing snakes.[32] The same skepticism will perhaps greet the rest of his argument on this point, which I need not summarize here. I only note that he sees the sexual nature of the assault on Medusa confirmed by the resulting births of Pegasus, Chrysaor, and various snakes from the drops of Medusa's blood.

Slater interprets Perseus' rescue of Andromeda and eventual marriage to her as essentially replays of his relationship with his mother. Slater emphasizes the visual element in Perseus' falling in love after he sees her enchained naked body, another fight with a monster in which he again uses a sword, another encounter with an older suitor, Andromeda's uncle, and another use of the Medusa head to immobilize the opposition. Slater sees as deeply significant the fact that Perseus brings both his mother and his new bride back with him to Argos. Slater's general assessment of the heroic pattern of Perseus' career emphasizes the hero's helplessness—his constant reliance on help from desexualized Athena and from multiple magic devices (flying sandals, cap of invisibility, etc.)—and the brutal violence of his solution to the problem of maternal sexuality.

Finally, Slater focuses briefly on the myth of Bellerophon, a figure also connected with Proetus and the winged horse born at the decapitation of Medusa.[33] Slater finds confirmation of the motif of fear of the mother's sexuality in Bellerophon's disastrous encounter with Proetus' wife, who seeks his death when he declines her sexual advances. He also notes that Plutarch preserves a story that the hero was stopped cold in his assault on a city when the women of the city came out and displayed their genitals to the bashful hero.[34]

32. For alternative interpretations of the myth see Edward Phinney, Jr., "Perseus' Battle with the Gorgons," *Transactions of the American Philological Association*, 102 (1971), 445–463; Thalia Feldman, "Gorgo and the Origins of Fear," *Arion*, 4 (1965), 484–494; Hazel Barnes, *The Meddling Gods: Four Essays on Classical Themes* (Lincoln: University of Nebraska Press, 1974), chapter 1: "The Look of the Gorgon." See Slater, *The Glory of Hera*, 318–319.

33. James J. Clauss, review of *Classics and Cinema*, *Bryn Mawr Classical Review*, 3.4 (1992), 305–310, chides me for not focusing on the many interconnections between the Perseus myth and other myths borrowed and adapted in the film. This is one connection that seems to me relevant to an interpretation of the *meaning* of the myth, an aspect often neglected by the collectors of parallels.

34. Slater, *The Glory of Hera*, 334. Cf. Plutarch, *On the Bravery of Women* 248.

306

CLASSICAL

MYTH &

CULTURE

IN THE

CINEMA

Clash of the Titans was generally panned by those critics who took any note of it, but it did reasonably well at the box office.[35] The screenplay was by Beverley Cross, who had earlier written *Jason and the Argonauts* (1963) for director Don Chaffey and other fantasy or historical adventures; the film was directed by Desmond Davis, whose films *Girl with Green Eyes* (1964) and *A Nice Girl Like Me* (1969) had earned him a reputation for "an empathy for women's plight in modern society."[36] Special effects were by Ray Harryhausen, whom reviewers often saw as the sole source of any interest in the film. At the time I first introduced it into the course, usually about half of my students had already seen the film. To my surprise that percentage has held or even increased in recent years. Such is the video revolution.

I discuss the details of the film's plot primarily in the context of the students' observations. But for those who have not seen it, I point out that the most striking innovation of the film over the myth is the nearly complete suppression of Danae from the plot: She is out of the picture after some five minutes. Secondly, the female monster, Medusa, although still central to the plot of the film, is presented as dramatically secondary to a male sea-monster, the Kraken, who is not even a figure from Greek myth. (*Kraken* is a German word for a giant octopus of the kind that appears in Jules Verne's *Twenty Thousand Leagues Under the Sea*.)

In asking students to compare Tripp, Slater, and *Clash of the Titans*, I juxtapose three very different entities: the already heterogeneous ancient evidence distilled in an eclectic handbook, an analytic academic discourse, and a popular film. I wish I could say that I substantially advanced the students' appreciation of the specificity of those different modes. For a modern student, film literacy should be a fundamental component of any cultural literacy worthy of the name, and there is a flourishing film studies program at my university. However, none of the students who have taken my myth class seems to have taken the introductory film studies course. Thus, apart from a scattering of comments directed at elements in the myth that are compatible or incompatible with translation to the filmic medium, I do not attempt to teach them film literacy.

35. Heavily ironic review titles were typical: for example, David Ansen, "Andromeda Strained," *Newsweek* (July 6, 1981), 75–76; Richard Corliss, "For Eyes Only," *Time* (June 22, 1981), 22; John Coleman, "Near Myth," *New Statesman* (July 3, 1981), 22–24.

36. Ephraim Katz, *The Film Encyclopedia*, 3rd ed., rev. and ed. Fred Klein and Ronald Dean Nolan (New York: HarperCollins, 1998), 337.

What do I want and what do I get from the students? On the simplest level I want to see the extent to which they have recognized how the film version radically cut, selected, transformed, and supplemented the available narrative data, most of which Slater had at least attempted to account for. On a deeper level I hope that they would explore the ideological implications of the most blatant omissions and additions in the film with a view to gaining some historical perspective on their own society's cultural production by contrasting it with that of ancient Greece. I do not expect, but would welcome, some exploration of the ideological aspect of Slater's emphases in his use of the ancient data. Alas, omitting social and political aspects of the interpretation of myth in favor of an exclusive focus on the sexual dynamics of the nuclear family comes as naturally to contemporary students as it does to Slater. My instructions to the students read as follows:

> Choose at least *five* mythemes (i.e. an action linked with a subject, a symbolic object, creature, or significant event) from the narrative material associated with Perseus (everything in the *Handbook* about the royal line of Argos). Consider whether these mythemes are typical of Greek myth as you have studied it: Do you see any suggestive parallels, and what sorts of concerns seem to be associated with these motifs? Examine what happens to these mythemes in Slater and in *Clash of the Titans*. What role do they play in Slater's interpretation? Are they included, altered, or omitted in the film? What are the *consequences for the myth's meaning* of the treatment of these elements in the film? Consider the changes—omissions, transformations, additions—and ask yourself what these reveal about the differences between Greek society and our own society. How much of the original meaning as you and/or Slater interpret it is left in the film? If the meaning of the film is different, what *does* it mean?
>
> The point of this exercise is to make as concrete as possible a comparison between Slater's and the filmmakers' use of the same material, to find out what you have learned about analyzing Greek myth and the myths of your own culture.

On the whole, the most successful aspect of the experiment is the students' application of the psychoanalytic approach to the film. While there are those who inevitably explain the relative absence of the mother as due to the fact that the Greeks liked incest whereas it is not so popular in America, many recognize the ways in which the film demonstrates the de facto return of the repressed unconscious material. They note the relentless imagery of flying, which begins with the credits and includes the addition of a monstrous turkey vulture carrying the virgin Andromeda through the air, Pegasus imported from the Bellerophon story, and the magic mechanical owl, an obvious import from the recent *Star Wars* (1977). Cumulatively this emphasis tends to confirm for many students

308

CLASSICAL

MYTH &

CULTURE

IN THE

CINEMA

Slater's focus on the element of phallic display in the myth and his insistence on the relevance of Bellerophon to the Perseus narrative. The repeated losses of the hero's sword, in particular to a snake, suggest the pervasive fear of sexual inadequacy that Slater stresses. Despite the heavy shift toward the romance of Perseus and Andromeda, some students note the carryover of misogyny in the film, focused in the mother obsessed with her son (Thetis and Calibos) and echoed in the vain mother Cassiopeia, who boasts not of her own beauty as in the ancient version but of her daughter's. Medusa is still a terrifying female, and the seemingly gratuitous addition of her long tail and phallic weapon (bow and arrows) escalates the threat she poses and shifts it from the otherwise exclusive interest in her stare.

At the same time many students notice the centrality of voyeurism, of unobserved staring with clearly erotic overtones when Perseus is spying on Andromeda asleep—not to mention the audience's spying on her bathing. The frightening stare of Medusa is echoed in the ferocious stare of the living stone of Thetis' statue. The panic of the cannibalistic Graeae when they lose their eye is vividly evoked in the film and duly noted by students. Despite the relative absence of the mother, some notice that the film's opening few minutes stress a heavily sexualized image of the mother–son relationship by her nude nursing of her son and by the flamboyantly nude stroll of mother and son along the sounding surf. Built into the narrative of the film, but opposed to the ancient material, is the precondition of the hero's facing the explicitly devouring Graeae and an immobilizing Medusa before he sexually consummates his relationship with Andromeda, whose appearance is most like his mother's when she is seen nude in her bath. In fact, some students even speculate on the possibility that a heavier-breasted actress than Judi Bowker, perhaps even the same actress who played Danae, stands in for Bowker in the nude bathing scene where the actress's face is invisible. Most note the film's striking emphasis on Zeus' relentless involvement in the fate of his son, whereas for Slater Zeus in the ancient myth is the quintessential absent father. Most students attribute this change to the "superiority of modern American fathers." Some add that the addition of Ammon, not a god but a ham tragedian, insists on the availability of a nonthreatening father figure who repeatedly offers decisive advice and encouragement. Indeed the film, which multiplies hostile or dangerous females (all the goddesses, but especially Thetis, the Graeae, and Cassiopeia) while omitting the "maternal" role of Athena and limiting "positive" female images to the dubious examples of Danae and Andromeda, is arguably more patriarchal and misogynistic than the Greek myth. One student noted that Andromeda's dream of flying with a bird to meet her former suitor suggests the dangerousness of female sexuality even in this most innocuous-seeming of virgins.

But despite the film's striking suppression of the lecherous uncles Proetus and Phineus and of Polydectes, who as suitor of Danae is the major and motivating hostile male in the myth, there are some hostile males (Acrisius, Calibos, the Kraken) whose function is, as in the myth, to block Perseus' access to the female object of desire. One student even argued that Calibos' association with downing the winged horse, an element completely lacking in the ancient material, confirmed his symbolic role as a potentially castrating father figure.

The appeal to the students of psychoanalytic elements is clear in their perceptive focus on the repetition of snake symbols. They note that snakes are at the base of Zeus' throne; that the snake gliding over Perseus' sword renders him temporarily impotent and is allied with the devouring threat of Cerberus; that Medusa, in addition to her writhing coiffure of snakes, has a long snaky tail; that Calibos not only has a long, frequently undulating tail but also uses a long whip as his prime weapon; that the Kraken, too, uses his enormous tail as a weapon against Perseus on his winged horse. To be sure, some of these are associated with clearly male phallic conflict. But Slater's insistence on the ambiguity of the snake symbol to include as well the engulfing female threat seems confirmed in some of these instances.

The most common, if not unanticipated, disappointment for me in the responses of students is their relative lack of critical distance from the contemporary ideology pervading the film. Despite the hopes raised for a more enlightened perspective from a classically educated screenwriter and a director noted for his empathy with women, the film celebrates traditional heterosexual romance in terms that completely objectify the nubile female while denigrating adult women. It celebrates American fatherhood under conditions which little justify it.[37] It reinforces the fetishism of mechanical gimmicks as the solution to all problems and indulges in blatant racism by adding the embodiment of evil in the only black character in the film, Calibos (whose name appears to be a mixture of Caliban and Setebos, perhaps influenced by Robert Browning's poem "Caliban upon Setebos"). Comments on the students' analyses and discussions in class offer an opportunity to explore some of these issues.

37. A study done in 1972 of the amount of time spent on child care in twelve countries came up with the startling conclusion that American fathers spend an average of twelve minutes per day on child care. See Carol Tavris and Carole Wade, *The Longest War: Sex Difference in Perspective*, 2nd ed. (San Diego: Harcourt Brace Janovich, 1984), 287. One would like to believe that there has been a dramatic improvement since then, but there is room for doubt. I am indebted to Judith de Luce for bringing this study to my attention.

310

CLASSICAL

MYTH &

CULTURE

IN THE

CINEMA

The pedagogical advantages of a film of an ancient Greek myth are more or less comparable in *Jason and the Argonauts*, although there are fewer psychoanalytically interesting details to which the students might respond. There is a close parallel in the film's censorship of the "uncanny" elements—the myth's powerful female and helplessly dependent hero are replaced by a helpless and vacuous female typical of Hollywood and an assertive macho hero.[38] The philandering of the hero and the revenge of Medea are completely repressed from the purely romantic narrative of the film, while both the psychoanalytic and political motivations for the quest for the Golden Fleece—its symbolic role in the fusion of sibling rivalry and dynastic intrigue so striking in the ancient mythic material—are omitted. Thus, like *Clash of the Titans*, it allows students an opportunity for assessing the concrete differences between the ideological norms of male–female relations in their own society and those explored in ancient Greek myth. At the same time I must acknowledge that the inherently transhistorical claims of the Freudian approach tend to undermine attempts to historicize such relations. Although Slater presents his study of Greek myth as a cautionary tale to suburban America with a clear sense that there are choices in how societies organize sexuality and gender identities, the intellectual excitement of a Freudian approach, particularly to those who are encountering it for the first time, derives in great measure from the discovery of similarities in human psychic responses to comparable situations.[39]

A modern version of an ancient myth initially seemed a good choice for my course because it offers clear grounds for comparison and contrast, but this choice had a number of potential drawbacks. The distancing implicit in an ancient myth, in which human royalty and the omnipotence of pagan gods are natural assumptions and the primary focus is on issues of family romance, makes it difficult to raise issues of ideology apart from those of gender roles without incorporating a far more serious study of ancient Greek society and history than I find possible in a single semester. Thus there seemed a built-in limitation to the private sphere in my sticking with these modern versions of ancient myths. This difficulty seems to me due only in part to the brevity, unavoidable in my course, of my focus on the political functions of ancient myth. More important, I think it stems from the heavy bias of ancient Greek myth itself toward

38. I allude here in particular to Freud's 1919 essay "The Uncanny," *Standard Edition*, vol. 17, 217–252.

39. A nuanced attempt to confront the ahistoricism of Freud while retaining some of his insights is in Page duBois, *Sowing the Body: Psychoanalysis and Ancient Representations of Women* (Chicago: University of Chicago Press, 1988; rpt. 1991).

the dynamics of personal affective relations. Perhaps because the close intertwining of the personal and political in the initial Mycenaean context was as unrecoverable for the Greeks of the historical period as it is for us, the reworking of the old stories was primarily ethical on the conscious level and on the unconscious level a vehicle for exploring in fantasy the tensions of ancient Greek relations between the sexes.[40]

5. Return of the Jedi

Focusing on contemporary mythic films like *Superman* or *Return of the Jedi*, which more explicitly subordinate the private to the public sphere, has the advantage of inviting students to take seriously the more overtly political implications of contemporary myth-making. Their prior introduction to psychoanalytic approaches enables them to see critically sorts of relationships in these films that they previously took to be "natural." Students are also less resistant to analysis of films from their own cultural context than was the case with their initial experience of *Clash of the Titans*. I am not sure whether I wear down their resistance or, as I prefer to believe, they are beginning to reap some of the pleasure of understanding how myths are trying to "think through us," in Lévi-Strauss's famous formulation.[41] There is, I hope, some compensation for the lost pleasure of spontaneous ideological recognition, that unconscious assent to the image of ourselves seductively proffered in the film, in the empowerment of exercising some critical control over the images that beckon

40. For an intriguing, if rather fanciful, attempt to reconstruct a historical Perseus see Cornelia Steketee Hulst, *Perseus and the Gorgon* (La Salle, Ill.: Open Court, 1946). In the wake of Martin Bernal, *Black Athena: The Afroasiatic Roots of Classical Civilization*, vol. 1: *The Fabrication of Ancient Greece 1785–1985* (New Brunswick, N.J.: Rutgers University Press, 1987; rpt. 1990), the attempt to find an Egyptian connection seems somewhat less fanciful. For the more blatant political uses of myth among the Greeks see Martin P. Nilsson, *Cults, Myths, Oracles, and Politics in Ancient Greece* (1951; rpt. New York: Cooper Square, 1972). For the Mycenaean foundations of Greek myths see Nilsson, *The Mycenaean Origin of Greek Mythology*. Some intriguing more recent explorations of the political use of myth are in *Myth and the Polis*, ed. Dora C. Pozzi and John M. Wickersham (Ithaca, N.Y.: Cornell University Press, 1991). I have explored the political use of myth in Pindar and Greek tragedy in *Sons of the Gods, Children of Earth: Ideology and Literary Form in Ancient Greece* (Ithaca, N.Y.: Cornell University Press, 1992), chapters 3–5. See also my "Historicizing Sophocles' *Ajax*," in *History, Tragedy, Theory: Dialogues on Athenian Drama*, ed. Barbara Goff (Austin: University of Texas Press, 1995), 59–90.

41. See Lévi-Strauss, *The Raw and the Cooked: Introduction to a Science of Mythology*, vol. 1, tr. John and Doreen Weightman (New York: Harper and Row, 1969; several reprints), 12.

us to subjection. What we lose in the assurance of a familiar world we gain in a new freedom to reject what Louis Althusser calls the ideological interpolations—the summons—to be the sorts of individuals who fit all too easily into an unsatisfactory status quo.[42]

As in *Clash of the Titans* and *Jason and the Argonauts*, the mythic element in George Lucas's *Return of the Jedi* (1983; directed by Richard Marquand) and in *Superman* is most obvious in the special effects that take us into a realm beyond the rules of everyday reality. At the same time a number of more or less obvious signs point to a historically real world; and it is not difficult, once the question is posed, for students to recognize some of them. In *Return of the Jedi* the helmets of Darth Vader and of the soldiers of the Evil Empire echo Nazi uniforms.[43] In conjunction with the authoritarian tone of those in power and the abject—even robotlike—obedience of the ruled, these visual elements reinforce other associations with the images of twentieth-century totalitarian societies. The focus on an ultimate weapon, the Death Star, to quell all resistance resonates with the origins of the atomic bomb and the increasing menace of the military industrial complex. Students in the 1980s readily associated the rebels with various media images of Nicaraguan "Freedom-Fighters" against "totalitarian Communism." Depending on their knowledge, often minimal, of the 1960s, they could see links between the centrality of the Force and the "consciousness revolutionaries" of that era. Most, however, saw the Force as a direct analogue to Christian faith asserting itself against godless Communism. To this extent students could feel a largely comforting recognition of the eternal verities of the Cold War's standard repertory of ideological representations. The nominal ending of the Cold War (nominal in that there has been only a token reduction in the military

312

CLASSICAL

MYTH &

CULTURE

IN THE

CINEMA

42. See Bill Nichols, *Ideology and the Image: Social Representation in the Cinema and Other Media* (Bloomington: Indiana University Press, 1981), 36–42 ("The Aesthetics and Politics of Recognition"). On "subjugation" and "recognition" see Louis Althusser, "Ideology and Ideological State Apparatuses," in *Lenin and Philosophy and Other Essays*, tr. Ben Brewster (New York: Monthly Review Press, 1971), 127–186.

43. On fascist and conservative overtones in the first *Star Wars* film see Dan Rubey, "*Star Wars*: Not So Far Away," *Jump Cut*, 18 (1978), 9–14. Obviously, much of what I say about *Return of the Jedi* also holds true of the first film, which inspired President Reagan to dub the Soviet Union the "evil empire" and his critics in turn to dub his fantasy-ridden Strategic Defense Initiative "Star Wars," revived recently by Republicans and Democrats committed to socialism for the rich, however far-fetched the rationale. My choice of the later film is due partly to its popularity at the time I was working out my approach to myth and partly to greater complexities arising from the presence of the Ewoks and a more elaborate focus on rebellion. On the Strategic Defense Initiative see now Penelope FitzGerald, *Way Out There in the Blue: Reagan, Star Wars and the End of the Cold War* (New York: Simon and Schuster, 2000).

budget) and the desperate attempt of Hollywood to replace the reliable villains of yesteryear with terrorists—Middle Eastern (James Cameron's *True Lies* [1994]), Irish (Phillip Noyce's *Patriot Games* [1992], Alan J. Pakula's *The Devil's Own* [1997]), and, yes, Russian (Wolfgang Petersen's *Air Force One* [1997])—has not yet produced a fully mythic response, at least not to my knowledge. On the contrary, just when I began to fear that the *Star Wars* material was getting dated for my students, Hollywood with its predictable penchant for predictable profits started re-releasing the old saga and even added another installment to it.

When, in dealing with *Return of the Jedi*, I raised the issues of Vietnam, Central American insurgency in El Salvador or Guatemala against United States–backed oligarchies, or the long record of United States support for apartheid in South Africa, the discussion would grow more heated and confused. What is the point of reference, for example, of the Ewoks, primitive peoples who triumph over the high-tech agents of empire both by stealing their own weapons and by imaginative acts of daring? If the rebellion stands for American democracy, why is it led by a royal princess, and why is the Force restricted to a hereditary elite?[44] Discussion along these lines can at least introduce students to the whole phenomenon of ideological messages that seem to be intentionally mixed in order to tap audience awareness of various contradictions in the world and allay anxieties by the sheer confusion of clear and unclear parallels to their own world.

A particularly striking instance of this mixed-message phenomenon may be illustrated by the echoes of American race relations in this film. On the one hand, Lando Calrissian, played by popular black actor Billy Dee Williams, is a loyal friend who is given the prestigious command of the attack on the Death Star. We seem to have a clear liberal image of complete and unproblematic integration of black people into white middle-class society. Yet the same character is portrayed as a cynical traitor earlier in *The Empire Strikes Back*. Moreover, some explanation needs to be given for the choice of James Earl Jones, one of the finest black actors in America, to do the voice of the very essence of evil, Darth Vader, who is always clothed in black from tip to toe. The racist symbolism seems all the more blatant when we see a white actor with a distinctly different, vaguely English voice representing the redeemed Vader, renamed Anakin. Students who notice or are confronted with these issues inevitably pro-

---

44. The inspiration of the saga in the Roman Empire is elaborated in Peter Bondanella, *The Eternal City: Roman Images in the Modern World* (Chapel Hill: University of North Carolina Press, 1987), 233–237. See also Martin M. Winkler, "*Star Wars* and the Roman Empire," in this volume.

duce very different explanations. But the entire experience introduces them to a level of consciousness about their own entertainment that is quite new to them.

314

CLASSICAL

MYTH &

CULTURE

IN THE

CINEMA

Furthermore, their rather extensive immersion in Freudian analysis from the earlier part of the course enables them to recognize the symbolism of Sarlacc, a very fleshy-looking hole in the sand, surrounded by rows of teeth reminiscent of the Greek monster Scylla. The comparably toothy devouring mouth of the monster Rancor and the hideously detailed mouth of Jabba the Hutt can give rise to a more elaborate interrogation of the film's gender politics. Like Perseus, Luke Skywalker is a young man without a father; but unlike Perseus, he has no mother figure in his life. His only female interest is Princess Leia, who turns out to be his sister. Students cannot miss the film's tantalizing play with the motif of incest familiar from Greek myth. Beside the extreme paucity of females in the film there is the heavy proliferation of father figures (Obi-Wan Kenobi, Yoda, and Anakin—the good, i.e., "white," side of Darth Vader) and the strong male bonding of Luke and Han Solo, the latter troubled only by the ambivalence of the only female figure's love for both. Luke's initial mission is to save Han; this is the portion of the film where Luke is most threatened by huge, toothy, devouring mouths and where the sexual aspect of Leia, heretofore predominantly cold, arrogant, and stereotypically bitchy in a full-length white dress, is heavily emphasized by her reduction to a scantily clad, chained appurtenance of Jabba the Hutt. On the other hand, female students sometimes see in Leia's power and initiative, together with the position of authority assigned a black woman in the rebel army command, a clear and positive reflection of the impact of the women's movement on popular culture. (My seventeen-year-old daughter described Leia as a "kick-ass woman.")

Luke's climactic confrontation, his "destiny," is with the evil father Darth Vader, and students again and again note the strong Oedipal pattern in this major part of the narrative. Some point out that the phallic Jedi weapon given Luke by another father figure, Obi-Wan Kenobi, allows him to retaliate for Darth's earlier symbolic castration of him. In *The Empire Strikes Back*, Vader had cut off Luke's right hand; now Luke cuts off the same body part from his father. Thinking about this invites students to consider just how "healthy" or "natural" an image of American family and of gender roles this particular myth evokes, one that clearly was and is enormously popular.

At the same time, they are made extremely uncomfortable by any discussion of the male bonding between Han Solo and Luke, and most find preposterous the idea that C3PO, with his high voice, slender, glitzy form, self-conscious display of vast knowledge, and constant maternal chiding of his companion, the fellow droid R2D2, makes fun of a particular gay stereo-type. The patronizing stereotype, however, of the "primitive" Ewoks, who mistake this fancy golden machine, C3PO, for a god, escapes no one. However, those students who attempt to analyze this juxtaposition of cultures tend to ignore any contemporary reference to Third and First World relations in favor of a completely unhistoricized invocation of Lévi-Strauss's opposition between nature and culture. This response suggests some of my difficulties introducing an unfamiliar and powerful critical model and then attempting to offer some qualification or critique of that same model. If students get it at all, they tend to adopt it hook, line, and sinker.

6. Superman

Finally, Richard Donner's *Superman* (1978) is particularly useful for stressing the historicization of myth. Indeed, one might even say that the film is in some sense *about* the historicity of myth. Beginning with a black-and-white evocation of the original appearance of the comic strip in 1938, the film constantly invites its older viewers to savor, however ironically, the historical disjuncture between the ideology of the 1930s and the realities of the late 1970s. On the simple narrative level, the comedy of Clark Kent's befuddled search for a phone booth, the traditional site of his quick-change act to emerge as Superman, in an age when phone booths have been replaced by small see-through plastic windshields, invites the audience to register the change. Similarly, the comic irony of Lois Lane's first comment on Clark Kent, when she overhears him arranging to have half his salary sent to his old mother back in Kansas ("Are there any more like you back home?"—to which the answer is a calculatedly simple "No") confronts an audience of the sophisticated present with the unabashedly hokey nature of the original concept of Superman. Finally, in her penthouse patio interview with Superman the full weight of the historical gap is spelled out when Superman offers his famous credo of "Truth, Justice, and the American Way" and Lois comments: "You'd have to come up against every politician in the country." Audiences who had lived through the hasty disappearance of Spiro Agnew from the vice-presidency in the face of serious fraud charges, the revelations of Watergate, the Saturday night "massacre" of the special prosecutor, the resignation of Richard Nixon in the face of certain impeachment, and the hasty pardon from his old ally Gerald Ford are here invited to an ideological recognition not entirely reassuring.

But observing the reactions of students in the 1980s to this film suggests just how deeply its nostalgia for what seemed the simpler politics of

316

CLASSICAL

MYTH &

CULTURE

IN THE

CINEMA

a bygone era anticipates the willful simplemindedness of politics in the 1980s, not to mention the relentless cynicism of politics in the 1990s. Younger audiences do not notice the little ironic reminders of a changed and corrupt present. Brought up on an endless diet of crime films and television police shows, they are inclined to participate in the simple Manichaean dualism of criminals on the one side and good policemen and prison wardens on the other. Nothing in the explicit politics of the film undercuts the public role of Superman as helpful adjunct of the status quo, which, apart from Lois Lane's cynical comment, is presented as unequivocally good.

On the other hand, the sexual politics of the film, especially when juxtaposed to comparable Greek myth, can suggest a historical slippage from the initial Superman myth that in turn sheds light on other sorts of politics. If one asks students for the nearest Greek parallel to Superman, it is usually only a matter of seconds before they bring up the name of Heracles. If then they are asked for the clearest differences between the two, a perception of a radically different role of sex in the careers of the two heroes virtually imposes itself, especially if they have read Sophocles' *Women of Trachis*. In the 1990s, with the establishment of a sex-symbol television Heracles who resists all sexual engagement, students may lose sight of the Greek version. In any case, the original conception of Superman underlines his "real-life" repression as a shy milquetoast, never able to communicate effectively with the ever inaccessible Lois Lane.[45] As such he is the direct antithesis of the relentlessly sexual Heracles, whose hyperbolic sexual accomplishments include sleeping with fifty virgins in a single night and murdering his host and destroying an entire city to win the object of his lust. On the psychoanalytic level, both Heracles and Superman appear as classic instances of overcompensation in fantasy for the hopeless inadequacy of real-life performance. But whereas Heracles' violent ambivalence toward an organized social role is a key component of his traditional mythic interest, the Superman–Clark Kent of the comic book is the epitome of desexualized submission to the order of his society. A contradiction, however, emerges fairly clearly in the first Superman film and is made explicit in the second, released in the United States in 1981, when Superman has to surrender his superpowers through a heavily elaborate ritual in order to have intercourse with Lois Lane. Apparently, by the early 1980s some explicit sex is so crucial an element in selling a film, even one presumably directed primarily at a preteenage

45. I am indebted to Bobby Seale, former leader of the Black Panther Party, for first bringing to my attention this aspect of Superman in an address delivered at Yale University in 1970.

audience, that the filmmakers had to scrap what is perhaps the single most essential feature of the original mythic conception of Superman, his desexualization.

Students who have studied Slater's analysis of the flying motif in the Perseus myth are quick to see the sexual symbolism of Superman's long flight with Lois. The use of his X-ray vision shortly before to reveal the color of Lois's underwear only confirms the strategic departure from the wimpy Puritanism of the original hero. Asking why these changes were necessary leads directly to questioning a society in which the overwhelmingly dominant ethical imperative is to make a profit—the American way far more clearly than anything to do with Truth and Justice. The economic imperatives of film production contradict both the loving ironies of eras juxtaposed in the film and the unlovely nostalgia for an era of overwhelming violence in support of simpleminded pieties. Needless to say, students are by no means inclined to acquiesce passively in such a reading of the film. My point, however, is not simply to convince them of my own views of the film but rather to engage them in a critical questioning of contemporary myths, which for most of them is essentially absent from the rest of their education. As one student wrote on her paper with obvious satisfaction: "For the first time, I've actually thought about what is important to us as Americans, instead of just sitting passively in front of a television screen and watching a movie as I would normally do."

At the end of the semester I am always distressed by all the fascinating points I was not able to fit in or get across in the time available. But insofar as I make conscious choices, I hope I have made clear why I am convinced that my emphasis on cultural difference is more enlightening for students than the potentially endless pursuit of continuities.

7. Summary

If twentieth-century linguistic theory has taught us anything, it is that meaning is not inherent in isolated objects of perception but arises from a linguistically mediated system of differences. I believe the same principle is relevant to the study of cultures. A genuine appreciation and critical assimilation of classical culture is only possible within the framework of an explicit juxtaposition to what it is *not*, a clear exploration of the ways Greek and Roman cultures differ from our own. This implies neither an idealization of Greek or Roman values nor a naive chauvinism about our own contemporary ones. On the contrary, the responsibility to contribute in whatever way we can to the formation of citizens capable of full participation in a true democracy requires that we take every opportu-

318

CLASSICAL

MYTH &

CULTURE

IN THE

CINEMA

nity to engage our students in an ongoing critical dialogue with the re-ceived conglomerate of ideas, beliefs, and ideological practices into which they are born and which are constantly reinforced and adjusted in most of their schooling and in all forms of popular culture. To me, film seems a particularly fruitful vehicle for helping students assess the otherness of Greek culture at the same time that they are empowered to use that other-ness to take a fresh look at their own culture. Films that either explicitly use Greek mythic material or offer self-consciously mythic narratives extrapolated from contemporary American culture offer teachers of an-cient myth who are inclined to use them a valuable tool for engaging their students in this critical enterprise. Teachers of genre courses, most obvi-ously comedy and tragedy, also have much to gain by directing their stu-dents' critical focus to film, the contemporary medium that most strongly fashions their own subjectivities. Although my own inclinations have led me toward Freudian and Marxist models of ideological critique, I do not think that the pedagogical usefulness of juxtaposing films with ancient myths or comedies requires any acceptance of those models—unless of course one accepts the proposition that only these models provide a ground from which to engage in a critical dialogue with the culture surrounding us, a culture that we as teachers must choose either to perpetuate or to interrogate.

XV

The Sounds of Cinematic Antiquity

Jon Solomon

Music is an integral part of most films, and this is certainly true for the hundreds of films set in Greco-Roman antiquity. But there is a special relationship between music and antiquity because, unlike literature, sculpture, or architecture, actual and audible examples of ancient music do not survive. The following essay, after tracing the history of the tradition of Greco-Roman music, will survey the variety of choices modern film composers have made in attempting to create or recreate a musical sound that could convey an atmosphere reminiscent of the ancient world.

Of the ancient arts, music stood apart from painting, sculpture, and architecture in that its end product was ephemeral. Such well-known masterpieces as Euphronius' calyx-crater showing the death of Sarpedon and the statue of Poseidon from Artemisium still reveal their original artistry. Surface chips and fissures, missing limbs, and added support struts might impair our total aesthetic perception of an ancient work of art, but at least it exists for our sense of sight to absorb, appreciate, and judge. This is actually less so for ancient literature. Most people who read, for example, Sophocles' *Oedipus the King* do so in translation because they lack knowledge of ancient Greek. Nonetheless, with the literary equivalent of those impairments or additions I mentioned, and in a language foreign to that in which it was originally written, the play exists in a condition quite satisfactory for both the lay public and the scholar.[1]

---

1. One might equate surface chips and fissures in a visual work of art to an alternate reading (*lectio varia*) of a word or phrase in a manuscript tradition, missing limbs or pottery fragments to gaps in literary texts (*lacunae*), and support struts to lines or passages added by a subsequent editor (interpolations). I am grateful to Kathleen Higgins for her bibliographical assistance and general expertise in musical aesthetics and to Stephen D. Burton for a critical reading of an earlier version of this essay.

320

CLASSICAL

MYTH &

CULTURE

IN THE

CINEMA

Modern interpretations of the drama certainly differ from one another, as well as from ancient analyses (of which we have only Aristotle's extensive critique in his *Poetics*), but Sophocles' tragedy can for the most part be read, visualized, and even staged in a way comparable to its original production.

The music that accompanied the poetry of Sophocles and the other Greek tragedians, however, as well as that which accompanied the poetic libretti of Sappho, Pindar, Terpander, and then also the tubal music which brought the Roman proconsuls home in triumph is lost, apparently and unfortunately, forever. Even if we have recovered over forty fragments of Greco-Roman music, numerous fragments of *auloi* (an instrument sounding somewhat like an oboe or Krummhorn), a few thousand depictions of musical instruments on vases, and a dozen ancient musicological treatises, in the end we do not know what ancient music in fact sounded like.[2]

2. The musical fragments have been collected in Egert Pöhlmann, *Denkmäler altgriechischer Musik: Sammlung, Übertragung und Erläuterung aller Fragmente und Fälschungen* (Nuremberg: Carl, 1970), and Thomas J. Mathiesen, "New Fragments of Ancient Greek Music," *Acta Musicologica*, 53 (1981), 124–132. For the auloi fragments see the bibliography in Denise Davidson Greaves, *Sextus Empiricus: Against the Musicians: A New Critical Text and Translation on Facing Pages* (Lincoln: University of Nebraska Press, 1986), 123 note 5; Annie Bélis, "Auloi grecs du Louvre," *Bulletin de Correspondance Hellénique*, 198 (1984), 14–22; and Martha Maas and Jane MacIntosh Snyder, *Stringed Instruments of Ancient Greece* (New Haven: Yale University Press, 1989). For the music theorists see Mathiesen, *Ancient Greek Music Theory: A Catalogue Raisonné of Manuscripts* (Munich: Henle, 1988). See also *Source Readings in Music History*, vol. 1: *Greek Views of Music*, rev. ed., ed. Leo Treitler (New York: Norton, 1998). For the Latin side: *Thesaurus Musicarum Latinarum: Canon of Data Files*, ed. Mathiesen (Lincoln: University of Nebraska Press, 1999). For recent scholarship on ancient music see, among other works, Giovanni Comotti, *Music in Greek and Roman Culture*, tr. Rosaria V. Munson (Baltimore: Johns Hopkins University Press, 1989); M. L. West, *Ancient Greek Music* (Oxford: Clarendon Press, 1992); Jeanette Neubecker, *Altgriechische Musik: Eine Einführung*, 2nd ed. (Darmstadt: Wissenschaftliche Buchgesellschaft, 1994); Warren D. Anderson, *Music and Musicians in Ancient Greece* (Ithaca, N.Y.: Cornell University Press, 1994); *Ancient and Oriental Music*, ed. Egon Wellesz, vol. 1 of *New Oxford History of Music* (Oxford: Oxford University Press, 1994); and John G. Landels, *Music in Ancient Greece and Rome* (London: Routledge, 1999). On music and the Greek stage see William C. Scott, *Musical Design in Aeschylean Theater* and *Musical Design in Sophoclean Theater* (Hanover, N.H.: University Press of New England, 1984 and 1996). One modern attempt at realizing the fragments' music is the 1978 recording *Musique de la Grèce antique* by Atrium Musicae, Madrid, under the direction of Gregorio Paniagua, which I reviewed in *American Journal of Philology*, 102 (1981), 469–471. It is now available as a compact disc on the Harmonia Mundi label. A brief discussion of ancient Greek music theory in relation to film music appears in Kathryn Kalinak, *Settling the Score: Music and the Classical Hollywood Film* (Madison: University of Wisconsin Press, 1992), 20–22 and 211 (references).

The extent of this loss should not be underestimated either in its scope or in its importance. We cannot hear how Hesiod, Homer, and the other archaic epic poets sang their hexameters, nor do we have the music that originally accompanied the great archaic poets from whom we have considerable literary fragments.[3] Of the approximately three hundred tragedies written by Aeschylus, Sophocles, and Euripides we have only a very fragmentary dozen or so lines of musical "score."[4] Of Pindar and Bacchylides we have nothing. Nor do we have any of the "revolutionary" music of Timotheus and the late-fifth-century avant-garde contemporaries of Euripides. We do not know what music Plato heard as a young man, nor do we know exactly what scales Damon must have been discussing in his ethical categorization of music.[5] All the music to the songs of Old, Middle, and New Comedy is completely lost.[6] Besides these lost collections of music, many great performances were heard only once. The Delphic performance of Sacadas of Argos, who musically described or imitated Apollo's slaying of Python, and that of the youthful Sophocles singing the part of Nausicaa would never again be heard.[7]

During the first few centuries of the Roman Empire, what we might properly call archaic, classical, and fourth-century Greek music were already passé. Only antiquarians studied the "music of the ancients."[8] One of them, Dionysius of Halicarnassus, even examined in a scholarly fashion a "score" of Euripides' *Orestes*.[9] At the advent of the Byzantine era

3. An easily accessible video recording of Irish and Turkic bards, whose musical and poetic arts resemble those of archaic Greece, can be found in part 3 of Michael Woods's BBC series *In Search of the Trojan War* (1985).

4. See Mathiesen, "New Fragments," 124–132, and my "*Orestes* 344–45: Colometry and Music," *Greek, Roman, and Byzantine Studies*, 18 (1977), 71–83.

5. See Mathiesen, *Aristides Quintilianus: On Music, in Three Books* (New Haven: Yale University Press, 1983), 27–28 note 135.

6. Some of this music probably imitated or parodied tragic music. Aristophanes (*Frogs* 1314) undoubtedly parodies Euripides' unusual proclivity for scoring more than one note to each syllable (*melisma*).

7. Solon Michaelides, *The Music of Ancient Greece: An Encyclopedia* (London: Faber and Faber, 1978), 294; Andrew Barker, *Greek Music Writings*, vol. 1: *The Musician and His Art* (Cambridge: Cambridge University Press, 1984; rpt. 1989), 213 note 60.

8. The term *archaic* in the study of ancient Greek music has traditionally been misused to refer to almost any period between the close of the Bronze Age and the beginning of the classical period. The antiquarians include Pseudo-Plutarch, Bacchius, and Alypius. If we include the extant treatises of Pseudo-Plutarch, Pseudo-Aristotle, Cleonides, Ptolemy, Nicomachus, Sextus Empiricus, Philodemus, Gaudentius, Bacchius, and Alypius within this Roman period, the number of antiquarians actively preserving "ancient" music theory is considerable.

9. A Vienna papyrus (*Pap. Wien G 2315*) contains the only extant copy of the second stasimon of *Orestes*; Dionysius of Halicarnassus, *On the Composition of Words* 11.58–63, examined the first stasimon. Pöhlmann, *Griechische Musikfragmente: Ein Weg zur*

322

CLASSICAL

MYTH &

CULTURE

IN THE

CINEMA

the scholarly tradition of ancient Greek music still dominated both the Western—via Boethius and, to a lesser extent, Ambrose and Augustine— and the Eastern empires, but the music itself for several centuries stagnated within the traditions and rituals associated with the Christian church. By the time of the Renaissance, ancient Greco-Roman music was virtually unknown.[10]

For centuries this never disturbed any practitioner or scholar of music. Even in the Renaissance, when most artists developed a passion for things ancient, music remained confined to the style and content of its day. The relative lack of understanding and dissemination of the ancient Greek musical notation, which would not be fully comprehended for several centuries, necessitated this neglect.[11] While writers and painters from Petrarch to Titian rediscovered, imitated, and expanded on ancient texts and artifacts, musicians for the most part would only continue and expand on the medieval tradition with its polyphony and modality, the main technical components of medieval music. There was for them very little ancient music to rediscover or imitate.

There were exceptions, of course. Ludwig Senfl and Petrus Tritonius attempted to engineer a genuine renascence in the sixteenth century. Their goal was to reproduce musically the quantitative value of ancient poetry, and they achieved respectable results, even if harmonically their recreations belong not to antiquity but to sixteenth-century chordal style. The other notable exception, the Florentine Camerata's nobly intended revival of Greek lyric monody, resulted in opera—no mean achievement, but still not ancient music.[12]

---

altgriechischen Musik (Nuremberg: Carl, 1960), 19–24, points out that the ancient commentaries on the play include references to its music.

10. Although it was for different reasons, the same is true for Greek vases. One of the earliest examples of a Renaissance artist using a Greek vase as a narrative examplar seems to be Titian, whose painting The Death of Actaeon (London, National Gallery 6420) seems to be influenced by a vase containing the same iconography as the Pan painter's version in the Boston Museum of Fine Arts (10.185).

11. See Mathiesen, "Towards a Corpus of Ancient Greek Music Theory: A New catalogue raisonné Planned for RISM," Fontes Artis Musicae, 25 (1978), 119–134; also published separately (Paris: International Association of Music Libraries, 1978). Study of the manuscript tradition of Alypius and Bacchius, both of whose treatises contain ancient Greek notation, shows that only scholars had access to this material. These scholars did not really have any significant effect on the practice of music in the period; see Claude V. Palisca, Humanism in Italian Renaissance Musical Thought (New Haven: Yale University Press, 1985), 1–50. Even in ancient Greece very few Greeks could read musical notation.

12. On this see Palisca, The Florentine Camerata: Documentary Studies and Translations (New Haven: Yale University Press, 1989).

For the next three centuries, hundreds of competent and dozens of significant musical compositions celebrated mythological and historical personages from the ancient world. In these three centuries alone, for instance, over seventy different operas entitled *Dido and Aeneas* were written and performed in England, France, Italy, and Germany.[13] Caesar, Dardanus, Jupiter, and Cleopatra came to life again and again. But all the baroque, classical, and romantic composers who recreated ancient plots, characters, or subject matter contented themselves with contemporary music. That is, they made no attempt to have their ancient characters, plots, or subject matter identified by or associated with sounds evocative of ancient music. To hear Jean-Baptiste Lully's *Theseus* is to hear Lully's music, not ancient music. The same can be said of Christoph Willibald Gluck's *Orpheus and Eurydice*, Wolfgang Amadeus Mozart's *Idomeneo*, Ludwig van Beethoven's *The Creatures of Prometheus*, and even Richard Strauss's *Elektra*.[14]

With the development of ethnology and ethnomusicology in the last quarter of the nineteenth century, it became popular to introduce and blend certain ethnomusicological stereotypes into the classical orchestral palette of Western romanticism. Hector Berlioz scored a sistrum for *Les Troyens*; Claude Debussy featured the syrinx prominently in his *Prélude à l'après-midi d'un faune*; an Egyptian "sound" produced by harp and soprano singing minor-third and semitone intervals emerged at the beginning of the second scene of Giuseppe Verdi's *Aida*.[15] Igor Stravinsky then took only a small step in scoring not only a harp motif for Orpheus in his 1948 ballet of that name but also a brief melody actually written in an authentically Hellenic Dorian mode.[16]

This modal technique became the most frequently employed method to evoke the musical sound of classical antiquity. Most composers had in their conservatory training at least been exposed to the Ptolemaic-

13. Listed in John Towers, *Dictionary-Catalogue of Operas and Operettas Which Have Been Performed on the Public Stage* (1910; rpt., in 2 vols., New York: Da Capo, 1967), vol. 1, 185–187.

14. This lack of interest in historical accuracy did not apply to music, particularly theatrical music, alone. In the visual arts it was regular practice to illustrate ancient mythological and historical characters in contemporary costume and style. Numerous examples from painting appear in Jacques Bousquet, *Mannerism: The Painting and Style of the Late Renaissance*, tr. Simon Watson Taylor (New York: Braziller, 1964).

15. Years after *Prélude à l'après-midi d'un faune* Debussy composed *Syrinx*, which depicts the death of Pan. He had also planned operas on Orpheus and Oedipus.

16. Yet in his *Orpheus*, as well as in *Apollon Musagète* and *Oedipus Rex*, Stravinsky intentionally incorporated dotted rhythms in conscious imitation of eighteenth-century style. His purpose was to "build a new music on eighteenth-century classicism." The quotation is from Igor Stravinsky and Robert Craft, *Conversations with Igor Stravinsky* (London: Faber and Faber, 1959), 21.

324

CLASSICAL

MYTH &

CULTURE

IN THE

CINEMA

Boethian modes (*tonoi*). For the most part its practitioners were European. Modal writing was common in the works of many composers from Debussy on, and film composers took it up in the silent era. The modes used were the ecclesiastical rather than genuine ancient Greek ones, and few film composers other than Miklós Rózsa—whose work I discuss later—have gone all the way back to the latter. A second and important example after Stravinsky was Nino Rota's Dorian melody for harp and flute, which he used as Gitone's theme in *Fellini Satyricon* (1970).

There was another mid-twentieth-century method for attempting to establish historical accuracy in music that described an ancient setting. By this time scholars had widely transcribed and published several dozen fragments of ancient Greek music, so composers could incorporate one of these authentic melodies into their works and thereby imbue them with an archaizing style. André Jolivet, companion and compatriot of Olivier Messiaen, did just this in his *Suite delphique*, composed in 1943. To the authentic-sounding melody of Pindar's *First Pythian Ode* Jolivet adds an awkwardly cacophonous rhythm section. On the other hand, in his attempt at music-historical accuracy he composed his work in the Phrygian mode to convey an appropriate dithyrambic *ethos*, that is, mood.[17]

Early attempts at composing music for films about antiquity were not nearly so carefully devised or successful as Stravinsky's and Jolivet's attempts at composing ancient-style concert music. Film composers, arrangers, and compilers made no special effort to establish a musical authenticity, and in this they parallel the films' often feeble attempts at establishing visual and historical accuracy. For instance, most costumes and settings of silent films set in Greco-Roman antiquity were modeled on theatrical or operatic examples. In most cases a grand romantic mood was all that was required. Much of this early film music is lost. (It is quite an irony that scores not even a century old are lost when fragments of ancient music survive twenty-three centuries.) One example that typifies the rest is the supplemental score to MGM's 1925 version of *Ben-Hur: A Tale of the Christ*, which was rereleased in the early 1930s with segments from Franz

17. Unfortunately, the melody to Pindar's *First Pythian Ode* is a composition by Athanasius Kircher dating to 1652; see Pöhlmann, *Denkmäler*, 47–49. In the field of classical music still other options were available. Peggy Glanville-Hicks gives her opera *Nausicaa* (1961) a neo-Hellenic sound, while some modern composers who have composed around ancient themes and subject matter remain within their neo-Romantic or modernist style. Included in these categories would be Othmar Schoeck, Bohuslav Martinů, Alexander Scriabin, Erik Satie, Hans Werner Henze, Vladimir Ussachevsky, and Giannis Xenakis. Carl Orff offered a very different solution by attempting in such works as *Antigone* (1949), *Oedipus Tyrannus* (1959), and *Prometheus* (1968) to recreate not so much ancient but elemental, primitive sounds of speech and music.

Liszt's symphonic poems.[18] Quotations from nineteenth-century romantic music adequately served the film's need for a grand and romantic musical background to an equally romantic nineteenth-century literary epic. *Ben-Hur* closes two decades of silent films set in the ancient world, a fashion that had begun modestly in 1907 with Kalem's *Ben-Hur*, blossomed in 1908 with Arturo Ambrosio's *The Last Days of Pompeii* (*Gli Ultimi Giorni di Pompeii*), and continued with a number of silent epics produced in the United States and, for the most part, in Italy.[19]

When the sound era began, there was some hesitation before any "ancient" films were produced. This hiatus paralleled and resulted from Hollywood's focus on modernity, particularly organized crime and Broadway musicals.[20] Nonetheless Cecil B. DeMille had already made so many successful films in the silent era that he was able to convince Paramount to finance *The Sign of the Cross* (1932) and *Cleopatra* (1934).[21] As one would expect, the music accompanying these relatively early sound films accords with the type of nineteenth-century music used to accompany silent films. Rudolph Kopp's overture to *Cleopatra* begins with a romantic theme of three notes played by the full string section, a theme borrowed from the orientalizing and in that sense exotic tradition authorized earlier by Mikhail Ippolitov-Ivanov, Sergei Prokofiev, and Aram Khachaturian. The film's title card, "Cleopatra," is accompanied by an additional series of semitones and minor thirds but now played on the requisite Verdiesque harp and flute; in fact, strumming on the harp produces precisely the same progression (in $\frac{4}{4}$: major, major, major, another one half higher) as that in the second scene of act 1 of *Aida*. The rhythm is similarly orientalizing, with a bass drum beaten (in $\frac{4}{4}$) every half beat for the first three, then on 4 alone (six eighth notes and a quarter). While the rhythm is not necessarily orientalizing in itself, the use of particular drums may imply an

18. A reconstruction of the original *Ben-Hur* score now exists, as does one of the original score for Cecil B. DeMille's 1923 *The Ten Commandments*. They are examples of musicologists' increasing interest in silent-film music. Not surprisingly, there is hardly any authentic "old" music in any of these scores, but they do contain some modal writing.

19. See the descriptive listings in my *The Ancient World in the Cinema*, 2nd ed. (New Haven: Yale University Press, 2001), 3–10.

20. Badly timed, therefore, was the establishment of La Itala Film Company di Hollywood and their 1931 production of *La Regina di Sparta*. Two films from this era that combine the cinematic musical with the tradition of ancient films are the Eddie Cantor vehicle *Roman Scandals* (1933), directed by Frank Tuttle and with musical numbers staged and directed by Busby Berkeley, and the German musical *Amphitryon: Aus den Wolken kommt das Glück* (1937), directed by Reinhold Schünzel.

21. Wilson Barrett's play *The Sign of the Cross* had been filmed earlier by Paramount in 1914 and still earlier (1904) in Great Britain. DeMille's *Cleopatra* was at least the tenth film by that name.

oriental sound. (Timpani originally came from India.) A martial fanfare both concludes this overture and leads, after a brief interlude on bass clarinet, to a scene with Cleopatra's chariot racing across the desert. This action music differs not at all from contemporary chase scenes in westerns or other genre films. Similarly, Cleopatra's triumphal entry into Rome, despite some attempt at historical accuracy by a visual presentation of lictors with their *fasces*, begins with a quasi-Wagnerian march scored for strings. It culminates with the return of the oriental theme, which appears again with full orchestration in the visually splendid barge sequence.[22]

The introduction to *The Sign of the Cross* was revised when the film was rereleased during World War II. Rudolph Kopp's brass fanfare leads to the title card, and then the music shifts to a sacral, ancient-style instrumentation of organ and harp, combining music associated with contemporary American religious services and the ancient world since the era of Verdi's *Aida*. This instrumentation in turn leads immediately and surprisingly into "The Wild Blue Yonder" to begin the modern military prologue, to which the rousing Air Force motif applies perfectly. This modern prologue concludes when Hitler is compared to Nero, at which point the film shifts back to antiquity. The music accompanying this abrupt historical flashback now reverts to a romantic *Sturm und Drang* to illustrate the burning of Rome. Whereas most ancient lyres contained seven or at most eleven strings, Nero's lyre here boasts twelve. Nonetheless, his lyre is actually mute; the soundtrack uses a concert harp playing f♯–g♯–a♯–g♯–f♯–g♯. (Incidentally, notes 1–2–3 are notes 2–3–4 of the "Merry Widow Waltz.") But the doubling at the root, fifth, and octave turns this into a stereotypical exotic motif. Similarly, the man who plays the double pipes (*biaulos*) in the initial scene by a fountain plays another stereotypically exotic or oriental motif (d–d–g–f–d doubled at a fourth below). This motif is modal, although not perhaps exotic in itself, in its use of the lowered leading tone F-natural instead of the modern Western scale F-sharp.

After World War II there was no immediate change of direction. In the film version of George Bernard Shaw's *Caesar and Cleopatra* (1946), directed by Gabriel Pascal, the filmmakers maintain the playwright's spirit of irreverence toward their historical characters. Consequently, the score by Georges Auric hardly makes an attempt at accurately recreating an

326

CLASSICAL

MYTH &

CULTURE

IN THE

CINEMA

---

22. Kopp uses the dramatic barge finale to vary his original oriental theme by alternating between the flatted and then the unflatted second. To this same period belongs Ernest B. Schoedsack's *The Last Days of Pompeii* (1935), the fourth cinematic version of Edward Bulwer Lytton's novel, for which Max Steiner used some of the themes he had composed two years earlier for Merian C. Cooper and Schoedsack's *King Kong*. Steiner's score for Robert Wise's *Helen of Troy* twenty years later is equally inauthentic but, appropriately, lusciously romantic.

ancient sound. In fact, it represents the type of film-scoring that puts style at a higher value than musical archaeology, whether this applies to an ancient or any other historical (or futuristic) film. It is at times capricious, at others stirring, and occasionally takes on an ethereal quality in its clustered but gently orchestrated high-pitched harmonies. This description applies as well to Auric's scoring of Jean Cocteau's Orpheus (*Orphée* [1949]), for it was a consciously devised style categorized by contemporaries as the musical style of "Les Six."[23]

After DeMille's extremely successful *Samson and Delilah* (1949), however, the next decade blossomed with a number of large-budget, high-profile films set in Greco-Roman and biblical antiquity. The music for *Samson and Delilah* differed little from that which had accompanied his previous productions. Victor Young was a tuneful composer, and he scored so many films that he rarely had the time to focus special attention on any one project.[24] These two aspects of Young's music help explain his scoring for *Samson and Delilah*. Borrowing heavily from his predecessors, he established with his very overture an enchanting, orientalizing theme of minor and augmented seconds to describe the romance of the two biblical figures, as Camille Saint-Saëns had done in his opera by the same title.

As mentioned earlier, classical music in the 1940s had produced Jolivet's *Suite delphique* and Stravinsky's *Orpheus*, which reflect an increasing awareness that a musical archaeology of ancient Greece and Rome was long overdue. But no serious composer ever became more conscious of recreating ancient Greco-Roman music in this era than Miklós Rózsa, and this is equally true for film composers. After all, Rózsa's cinematic predecessors had hardly attempted to recreate genuine ancient music. Their interest was to maintain their own style or to create an oriental, romantic, or martial ambience. Established romantic instrumentations and melodic motifs sufficed for this purpose, and such films generally did not demonstrate any serious or consistent attempts by their creators to portray the ancient world accurately.

The task Rózsa set for himself with *Quo Vadis* (1951), directed by Mervyn LeRoy, was quite different.[25] The screenwriter, Hugh Gray, an

23. The other five were Darius Milhaud, Louis Durey, Arthur Honegger, Francis Poulenc, and Germaine Tailleferre. They were labeled as such by Henri Collet, music critic for the Parisian *Comoedia*, in 1920.

24. He scored over 350 films in his twenty-year career, at least eleven in 1949 alone. See Tony Thomas, *Music for the Movies* (South Brunswick, N.J.: Barnes, 1973), 43–48.

25. MGM decided to film an epic version of Henryk Sienkiewicz's 1905 Nobel Prize–winning novel soon after DeMille's highly successful *Samson and Delilah*, made for Paramount. Earlier versions had been made by Enrico Guazzoni in 1912 and Arturo Ambrosio in 1925.

328

CLASSICAL

MYTH &

CULTURE

IN THE

CINEMA

Oxonian educated in the classics who later co-wrote the screenplays to Mario Camerini's *Ulysses* (1954) and Robert Wise's *Helen of Troy* (1955), had already filled several notebooks with historically accurate material to be incorporated into the film. Rózsa, too, perceived part of his task to be the accurate recreation of an ancient sound, and so he rejected the approach of his immediate predecessors and rethought completely how to score a modern film with ancient music.[26] In Rózsa's own words:

> A motion picture with historical background always presents interesting problems to the composer. There have been innumerable other historical pictures produced before *Quo Vadis*, and they were all alike in their negligent attitude toward the stylistic accuracy of their music. When *Quo Vadis* was assigned to me, I decided to be stylistically absolutely correct.[27]

Rózsa's solution was to orchestrate with a particular concentration on brass, to employ the same authentic ancient modal constructions (*tonoi*) used less than a decade before by Stravinsky and Jolivet, to avoid triads and counterpoint as much as possible, and to adapt authentic melodies from the extant fragments of ancient Greco-Roman music. He even had a number of *citharae*, lyres, *auloi*, and *tubae* reconstructed. For his marches he consciously eschewed the use of strings and built his melodies almost entirely on Pythagorean fourths, fifths, and octaves, although he harmonized this authentic foundation with the sevenths, ninths, and seconds that give his compositions their characteristic sound.[28] The piece he adapted for Nero's cithara is that from the Seikilos Inscription, a funerary monument found in Turkey in 1883 and dating to the first century B.C. On it was inscribed a haunting dirge.[29] Nero's poem ("O lambent flame") is substituted for the original funeral song and expresses his desire to destroy Rome by fire, in this way creating both a new city and a worthy epic. Into the otherwise typical dance interlude at Nero's court Rózsa incorporated a prestissimo version of Athanasius Kircher's recreation of the music to Pindar's *First Pythian Ode*, which he described in these words:

---

26. See, for example, Mark Evans, *Soundtrack: The Music of the Movies* (with an introduction by Rózsa; 1975; rpt. New York: Da Capo, 1979), 131–132; Roy Prendergast, *Film Music: A Neglected Art* (New York: New York University Press, 1977), 123–130; William Darby and Jack Du Bois, *American Film Music: Major Composers, Techniques, Trends, 1915–1990* (Jefferson, N.C.: McFarland, 1990), 328–331 and 339.

27. Quoted from Evans, *Soundtrack*, 131.

28. For Rózsa's own description of his contribution to the film see his "The Music in *Quo Vadis*," *Film Music*, 11 no. 2 (1951), 4–10, and Thomas, *Music for the Movies*, 98–100. See also Darby and Du Bois, *American Film Music*, 311.

29. See Pöhlmann, *Denkmäler*, 54–57. A recording appears on *Musique de la Grèce antique*. The inscription has been lost since 1923, when it disappeared in the fire of Smyrna.

"Its authenticity is doubtful, but it is constructed entirely on Greek principles, and it is a hauntingly beautiful melody."[30] For the chorus of Christian martyrs in the arena he adapted the extant *Hymn to Nemesis* by Mesomedes, court musician to the second-century A.D. emperor Hadrian. Rózsa also adapted the ancient *Hymn to Helios*, preserved in several Byzantine manuscripts, for the music accompanying a chase sequence.[31]

Rózsa's solution to the quest for musical authenticity might be labeled the "Rózsa synthesis," for he synthesized ancient musical fragments, theory, and instrumentation with melodic lines, harmonies, and orchestrations suitable to modern ears and capable of evoking familiar emotional responses in modern audiences. Such a synthesis became for some composers the sine qua non for the scoring of ancient films in the 1950s. It influenced even such honored film music composers as Alfred Newman for Henry Koster's *The Robe* (1953) and Bernard Herrmann for Don Chaffey's *Jason and the Argonauts* (1963). For Rózsa himself, the next decade was filled with assignments to score ancient films and medieval epics.[32] For *Ben-Hur* he won an Academy Award, the only film score of this genre to be so honored, although this time he quoted no ancient Greco-Roman musical fragments in his melodies.[33] In addition, it was the first film score to have not only its soundtrack but an additional album issued.[34] With the exception of Max Steiner's score for Victor Fleming's *Gone with the Wind* (1939), which did not win the Academy Award, few films scores had ever been as successful and influential until the advent of John

30. The quotation is from Thomas, *Music for the Movies*, 127–128.

31. See Pöhlmann, *Denkmäler*, 18–19 and 16–19, respectively. Performances of the music for the *First Pythian Ode* and for the two hymns appear on *Musique de la Grèce antique*.

32. Joseph L. Mankiewicz's *Julius Caesar* (1953), William Wyler's *Ben-Hur: A Tale of the Christ* (1959), Nicholas Ray's *King of Kings* (1961), and Robert Aldrich's *Sodom and Gomorrah* (1963); Richard Thorpe's *Ivanhoe* (1952) and *Knights of the Round Table* (1953), and Anthony Mann's *El Cid* (1961). On his score for *Julius Caesar* see Rózsa, "Julius Caesar," *Film Music*, 13 no. 1 (1953), 7–13, and Evans, *Soundtrack*, 133.

33. Rózsa reused one of his marches from *Quo Vadis* in *Ben-Hur*, just as he was to reuse music from *Ben-Hur* in *King of Kings*; cf. "The Procession to Calvary" and "The Bearing of the Cross" in *Ben-Hur* with "Way of the Cross" in *King of Kings*. On Rózsa's score for *Ben-Hur*, the longest ever written for a film, see Mark Koldys, "Miklós Rózsa and 'Ben-Hur'," *Pro Musica Sana*, 3 no. 3 (Fall 1974), 3–20; Steven D. Wescott, "Miklós Rózsa's *Ben-Hur*: The Musical-Dramatic Function of the Hollywood *Leitmotiv*," in *Film Music 1*, ed. Clifford McCarty (New York: Garland, 1989), 183–207; and Darby and Du Bois, *American Film Music*, 331–334. The latter conclude that "Rosza's music emerges as one of the central strengths of the film" (334).

34. A two–compact disc set of the music of *Ben-Hur*, with extended versions, outtakes, and background information about composer and music, appeared in 1996 on Rhino Records.

Williams's fully orchestrated adventure and science fiction scores in the 1970s.

The scores for the spate of ancient films that appeared in the wake of the success of *Samson and Delilah* and *Quo Vadis* followed Rózsa's approach to a reasonable extent, particularly in their martial sequences.[35] But several influential composers in the subsequent decade resisted or felt no obligation to adhere to this renewed authenticity in favor of their own musical styles. Film music, after all, is a creative art, and the Rózsa synthesis could influence other composers only to a certain extent, particularly those who would have difficulty adapting their own styles to his model. Also, as Rózsa himself discovered, only a limited number of fragments of Greek music are extant, and *Quo Vadis* had already consumed the more adaptable ones. As a result, such composers as Dmitri Tiomkin, Alex North, and Nino Rota developed two other noteworthy approaches.

The first is that employed by Dmitri Tiomkin and Alex North. Tiomkin, who earlier had scored Howard Hawks's *Land of the Pharaohs* (1955), was hired toward the end of his extremely productive career to score Anthony Mann's *The Fall of the Roman Empire* (1964), replacing Rózsa. North was considerably younger than Tiomkin, and although he had spent his career scoring such challenging and dramatic contemporary masterpieces as Elia Kazan's *A Streetcar Named Desire* (1951) and Martin Ritt's *The Long Hot Summer* (1958), he was hired for both Stanley Kubrick's *Spartacus* (1960) and Joseph Mankiewicz's notorious *Cleopatra* (1963), which caused a financial disaster for Twentieth Century–Fox.

Predictably, *Spartacus*, the earliest of these three epic scores, begins with a martial snare drum.[36] Its beat, again predictably, supports a melodic fanfare scored primarily for brass, and this melody is still based on fourths and octaves. To this point Rózsa's influence is still marked. But within seconds of this beginning we hear dissonances, as North suspends one fourth upon another. He takes us through a series of keys, and each harmonization transcends the simple Pythagorean consonances that Rózsa had reestablished for the genre. This and other martial passages were not designed to create grandeur or to arouse patriotism for the Roman state. Instead, they create a disturbing and perplexing consciousness, as befits a score accompanying a screenplay by once blacklisted Dalton Trumbo, based on a novel by left-wing author Howard Fast. Indeed, *Spartacus* is "the thinking man's epic," as it has often been called; it celebrates not the glory and might of Rome but an individual who dared oppose it in his struggle for personal freedom.

35. For a list of these films see my *Ancient World in the Cinema*, 13–15.
36. On the music for this film see Darby and Du Bois, *American Film Music*, 401 and 409–413.

When *Spartacus* turns to the plight of the suffering, North's score excels in instilling in the viewer the pathos inherent in such scenes. At one point before the great battle against Crassus' legions, Kubrick eliminates all dialogue and leaves us with only images and music with which to observe the human faces and to experience personal relationships between ourselves and the fugitive slaves in their camp. Whereas the score's martial passages had Rózsa as their progenitor, these more intimate sequences have no direct predecessor.

For the almost contemporaneous *Cleopatra* and *The Fall of the Roman Empire*, North and Tiomkin seem to have approached the same problems with essentially the same solution. Films such as *Samson and Delilah* and *Quo Vadis* no longer exerted direct influence, and the two later huge and enormously expensive epics were projects conceived and executed after the genre had reached its zenith. The problem was to allot to these two epics something lacking in *Quo Vadis*, *The Ten Commandments*, *Spartacus*, or *Ben-Hur*. The Christian martyrs, armies, miracles, and mad emperors that had been the stock in trade of Roman epic films had all been exploited more than enough, so in *Cleopatra* emphasis was to be given to the love affairs of powerful but ill-destined rulers, while *The Fall of the Roman Empire* aimed to illustrate its momentous historical plot through a focus on the love affair between ineffective but well-intentioned powers behind the throne of the evil emperor Commodus. North's and Tiomkin's musical solution was to revert to romantic music of epic proportions.[37]

While Rózsa had by no means neglected the romantic elements in *Ben-Hur*, these two later films were predominantly romantic. Consequently, the Pythagorean intervals, ancient instrumentation, and modal restrictions were all abandoned. The composers found that progressive and at times even avant-garde dissonances scored for large string ensembles could convey both the larger-than-life scope of the romantic protagonists and the depth of the human feelings shared or lost between them, yet at the same time the music of both films gives us an unmistakable sense of isolation from their period of history. Their avant-garde harmonies are liable to modify an audience's emotional involvement to such an extent that some viewers may feel only detached sympathy for the heroes' plight.

Even more than George Stevens's mammoth 1965 film about the life of Jesus, *The Greatest Story Ever Told* (with a reverent score by Alfred Newman), *Cleopatra* dealt a mortal blow to the ancient epic in the cinema. Cost overruns, the scandalous affair between costars Elizabeth Taylor and Richard Burton, and a final product that was not well received by the critics

37. On the music for both films see Darby and Du Bois, *American Film Music*, 257–263 (Tiomkin) and 413–414 (North).

332

CLASSICAL

MYTH &

CULTURE

IN THE

CINEMA

shifted the genre from Hollywood back into the hands of European and especially Italian directors. Because the very nature of their films differed from those produced in the 1950s and early 1960s, their music had to emphasize a new, nonepic atmosphere and fresh artistic perspectives. Pier Paolo Pasolini's *Medea* (1968) and *Fellini Satyricon* demonstrate these different perspectives, the former creating a metahistorical, anthropological environment for Medea's revenge on Jason and Creon, the latter an entirely different world.

For his film version of Petronius' *Satyricon*, Fellini chose two types of music, both intended to belong to what he himself described as a "different" world.[38] Nino Rota composed not his characteristic Neapolitan street and plaintive circus tunes but unfamiliar and synthesized sounds produced electronically. These were complemented by a number of ethnomusical recordings, including frequent segments of *sansa*, the Balinese Ramayana chants, for the Minotaur scene, and the central African *niegpadouda* dance. As Kubrick earlier in the decade had rejected the stereotyped glorification of Roman grandeur in *Spartacus*, so Fellini wished to present and critically examine a culture unfamiliar to our own. In his own words, the *Satyricon* "is a kind of essay into the science fiction of the past, a journey into a mysterious world . . . a film outside of time."[39] The one relic of the Rózsa synthesis is Giton's lyre piece, composed in a Dorian mode.

Pasolini had also attempted to create an alternative world for his *Medea*, but his approach to antiquity in this film resorts to a Bronze Age world in which earth, sun, death, and rebirth have genuine significance. He had previously focused on antiquity in *The Gospel According to St. Matthew* (*Il Vangelo secondo Matteo* [1965]). His Medea killed her children because human sacrifice was a part of Colchian ritual. Calling on her grandfather Helios, the sun god, she performed one last act of ritual sacrifice with divine approval but full of human horror.

In Pasolini's opinion, to compose a soundtrack for a film that attempts to describe ancient ritual sacrifice was not possible, so he, too, selected a number of ethnomusical compositions for symbolic effect.[40] For the rituals in Colchis he selected Tibetan chant for the elders, Persian *santur* music for general Colchian atmosphere, and Balkan choral music, characterized by a female chorus doubling in two parts a second apart, for the

---

38. See *Fellini's Satyricon*, ed. Dario Zanelli, tr. Eugene Walter and John Matthews (New York: Ballantine, 1970), 4–9.

39. The quotation is from *Conversations with Fellini*, ed. Costanzo Costantini, tr. Sohrab Sorooshian (San Diego: Harcourt Brace, 1995), 74.

40. Ethnomusicology was becoming generally popular at that time. Folkways and Nonesuch records issued numerous samplings from around the world. The scholarly journal *Ethnomusicology* had begun publication in 1953.

women promoting the growth of new crops with the blood of the young victim of *sparagmos*, the Greek Dionysiac ritual of dismemberment.

In the wake of the *Cleopatra* fiasco and the shift in popular taste in adventure films from sword-and-sandal epics to spaghetti westerns, Kung Fu movies, and science-fiction films, to name only the most notable genres, very few ancient films of note were made.[41] There have been a considerable number of made-for-television miniseries, whose scores are as excessively derivative, tedious, and unimaginative as the four-to-twelve-hour teleplays they accompany.[42] There were only two large-scale theatrical releases, the infamous *Caligula* (1980), directed by Tinto Brass, and *Clash of the Titans* (1981), directed by Desmond Davis. The most exquisite music of the former derives, ironically, from Khachaturian's ballet *Spartacus*, and some of it is played in its original orchestral form. It is ironic that one of the most monstrous Roman emperors has his story told to the music of a ballet about the Thracian slave who could not stomach the stifling authority of the Roman aristocracy, although this was comparatively benign if compared to later imperial excesses. Added irony lies in the fact that a romantic orchestral piece in the film had originally been created for the 1925 *Ben-Hur*.

Laurence Rosenthal's score for *Clash of the Titans* also makes no attempt at authenticity. Finding no use for it in scoring this pseudo-mythological tale, he easily rejects the marches, lyre solos, and Pythagorean harmonies Rózsa had employed. The full orchestrations and rousing themes of the film, and particularly the luscious music accompanying the winged horse Pegasus soaring above the mountains, reveal Rosenthal's debt to the immensely successful style made popular by John Williams in George Lucas's *Star Wars* (1977), Richard Donner's *Superman* (1978), and Steven Spielberg's *Raiders of the Lost Ark* (1981) and, of course, to their common predecessors such as Max Steiner and Erich Wolfgang Korngold, among others, and *their* models, Richard Wagner and Peter Ilyich Tchaikovsky.[43]

41. For a list of films produced since the 1960s see my *Ancient World in the Cinema*, 15–21.

42. These began with *The Adventures of Odysseus* (*L'Odissea* [1969]) and continued with, among others, *Moses the Lawgiver* (1975), *The Story of David* (1976), *Jesus of Nazareth* (1977), *Masada* (1981), *A.D.* (1985), and *A Child Called Jesus* (*Un Bambino di Nome Gesù* [1987]). New large-scale television adaptations of *Quo Vadis?* the *Odyssey*, and *Cleopatra* appeared in 1985, 1997, and 1999. The 1990s also saw popular serials based only loosely on ancient sources: *Hercules: The Legendary Journeys* and *Xena: Warrior Princess*. Disney's animated feature *Hercules* (1996) led to an animated musical television series.

43. On this see Kalinak, *Settling the Score*, 188–191 and 198–199.

334

CLASSICAL

MYTH &

CULTURE

IN THE

CINEMA

There are no categorically proper or improper ways to score Greco-Roman films. To consider the Rózsa synthesis in *Quo Vadis* to be the most appropriate, accurate, and influential of "ancient" scores might only lead us to assume that it established the "classical" form of such music and that every score before it was preliminary and therefore inferior, every one after derivative and equally inferior. But this assumption too easily fits a preconceived notion of stylistic development. While it might be admirable or uplifting to have an entire film score consist of actual pieces of ancient music played correctly on properly reconstructed instruments, such musical authenticity might not appropriately reflect the character or intent of the film itself. In addition, from a more pragmatic perspective, the size of our present corpus of ancient music, only forty brief fragments, and our present lack of knowledge about ancient musical performance techniques greatly limit film composers in their attempts to recreate ancient music.

One reasonable substitute is the solution adopted by the New York Greek Drama Company, which has employed Eve Beglarian specifically to score, that is, to compose, "ancient Greek music" based on the Aristoxenian-Ptolemaic *tonoi* and the types of melodic and intervallic movements revealed in the extant fragments.[44] The company has produced Euripides' *Medea* and *Songs of Sappho* on video. Because these scores accompany academic performances of ancient Greek tragedy and poetry in the original Greek language, they must be as authentic as possible.

When we hear authentic Renaissance masses incorporated into Alex North's score for Carol Reed's *The Agony and the Ecstasy* (1965) or the authentically Mozartian soundtrack of Milos Forman's *Amadeus* (1984), we have a secure feeling of historical accuracy. Yet with a musical corpus as generally unrecognizable as that of classical antiquity, our appreciation of the Seikilos Inscription intoned by Nero in *Quo Vadis* depends not on the authenticity or inauthenticity of the words or melody but on the irony revealed in the sycophantic kudos given by his courtiers to this barely tolerable monody sung by a hopelessly untalented tyrant.[45] This rendering of the song is intended to displease us. In fact, it is meant for both artistic and political ridicule, and it is worthy of such ridicule on both accounts. In a sense, its authenticity is wasted, even detrimental to the

44. On Aristoxenus' *Elements of Rhythm* and his Aristotelian background see Annie Bélis, *Aristoxène de Tarente et Aristote, le Traité d'harmonique* (Paris: Klincksieck, 1986), and Lionel Pearson, *Aristoxenus: Elementa rhythmica: The Fragment of Book II and the Additional Evidence for Aristoxenean Rhythmic Theory* (Oxford: Clarendon Press, 1990).

45. Darby and Du Bois, *American Film Music*, 331, note the "appropriately skewed fashion" of Nero's playing and add: "The wicked emperor even dies to a dissonant figure on the harp, a gentle reminder of his lack of talent."

employment of ancient Greek musical fragments. On the other hand, we sympathize with Miklós Rózsa, who threatened to leave *Ben-Hur* when he was initially instructed to adapt, anachronistically, "Adeste Fideles" for his scoring of the nativity scene.[46]

Rózsa, in the sense discussed earlier, created a high classical standard against which all other scores to films set in antiquity can be measured. It is not an exaggeration to say that for a full decade he established the norm in the genre because of his achievements in *Quo Vadis* and *Ben-Hur*. But just as Rózsa's music appropriately echoed the well-intended authenticity of MGM's production of *Quo Vadis*, so did the various ethnomusics effectively convey the artistic messages and unique ambiences that Pasolini and Fellini attempted to establish in *Medea* and *Satyricon*. Even the romantically dissonant scores of North's *Spartacus* and *Cleopatra*, the fulsome score of Rosenthal's *Clash of the Titans*, and, much earlier, Kopp's orientalizing scores for *The Sign of the Cross* and *Cleopatra* appropriately reflect the atmosphere and intended emotional stimuli of these films.

Like the cinema itself, historical film music depends to a large extent on illusion. It is the viewer, not the historian or history itself, who determines the effectiveness of the cinematic recreation of history. But because the viewer's aesthetic judgment ultimately determines the value of the film's historicity, the basis for such a judgment is neither consistent nor universal. John Williams's score for *Star Wars* does not authentically, one may presume, recreate the sound of music in a galaxy far, far away, yet it enhances and is an essential part of George Lucas's artistic intentions. Along with special effects, costumes, and the film's overall design, the music helps create in us the illusion of outer space.[47] If the visual and emotional sweep of a film is sufficient, be it action-packed as in *Star Wars*, romantic as in *Cleopatra*, or religious as in *Ben-Hur*, the viewer will be convinced that the engrossing story is realistically, appropriately, and even authentically enhanced by the music.[48]

It is the combination of hearing Rózsa's music and seeing the ancient armaments, costumes, and architecture on the large screen that creates in

46. A famous anecdote, mentioned or described frequently, for example by Prendergast, *Film Music*, 126.

47. Stravinsky discusses the space element in music in Victor Zuckerkandl, *Sound and Symbol*, vol. 1: *Music and the External World* (Princeton: Princeton University Press, 1956; rpt. 1969), 69.

48. On authenticity as opposed to emotional response see Peter Kivy, "On the Concept of the 'Historically Authentic' Performance," *The Monist*, 71 (1988), 278–290. As Rózsa said in a 1988 interview: "the final function of film music, at least for me, is to complete the psychological meaning of a scene. And that's what I've tried all the time." The quotation is from Royal S. Brown, *Overtones and Undertones: Reading Film Music* (Berkeley: University of California Press, 1994), 271.

336

CLASSICAL

MYTH &

CULTURE

IN THE

CINEMA

the viewer the illusion of an ancient setting. Rózsa's film music, composed for other historical periods and omitting both the brass instruments and the adaptations of actual Greek musical fragments, sounds stylistically uniform. A hearing of his overture to *Ivanhoe*, for instance, would not pass a blindfold test: The listener, exposed to the music alone, could easily envision any other magnificent setting, whether medieval or ancient. This applies equally to other scores by Rózsa, to those of North or Rota, and even to operas in ancient settings, either of the Baroque era or later.

What, then, are the sounds of cinematic antiquity, and how do they strike viewers? The score becomes "ancient" if the filmmaker creates for the viewer a captivating ambience that successfully establishes a sufficiently different world that is then subjectively perceived to be ancient, and if the music itself is an appropriately influential part of this ambience.

Contemporary aestheticians and ethnomusicologists have demonstrated through cantometric analysis that music originates in and creates certain illusions and patterns, which are almost always culturally conditioned and affirmed.[49] It aids a composer to describe another, unfamiliar world if both the patterns and illusions are equally unfamiliar. But just as speech can be used to communicate intellectual stimuli, music can be used to communicate emotional ones. The process of establishing an ancient sound depends on the socially interactive process of reality construction.[50] In his *Quo Vadis* score Rózsa established just such a process. Once it became familiar enough, it could be reused and adapted by Rózsa himself and by subsequent composers now familiar, as were audiences, with the newly recreated aesthetics of "ancient" cultural norms. Ironically, attempts at musical authenticity came to be not nearly as important as did the expectation to meet this new and by now required aesthetic. Rózsa's musical innovations, based on his research on ancient music, led not to renewed interest in that music but to a musical stereotype heard today in any films or film segments set in antiquity, not least in parodies of ancient films.[51]

These observations call into question the view that, in general, the filmmakers who took greater care to make their ancient films authentic also took greater care to make them better as works of popular art. Clearly such an opinion depends on one's bias toward a classical ideal. If authen-

49. On this see Alan Lomax, "Song Structure and Social Structure," in *Readings in Ethnomusicology*, ed. David P. McAllester (New York: Johnson, 1971), 227–252, especially 251; and Steven Feld, "Communication, Music, and Speech about Music," *Yearbook for Traditional Music*, 16 (1984), 2–6.

50. See Charles Seeger, *Studies in Musicology 1935–1975* (Berkeley: University of California Press, 1977), 16–44.

51. Such as Terry Jones's *Monty Python's The Meaning of Life* (1983) and Edward Bernds's *The Three Stooges Meet Hercules* (1962).

ticity in music belongs to that ideal, then the music of *Quo Vadis* must be superior to all scores that precede and follow it. But it was not until Rózsa ceased quoting actual ancient melodic fragments that he was able to write his award-winning and deservedly acclaimed music for *Ben-Hur*. Not historical authenticity but his ability to provoke martial, pious, and romantic responses in the viewer-listener makes his score outstanding. Since then, critics and scholars have developed new intellectual and aesthetic approaches to the arts and now employ different criteria. Literal authenticity no longer has the same value as it did forty or fifty years ago. This makes the desirability or justification of historical accuracy questionable. The ethnomusics used by Fellini and Pasolini thereby earn greater critical validity, and so do the romantic scores of the 1930s and the operas of the Baroque. In the cinema, there is no permanently "correct" sound of antiquity.

Index